American Organic

A Cultural History of Farming, Gardening, Shopping, and Eating

Robin O'Sullivan

University Press of Kansas

Published by the
University Press of
Kansas (Lawrence,
Kansas 66045), which
was organized by
the Kansas Board
of Regents and is
operated and funded
by Emporia State
University, Fort Hays
State University,
Kansas State
University, Pittsburg
State University, the
University of Kansas,
and Wichita State
University

Library of Congress Cataloging-in-Publication Data

O'Sullivan, Robin, author.

  American organic : a cultural history of farming, gardening, shopping, and eating / Robin O'Sullivan.

     pages cm. — (CultureAmerica)

  Includes bibliographical references and index.

ISBN 978-0-7006-2133-0 (cloth : alk. paper) —

ISBN 978-0-7006-2158-3 (ebook)

1. Natural foods—United States—History. 2. Organic farming—United States—History. I. Title. II. Series: CultureAmerica.

TX369.O88   2015

641.3'02—dc23

                                                    2015020382

British Library Cataloguing-in-Publication Data is available.

Printed in the United States of America

10 9 8 7 6 5 4 3 2 1

The paper used in this publication is recycled and contains
30 percent postconsumer waste. It is acid free and meets the
minimum requirements of the American National Standard for
Permanence of Paper for Printed Library Materials Z39.48-1992.

Contents

American Organic

Introduction

"The Revolution has begun," pronounced J. I. Rodale, the editor of *Organic Gardening* magazine, in 1947. Brimming with optimism, he told his sixty thousand readers that the burgeoning organic farming and gardening movement was "gaining strength and numbers each year."[1] Rodale's troops rallied, touting the benefits of food grown with all-natural humus, decaying organic material. The avenues to success seemed paved with (pesticide-free) gold. The organic crusade was miniscule, but it implied a contrarian critique of conventional agriculture. As such, it drew fury from sovereignties that felt threatened by organic "extremists." The chemical-laden agricultural regime excoriated compost aficionados. In 1950, an organic farmer who had learned from Rodale's advice acknowledged that his own evangelical exertions were being mocked as "the silly outpourings of some new kind of crackpot."[2] Organic farming was bashed as a harebrained fallacy, fatuous pastime, and logistical failure. A report from 1960 from the Super Market Institute scoffed at "faddists" for falsely claiming that modern farmers using chemical fertilizers were undermining public health.[3] US Secretary of Agriculture Earl Butz declared in 1971 that "before we go back to organic agriculture, somebody is going to have to decide what 50 million people we are going to let starve."[4] News articles often included the words "cult" or "craze" when writing about organic food. The paths of the gilded organic "revolution" were more arduous to traverse for those marching down them than Rodale had expected.

Though scorned as hokum for decades, organics did make inroads from the periphery. Between alternating spells of passion and hyperbole, the organic movement seized credibility. As "sustainability" became a buzzword among environmentalists, organic farmers found themselves on an ecological and agricultural pedestal. Foodies revered organic baby-leaf mesclun greens. Gourmands began eating organic heirloom eggplants with gusto. Ethicurian eaters showed proclivity for socially responsible labels, while ecophiles meticulously hunted down earth-friendly ingredient lists. The cocktail cognoscenti drank small-batch spirits distilled from 100 percent organic grain, while the juice bar crowd sipped fruity organic elixirs. Farmers' market shoppers doted on organic red cored chantenay carrots. By 2009, First Lady Michelle Obama was enthusiastically planting seedlings for spinach, onions, cucumbers, and peas in the new White House organic garden. Celebrity chefs Bobby Flay and Emeril Lagasse were touring organic farms and cooking organic meals on their Food Network television programs. Supermodel Claudia Schiffer swore that she would eat *only* organic food. Highbrow culinary circles were obsessed with organic Russian Banana fingerling potatoes, organic ancient spelt, and organic baby back pork ribs. Upscale resorts were cultivating organic herbs, flowers, and vegetables for their posh restaurant and spa guests. Oprah Winfrey was tilling the fertile soil on her organic farm in Maui and donating the organic radicchio, beets, turnips, and Swiss chard to charities. The Organic Trade Association (OTA) launched "Organic. It's worth it," a national consumer education and marketing campaign that included a contest searching for an "Organic Idol" who would serve as an ambassador and spokesperson on behalf of organic products: an organic superhero.

Rodale's indomitable magazine, *Organic Gardening*, maintained that it was still leading "the charge toward a sustainable future."[5] Consumer sensitivity to food safety, distaste for the corporate "foodopoly," and trepidation about genetically modified crops were among the motivations that kept spurring even more growth in the organic industry. At the same time, misapprehensions about compost lingered, prickly questions about allowable substances were unresolved, and confusion about exactly what "organic" meant remained. Organic farmers were still outliers, if not outcasts. Some detractors thought organic food was no better—and perhaps even worse—than conventional food. The organic label was assaulted as a wanton marketing scam and condemned as extravagantly elitist. Popularity itself was a double-edged ballast. Cynics alleged that agribusinesses seeking to profit from an ambience of haute health food had hijacked the incandescent movement.

American Organic analyzes the history and significance of organics as a cultural movement in the United States. It illuminates how organic production and consumption are entrenched in the lives of all Americans, whether they eat organic food or not. It pays special attention to the durability of early publications that have been intertwined with social changes as they influenced the movement. Rodale's goal was improving individuals and the world, but the organic movement has been more successful in meeting the first objective than the second. From agricultural pioneers in the 1940s to hippies in the 1960s to consumer activists today, the organic movement has preserved connections to environmentalism, agrarianism, and nutritional dogma. Organic growing and consumption have been everything from a practical decision, a lifestyle choice, and a status marker to a political deed, a subversive effort, and a social philosophy. The organic movement has exhibited split personalities, alternating between highfalutin or down to earth. The movement's complex messages have been manifested in the trifecta of growing, buying, and eating organic food. *American Organic* embraces that multiplicity and expounds on the nuances of what the organic zeitgeist has meant in American culture. I do not tell the reader what to eat, nor do I state whether organics are "good" or "bad." My holistic approach examines intersections between farmers, gardeners, consumers, government regulations, food shopping venues, advertisements, books, grassroots groups, and megaindustries involved in all echelons of the organic food movement.

The first four chapters are arranged chronologically, but the sequences of events are not strictly linear within each. Overlapping themes reappear in each chapter. Chapter 1 examines the work of Jerome Irving (J. I.) Rodale, a foundational figure in the organic canon. Rodale zealously popularized organic agriculture in the United States through his books, magazines, and research sponsored by Rodale Press. The chapter looks at his role as an organic envoy and investigates his work in a cultural context, from the 1940s into the 1950s. It considers the contrast between the budding organic movement and government-supported conventional agriculture during the chemical boom. The second chapter focuses on the 1960s and early 1970s, taking account of organic farming's prevalence among environmentalists, homesteaders, the counterculture, and antiestablishment converts. It delves into the culturally resonant ideals of country life, family farms, and agrarianism featured in organic texts. It also situates the pursuit of physical well-being through organic food within broader American inclinations toward health food. Chapter 3 highlights the late 1970s and 1980s, the ongoing health and environmental traits of the organic movement, food safety concerns, the continuing activities of Rodale Press, and new organic business ventures. The fourth chapter picks up in the 1990s, with federal organic legislation, statutory impediments, the spectacular intensification of the industry, corporate power plays, fissures between devotees, and the repercussions of all those developments. It traces how the organic movement's ostensibly subversive impetus became more routinized and less insurrectionary. Chapter 5 focuses on organics as a health food movement and the interconnected issues of chemicals, GMOs,

Cascadian Farm (Photo courtesy of Lisa Powell)

"junk" food, and food scares. The last chapter inspects organic food consumption, including shopping landscapes, gentrification, "green" consumerism, and identity construction through purchases. It discusses the acclaim that has bolstered organic revenues and the skepticism that has plagued the organic food clan.

SCHOLARLY ENGAGEMENTS

By examining the organic movement in an interdisciplinary fashion, I engage with several branches of scholarship, including environmental history, consumer studies, and food studies. These intertwined areas of inquiry have seen modifications and new angles in recent years. *American Organic* contributes to the existing literature in these fields, transcends methodological limits by considering them in tandem, and makes fresh critical interventions by presenting a more complete understanding of how the environment, consumers, and food are inextricable. It is impossible to study organics without this multidimensional strategy.

The first major subject, environmental history, contemplates the reciprocal relationship between humans and the environment by charting physical nature itself, the human socioeconomic sphere, and the intellectual domain. Environmental history unites history, economics, geography, ecology, politics, and cultural studies in meaningful dialogue about the profound effects humans and the natural world have wrought upon each other. Environmental historians have examined topics such as the biological magnitude of colonization, the cultural causes of natural disasters, the ecological results of industrialization, and the varying definitions of nature.[6] The environment has been a structuring agent that constrains options for human activities. At the same time, human biases, preconceptions, morals, and laws have impinged on physical places. Since the 1980s, environmental historians have engaged in copious deliberations about the denotations and connotations of "nature." Historian William Cronon spearheaded a corpus of scholarship that clarified links between city and country, placing the "hinterlands" in a metropolitan perspective and divulging how market forces were also prevailing over environmental forces. Cronon also asserted that the very idea of "wilderness" was a human concoction, not an essentialist category, and rejected the fundamental dualism placing urban industrialism in opposition to rural nature.[7]

Americans have long contended that nature was an asylum from hectic urban-industrial life and preferred not to unravel the knotty web strung between those concepts. However, challenges to the romantic tradition that artificially separated ideal, sublime nature from corrupt, human culture have become de rigeur in environmental history. Nature and culture are intimately enmeshed, since even "untouched" natural panoramas have a human history. Poststructuralist philosophy has interrogated the strict dichotomy between nature and culture. Many environmental scholars have addressed the conjoined boundaries of the human and nonhuman and of nature and culture. Cultural geographer David Harvey has dissented from nature "fetishization" or "idolatry," insisting that unspoiled nature had to be saved from human damage. Other scholars have emphasized the fluidity of categories like "natural" and "artificial."[8] Greater recognition of nature-culture hybrids has developed in environmental history, exposing the natural or wild elements of cities and the human histories of "pristine" landscapes.[9] These approaches suggest how the human relationship with the environment might be reinvented to incorporate a more calibrated view of nature and culture.

American Organic complements previous literature in environmental history by scrutinizing the mélange of the natural and the human that organic gardens and farms encompass. My work recognizes the environment as a historical actor while also acknowledging the material consequences of human behavior. Globally, agriculture has tremendous ecological and social aftereffects. *American Organic* demonstrates how the very word "organic" has united growers, consumers, businesses, and mass media—and how it has divided them. It grapples with the quandary of what kind of agriculture can best reduce carbon emissions, increase biodiversity, improve human health, and still "feed the world."

Consumer studies, the second area of analysis, considers commodities, consumers themselves, and social corollaries of consumption. Economists, anthropologists, sociologists, and historians have all contributed to consumer studies. In appraising the capitalist system, Karl Marx described the "commodity fetishism" that arises when money instead of labor power is bestowed the value of a commodity. Thorstein Veblen's *The Theory of the Leisure Class* (1899) drew attention to "conspicuous consumption," denigrating people who used goods to signal their status. Subsequent scholars were less judgmental but still underlined the symbolic character of consumer goods. Jean Baudrillard's *The System of Objects* (1968) defined consumption as an active relationship that operated as the foundation of our entire cultural system and consisted of the "systematic manipulation of signs."[10] In *The World of Goods* (1979), Mary Douglas and Baron Isherwood analyzed consumption from an anthropological bent, as part of the social system. They asserted that goods were neutral, but their roles were social. Consumption was a way of using goods to make judgments and classifications visible. Douglas and Isherwood saw goods as an information system, endowed with value by fellow consumers, and they disputed the notion of a "puppet consumer" manipulated by wily advertisers.[11] Michel de Certeau's *The Practice of Everyday Life* (1984) similarly examined the "tactics" of consumption that individuals employed to appropriate and personalize products of mass culture. Consumption was another form of production, revealed through what de Certeau called "*ways of using* the products imposed by a dominant economic order."[12] He believed that tactics of consumption were ingenious techniques of lending "a political dimension to everyday practices."[13] Expanding on the politics of consumption, historian Susan Strasser's *Satisfaction Guaranteed* (1989) explored the creation of powerful mass markets for manufactured goods but maintained an emphasis on consumer agency.

Sociologists and economists have studied how consumption and class position were connected. Pierre Bourdieu thought that each class fraction had a system of dispositions, or an "internalized form of class conditioning," known as *habitus*.[14] One's habitus generated particular practices and thoughts. People and classes distinguished themselves by their cumulative aesthetic preferences, which constituted a lifestyle.[15] Consumer choices were attempts to acquire cultural capital, which defined class membership and served as an instrument of power.[16] Historians have examined evolving attitudes toward consumer culture and American character, shifts in aesthetics and design, and technological transformations.[17] Additional work has analyzed the expressive function of consumer decisions, the implications of choice on personal satisfaction, and the social psychology of shopping.[18] Much work has noted the importance of advertising and branding.[19] Surveys and market researchers have shown a hierarchy of assorted motives as factors in consumption decisions. Scholars have discussed how some consumers have viewed shopping as activism, while others have been acting only on a singular level.[20] In mainstream media, anticonsumerist texts have urged people to reduce material possessions,[21] while proponents of "responsible consumption" have encouraged people to buy "eco-conscious" goods in order to help "change the world."[22] Keener attention to resource use, commodity chains, and the externalities of consumption has been a key development in the field.[23] My work contributes to this body of literature by demonstrating the dynamic disposition of organic consumption, the utilitarian and performative functions of organic food, the motivations for purchasing and the values consumers have assigned to it, differences between sites of consumption, the larger cultural systems in which consumption takes place, and linkages between production, marketing, and procurement.

The third thematic strand, food studies, looks beyond the dominions of cooking and nutrition to examine food practices, systems, cultures, symbolism, material artifacts, folklore, literature, and social relations. Blossoming scholarship in food studies includes work by anthropologists, sociologists, food historians, and geographers who use ethnographic, quantitative, and qualitative methods. One of the earliest paradigms for food studies was a structuralist approach. Roland Barthes analyzed the "grammar of foods," in which food was a sign, a system of communication, a body of images, and a protocol of behavior.[24] Anthropological studies of food practices have underscored how food is employed in symbolic, materialist, and economic ways.[25] Many scholars have assessed how food serves as a signifier of the social environment, and their work has shed light on how food is alternatively a badge of identity, an apparatus of power, and a symbol of resistance.[26]

The culturalist angle to food studies has explored subjective experiences, social cognition, and historical trends.[27] Several works have examined how national cuisines have been shaped by geography, subsistence needs, environmental factors, cultural taboos, technological developments, immigration, industrialization, and urbanization.[28] Scholars note that foodways are entangled with gender, race, ethnicity, religion, and class.[29] Despite fears that have been voiced about homogeneity in a globalized marketplace, some work has emphasized that the rise of mass-produced food and international chain restaurants didn't occasion culinary uniformity.[30] Many historians have spotlighted particular foodstuffs, prepared foods, and food rituals.[31] Others have delineated the commodity chains that connect disparate locales and bring goods "from farm to table" in the industrial food infrastructure.[32] Media attention to food sustainability has grown exponentially, and journalists like Eric Schlosser, Michael Pollan, Marion Nestle, and Mark Bittman have produced best-selling books on food safety, the politics of food, and the health repercussions of dietary choices.[33] *American Organic* builds on scholarly attentiveness to the assembly of meanings and identities through food. It explores organic food as a nexus of concerns about health, ethics, taste, prestige, purity, and authenticity. My research notes parallels between the organic movement and other food networks that highlight cause-driven consumption, such as vegetarianism, local food, slow food, and fair trade.

Overall, my research combines perspectives from the interrelated disciplines of environmental history, consumer studies, and food studies, providing an expansive assessment of the organic movement. Much that is written about organics has a narrow slant: there are case studies of businesses, ethnographies that track specific organic farms, and consumer guides to organic shopping. Unlike these, *American Organic* presents a new critical paradigm and offers a discerning vantage point. My study entails the collection and scrutiny of historical and contemporary data, including archival, regulatory, literary, and promotional documents. It applies discourse analysis, semiotics, iconographic study, and cultural hermeneutics to exemplary texts and historicizes them. Observations of organic sites of consumption also enhance the historical and theoretical evaluations. Although organic agriculture is an international phenomenon, with cross-cultural exchange between nations, my investigation concentrates on the United States. This study contributes to ongoing debates over sustainable agriculture, green consumption, nutrition and health, identity formation, and popular constructions of nature. It informs explorations of the dialectic between cultural production and consumer agency. The result is relevant to academics as well as to the general public, since it casts the organic movement alongside wide-ranging environmental, economic, cultural, ethical, scientific, and historical issues on the American stage.

ORGANICS AS A SOCIAL MOVEMENT

Organic farming has been classified as a mere hobby, as an indulgent luxury, and as a minor constituent of agribusiness; organic food has been dubbed a hollow preference and an exploited industry sector. Fundamentally, though, I argue that organic farmers and eaters are part of a social movement with a vibrant group identity. Sociologist Alberto Melucci defined a social movement as collective action that involved solidarity, was engaged in conflict, and broke systemic limits; actors recognized that they were part of a "single social unit."[34] The organic movement does have its own history of solidarity, conflict, and violation of boundaries. However, a movement is a transitory network of interaction among individuals and organizations, not a permanent monolith of robots acting in unison. Its personality is mobile and fragmented, not fixed or unified. The organic movement often reinvented itself while adapting to changing circumstances. Internal tension sometimes boiled over, affecting the movement's configuration. Cultural theorist Stuart Hall noted that identities are always "in process," never completed. They are constructed by enunciative strategies marking difference and exclusion.[35] Though it has never been static, the organic movement did indeed maintain distinct characteristics. It coalesced through core maxims that provided internal guidance. This ideology also offered an "official" view of the movement to society at large.[36]

Social movements begin when contrasting value systems come into conflict, and one group makes a meaningful attempt to alter existing norms. In promoting or opposing social change, a social movement tends to fluctuate between phases of intensity and latency.[37] Over time, radical aims may give way to moderate ones, and successes may trigger backlashes. This is very much the story of organics. Organics can be categorized as one of several contemporary new social movements, which differ from models of earlier mass social movements in their emphasis on consumption. Many of these collective initiatives deal with nonpolitical terrain, focusing instead on "self-realization" in daily life.[38] The organic movement has often been more personal than political, but it has continued to partake in its own cultural conflicts. While the commercial organic food industry has become a salient component of the movement's structure, the organic movement as a whole has maintained a rank-and-file base and a social agenda.[39]

Organic movement participants have been engrossed in a series of differentiated acts against antiorganic opponents, which have reinforced their sense of belonging.[40] While acting as a social movement in this respect, the organic legion could also be described as a community. Social anthropologist Anthony Cohen noted that a community was largely a mental construct, something people made into "a resource and repository of meaning, and a referent of their identity."[41] The community of organic farmers and consumers lacked homogeny, yet it crystallized through communal consciousness. There was infighting but also cohesion. Organic community members simultaneously belonged to other associations. Still, they did form a cadre of people who shared actions and symbols, however malleable these might have been, that significantly distinguished them.[42]

While decoding the organic movement, I have interpreted books, magazines, newspapers, advertisements, catalogues, websites, blogs, podcasts, regulatory documents, and other discursive sources. In the missives heralded

Farmers' market (Photo courtesy of Colleen Freda Burt)

by organic emissaries, I have found coherent anchors and common themes. Dominant discourses about organics have impinged on public consciousness, and some dictums have gained precedence over others. There have been battles between master narratives and alternative dialects in the organic psyche. Social movements are polyphonic, churning contradictory voices and subtexts within every utterance. Semiotician Mikhail Bakhtin conceptualized every text as a dialogue, in which compound discourses interacted. Like texts, movements rarely speak as univocal entities; they are dialogically oriented. Not all actors participate equally or fully in the articulation of movement identity. While the organic movement has had no single or conclusive precept, some notable players have spoken vociferously. Certain "movement intellectuals" have been more visible and legible as organizers, spokespeople, or visionaries.[43] *American Organic* includes analyses of rhetorical strategies utilized by organic farmers, business leaders, chefs, consumers, writers, organizations, and stakeholders who have engaged extensively with the "organic lifestyle" and served as attachés. Unraveling the controlling organic discourses provides insight into the movement's epicenter. Some prominent trailblazers on the organic front lines consciously aligned with discernible viewpoints. *American Organic* interrogates the manifestations of these resilient ideals to reveal pivotal tenets of the movement.

WHAT IS "ORGANIC" ANYWAY?

Since the 1940s, the concepts of holism, health, natural cycles, and balance have been integral to the organic ethos. Organic farming was predicated on approaching the soil as a living organism and using nonsynthetic materials to build fertility. At a time when the chemically based approach prevailed, the organic ambassador, J. I. Rodale, felt that the organic method was a way of "bringing nature back into balance."[44] Addressing doubts about what "organically grown" really meant, he defined it in 1953 as food and crops that had been "raised on soil fertilized by organic methods only." In particular, he said the term indicated that "no chemical fertilizers, conditioners, insecticides or any such type of spray, pesticide or preservative has been used at any time in the growing or preparation of these products."[45] "Organic" was delineated as both an oppositional and a positive label; it was anticonventional and pronatural. Rodale's definition was never legally sanctioned; he and other organic diplomats modified it repeatedly. I argue that organic protocol was dynamic, evolving to accommodate new research and practices. In this respect, it was suited to longevity. However, the meaning of the term "organic" was fuzzy for decades, and the discourses surrounding "organic" have shifted, conveying fluid connotations to successive eras. This opacity has thrown off consumers unfamiliar with organic standards. The individualization of responsibility has been the movement's primary tactic. Still, elements of subversiveness have always been part of the movement.

The organic movement was (and is) in perpetual flux, molded by social and historical contexts. Still, amid the breadth of doctrines motivating organic gardeners and farmers, common threads recurred. Persistent tropes offered by organic advisers included the poetic veneration of primitive "Nature"; a yearning for "wholeness" and simplicity; the hunt for independence, sustainability, plentiful harvests, and abundant health; antiurban sentiments; celebrations of idyllic agrarianism and earthy pastoralism; the assertion of a purpose higher than a paycheck; and a respect for honest, wholesome hard work. Organic iconography has relied extensively on illustrations of backyard gardens, charming family farms, peaceful natural vistas, and sustainable "green" lifestyles. These visual organic emblems are significant because landscape representations found in popular culture bear metaphorical importance. Discursive analysis indicates how organic farmers have long resolved to work in "harmony with nature," and grandiloquent descriptions on organic labels have mimicked this leitmotif.

Organic breakfast options (Photo courtesy of Colleen Freda Burt)

When J. I. Rodale championed the term "organic" as indicating a fundamental farming practice imitating the "balance of nature," he implied that this symbiosis was in stark contrast to the domineering means of corporate agriculture. Rodale maintained that organics called for "a study of the phenomena of Nature," so that it would "not depart too far from her methods."[46] An *Organic Gardening* article in 1952 said that every organic gardener knew that "the balance of nature must not be overlooked."[47] Another organic farmer in 1954 discussed his aspiration to "raise in Nature's own way the kind of food required for our well-being."[48] Much later, in *The Organic Garden Book* (1993), Geoff Hamilton pronounced that organic gardening was still "simply a way of working with nature rather than against it"; basic organic cultivation principles followed "those found in the natural world."[49] Contemporary organic farming expert Eliot Coleman said that true organic farmers understood how "nature's elegantly structured system" had to be "studied and nurtured."[50] Diverse templates of knowledge among organic missionaries have coexisted, and "nature" has had a range of meanings for participants. Nonetheless, descriptive literature, attitudes about the environment, and guiding moralities such as "cooperating with nature" have affected how organic farming has been performed and perceived. Furthermore, J. I. Rodale epitomizes the mercurial movement and the shift from organic farming to organic consumerism that has occurred in the past eighty years. Whether you love him or hate him, Rodale and his descendants have played, and continue to play, a vital role in the US organic movement.

The way people have understood "organic" as a cultural designation has often differed from what has become a stringent legal definition. There were contentious struggles over pinning down precisely what the pillars of organic agriculture were. Notwithstanding habitual claims that organics were the way farming had "always" been done, it was actually a new, discrete technique advanced by Rodale and other pioneers. Organic practitioners deliberately crafted their game plan. Though some of its methods were centuries old, organic farming was also innovative in its incorporation of unique features. In the United States, it was not until 1990 that the Organic Foods Production Act (OFPA) established national parameters for marketing organic agricultural products. This culminating legislation assured consumers that organically produced goods met a consistent standard.[51] Items that had long been tinged with an aura of virtue acquired administrative approbation. By 2001, the National Organic Program (NOP) rules were finalized, providing national criteria for the term "certified organic." Any person or retailer who misappropriated the term "organic" became subject to a penalty of up to $10,000.[52]

Federal organic standards developed by the US Department of Agriculture (USDA) went into full effect on October 21, 2002. Only certified organic products containing at least 95 percent organic content could be labeled "organic" on the primary label panel and carry the USDA seal. Those with at least 70 percent organic ingredients could read "made with organic ingredients" but not bear the seal. To warrant certification, organic farms had to prove that they omitted certain customs and adopted others. From that point on, all the intricate details were revised as new disputes arose. The recognizable USDA Organic seal was a process claim, not a product assertion; it referred to how the merchandise was made, not what it promised to do. The formal classification was forged, in part, to dispel mystification about organics. The seal's trustworthiness was crucial to the success—and profits—of organic food sales. However, quarrels about which modus operandi warrants the seal have affected the praxis of organic growers.

Jeremiads applying the "conventionalization thesis" to organic farming have lamented that the growth of organic food from a small niche into a multibillion-dollar global industry insinuates that there has been corporate co-optation. It has seemed that the movement's linchpin ideals have dissipated into profiteering. Critics have alleged that, by "selling out," organics have moved from the moral high ground to the crass bargain basement. The transition from grassroots nirvana to mainstream nightmare has been well publicized in declensionist story lines, which have often made facile suppositions. There are fractures in the spectrum of categorizations between large, disingenuous, and hollow organics and small, sincere, and meaningful organics. Finger-wagging decriers of organic food's metamorphosis often ignore how motifs ingrained in organic rhetoric have, since their inception, reconciled the movement to the orthodox food framework. The movement grappled with the drawbacks and advantages of obliging the commercial market for decades. I argue that the organic fraternity in the United States was never as wholly radical or seditious as some votaries profess. Organic farmers were not raising citizen armies to supplant conventional agriculture; rather, they developed stand-ins for the chemical model. Organic consumers "voted" with their dollars but did not overhaul the entire regime, however much they detested it. This book analyzes the tension between subcultural and mainstream facets in the organic movement since the 1940s. No true revolution ever took place, but some sects within the organic movement continue to clamor for one.

At times, organic farming has indeed posed a formidable challenge to conventional farming's axes of power. For the most part, though, organivores have banked on nonconfrontational language, indirect protests, and individualized responsibility. They have demonstrated the pleasant—often intangible—benefits accruing to those who engage in organic activities. The underlying motivations of people doting on organics have included the improvement of physical health, personal fulfillment, and the achievement of internal purity. Those growing and consuming organic food have pragmatically expressed displeasure with pesticides through defensive self-protection. Some organicists have had lofty goals to change the world but pursued these through a quest for private satisfaction. Despite the periodic theme of "revolution," these acts have often been limited ripostes. Consumers were expected to assume the individual "burden" of purchasing organics. Backyard gardening and routine shopping decisions were less effective than other kinds of activism could have been, such as large-scale political lobbying demanding greater legislative reform, which could have pressured "the establishment" and facilitated the enlargement of organic agriculture. Chronic dependence on the behavior of individuals restricted the organic movement's capacity for comprehensive social insurgency. Individuals purchasing organic food have rarely campaigned intensely for an overhaul of the mainstay assumptions underpinning conventional agriculture. Organic farmers did not raise their fists to overthrow the chemical industry. Yet, even as autonomous organic businesses succumbed to corporate mergers and the ringing cash registers of Wal-Mart, the movement retained transgressive ingredients.

The insights in *American Organic* matter to those who eat organic food—and those who don't. They matter to those who buy Martha Stewart Living 100 percent organic herb and vegetable seeds for their window boxes—and those who buy Roundup Weed & Grass Killer to spray their tomatoes. This book does not attempt to judge or to sway you. I do not tell the reader what to eat or whether organics are unabashedly good or bad. I am a historian, not a demagogue. Plenty of partisan publications have weighed in, but few have carefully pondered the organic movement's trajectory. The term "organic" has often been malleable enough to be pulled and twisted by rival factions, leaving a trail of misconceptions. Its elements were ideologically charged. My research unmasks planes of contention and complacency, resistance and accommodation. The organic movement's interdependent creeds have had a formative influence on its status and stupendous growth in American culture. The lived experiences of farmers, the convictions of consumers, the semantics of promoters, and the undertones of disparagers have been inseparable in steering how the movement has been branded and encountered. *American Organic* traces that history and chronicles how competing, oppositional axioms have affected the daily conundrum of "what should I eat . . . and why does it matter?"

CHAPTER ONE

Organic Destiny

Jerome Irving (J. I.) Rodale began making compost heaps in 1941, as he commenced farming on the sixty acres he had purchased near Emmaus, Pennsylvania. Compost piles included layers of vegetable material and grass clippings or animal manure as a nitrogen source. They had to be kept damp and rotated every few weeks with a pitchfork or shovel. Heat, worms, and fungi helped to break down the organic matter over the course of several months into rich black humus, the stable remains of decomposed plant tissue. This humus, or "mature" compost, would then help soil retain moisture, nutrients, and essential organisms. Rodale boldly believed that healthy soil—awash with organic matter—would produce healthy food and, in turn, healthy people. He used the term "organic" in reference to the crops he grew without artificial fertilizers or chemical sprays. He accentuated farming in "imitation of Nature."[1] His pesticide-free method, he discovered, could compete financially with the chemical bastion that governed agriculture at the time.[2] Heartened by his bountiful crops and the physical vigor they spawned, Rodale was not content to be a reclusive gardener. With crusading zeal, he propagated the organic gospel and became the first major advocate for organic growing in the United States. For this, Rodale is frequently cited as the de facto founding father of the US organic movement.[3] He was a pivotal—albeit colorful and controversial—figure who left his mark on much of the organic canon. This chapter examines Rodale's goals, activities, and interactions with other prominent people connected to the birth of organics. It illuminates perspectives on the intertwined themes of "natural" farming and gardening, homesteading, environmentalism, health, and commercial growth that emerged in the 1930s, blossomed in the 1940s, and expanded in the 1950s, and would persist throughout the organic movement. It also argues that Rodale never wanted to brazenly sabotage chemical agriculture or to meekly till the soil. Heralding the good word, earning revenue, and cultivating middle-of-the-road appeal were among his earliest ambitions.

"TOUCHING OFF A POWDER KEG": J. I. RODALE'S ORGANIC MISSION

An innovative, self-made man, Rodale was a quintessential Benjamin Franklin character: he was the architect of an organic printing empire, if not of organic farming itself. He had no background in agriculture or agronomy, but he was a novice who possessed ample enthusiasm. In the first year after procuring his land, Rodale received "such a wonderful crop that it was a joy to behold." Seeing the promising results and convinced that "this compost system was nothing short of magic," Rodale thought that "it would be a crime" not to teach others about it. Deciding to share his knowledge of "this simple method of farming," he unearthed his calling.[4] Rodale established *Organic Farming and Gardening*, touting it as a "New Kind of Agricultural Magazine." It was a milestone. Upon later reflection, Rodale said, "I did not dream at that time that I was touching off a powder keg."[5] The initial spark igniting that powder keg was unassuming and unpretentious. The magazine's inaugural issue in May 1942 included articles on composting, earthworms, soil fertility, and the superiority of mature (composted) animal manure over chemical fertilizers. From the beginning, it covered both gardening and farming. Doing things "Nature's Way" was a recurring typology. Each issue played an instrumental role in ardently articulating organic philosophies for acolytes.

Rodale's multifaceted magazine had far-reaching power with early organic growers; it carved out a niche partly due to the dearth of other data sources. It tackled topics like how to enliven the soil's microbiological activity with organic matter. However, the publication was never just about farming and gardening. Rodale wished to connect with the general public and address its apprehensions about food. In his first editorial, he discussed how synthetic fertilizers altered the nutritive value of food. Touting the impressive quality of eggs, meat, and vegetables raised by organic methods, he wrote, "The better-earning class of the public will pay a high price if they can be shown its value, and that they will save on doctor bills."[6] Throughout his life, Rodale displayed keen gravitas in alerting people to health hazards and organic blessings. In an issue of *Organic Farming and Gardening* from 1944, Rodale wrote that if all the food-producing soil in the country were "intensively treated in the organic manner," then "we could become a race of super-men and super-women."[7] He supported the commonplace allure of wholesome food for all and the bounteous profits it could reap for clever farmers. He wrote several seminal books, beginning with *Pay Dirt: Farming and Gardening with Composts* (1945). *Pay Dirt* proved to be an apt title for the book that launched

Organic heirloom tomatoes (Photo courtesy of Colleen Freda Burt)

Rodale on the path to being healthy, wealthy, and wise (in some circles, at least). He felt that organic gardening could remedy mineral deficiencies in crops, nutrient deficiencies in humans, and happiness deficiencies in society. Rodale was a passionate organic ambassador; he knew that savvy Americans were far more spellbound by optimum health and tasty tomatoes than by horticultural jargon about how lime in their compost would maintain good tilth and proper soil alkalinity. He started numerous other periodicals, and his compelling writing pioneered the vibrant organic movement in American culture.

Chemical agriculture reigned in the 1940s, when Rodale began his crusade. German chemist Justus von Liebig's assertion that plants needed only a straightforward arrangement of nitrogen, phosphorus, and potassium (NPK) was the dominant paradigm. Endorsing an NPK ratio that could be manufactured and applied artificially, agronomists downplayed the merits of humus. The chemical industry eagerly produced synthetic nitrogen fertilizers, promising to feed the world. Rodale obdurately disagreed with this mechanistic approach. He felt that the soil was a living organism, and that chemicals wrecked beneficial bacteria. Rodale yearned to "saturate every segment of American life with the realization that there is something radically wrong with the foundations of our civilization."[8] An agrichemical substratum was a blunder; true organic farming, the art of cooperating with nature, was the only suitable bedrock. At first, skeptics vilified Rodale as an incendiary "crackpot" and "food faddist."[9] Though he couldn't fully displace the disposition toward using chemicals, he was the vanguard actor in the cultural revision of attitudes toward organic farming. He eventually achieved a measure of legitimacy and renown as organic food came into vogue. When the number of organic gardening adherents ultimately boomed, Rodale would stand tall as the "leading apostle" of organically grown food.[10] Though no one person "invented" organic farming, Rodale's ability to capitalize on the organic explosion and parlay it into personal success would prompt some critics to impugn his motives. He may have been America's first "ecopreneur," with panache for both marketing and farming. In both capacities, when the stars aligned, Rodale thrived. He combined a genuine concern for educating Americans about organic farming and healthy living with an aptitude for making money by publishing that information. More than any other form of publicity, his magazines and books lifted public awareness of what "organic" meant.

SEEDS PLANTED

Rodale could be categorized as an archetypal rags-to-riches hero torn from the pages of a Horatio Alger novel. He was born in 1898 as Jerome Irving Cohen, one of eight children raised in what he called "the slums of New York City."[11] He grew up in a small flat at the rear of his father's grocery store. In his youth, he suffered from nagging headaches and colds.[12] Heart problems ran in the family; his father and five of his siblings died in their fifth or sixth decade due to heart attacks. He described himself as "mildly health-conscious since young adulthood."[13] To augment his fitness as a teenager, he followed self-improvement courses, such as the bodybuilding regimen of Bernarr Macfadden (1868–1959).[14] He worked as an accountant and federal tax auditor after graduating from high school. Feeling that a Jewish name would hinder his aspirations to enter the writing and publishing business, he changed his last name from Cohen to Rodale in 1921.[15] He married Anna Andrews in 1927 and had three children with her. After Rodale abandoned accounting, he initiated an electrical equipment manufacturing business with his brother and moved their plant to Pennsylvania in 1930. From this unlikely background, Rodale suddenly found himself "part of an agricultural scene." Observing farmers at work in the fields, he began to covet his own piece of land.[16] Farming was, at first, merely a hobby; his other diversion was publishing. With the revenue he earned from the factory, Rodale began a publishing company that issued magazines and pamphlets on humor, health, and etiquette.[17] In these short-lived and mostly unprofitable publications was the birth of Rodale Press. The erstwhile urbanite soon sought to disclose what he was learning on his farm too.

Rodale's fascination with organics began inadvertently when he stumbled upon the work of British agriculturist Sir Albert Howard (1873–1947), widely considered the "grandfather" of contemporary organic farming. Howard had served as a mycologist and agricultural lecturer in the Imperial Department of Agriculture for the West Indies, garnering knowledge of tropical agriculture. He then studied nutrient cycling in central India, at the Institute of Plant Industry in Indore, where he observed how the "methods of Nature" restored soil fertility. Howard developed the idea of emulating nature scientifically with an aerobic composting system. In the 1920s, he devised the "Indore Process," a practical way of making compost in which high-quality humus determined soil quality. The Indore Process manufactured humus from vegetable and animal wastes, with a base to neutralize acidity, and managed the admixture so microorganisms could function effectively.[18] Howard focused on building fertile soil according to "Nature's dictates." He came to believe that plant disease was "punishment meted out by Mother Earth for adopting methods of agriculture which are not in accordance with Nature's law of return."[19] Howard was knighted in 1934 for his contributions to agriculture. Gardeners who adopted his Indore mode of making compost discarded customary commercial fertilizers formulated with inorganic chemical compounds. Howard's Law of Return was his great principle underlying "Nature's farming." Animal and vegetable wastes had to be returned to the land. Nature provided the prototype for transforming wastes into humus, and this was the key to agricultural prosperity.[20]

The organic school often looked to Franklin King's classic *Farmers of Forty Centuries* (1911), which extolled the agricultural practices of China, Korea, and Japan, as an authoritative text. King urged the United States to adopt the ways of these "old-world farmers" for maintaining soil fertility, including the use of organic material as plant food.[21] Albert Howard also felt that the peasants of China, who returned all wastes to the land, came nearest to "the ideal set by Nature."[22] Howard believed that "Nature, the supreme farmer, manages her kingdom."[23] In *An Agricultural Testament* (1940), a founding text for organic farming, Howard predicted that at least half the illnesses of mankind would disappear once food supplies were raised from fertile soil and consumed fresh.[24] Rodale appreciated this adulation of "Nature" and the critique of NPK scripture; he became Howard's protégé. The link Rodale began to forge between organic farming and health would be a turning point in his vocation.

Other early organic advocates who coupled healthy humans with healthy soil also influenced Rodale. Sir Robert McCarrison (1878–1960), an English physician serving as director of research on nutrition in India in the 1930s, ascertained that farmyard manure produced foodstuffs of higher nutritive quality than those grown with chemicals on the same type of soil.[25] During lectures on his findings before the Royal Society of Arts in 1936, McCarrison stressed that the quality of vegetable foods depended on the manner of their cultivation, including soil, manure, rainfall, and irrigation conditions. He was adamant that "perfectly constituted food" was the greatest single factor in the acquisition and maintenance of good health.[26] Similarly, Weston A. Price (1870–1948), a dentist who examined isolated cultures in the 1930s, deduced that tooth decay and other diseases indicated divergence from "Nature's fundamental laws of life and health."[27] He demonstrated how the adoption of a "modernized" diet led to declining levels of health among "primitive" clusters. In *Nutrition and Physical Degeneration* (1939), Price avowed that people were actually malnourished with industrial foods like refined flours, canned goods, sweetened fruits, and chocolate. Orthodox medical professionals largely ignored Price, but he gathered followers. Rodale read Price's work and accepted the inference that dental conditions were "almost perfect" among groups eating a "simple primitive diet" of food from soil without chemical fertilizers.[28] William Albrecht (1888–1974), chief soil scientist at the University of Missouri, also expounded on the connection between soil, food, and health in the 1940s. He rebuked the artificiality of the NPK dogma and viewed organic matter as the lifeblood of the soil. He reported a rise in diseases due to poor crops grown in soil treated as a commodity. In one speech to the American Chemical Society, Albrecht claimed that "the human species is degenerating because of a decline in soil fertility."[29] His audience was dubious, but Rodale and the nascent organic movement shared much of Albrecht's gloom.

Nutrient-rich organic soil seemed to account for the benefits of what became known as organic food. In 1941, Rodale read an article in an English health magazine about an experiment demonstrating the advantages of feeding children food grown by Albert Howard's organic composting technique. Intrigued, Rodale learned how the health of boys in a boarding school near London had improved when they were fed vegetables grown in this natural humus. The taste and quality of the vegetables also increased. The theory that the way food was grown could affect its nutritional quality was a new concept, unsupported by physicians. Yet, the evidence persuaded Rodale and seemed like common sense. Plagued by colds and regular headaches, he had tested various remedies but deemed none to be effective. Organically grown food appeared to be his salvation. Rodale was profoundly affected by reading *An Agricultural Testament* and contacted Howard.[30] Rodale said, "I could not rest until I purchased a farm in order to assure for ourselves a supply of food raised by the new method."[31] Howard and Rodale began to correspond, and Rodale later published many of Howard's writings. After Howard's death, Rodale professed that the world owed Howard an immense debt, because "it was he who first detected the pathetic fallacy of present-day chemical fertilization."[32] Rodale aspired to "carry the torch aloft for the spread of his ideas in this country."[33]

Rodale imported to the United States the Law of Return and principles of soil fertility that both Howard and Lady Eve Balfour (1899–1990) were circulating in England. Like Howard, Balfour had studied agriculture but questioned the farming methods of the day. After reading Howard's work, Balfour initiated experiments at the 210-acre Haughley Research Farm in Suffolk to scientifically compare the performance of chemical fertilizers with compost. Balfour endorsed Howard's Indore Process of manufacturing humus and asserted that "composting is as old as agriculture."[34] She also agreed with Franklin King's work and noted that "sooner or later all advocates of organic farming cite the Chinese," calling them "the Fathers of good husbandry."[35] Balfour insisted in *The Living Soil* (1943) that a "complete revolution in outlook" was necessary. A nation's health depended on the way food was grown, and agriculture should be looked upon as "the primary health service."[36] Balfour further argued that chemicals found to injure the soil should be forbidden and that governments should recognize the threats posed by the loss of fecundity in soil. Her overall purpose was to present evidence that affirmed "the wholeness of the cycle of life," which encompassed the correlation between soil fertility and full health.[37] Balfour began traveling the globe, hoping, as Rodale did, to diffuse the organic message.

Howard and Balfour highlighted the relationships between healthy soil, plants, livestock, and people. Both were connected to the nonprofit Soil

Association, which was founded in 1946 to promote health and organic agriculture, and which played a central institutional role within the British organic movement. Their cohort included Lord Northbourne (1896–1982), an agriculturalist born as Walter E. C. James, who was the first to use the term "organic" with respect to a farming system that was an "organic whole." Northbourne felt that the farm had to be "organic in more senses than one."[38] He wrote in *Look to the Land* (1940) that, if "wholeness" was to be attained, the farm must have "a biological completeness; it must be a living entity, it must be a unit which has within itself a balanced organic life."[39] He believed that adopting "true mixed farming" was "the first step towards the perfection of the individual farm," and it would be "a healthy organic whole yielding a true profit rather than only a financial profit."[40] For Northbourne, as for Howard, the "Rule of Return" is the essence of farming, and the farm should be a symbiotic unit. Lionel Picton, another founder of Britain's Soil Association and an associate of McCarrison and Howard, wrote about nutrition and food quality in his essay "Medical Testament" (1939). Picton blamed poor food from factory-made fertilizer for bad teeth, rickets, and anemia. He suggested that organic agriculture could transform national health.[41] Picton began editing *The Compost News Letter* in 1941 and writing books on medicine, soil fertility, diet, and the principles of organic farming.[42] Organic farmers like Picton and Rodale suspected that they alone could rescue mankind from the unhealthy sinkhole of conventional agriculture.

A nonchemical but more celestial agricultural method predating organics was the biodynamic approach, based on lectures given by Austrian philosopher Rudolf Steiner (1861–1925). In a lecture delivered in 1923 on beekeeping, Steiner stated that men had "yet to learn much from Nature" and ought to "recognize the spiritual in Nature."[43] Steiner incorporated working with the natural environment, special herbal preparations, and the movements of the moon in the mystical views of anthroposophy. Biodynamic farming, by extension, used organic processes like manure but embraced cosmic tenets, such as planting seeds by lunar rhythms and applying elixirs to plants. Each farm was an organism affected by unseen forces but capable of self-healing. Dutch soil scientist Ehrenfried Pfeiffer (1899–1961) worked closely with Steiner and was a key player in bringing Steiner's opinions to the United States. Pfeiffer ran a biodynamic farm and training center in Kimberton, Pennsylvania, and helped found the Biodynamic Association (BDA) in 1938. In *Bio-Dynamic Farming and Gardening* (1938), Pfeiffer wrote that sound agriculture could only be achieved through "the principle of an Organic

A small organic garden (Photo courtesy of Colleen Freda Burt)

Whole."[44] Pfeiffer studied the role of earthworms in enriching the soil, and the *New York Times* reported that the "bio-kinetic farming" school favored earthworm multiplication in lieu of strong chemical fertilizers to produce bigger plants.[45] Rodale met Pfeiffer at Kimberton Farm; though Rodale did not adopt Steiner's numinous teachings, he did espouse the perspective of treating the farm as a biological organic unit. *Bio-Dynamics*, a periodical first published in 1941 by the Bio-Dynamic Farming and Gardening Association, featured articles on organic farming, since there were many parallels between the two standpoints: both favored compost heaps, the inclusion of manure, and the "natural balance of nature."[46] Pfeiffer also became a regular contributor to Rodale's farming magazine, in which he wrote about his own practical research. Biodynamics was in Rodale's organic cognizance, but he moved in a discrete direction. Rodale's direction was decidedly away from the chemical-dependent approach of American agriculture.

From the 1930s onward, a "get big or get out" mentality had been the agricultural norm. Carey McWilliams coined the term "factory farming" in 1939 to describe the highly industrialized agriculture emerging in California.[47] Tractors, combines, mechanical pickers, and other gasoline-powered equipment replaced horse-drawn plows by the 1940s. Fewer family members were needed to perform physical labor as farms became more productive. Machines made mammoth, specialized farms more practical. Higher operating costs squeezed out many farmers, so ownership was concentrated in fewer hands, which enlarged profits for those willing to make the capital investment. King-size farms hired temporary employees during the planting and harvesting seasons, and some exploited migratory workers. Government policies facilitated the trend toward gigantic farms, and World War II accentuated it.[48] The Future Farmers of America (FFA) and 4-H groups joined federal and state departments of agriculture to promote home gardening as a vital contribution to the war effort. The US Department of Agriculture "Food Fights for Freedom" campaign inspired millions of Americans to plant "Victory Gardens." Vegetable patches appeared on front lawns, while kitchen gardens became badges of patriotism. A flood of people dove into homesteading and farming. However, these groups also pressed for intensive tilling to upgrade farm capacity after the war ended.[49] Chemical fertilizers seemed indispensable. At the other end of the spectrum, Rodale had a blueprint for the future of agriculture.

TOUCHING OFF A MOVEMENT

In February 1942, Rodale produced a special issue of his small magazine *Fact Digest* with the headline "Present Day Crops Unfit for Human Consumption!" This issue, unlike previous ones, "flew off the racks and resulted in a deluge of letters calling for more such articles."[50] Rodale discontinued *Fact Digest* and created *Organic Farming and Gardening* instead. Albert Howard would be an associate editor. Rodale said, "Little did I realize what I was touching off—that I would be the one to introduce this great movement into the United States." The first issue, in May 1942, was "a slim thing with a self-cover and 16 pages of coarse newsprint."[51] "Back to Nature in Agriculture" was the headline on the cover. Rodale promised readers that, although learning to make compost heaps from manure would mean extra labor, the farmer would be "more than repaid by getting better crops and selling them at higher prices."[52] He mailed out about fourteen thousand free copies of the first issue to farmers, soliciting subscriptions at $1 a year, but received only twelve responses. The whole thing might have petered out right then. There were other ways to farm. America didn't *need* an organic movement . . . or did it? Though the "prospects looked bleak," Rodale was undeterred.

After sending out circular letters instead, the list of subscribers began to grow.[53]

The cover of *Organic Farming and Gardening* for October 1942 featured a warning that "the U.S. Government has admitted that the reason 50 percent of the men called for the draft were rejected was because they were undernourished."[54] The magazine swore to tell readers how to make organic fertilizer that would "remedy this condition." Howard contributed an article with instructions for assembling a backyard compost heap. Agronomist William Albrecht wrote about the effect of sick soils on animals. Ancillary articles addressed seaweed as fertilizer, the benefits of earthworms, and the increasing number of abandoned farms that were becoming "eye-sores" in the countryside.[55] One page in the issue promoted a course of practical study to be offered by Ehrenfried Pfeiffer in January 1943, which would cover soil chemistry, tilling, botany, farm economics, dairy management, and other topics. The "Reader's Correspondence" section included letters from readers in Ohio, Nebraska, Illinois, Pennsylvania, and New York who had questions about chicken manure, weeds, and compost piles. There was a full-page advertisement for Hoegger Goat Supplies, along with smaller classified ads for compost equipment, earthworms, biodynamic farming books, and rabbit market magazines. Articles by Edward Faulkner, Lord Northbourne, and Charles Darwin were reprinted with permission from other books or journals. Rodale acknowledged in his editor's note that most of these pieces were "heavy reading."

Edward Faulkner, an organic farming proponent who caused a ripple of excitement in the agricultural world by snubbing standard plowing practices, was an influential friend of Rodale's. Faulkner gained national attention with his controversial book *Plowman's Folly* (1943). He critiqued what he regarded as the misguided use of science and technology in prevailing farming customs. He buttressed the notion that moldboard plows were damaging the soil by pushing organic material down too deeply. Instead, disk harrows should be used and applied only to the upper surface of the soil. He felt that organic management of soil could evince fertility. Rodale praised *Plowman's Folly*, which rapidly sold fifty thousand copies. Both Faulkner and Rodale seemed like sinners in the establishment's agricultural temple. Implacable resistance to organic farming came from several members of the USDA, which had been responsible for directing federal policies on farming and food since the nineteenth century. Faulkner's book was classified as heresy for violating the divine right of plows. Many eyebrows were raised at organic farming, which seemed fanciful and even outrageous.

Organic Farming and Gardening did not initially entice professional farmers. By 1943, Rodale realized that he "had better leave the farmer for later" and changed the name to *Organic Gardening*. Progress was more rapid from that time on, and Rodale saw that "people gave more respect to the publication."[56] In the February issue that year, he discussed how organic fertilization was "a far more natural method for raising crops than doping the soil with high-powered, concentrated chemicals."[57] A reader from Oklahoma wrote in approval of the magazine's viewpoint, because it was "quite at variance with the orthodox traditional attitude" that had developed under the "influence of commercial high pressure salesmanship" in American farming.[58] Several issues remarked on the ongoing war. The cover in August 1943 decreed "Help the War Effort: Use Only Home-Made Organic Fertilizers." Rodale's editorial suggested that the creation of a "land army" after the war could preserve organic wastes for the "enrichment of the land." He felt this would combat unemployment and also "save the soil of our country."[59] An article in July 1944 pinpointed how Victory Gardens were supplementing wartime foodstuff shortages and creating a greater interest in plants. In the issue from September 1944, Rodale enumerated forty reasons why farming with compost was superior to using artificial fertilizers. The first reason was that it improved "the general fertility level of the farm and garden"; number twenty-four was that it mitigated "the weed menace"; and reason thirty-six was that "foods raised organically taste better." As a bonus, Rodale added that compost farming actually entailed less work overall.[60] In the early years of *Organic Gardening*, the covers were plain and the only illustrations were hand sketches. Some black-and-white photographs appeared in 1944, and then covers over the next two years featured rustic photos of things like butterflies, cows, farmhouses, trees, horse-drawn buggies, birds, flowers, children, vegetables, bunnies, and swans. The magazine lost money for the first sixteen years, but Rodale persevered, retained loyal readers, and found an avid audience among home gardeners who believed in his cause.

Rodale couldn't refrain from giving healthy-eating advice, which often strayed from what the government proffered. The United States had developed Recommended Dietary Allowances (RDAs) of calories and nutrients (for example, protein, iron, calcium, vitamins A, D, and C, and so on) in 1941, providing nutritional guidance for citizens with a "margin of safety" that took the availability of food during rationing years into account. The USDA released a National Wartime Nutrition Guide in 1943, with counsel for meeting the RDAs, despite limited food supplies. A war-themed ad in

McCall's magazine in 1944 showed a bottle of Ovaltine pulling a solider in a wagon, with other wagons labeled Vitamin B_1, Vitamin D, Vitamin A, and Iron behind them. The ad headline promised that Ovaltine gave you "all the *Extra* vitamins and minerals you need."[61] To Rodale, Ovaltine and the RDAs seemed inadequate; he had a few atypical suggestions for people seeking a health boost. In October 1944, he devoted his *Organic Gardening* editorial to the relationship between health and soil. Instead of the millions spent annually on vitamin pills, the best investment for public well-being would be funding for farmers making humus. Organic food, he said, was the secret ingredient for "a veritable fountain of youth."[62]

In 1944, Rodale exhorted people to "demand food that is raised with organic fertilizers" in order to "achieve the ultimate in the perfection of health."[63] Only organic food, he told an audience in 1948, had "the maximum amount of vitamins and minerals."[64] Rodale's ideology was derived from American health food rhetoric and, in turn, swayed it. With his intense opinions about health and sustenance, Rodale followed in the footsteps of dietary reformers and fitness evangelists like Sylvester Graham (1794–1851), William Andrus Alcott (1798–1859), Wilbur Atwater (1849–1907), Horace Fletcher (1849–1919), John Harvey Kellogg (1852–1943), and Bernarr Macfadden. Despite hard times, American diets grew more nutritious throughout the 1930s, due largely to supplemental home canning, truck farming, and government distribution of vitamin-rich foods. However, the average US diet still had plenty of room for improvement in the 1940s.[65] Nutritionists Samuel and Violette Glasstone lamented the pervasiveness of "devitalized foods" like white bread, white sugar, oleomargarine, coffee, canned beans, preserved meats, and overcooked vegetables. Americans were baffled about how to apply nutrition discoveries to their daily lives.[66] Rodale recognized this and sought to fill a vexing informational void with his books and magazines.

Rodale published fervent treatises on the nutritional capacities of organic food all through his life. He first theorized that organic fare aided human health because it encouraged indispensable bacterial and enzyme life in the stomach, whereas food produced with chemical fertilizers inhibited the growth of bacteria meant to succor the digestive process.[67] Catering to health-inclined readers, Rodale wrote an advertisement soliciting magazine subscribers that promised: "You can help mightily to avoid rheumatism, arthritis, gall stones and kidney troubles by growing your own GOOD food . . . Learn how by reading ORGANIC FARMING AND GARDENING."[68] He expounded on a host of other explanations for organic food's supremacy in the ensuing years. In May 1945, *Organic Gardening* cautioned readers about poison sprays on apples and envisaged a day "when only organically grown fruit, carefully picked, will be marketable."[69] This correlation between organics and health would never fade, as consumers began to associate better health, purity, and integrity with organic food. They tended to believe organic foods were more nutritious than their counterparts, though there would never be much substantiated evidence for this. In the 1940s, the field of clinical nutrition was still in its infancy, and Rodale's assertions seemed nothing short of outlandish to medical professionals.

Organic Gardening's readers continued to write in with testimonials. In February 1945, a man from Maine thanked Rodale for the "wonderful magazine" and stated that several men in his community were forming an organic gardening club. Rodale printed the letter, hoping it would foment other similar clubs.[70] A woman from California wrote in March 1945, sending snapshots of her own compost heaps crafted by the Indore Process and expressing appreciation for the "education and moral support" she obtained from the magazine.[71] Some readers had quite specific questions: "What causes leaves of African violets to become spotted with yellow spots?" "Are eucalyptus leaves dangerous to earthworms?" "How many pounds of phosphate rock would I need for 9000 square feet of space?"[72] A Florida man beguiled by the magazine wrote in April 1945; he felt that organic gardening was "the answer" but warned that "yours is a crusade, and as you grow you will meet many obstacles."[73]

There were, undeniably, obstacles to the budding organic crusade, which only made inroads into agricultural colleges and USDA experiment stations slowly. Skepticism was a foremost impediment. Alex Laurie of Ohio State University wrote a piece in the issue of *Garden Path* from December 1945 contending that, although the new *Organic Gardening* had instigated "a revival of the old theory that 'chemicals' are injurious," there was nothing wrong with commercial fertilizers.[74] Albert Howard agreed that Rodale's "army of compost-minded crusaders" was certain to encounter opposition from the manufacturers of artificial manures and poison sprays and their "disciples in the administration, in the research stations and agricultural colleges, in the press, and in broadcasting."[75] The antagonism from those who excoriated organics was daunting but not insurmountable. Despite the hindrances, *Organic Gardening* also reported that it was making headway in the burgeoning movement. When a farm shop in London selling organically grown food opened, Rodale called it the first in developing the "commercial possibilities" of organics.[76] Heinrich Meyer, the magazine's assistant editor, was cheerful about a radio program with "a wide audience among gardeners" that had recommended *Organic Gardening* over the air.[77] Howard pointed out in *The Soil and Health* (1947) that he had been involved with the magazine since its beginning, and the number of subscribers had grown to fifty-one thousand by August 1946, despite wartime publishing difficulties and paper shortages. Howard commended Rodale's efforts and affirmed that "a definite trend towards organic farming and gardening is well under way in America."[78] Rodale, he said, had "started a movement in the New World which promises soon to become an avalanche."[79]

The avalanche would not bury any chemical leviathans, but Rodale himself was similarly sanguine; he felt that *Organic Gardening* represented "a major revolution in the matter of producing the food of America." Having "educated thousands of people to practice this new agriculture, and to go out and preach this new gospel," seemed like a coup.[80] As more organic garden clubs formed across the nation, the magazine introduced a column devoted to their news. The San Diego club recounted that forty-two people had attended its first meeting, local attentiveness was "quite keen," and some members were "carrying forward the good word of Organics" by giving lectures and classes.[81] Rodale thanked readers who took the trouble of sending in clippings from all over the country showing that "the organic method is spreading."[82] While he suspected that "before long a considerable segment of the public will obtain their food from farmers who are pursuing organicultural practices," Rodale sensed that "this revolution will take time."[83]

Rodale's ebullience for health was potent, but he acknowledged glitches that could derail the movement. He said in 1947 that it would be "a long time before even appreciable amounts of organically grown foods are available generally in the public markets." In the meantime, he prescribed the "Rodale Diet" for the betterment of health, which included kelp, mushrooms, coconut, watercress, palm cabbage, wild rice, cranberries, honey, maple syrup, nuts, fish, and wild game that were "free from the taint of chemical fertilizers."[84] He extolled the basic diet of "primitive peoples" that was unlike the adulterated, fragmentized, dehydrated food "not fit to be eaten by human beings" that had appeared in the last few generations.[85] Rodale did see incremental growth in the magazine's circulation. There were sixty thousand subscribers to *Organic Gardening* in 1947, each paying $3.00 per year, and Rodale thought they represented "a vital force in our National community."[86]

With ninety thousand paid subscribers in 1948, Rodale was confident enough to declare organiculture "a vigorous and growing movement" that was "here to stay."[87]

PAY DIRT, EARTHWORMS, AND NATURAL FOOD

Rodale's first full-length book, *Pay Dirt: Farming & Gardening with Composts*, is a benchmark text of the organic canon. As a practical guidebook for aspiring organic farmers and gardeners, it discussed the biology of soil, the theory and practice of compost, the dangers of artificial fertilizers, and the connections between health, disease, and food. *Pay Dirt* also drew upon culturally resonant ideals of natural food, family farms, and harmony with the earth. Throughout the book, Rodale emphasized that organic farming was more humane, benign, and concordant with the natural world than chemical-intensive agriculture. He railed against the "assembly-line, machine-run agriculture" that was in its heyday.[88] Organic farming, in contrast, was a superior and straightforward "imitation of Nature."[89] Rodale subscribed to a pervasive opinion in American culture that each man ought to own a piece of the earth. Engaging with nature carries ethical connotations, and, customarily, agriculture has figured prominently as a conduit for postulations about humans and morality. Man's ability to cultivate the earth has long been seen as a "civilized" trait. To subdue the land through agriculture meant the conquest of the chaotic, depraved wilderness. Rodale acclaimed "a country of prosperous farms and a healthy, vigorous people creating a fine, new community life."[90] His insistence that a "healthy society" must be "in touch with the land" embodied a cultural preference for a preindustrial agricultural golden age.

Entrenched views about humans and nature are often grounded in value judgments, and organic farming was thus endowed with particular moral weight. The last chapter of *Pay Dirt*, titled "Good and Bad Farming Practices," was ensconced in assumptions about balance and equilibrium in "Nature." The emotive themes of harmony, constancy, and order recurred in *Pay Dirt* and other works on organic farming. The organic movement upheld positive correlations between uncomplicated farming methods, natural cycles, and unmutilated landscapes. There were habitual references to "Mother Earth," "Mother Nature," "wholeness," and the "cycle of life." In the 1940s, the succession model of plant communities, advanced by Henry Cowles and

Frederic Clements, governed ecology and agriculture. This theory posited that systems reached a climax of general stasis.[91] Employing this esteem for untainted nature, Rodale described organic farms as ones that emulated the stable structure of natural systems. *Pay Dirt* dispensed unabridged details on the process of organic farming, beginning with the biology of the soil. Rodale explained that soil was a living substance in which vital microbes lived together in "a delicate, balanced relationship closely controlled by Nature."[92] He argued that chemical fertilizers, pesticides, and herbicides deprived the soil of organic materials that fostered the healthy growth of plants. Chemicals indiscriminately killed beneficial fungi and bacteria, making them counterproductive to soil health. He paid homage to those unsung heroes, earthworms, which functioned as "Nature's plow" and were necessary to maintain soil fertility. Artificial fertilizers killed earthworms; this was dangerous because "Nature consists of a chain of interrelated and interlocked life cycles. Remove any one factor and you will find that she cannot do her work efficiently."[93] Agriculture needed to take a holistic approach. An emphasis on the primacy of "Nature" and its intricate, interdependent processes resurfaced throughout *Pay Dirt*. Rodale reiterated that dedication to increasing the soil's organic matter would pay rich dividends in the long run.

Organic farming implied continuity with the past as it rejected commercial agricultural dogma. Rodale believed that organic farms emulated "old-fashioned farms," because they used animal manure instead of chemicals, were self-contained, and relied on equilibrium between crops and livestock. Organic farms were consciously *not* run as factories. Rodale proposed that "vast-acred, assembly-line, single-crop farms ought to be outlawed."[94] Yet, he did not see modernization itself as his nemesis. He buoyed the use of certain machines, like manure-loaders, that could take "the back-breaking labor out of making and turning compost heaps."[95] Nonetheless, Rodale upheld timeless apparitions of organic farming, affirming that he belonged to a "cult" in which membership had been held by "good practical farmers from Adam's time on down the centuries."[96] He preferred time-honored agronomic strategies like cover cropping and crop rotation over forceful, chemically induced devices for soil fertility. Rodale criticized the ignoble character of corporate agriculture, stating that large farms were reprehensible. Raising chickens had become "Big Business," dependent on an "assembly line sort of production" in which the birds were merely "egg machines" in the "laying factory."[97] Concurrently, farmers who bred chickens organically were penalized because the eggs looked odd. Rodale saw "fashions in eggs as in clothes."

Organic eggs for a toddler (Photo courtesy of Colleen Freda Burt)

He found it ironic that "the public by its own fickle whim encourages practices which give it foods of dubious nourishing qualities."[98] However, Rodale advised organic agriculture entrepreneurs to trust that, like other fashions, this one was likely to change.

Rodale was especially concerned about nutrition and health, asserting that food raised organically tasted better and also contained more vitamins and minerals.[99] Using alarmist language, he warned about the dangers that synthetic weed-killers posed to soil, animals, birds, and humans. Rodale insisted, "We cannot go on forever treating the soil as a chemical laboratory and expect to turn out *natural* food. What we are getting is more and more *chemical* food."[100] He castigated the "continuous propaganda of the chemical interests."[101] Rodale cited doctors who decreed that artificial fertilizers caused cancer, and he quoted scientists who acknowledged that poison sprays killed birds. Denouncing the deleterious effects of insecticides that were destroying wildlife and bird havens, he said, "The balance of Nature is upset."[102] Rodale also alerted consumers to risks from bleaches in white flour and arsenic on fruit polluted by poison sprays. The only way to counteract these perils, Rodale insisted, was to use organic composts and adopt safe routines for checking for garden insects. Although he admitted that "if you tell a farmer that he can raise fruit without spraying he will look at you with that queer expression that seems to question your sanity," Rodale averred that "actual results show it can be done."[103]

In the introduction to *Pay Dirt*, Albert Howard praised Rodale's "audacity" and courage in acquiring a farm, experimenting with compost on his crops, and offering the results to his countrymen.[104] *Pay Dirt* struck a chord with members of the general public entranced by farming and gardening. One—albeit biased—reviewer in *Organic Gardening* called it the "garden book of the year" in 1946, because it explained "a substantial aspect of the revolution in farming and gardening which is going on all over the world."[105] Decades later, a *New York Times* column on garden books said that *Pay Dirt* had been "met with well-earned popularity" and dealt "lucidly with the all-important subject of compost for farm and garden."[106] Commercially, though, Rodale deemed *Pay Dirt* a "dismal failure," since it had sold only 36,432 copies by 1953.[107] Like Aldo Leopold's *A Sand County Almanac* (1949), it was ahead of its time as an ecological treatise. Most Americans were not yet attuned to the anticorporate farming sentiments Rodale articulated. After World War II, leftover chemicals and new technologies were revamping agriculture. The USDA regularly insisted that farm chemicals were entirely safe. The scourge of ubiquitous synthetic pesticides tormented the organic movement. Biodynamic farmer Sterling Edwards complained in 1948 about how the government had "done so little to inform the farmer of the advantages and present stages of the art of organic soil treatment."[108] Rodale also grumbled that agricultural scientists in the government and state colleges "seem to be fighting the spread of the organic method of farming. They say it is impractical and impossible without ever making a move to try it out."[109] Rodale believed that technological expertise was a poor substitute for the complexity of organic nature, but the postwar climate was infused with optimistic faith in futuristic scientific miracles that ran counter to Rodale's old-fashioned proposals. He could not add ratification from the agricultural powers-that-be to his arsenal. *Pay Dirt* later went through multiple printings and was published in Japan in 1951 under the title *Ogon No Tsuchi* (Gold in the Earth). The publishers stated that it was "creating a sensation" among farmers who had been heavily burdened with payments for chemical fertilizer.[110] Few organic adherents read *Pay Dirt* in the ensuing decades, because a plethora of updated guides on how to farm organically were published. Nevertheless, it was a groundbreaking book, setting the tenor for the route that organic agriculture would travel in the United States.[111]

Pay Dirt and other garden instruction books that followed conveyed practical and symbolic organic credos. For myriad people attracted to the countryside, organic farming became a critical element of the do-it-yourself lifestyle known as homesteading. Homesteading was a deliberate, self-conscious choice to move from an urban to a rural setting. Individually or collectively, it could be seen as an act of both rebellion and revitalization.[112] Organic handbooks and narratives shared characteristics with a reservoir of prescriptive homesteading literature in American culture. Authors in this vein have produced manuals for the general public that were permeated with references to the superiority of countrified life. Much of organic farming's lexicon was built on the foundation of homesteading texts. Though he predated contemporary visions of organic homesteading, Henry David Thoreau was the archetypal character in the rituals of "living deliberately." Thoreau's aspirations in going to Walden Pond were liberation from materialism and communion with the natural world. He praised the "innocence and beneficence of Nature."[113] Part of the lasting appeal of *Walden* (1854) has been the allure of being in "undisturbed solitude and stillness" next to a placid pond, listening to singing whip-poor-wills and eating handpicked huckleberries.[114] Thoreau provided his readers with lists and figures on the economic advantages of an unembellished life. Simplicity and self-sufficiency were within reach for everyone. Thoreau chopped down white pines to build his house and planted a garden. He spent many hours hoeing, harvesting, threshing, picking, and eating the beans he planted. Both literally and metaphorically, he came to cherish the beans, because, he wrote, "they attached me to the earth."[115] Thoreau, like Rodale and a host of others after him, perpetuated a long-standing belief that connecting with the source of one's food bred a heightened sense of health and happiness.

Thoreau was an exemplar of the American pastoral tradition. In the early twentieth century, the "Country Life" creed depicting cities as crowded and diseased reflected Thoreau's legacy. The Country Life Commission saluted agriculture as the backbone of national virtues. Liberty Hyde Bailey (1858–1954), a Cornell University botanist and horticulturalist, was the primary spokesman for this impetus in the United States. Bailey served as editor of *Country Life in America*, launched in 1901, which presented the joys of rural residence, both permanent and seasonal. The magazine was full of images and stories about gardening and farming, birds, poultry, county fairs, automobile travel, country homes, outdoor sports, and wild nature. John Burroughs contributed a poem, "The Cuckoo," to the first issue; the issue from July 1905 included a balance sheet of expenses on a gentleman's estate; the issue from February 1907 had pieces titled "The Show Dog," "Egret Murder," and "The Coming Fruit—the Mango." *Country Life* noted how the social and intellectual plusses of the city could combine with the humble joys of the country. Bailey believed that the simple life was "a state of mind."[116] Objecting to mindless nostalgia, he argued that both urban and rural forces should shape civilization. Encouraging people to remain in agriculture, he resolved that it had to be a lucrative business. Bailey plugged conservation-minded farming, the elimination of the middleman system to increase profits for farmers, and a general revitalization of the countryside. He said the farmer not only "feeds the world" but also "saves the world."[117] President Theodore Roosevelt appointed the Country Life Commission in 1908 to investigate the lives of the nation's rural population. In a letter to Bailey, he wrote of how the "great farmer class" was vital to national economic and moral welfare. Roosevelt felt the commission's inspection could expose deficiencies in country life that needed to be remedied.[118] The *Report of the Commission on Country Life*, published in 1911, expressed the view that country life must be made attractive, satisfying, and remunerative.[119] In its findings, the commission underscored the need for the formation of organized business interests among cooperating farmers, the development of new schools with outdoor lessons to prepare children for country life, and improvements in roads and mail delivery to facilitate communication among country people.

Other spokesmen for country living accentuated the potential for homesteads and small-scale farms to prosper, offer personal contentment, and revive the countryside. Land reformer Bolton Hall advocated intensive farming on small city plots. He also cheered people on to leave overcrowded, unhealthful metropolitan life and move to the nearby country. Hall's series of how-to books included *Three Acres and Liberty* (1907) and *A Little Land and a Living* (1908). He hoped to convince young men who saw agriculture as a stagnant profession that it could, in fact, be profitable and rewarding for those who approached it intelligently. Hall was part of a back-to-the-land movement that stretched from early in the twentieth century through World War II. Untold Americans were hungry for a preindustrial, bucolic world. Media sources that discussed the virtues of farm life educated those who wanted to move to the countryside. Alongside *Country Life in America*, mass-circulation magazines like *Collier's*, *Sunset*, and the *Atlantic Monthly* offered articles on how to find rural property and first-person accounts of thriving on small acreages.[120] Liberty Hyde Bailey wrote in 1923 that homesteading, as an "integral part of farming," encompassed "the art of living."[121] To homesteaders, growing food was a prudent practice that sustained an autonomous existence. Participants tended to assume that their acts would yield freedom, security, simplicity, and a meaningful relationship with nature. Their goal was to decrease commercial consumption levels yet increase their quality of life. In pining for a "middle ground," the flawless balance of sociable culture and peaceful seclusion, some set up cloistered retreats; others maintained communal connections.[122] Homesteading was fundamental to the art of living organically, and organic food was woven into the fabric of homesteading.

RALPH BORSODI AND THE SCHOOL OF LIVING

Notwithstanding Thoreau's solitary experiment, families and communal groups have often partaken in organically inclined homesteading. Ralph Borsodi (1886–1977), an economist and philosopher of sorts, moved his family two hours away from New York City to an expansive country farm in 1920. This groundbreaking homesteader intended his shift to be a critique of overindustrialized tendencies in "this ugly civilization." Borsodi described in *Flight from the City* (1933) how his family began producing fruits, vegetables, milk, eggs, and nearly everything else they needed for a "more independent, more expressive way of life."[123] Borsodi popularized the idea that any man facing unemployment or financial difficulties in Depression-era America could greatly improve his quality of life by choosing an agricultural mode of existence in place of an industrial one. He thought autonomous farm life and "family security" were accessible to anyone willing to make the effort.

Economic security, private satisfaction, and harmony with the earth were the incentives that compelled Borsodi to undertake modern homesteading. The farm enabled Borsodi to appreciate the beauty that came from "contact with nature and from the growth of the soil, from flowers and fruits, from gardens and trees, from birds and animals."[124] It also convinced him that factories and mass manufacturing were more wasteful than individual production. Through homesteading, Borsodi developed an appreciation for "pure and unadulterated foods" and a "distaste for the commercialized foodstuffs" his family had been eating. He opposed commercial products for both economic and nutritional reasons, craving "pure and fresh food" instead of white bread, polished rice, or white sugar.[125] Borsodi reinforced traditional gender roles, insisting that cooking was an artistic endeavor through which the American housewife could exercise her creative talents. However, he supported the use of domestic equipment—like pressure cookers, laundry machines, and home gristmills—to eliminate drudgery. He claimed that "we are masters of machines instead of servants to them."[126] Borsodi sought the comforts of the city as well as the ease of country existence, rather than a "return to primitive ways of life."[127] Borsodi stressed the responsible use of natural resources and supported the blooming organic agriculture movement. He wrote articles for Rodale's *Organic Gardening* magazine in the 1940s, including "How You Can Save $1.12 an Hour by Making Your Own Fertilizers," a series titled "Humus Manufacture in the Orient," and pieces on soil depletion. He directed an experiment that compared the costs of buying and using artificial fertilizers to the costs of organic composts made with Albert Howard's Indore Process; this experiment revealed a net saving of $4.10 per acre with the organic method. Borsodi concluded that it was unnecessary for farmers and gardeners to use chemical or commercial fertilizers and published his results in an issue of *Organic Gardening*.[128]

Borsodi also championed decentralized communities based on local control; he solicited government loans for homestead development projects. Grassroots autonomy and cooperation were key aspects of the communal homestead undertakings Borsodi engaged in. He created the School of Living in Suffern, New York, to teach other families how to achieve greater self-sufficiency and fulfillment. For decades, the School of Living was a center for research and education in community development, ethical land tenure, and homesteading. The school's journal, *Green Revolution*, touted itself as a voice for "modern homesteading, family-farming and decentralized culture." It distributed how-to pieces, such as those on cheese making, beekeeping, and building compost piles, but it also focused on politics. Articles in the journal propped up the principles of decentralization, egalitarianism, and ecology. The School of Living relocated to Ohio in 1950 and continued to offer workshops in organic gardening, alternative energy, anarchism, forestry, holistic health, midwifery, poetry, therapeutic massage, prison reform, and tax resistance. Most homesteaders were less active on a national level than Borsodi, but many still embarked upon peregrinations away from what seemed to be an "ugly civilization," gravitating toward a more beautiful—and organic—scene.

Though not a full-fledged homesteader himself, Rodale supported back-to-the-landers, because "the majority of human beings need some contact with country life, to restore the soul."[129] He asserted that nations, like people, "need to renew their strength by contact with the earth."[130] He affirmed that the straightforward procedure of organic farming was perfectly suited for adaptation by amateur homesteaders, who would become an integral part of America's "sturdy, healthy population." The opposite trend—what Rodale called an "away-from-the-land" movement—extended "large-scale mono-cultural practices" and a "plantation kind of commercial farming," which would only end in "disaster to the land."[131] Attempting to impose uniformity with the indiscriminate use of pesticides was pure foolhardiness. The phantoms of dust storms and abandoned farms that had materialized during the crises of the 1930s loomed behind Rodale's admonition. While the USDA's Soil Conservation Service attempted to initiate new farming programs "on a basis of efficiency," one of Rodale's goals was to demonstrate how to naturally rebuild deteriorating soil fertility.[132]

After suffering in the profound agricultural depression, Dust Bowl refugees Albert and Frances Lundberg were among those eager to learn. The farmers had moved their family from Nebraska to California's Sacramento Valley in 1937, seeking more fertile land. They focused on soil management and began experimenting with organic and eco-friendly farming practices. The Lundbergs and their four sons used clover and beans as cover crops to provide nitrogen, instead of falling back on chemicals. Rather than burning the field after harvest, they turned it over and let the rice waste fertilize the soil.[133] The family developed new rice varieties—including Wehani, Black Japonica, and Arborio rice—that would become part of the Lundberg Family Farms repertoire (these organic rice products would be branded decades later under their nationwide "In Harmony with Nature" tagline).[134]

In more of a flight from the city than the Lundbergs, Carolyn and Ed Robinson moved from New York City to a Connecticut homestead in 1942. Feeling "restricted" by their urban environs, they hankered to begin country living on a piece of land that would furnish them with food, recreation, health, security, "fullness," and extra income.[135] In The "Have-More" Plan: A Little Land—a Lot of Living (1944), the Robinsons promised that families could raise up to 75 percent of their food in their spare time while finding real pleasure in doing so. Their proposal called for home ownership on at least an acre of land, a source of cash income, and a willingness to raise a variety of vegetables, fruit, poultry, meat, and dairy products. While staying close enough to the city to retain a job and reap its advantages, the "Have-More" family would be self-reliant and happy in the country. Their food would be cheap and healthy, rich in vitamins and minerals.[136] The Robinsons offered tips on managing fruit trees, berries, hens, geese, turkeys, dairy goats, and beehives. Addressing housewives, Carolyn sympathized with city women who found housekeeping boring but claimed that her daily tasks were "stimulating, creative and varied."[137] While the Robinsons did not explicitly prescribe organic farming methods, they were recognized homesteaders whose ideals matched those of numerous participants in the organic movement. Advertisements for *The "Have-More" Plan* ran in *Organic Gardening* in 1944, and the Robinsons offered a booklet titled "The New Science of Miniature Farming" specifically to readers of the magazine in 1947.

In most homesteading cases, husband-wife teams like the Robinsons tackled the project. After a lengthy career in the city, Harold Richmond and his wife moved onto three acres in a small Florida village in 1942. They began converting the chemical citrus grove into an organic farm. Their primary crops were pineapples, oranges, grapefruit, and tangerines. The early years were discouraging, so the Richmonds wrote to agricultural expert Ehrenfried Pfeiffer for guidance on organic methods. With soil improvements attributable to the practice of composting, the Richmonds observed steady advances on their farm. These homesteaders accomplished their longtime dream to get back to the land and support themselves.[138] In experiences of returning to the land, the choices people made of which location to settle in or which crops to grow were far from homogenous. Some homesteaders acknowledged their contribution to a cultural phenomenon, while others made more intimate choices. Some aimed simply to provide for themselves; others developed small-scale enterprises to supplement their income. Almost all agreed on the importance of growing their own food as Mother Nature would, and forging an organic oasis was an instinctive choice.

Agriculture is inherently a manipulative activity, since any form of cultivation disturbs the alleged equilibrium of the natural world. Farms and gardens are domesticated, not wild, landscapes. However, the ethos of organic farming and gardening is to manage crops and pests in a way that is less taxing on the environment than the aggressive intrusions of conventional methods. In contrast to techniques that aim to control nature, organic farming is said to cooperate with nature. Florid organic rhetoric by and large refers to farmers "guiding" the land, as opposed to callously intruding on it. Farmer F. H. Billington offered a typical explanation in 1943: "Organic husbandry is based on those methods which have been employed by nature to crop the major portion of this planet for countless centuries. From this it will be seen that organic methods of farming and gardening are largely biological and *con*structive—as opposed to currently used orthodox methods which are predominantly chemical and *de*structive."[139]

Farmer Wilfred Wellock said he composted by the Indore Process because "Nature is man's finest teacher." After eight years of gardening, he testified to the vitality and enjoyment he derived from eating compost-grown food.[140] Another longtime organic farmer said in 1949 that man could avoid all kinds of troubles if he consciously tried to "work with nature" and recognized "life in its wholeness."[141] Allusions to the hubris of conventional farming were common in organic factions. When Fairfield Osborn expressed his alarm about the misuse of the land through chemical fertilizers in *Our Plundered Planet* (1948), he warned humans to "recognize the necessity of cooperating with nature. . . . The time for defiance is at an end."[142] Organic farming may have been gentler than ruthless toxic chemicals, but it did require the utilitarian management of landscapes (and a bit of defiance). Partisans of organic or "traditional" farming who compared it to industrialized agriculture rarely discussed the extent to which *all* farming entailed the modification and domination of the land. Nature did not spontaneously till soil or meticulously build compost heaps. Still, exaltations of serene natural harmony recurred throughout organic farming texts and lent an air of tranquility to the movement.

By 1948, the combination of erosion and bad cultivation practices had caused the United States to lose one hundred million acres of cropland. Despite increased mechanization, the yield of corn, cotton, and oats in bushels per acre was down. In places like eastern Oklahoma, so much topsoil had been lost that agronomists predicted it would take "300 years of intensive soil rebuilding" to restore its richness.[143] The crisis of impoverished soil had prompted the Soil Conservation Service to increase its educational efforts for farmers. Even these exertions seemed negligible to Rodale, who reflected that "to subdue nature, to bend its forces to our will, has been the acknowledged purpose of mankind since human life began." But, for him, "the question still remains: who is winning the battle?"[144] Rodale felt that the real winning strategy was a restrained organic approach.

LOUIS BROMFIELD AT MALABAR FARM

Recognized American novelist Louis Bromfield (1896–1956) bought five hundred Ohio acres in 1939 and launched Malabar Farm as a unique agrarian experiment. Bromfield pursued humus-building biological techniques and, for a time, was a leading exponent of organic ideas. He wrote four books about his work, and his fame as an author and farmer established him as an important spokesman for Howard's Rule of Return.[145] Bromfield wanted to prove that worn-out farms could be restored. Self-sufficiency was integral to his plan. He blamed the "sickness of American agriculture" on the "great mechanized farms which were more like industries than farms," since these had caused the gradual disappearance of the "family-sized farm."[146] In 1945, *Organic Gardening* published a favorable review of Bromfield's *Pleasant Valley* (1943), a book articulating the "profound belief that farming is the most honorable of professions and unquestionably a romantic and inspiring one."[147] Like Rodale, Bromfield paid tribute to Howard's Indore Process. He assessed his accomplishments on the farm by saying, "We have sought merely to build as Nature builds, to plant and sow and reap as Nature meant us to do."[148] He seemed to espouse organic methods.

Bromfield's perspective had changed by the time he wrote *Malabar Farm* (1947), in which he decreed a more productive, efficient agriculture. After initially backing organics, Bromfield began to believe that some artificial fertilizer was necessary. Bromfield still echoed Rodale and Howard in idealizing "primitive" lifestyles; and he felt a need for "working *with* Nature rather than *against* her" in agriculture.[149] He said, quite simply, "a farm life is a good life."[150] Yet Bromfield candidly admitted that many of his "utopian" ambitions for achieving self-sufficiency on the farm had been abandoned. Resigned to the realities of economics, the farm moved toward specialization and concentration. While Bromfield felt that barnyard manure was the best source of fertilizer, he didn't see how it could be produced in sufficient quantities for large farms and therefore accepted complementary commercial fertilizers to maintain yields. He used sprays and insecticides to restore the "worn-out land."[151] This shift caused organic purists to split from him; in turn, he began to consider them "cultists."

Unlike Rodale, Bromfield avowed that chemical fertilizers in "reasonable quantities" would not agitate living creatures. He accused "the fanatics of the organic material school" of erroneously assuming that vegetation grown on depleted soil could produce substantial quantities of calcium, potassium, phosphorous, trace elements, and nitrogen.[152] Instead, there was a requirement for "natural" mineral replenishments, such as limestone and phosphate rock. Bromfield did not acknowledge that Rodale also insisted upon mild types of ground rock fertilizers as adjuncts to compost. The topmost point of contention between the two was that Rodale approved *only* of safe, nonchemical enhancements for exhausted soil. Rodale used "not an ounce of artificial fertilizers or poison sprays."[153] Bromfield addressed the debate by saying, "None of us at Malabar Farm are fanatic advocates either of the chemical fertilizer or the organic school."[154] He said the dispute was a question of balance. Practical economics came to govern Bromfield's decisions for the course his farm would take, so he was disposed to abandon what he perceived as organic "fanaticism" and its romantic specters of tiny family farms. The farmer, he said, had to be a businessman who would "specialize and do well and efficiently a few things rather than attempting to do too many things inefficiently."[155] Bromfield thereby aligned himself with the general direction of American agriculture in the 1940s and 1950s.

Still, similar to that of organic adherents, Bromfield's guiding philosophy was that "Nature has provided the means of producing healthy and resistant plants, animals and people," so if these were put to use, "the need for 'artificial' and curative as opposed to preventive methods is greatly reduced."[156] In 1951, he testified to a congressional committee investigating chemicals in food. Though he was willing to use chemical fertilizer, insecticides, and fungicides, he claimed to choose the forms that were "comparatively harmless to animals and humans" as much as possible. Summing up his perspective in *From My Experience* (1955), Bromfield explained that "one of our constant struggles at Malabar is to avoid becoming kidnapped by the organic extremists and even the cranks."[157] Those "organic extremists" became disenchanted with Bromfield's tolerance for chemicals but continued to share his confidence in the redemptive merits of "Nature" and farming.

"A SCIENTIFIC STAMP"

Offering his definition of "organic" in 1945, Rodale called it "gardening in a way as close to nature as is practical under present day conditions." This meant rotating crops to uphold balance and using a mixture of animal and plant debris as fertilizer, instead of strong chemicals.[158] Every action was meant to mimic the natural cycles of soil and life. Not all organic gardeners toed the or-

A pastoral farm scene (Photo courtesy of Colleen Freda Burt)

ganic party line, but many agreed with Rodale's platform and credited *Organic Gardening* for its formative function. A reader who wrote to the magazine in 1946 was thankful that it had started him on the "Organic Trail" and said, "May God bless your efforts."[159] An *Organic Gardening* article in 1946 called composting "a return to the great crucible of Nature," to agriculture that was "as old as Nature" and "older than Man."[160] In a speech in 1947 about his experiences, organic farmer John Hershey said that the "returning to nature" way of farming was "known today as organic farming."[161] But achieving this "natural" stasis did not mean that organic gardening was impractical or anachronistic. Rodale refuted charges in 1948 that the organic movement was a backward "religious cult," saying instead that "the organic farmer must be scientific."[162] Rodale was not trying to revive ancient practices without updating them. Organic farmers put naturally occurring substances like limestone, phosphate rock, legumes, and animal manure to work—they did not let "Mother Nature" have free rein in their fields. Tradition and innovation were not mutually exclusive; both were part of the organic repertoire, and organic principles became more high-tech over time. Rodale's own lack of scientific training and rigor, however, left him susceptible to reproof; his tendency to veer away from even-keeled rhetoric only perpetuated stereotypes and exacerbated criticism.

Along with his own writing and farming, Rodale began to augment *Organic Gardening* magazine with related ventures. Appropriately, J. I. Rodale's granddaughter, Maria Rodale, would remember him as "not a sun-weathered guy in dirty overalls, but a man who strolled his fields deep in thought wearing a gray suit and a pressed white shirt."[163] Rodale was usually planning or analyzing, not hand weeding his furrowed fields. In 1947, he established the Soil and Health Foundation to fund agronomic research on the interrelationships between the earth's surface, food, and human health. The foundation encouraged the use of humus and other organic matter to enhance soil fertility and "improve the health of man." Its goals were fostering scientific studies, educating the public, and publishing findings on how organic and artificial fertilizers affected soil, plants, animals, and man.[164] Rodale announced that "we in America must take the lead" in battling the "unnatural methods" of commercial agriculture, which, he said, were "ruining soil and begetting degenerative diseases."[165] The foundation's first grant was for a University of Missouri Agricultural College study of how potash from rocks compared to chemical forms of potash. Rodale hoped researchers would prove the preeminence of the organic method, giving the organic camp "a scientific stamp so that our critics will stop calling us cultists and crack-pots."[166] The unfavorable opinions, however, lingered for decades. The Chemical Publishing Society printed *Chemicals, Humus, and the Soil* in 1948, giving Donald Hopkins a platform to repudiate the misconception held by "the humus school" that chemicals were intrinsically harmful to soil health. In making the case for chemical fertilizers, Hopkins wrote that producing enough food with the exclusive use of humus manures could be done "only by a truly colossal effort in terms of labor, transport, and planning," and this was not only wasteful but unwarranted, because there was not enough "concrete evidence" demonstrating that chemicals were poisoning the soil. In the end, Hopkins predicted, "It is the scientific opinion which will prevail."[167]

Rodale, undaunted, wrote *The Healthy Hunzas* (1948), which fixated on the "marvelous health" of the tribe living in the isolated Hunza region of the Himalayan Mountains. His study was based on the work of the aforementioned Sir Robert McCarrison, who had visited the area and had been particularly impressed by the Hunza people's health and immunity record.[168] According to McCarrison, cancer, diabetes, heart disease, and even common colds were unknown there. Rodale asserted that "the hardiness of the Hunzas is closely associated with their method of tilling the soil."[169] They used no chemical fertilizers but applied composted manure in raising food. Another factor in their "health and physical prowess," Rodale said, was that they ate only the "unsophisticated foods of Nature: milk, eggs, grains, fruits and vegetables."[170] Primarily, though, Rodale tied the well-being of the Hunzas to soil fertility, and this connection influenced his embryonic hypotheses about organic agriculture. He buoyantly proclaimed that following the Hunza procedure of soil cultivation would "begin the process of Hunzarization of our bodies which will result in nothing but favorable consequences."[171] In the back of *The Healthy Hunzas*, Rodale printed letters that he had received from readers attesting to the "astonishing benefits" of eating food raised in rich organic humus. He insisted that these letters proved how the health of the Hunzas was "definitely tied in with the element of soil fertility."[172] Each evocative letter described a host of ailments that had plagued the writer but dissipated after he or she began to eat organically grown fruits and vegetables. One such letter said: "*Organic Gardening Magazine* is truly a blessing to mankind and to our nation. Results obtained from your methods are remarkable and frequently I bow my head in prayer for the success of your magazine."[173] Those prayers seemed to be working in the late 1940s, though the term "Hunzarization" never quite caught on.

Rodale wrote *The Organic Front* (1948) to elaborate on the intrinsic worth of organic farming and discuss problems that had arisen since the publication of *Pay Dirt*. A note to readers in the back told those who "genuinely love the soil" to subscribe to *Organic Gardening*, which would teach them how to treat the soil as a "living organism." Chemical fertilizers and poisonous sprays were ruining the soil; this infertile state produced "unhealthy plants and animals," which, in turn, led to "unhealthy people." The wiser remedy, Rodale said, was homemade organic fertilizer, which would turn out "better-tasting food that contains more minerals and vitamins."[174] It would be decades before any substantial studies were published to support Rodale's early oaths, and even these were still not uncontested. But he was relentless. In the meantime, Rodale's technical guide, *Stone Mulching in the Garden* (1949), advised people to "make and apply as much compost as possible" in order to build up safe soil in the organic way.[175] Rodale said that he had received an "avalanche of letters" from readers of *Organic Gardening* who had secured "encouraging results" from stone mulching.[176] To the aficionados, organic farming seemed reasonable and serviceable.

Rodale was not operating in a vacuum; some people and groups used parts of organic theories but did not adopt them fully. Friends of the Land—a nonprofit conservation organization in which Louis Bromfield served as an officer—held a National Nutrition Conference in 1948 in Ohio to discuss soil, food, and health. One of the presenters, Jonathan Forman, argued that "robust personal health" came from "nutrient-rich soil," which was also the basis of national plenteousness.[177] Forman acknowledged that organic matter was the basis of good soil structure and offered William Albrecht's advice on how to build a compost pile.[178] He was concerned that farm mechanization emphasized food as a market commodity instead of elevating its nutritive value. Like Rodale, Forman felt that the overrefining of processed food depleted vitamins and minerals. People needed to respect the food "Nature and Nature's God" provided, instead of eating "devitalized" products. Food had to be grown in rich soil if people hoped to be healthy.[179] Health was "in the hands of the farmer."[180] Forman professed that more knowledge had to be disseminated about the relation of soil to human health and behavior. Like Rodale, he felt that the soil in which crops were grown could affect the physical properties of food. Other farmers who dabbled in organics—or at least did not rebuff the premise entirely—were in agreement.

According to the New York Botanical Garden's librarian, among the top garden books for 1948 were *The Earth's Face and Human Destiny* by Ehrenfried Pfeiffer and *The Earth's Green Carpet* by Louise E. Howard, both published in the United States by Rodale Press; most of the other books on the list, however, were less organically oriented.[181] Louise Howard was the wife of Albert Howard, and her book's preface mentioned that the body of thought inspired by her late husband—what she called the "School of Organic Farming and Gardening"—was characterized by "courage, cheerfulness and the willingness to dare." She said that her husband's trenchant views had served as an essential inspiration to the organic school, and these "reformers" were now certain that the earth could be "cultivated prosperously."[182] Rodale Press also published that year a new edition of Franklin King's *Farmers of Forty Centuries: or Permanent Agriculture in China, Korea, and Japan*, which held ceaseless appeal for Rodale's fellow organic farmers. American publisher Devin-Adair printed several books connected to organic agriculture in 1949: Leonard Wickenden's *Make Friends with Your Land*; Joseph Cocannouer's *Weeds, Guardians of the Soil*; and Lady Eve Balfour's *The Living Soil*. Devin-Adair also published Lionel Picton's *Nutrition & the Soil: Thoughts on Feeding* (1949). Picton, a doctor, hoped to "sow in the public mind" how human nutrition depended on the soil.[183] He felt that treating the soil with natural, not artificial, manure made a difference in the vitamin content of foodstuffs. Like Rodale, Picton issued warnings about the "famine of quality" in human nutrition resulting from the "ignorant" use of artificial inputs meant to improve upon "Nature." To endow humanity with healthy food, organic wastes had to be completely utilized. In his book, Picton praised the superb health of the Hunzas and criticized the "industrially-minded generation."[184] He described the "organic origin" of civilization—it was "alive," not something to be treated as a machine.[185] Picton called Albert Howard "the warrior at the apex of the phalanx who fights for positive health."[186] He wrote about the superiority of compost over chemicals, the "wheel of life" that farmers should base their activities on, the micorrhizal partnership between roots and fungi, and "the leading role" humus played in "the drama of the soil."[187] In the organic spirit, Picton said that the "whole hope of the future" lay in the replenishment of the "soil of our fields."[188] Organicists continued to juxtapose "natural" (less altered) and "artificial" (highly processed) foods and farming methods.

THE HARD-FOUGHT BATTLE

J. I. Rodale declared in 1948 that organiculture was "destined to alter our conceptions of the farm and the garden and to revolutionize our methods of operating them in order to secure for ourselves and others more abundant and more perfect food."[189] Rodale's overconfidence in alluding to "destiny" belied the fact that the triumph of organic farming was far from inevitable. Predicting a "revolution" was ambitious, since the advent of organic food did not overturn all accepted wisdom about farming and gardening. Predicting the onset of "more abundant and more perfect food" was exceedingly optimistic, since shortages still occurred and contamination issues did not abate. Yet Rodale used the term "movement" even when his crusade was in its incipient stages, and he did feel that he was at the helm of something monumental. With his kinetic can-do mentality, he was upending axiomatic notions.

In Britain, several organizations endorsed organic food. The Soil Association was publishing a journal, *Mother Earth*, and putting growers of organic products in touch with consumers. Officers of the Food Education Society were telling people that man had to "Copy Nature" in order to restore soil fertility and produce foodstuffs that could convey "health, vitality and resistance to disease."[190] Supporters of the Law of Return formed the Albert Howard Foundation of Organic Husbandry to persuade people that they could maintain soil fertility with organic manures instead of artificial fertilizers. Members felt that "if the soil is fed as designed by Nature the result is fertility and good health all along the line." Returning all animal and vegetable wastes to the land was the only way to heal exhausted layers of soil.[191] At the same time, farmer Frank Newman Turner established the Institute of Organic Husbandry to provide instruction and advice on "natural basic principles of farming." He published a journal, *The Farmer*, to criticize "artificial methods" that were "boosted by immense vested interests" but that were "insidiously ruining the health of our animal and human communities."[192] Turner had restored the diseased fields and cattle of Goosegreen Farm in Somerset, England, by using organic manure methods and long rotations. He hoped to demonstrate that "farming by the laws of nature" was simple and effective; chemicals were superfluous in achieving soil fertility.[193]

Meanwhile, organic gardening continued to make headway in the United States without oversight from a formal union like the Soil Association in Britain. Rodale had fewer organizational colleagues, but he was driven and tireless. He introduced the concept of engaging in a sacred mission to achieve natural balance—the organic nirvana. He saluted the virtues of compost and manure. The organic movement mobilized, gained momentum, and permeated American society. Yet Rodale was always willing to modify organic practices, feeling that "we organiculturists must not become too set in the stubborn tenets of our theories."[194] Flexibility was one of his strengths. Having already made some alterations in 1949, he predicted that "there will be further changes."[195] The lively renovations and exponential growth of organics would be part of Rodale's durable yet mutating legacy.

In 1949, Rodale said that "the introduction of the organic method into the United States may be likened to a war." Through a "hard-fought battle," the subscriber list of *Organic Gardening* had reached one hundred thousand names, and organic gardening had received recognition in "some powerful quarters." Still, Rodale was "aiming at higher stakes" by "fighting for farmers to join our movement," hoping to "make a substantial dent in this rotten citadel of artificial farming methods."[196] Though Rodale was resigned to directing his first magazine to gardeners, he still aspired to wean more people engaged in agriculture away from chemical methods. He felt that sufficient tests had proved that the organic method was practical and profitable on a farm scale.[197] Rodale said that he had received requests for a publication that reached out exclusively to the needs of farmers, so he sent out pamphlets in 1948 about the *Organic Farmer*, "a new magazine that attacks chemical fertilizers and poison sprays." He received enough advance subscriptions to furnish all the necessary start-up capital.[198] The *Organic Farmer* pledged to run "articles that most other farm magazines wouldn't dare print."[199] These daring pieces had titles like "Why I Disk," "Winter Care of Geese," "How Glaciers Make Soil," "War: Some Agricultural Implications," "5 Steps to 100 Bushel Corn," and "The Insecticide Makers Are Going Too Far." Albert Lesle, winner of the magazine's "How I Practice the Organic Method" contest in 1950, described how production on his California lemon grove had gone from under four hundred boxes per acre to over six hundred when he went organic.[200] One reader in 1952 told Rodale he "would pay four times the price that you are asking for this magazine, if necessary, in order to get this extremely valuable information obtainable nowhere else."[201] The *Organic Farmer* had fifty thousand subscribers that year. For a time, Rodale produced these separate periodicals for gardeners and farmers but then merged them in 1954, adding *Farming* back to the title for a while (then dropping it again later). *Organic Gardening and Farming* had heuristic value to growers at all levels of experience; it was teeming with advice, inspiration, and responses to ongoing questions. Although the distinction between *farming* and *gardening* is critical, Rodale often viewed the terms as somewhat interchangeable, because, despite differences of scale, his organic principles applied to both practices.

As Rodale and other organic advocates gathered composting converts, they promoted the link between ecologically healthy soil and human health. A commentator on the "crucial crusade" avowed that organic food was "food as Nature intended," containing "all the life-needed elements."[202] The organic method promised to bring wellness and environmental benefits. Rodale's media empire and cadre of devotees managed to grow. However, these compost-lovers were diverging from the surge of machine-slanted agriculture dependent on synthetic inputs. In the 1950s, the government attempted to bolster the nation's nonorganic food supply. Fewer—but larger—farms were producing more per acre than ever before.[203] Exhortations for elevated food production in order to celebrate prosperity at home, help wage the Cold War abroad, and demonstrate American strength in the "free world" were correlated with the acceleration of farming that was technologically and chemically intensive.

FACTORY FARMS, FAMINES, AND FUMIGANTS

Dwight D. Eisenhower, before his election as president, sought support for a proposed nutrition center at Columbia University, and he spoke assertively about the "possibility of doubling the world's food supply."[204] In 1953, the Senate Agriculture Committee proposed that President Eisenhower should be permitted to give surplus farm commodities as gifts to "friendly nations." Several senators felt that this was an "ideal opportunity to spread good will for America to starving people beyond the Iron Curtain." The wheat, butter, and other foods stockpiled in government warehouses could be efficacious Cold War weapons.[205] In the context of geopolitical rivalries, the single biggest reason that the Soviet Union's crop output lagged far behind that of the West was said to be "poor progress in farm mechanization." Though Soviet farms encompassed 40 percent more acreage than those in the United States, they had 20 percent fewer tractors for plowing and harvesting.[206] Business analysts scolded Soviet collective farms for stifling the "scientific open-mindedness" and "spirit of initiative" that were integral to successful (democratic) farming.[207]

The US government also promoted leftover wartime chemicals, some of which had performed imposingly overseas against disease-carrying insects, as agricultural pesticides and herbicides. The introduction of DDT (Dichloro-diphenyl-trichloroethane) in 1942 had opened a new era for tenacious synthetic compounds. Ammonium nitrate, organophosphate nerve gas, and DDT were used to manufacture fertilizers and potent insecticides. State agricultural colleges and research stations experimented with DDT and other insecticides before making them available to the public. The US Bureau of Entomology and Plant Quarantine said in 1945 that DDT formulations could be used "safely and effectively" by home gardeners. The bureau advised that vegetables and fruits sprayed with DDT should be washed before eating, that DDT was harmful to honeybees and other "good" insects, and that residue in the soil might "retard the growth of some crops." Still, the bureau predicted that DDT would be important in restraining Japanese beetles, cabbage caterpillars, pea aphids, grape berry moths, apple leafhoppers, gypsy moths, and other pests.[208] In *Pay Dirt*, Rodale cited articles from the American Medical Association confirming that DDT was a "definite health hazard," even as it was being extensively used.[209] Rodale also critiqued how dastardly chemical industry representatives had influenced the USDA's position on artificial fertilizers. The agency's denial of organic agriculture's feasibility would not subside. Rodale's voice was a contrary one from a faraway island. In the chemical manor, farmers and gardeners continued to hear about how powerful DDT and the compositions derived from it were against pests.[210] Having crowned "King Productivity," agronomists worshipped the pesticides that seemed to serve so faithfully. American farmers were told that petroleum-based chemicals were essential for boosting agricultural production to unprecedented levels. Hybrid seeds, "modern" fertilizers, and pesticides were the leading-edge farming tools. The USDA's agricultural extension service also praised mechanical improvements that enabled each farmer to work concertedly on more enormous units.[211] After Norman Borlaug (1914–2009) developed a disease-resistant, high-yield wheat variety in the 1940s, he led efforts to introduce what became known as the "Green Revolution" in India and Pakistan; increases in food production were praised for helping to avert famines abroad. Techno-agriculture seemed economically advantageous but had ecological and social repercussions.

By 1950, farm mechanization and the latest chemical concoctions were said to have reduced the "stoop labor" required for weeding and picking crops by 50 percent. The American Cyanamid Company began marketing a contact insecticide with "toxic action" to which "no species of insect or mite among those tested" had demonstrated resistance. Researchers said that there were approximately four million species of insects that needed to be controlled.[212] The "federal bug-fighters" were expected to spend $4 billion in 1950. Insecticide makers like DuPont and Standard Oil were ready with new "lethal sprays, powders and fumigants."[213] North Carolina State College held its third annual two-day Pesticide School in 1951 to inform attendees of all the latest research and recommendations on insecticides, fungicides, rodenticides, and herbicides. Workshops were conducted by the college's agronomy, plant pathology, and entomology faculty in the school of agriculture; among those who registered were employees of Dow Chemical Company, U.S. Rubber Company, Standard Fertilizer Company, Taylor Chemical Company, and American Cyanamid Company.[214] Throughout the United States, borax derivatives were being used for preventing mold on fruits, and the Pacific Coast Borax Co. said in 1954 that its fertilizers would improve "the yield and quality of apples" and "double the per-acre yield of alfalfa."[215] Chemists hailed the wonders of "systemic" insecticides. By 1955, the *Wall Street Journal* reported that the USDA was testing DDVP (dimethyl-dichlorovinyl-phosphate), a new phosphorous-compound insecticide, as a "possible successor to the popular DDT." Although the research chief for one pesticide maker admitted that the first insecticides made from phosphorous compounds were "pretty toxic to humans," he gave his word that "newer, less risky ones" would be coming out.[216] The amalgamation of pesticides and policies incited the overproduction of concentrated crops on megafarms.

From a global food supply perspective, the widespread adoption of fertilizers, synthetic pesticides, herbicides, and petrochemicals made dizzying increases in yields per acre possible. The Food and Agriculture Organization of the United Nations estimated that the agricultural production of the noncommunist world was 25 percent greater in 1954 than in 1946. Many nations had surpluses of wheat, sugar, and cotton.[217] In the United States, seed varieties were tailor-made to create vegetables that consumers were fond of; hybrid corn and onions provided yields double and triple those of timeworn seeds. Government price supports were in place for wheat, corn, rice, peanuts, cotton, and tobacco. Au courant insecticides and fungicides drenched the soil from which market crops sprouted. Farmers were applying 60 percent more pounds of fertilizer per acre per year in 1957 than they had in 1940.[218] The farmer who specialized in streamlined crops on consolidated landholdings became "more like an industrial engineer every year." Cargill Inc. offered at least eighty distinct feed formulas for animals at various developmental stages, and farmers chose prepared feeds to maximize growth. Farmers also used antibiotics to prevent diseases in livestock.[219] Chemical and technological advances—like more stalwart tractors, formidable fertilizers, and vigorous irrigation systems—amplified output. Agricultural extension services pointed out that "today's farmer is a specialist—a producer of food or fiber. His efficiency is steadily increasing."[220] Efficiency also meant uniformity. In 1959, John Deere showcased a state-of-the-art cotton picker designed to do the work of eighty field hands, and International Harvester announced a corn picker that could grab twice as many ears at a time, in addition to husking and shelling the ears in the field. Tractor-drawn spray equipment could kill twenty million weeds in an hour; hormones and chemical additives could fatten more livestock on less feed.[221] One farmer—who boasted of using more chemical fertilizer per acre than anybody else in the nation—crowed that "farming is a science and profession today. It's not a way of life anymore."[222] Many farmers were willing to spend billions on grandiose equipment that could slash steep labor costs.

Ezra Benson, who served as US secretary of agriculture from 1953 to 1961, notoriously opposed high government price supports for farmers. Critics said that he hastened the demise of small farmers by favoring factory farms and obstinately refusing to aid farmers who were suffering economically.[223] Benson's controversial "flexible price supports" were dubbed "antifarmer" by members of Congress from both parties, who repeatedly called for his resignation.[224] Inflation and dropping prices added to the ferment, as the net

Raising organic chickens (Photo courtesy of Colleen Freda Burt)

income of farmers slumped. Dissatisfied South Dakota farmers splattered Benson with eggs during a speech in 1957.[225] For those getting pushed off the land, the agricultural revolution was having "painful consequences." In 1958, 2.1 million commercial farms produced 91 percent of agricultural dollars, while 2.7 million farms struggled for the remaining 9 percent. Still, Benson insisted that "inefficiency should not be subsidized."[226] Benson wanted growth and specialization, not quaint barns and scenic silos. Overflowing grain bins were the apotheosis of agricultural achievement, hailed as the "triumphant symbol" of the chemical revolution in farming.[227] While food surpluses kept piling up, small-scale organic farms were brushed off as ineffectual.

As turnout from conventional methods swelled, the organic school appeared too irrelevant, impotent, and labor-intensive to detractors. The monocultures and conglomerates of "modern" agriculture, not "antiquated" organic farms, were producing the desired level of US food exports. If anything, organic farming seemed best suited to diversified plantings on pint-sized plots, but "mined and manufactured chemicals" were already key ingredients in plant food for suburban lawns and gardens. Sales of lawn and garden fertilizers had become a lucrative "little brother of the giant farm fertilizer industry."[228] The Monsanto Chemical Company's first soil conditioning resin, Krilium, was said to be a thousand times more effective than compost.[229] Soil conditioners were dubbed "miracle" chemicals, for doing "synthetically what rich humus does naturally," and their popularity "snowballed."[230] Defenders of the manmade fertilizers spoke up vociferously on behalf of the status quo. Nevertheless, protests against industrial agriculture could not be quashed. One newspaper editorial lamenting the plight of farmers contended that, under programs favoring crop culture instead of grazing land, "soil ruiners are rewarded, and soil conservers penalized."[231] Expressing disquiet about economic justice for small farmers, a report in 1955 by the Conference on Economic Progress noted that, since the aggregated wealth of "factory" farms was overtaking "an increasing share of farm production and income, abetted to a considerable degree by national policies," inverse action should be taken to augment the income of the "family-type farm."[232] Organicists could not stem the tide of pesticides, but a counterattack against the chemical-laden deluge was percolating.

THE "MISGUIDED" CULT: ORGANIC DISCIPLES AND DOUBTERS

Initially, believers in organic soil's clout were vexed by stone-faced listeners when proselytizing to the general public. Rodale testified to a congressional committee formed to investigate chemical fertilizers in 1950. He cited Ehrenfried Pfeiffer's recent research at Threefold Farm in New York, which proved that a group of mice fed with organically produced food was far healthier and more amicable than a group eating food raised with chemical fertilizers.[233] Rodale referred to other experiments corroborating that organic food had more vitamins. He pointed out that several physicians had written about the repercussions of chemical fertilizers on human health. In spite of all this verification, Rodale felt thwarted by agricultural scientists at American institutions who pronounced that there was "no evidence that the organic method of producing food gives people better health."[234] These authorities seemed to think his testimony was rubbish and stymied any potential enlargement of organic farming research.

In the 1950s, everyday gardeners were riven between organics and chemicals. The lines of this rift that was "shaking the gardening world to its foundations" were drawn as "chemicalist versus organiculturist," said Rodale.[235] This house divided against itself could not stand, since each side deemed the other to be both implausible and menacing. There were no impartial referees. *Or-*

ganic Gardening's circulation reached 250,000 by 1950.[236] It was the premier kitchen gardening magazine, brimming with hands-on advice, but the established press ridiculed it. Mainstream gardening journals were scathing. The *Country Gentleman*, which dubbed itself "The Magazine for Better Farming" and had been tackling the business of farming since 1911, certainly did not sanction organics. The cover story in May 1950 was "A Poison for Every Bug"; in August 1950 it was "New Chemical Weapon for Farms." R. I. Throckmorton, dean of Kansas State College, wrote "The Organic Farming Myth" in the *Country Gentleman* in 1951, calling organic farmers "a cult of misguided people" who relied on "half-truths, pseudo science and emotion."[237] In response, Rodale said that "gloom enveloped the heart of every organically-minded person," but he did receive thousands of encouraging letters and "took heart in realizing that the organic movement had become important enough to deserve the attention of big-time publications."[238] One subscriber to the *Organic Farmer* egged Rodale on in a letter, expressing "hope that the frothing at the mouth of the enemies of organic methods won't get you down" and adding that "the truth always has enemies, but it will triumph in the end."[239] At the time, though, if an end was in sight it was rather inauspicious.

America's oldest garden magazine, *Horticulture*, was another one of Rodale's antagonists. It referred to "extreme organic gardeners" as "cultists" who were prone to discard scientific knowledge because of "fancies or whims." *Horticulture* considered commercial fertilizers to be "one of the greatest gains of the nineteenth century" and thought gardeners ought to be indebted to the fertilizer industry.[240] The *Dallas Morning News* chastised organic farmers for being "blind to evidence" and "well intentioned but gullible" for subscribing to their "folly." Though the "organic cultists" had the "zeal of apostles," there was "no shred of evidence" to support their claims. Field tests by food packers—such as the Campbell Soup Company—demonstrated that "chemical plant foods made more and better tomatoes than did manure alone." The editorial concluded that "to banish commercial fertilizers would be to put American farming back in the Dark Ages."[241] Similarly, both the *Progressive Farmer* and the *Montana-Farmer-Stockman* belittled organic claims in 1952 as nonsense. The *Rural New Yorker* indicted the movement for simply trying to sell magazines. Rodale felt that these "vicious articles" were part of a "planned attack of the chemical fertilizer interests." He could not corral the wave of name calling. His response to the abuse was to say that "if it is being a cultist to farm by the organic method and beat the yields of the chemical farmers, then I am glad I am a cultist."[242] Historian Warren Belasco later noted that the "much-maligned but indefatigable" Rodale didn't seem to mind his "marginal status as intellectual gadfly."[243] Rodale was a pariah convinced of his own principles, a perpetual thorn in the chemical corpus's side.

Addressing "emotional outbursts on both sides of the argument" in 1952, Ehrenfried Pfeiffer reported on how many publications tended to maul the organic movement as "fanatical." Organic naysayers avowed that "this country has about doubled its acre yields with chemical fertilizers."[244] Pfeiffer agreed that insecticides and weed killers had "done wonders," but they had also backfired, making insects immune to DDT and killing natural enemies of pests. While fertilizers increased yields, soil structures declined. Organic matter, on the other hand, fed the "microlife of soils" and was "the savings account of the soil."[245] Like Pfeiffer, Rodale was unrelenting in plugging his case that organic soil inputs led to agricultural productivity and robust health, while inorganic supplements and chemical pesticides degraded the soil. In spite of the "disgracefully inaccurate" press reports, "the organic method goes on!" he exclaimed.[246] Rodale said that his magazines seized "only a small share of the credit for the snowballing organic movement," because it was more "the case of the idea being sound."[247] The idea was not sound to university and government research institutions, who pilloried Rodale and derided "organic cranks, manure farming faddists, the muck and mystery school, the muck and magic school, and apostles of dung who indulge in the hocus pocus of the cult."[248] Rodale observed how "chemical people" were hauling up "heavy artillery" and pelting organics with a "vicious barrage" of "misguided journalism."[249] Those haughty, belligerent "chemical people" thought organics were bogus.

An advertisement for pheasants in the *New York Times* in 1950 used the fact that they "led a pampered life on an organic farm," eating "only the food that nature provides," as a selling point.[250] It was an alluring message. But Rodale faced as much heavy artillery when propping up the realm of natural food as he did when propagandizing natural gardening. In 1950, Rodale began publishing *Prevention* magazine, which espoused exercise, nutrition, and a system for better health based on deterring diseases. *Prevention*'s purpose was to reach the general public that neither farmed nor gardened, so they, too, could learn the "evils of chemical fertilization" and help "build the organic movement stronger and stronger." The magazine accepted no advertising for medical or health products but did make editorial comments on worthy goods. Rodale hoped that people would consider the cost of subscribing to be a "medical fee," as an alternative to paying the doctor.[251] *Prevention* magazine was dedicated to promoting a healthy-living ideology known as the "*Prevention* System for Better Health." The system was meant to restore a "natural" diet of organic foods, expunging chemical additives and refined foods. It advocated natural vitamin supplements to make up for the poor nutritional status of modern foods. This magazine gave Rodale a forum for news on nutrition and wellness that was more tangential to *Organic Gardening*, since some readers had complained that Rodale's articles on cancer did not belong there. Within two years, *Prevention* had over sixty thousand subscribers, and most were nongardeners who might have found pontifications about mineral particles in the soil substrate to be soporific.[252] Still, it was consistent with the organic agricultural philosophy that a long-term preventative routine was the best approach to warding off plant and human diseases, rather than treating defects with quick fix solutions. Finding the root of a problem and applying a natural solution to mend it were always the goal. Rodale felt that chemical fertilizers were a "shot-in-the-arm method, like taking medicines," and he disapproved of taking the easy way out.[253]

The *Prevention* system bucked the fast-paced trend in the 1950s toward technologically sophisticated food processing, packaging, and handling techniques. Foodstuffs like the iconic Swanson Salisbury steak TV dinner, Birds Eye frozen cod fillet, Jell-O lime gelatin, Post's sugar crisp cereal, Chef Boy-ar-dee canned spaghetti and meatballs, Campbell's condensed tomato soup, and Peter Pan peanut butter were decidedly *not* "primitive" or organic. As hundreds of new synthetic chemical additives were injected into much-ballyhooed products for the "happy housewife," James Delaney, a US representative from New York, began campaigning for restrictions on injurious food additives. He was rewarded with the Delaney Clause, a proviso to the 1958 Food Additive Amendment that prohibited the approval of additives shown to have caused cancer in animals or people. It was a notable step toward the government regulation of food safety but one that irked many food scientists, who reckoned that it was a senseless emotional response to a scientific affair. Meanwhile, carcinogens were not on the radar screen of most Americans, and the chemical onslaught proceeded unabated in agriculture.

From the 1950s onward, researchers did investigate more closely the relationship between nutrition and degenerative diseases, and some landmark studies were published.[254] The *American Journal of Clinical Nutrition* began to publish peer-reviewed research in 1952, though it was hardly cutting edge. A more avant-garde group of doctors and citizens formed the Natural Food Associates (NFA) in 1952 to broadcast the belief that proper farming practices fostered good nutrition and health.[255] The founders, inspired in part by the writings of both Louis Bromfield and Lionel Picton, were concerned about chemical pesticides. Physician Joe Nichols, the first NFA president, collaborated with William Albrecht on a book about the relationship between soil, food, and health. Biodynamic farmer Sterling Edwards expressed pleasure in 1952 that it was "slowly dawning on many basic food nutritionists that the food industry all too often substitutes manufactured junk and general trash for healthful home prepared dishes." In place of this "devitalized stuff" that had been sprayed with poisonous chemicals, the best natural foods for good health were organic products like "fresh goat milk, natural figs, sunflower seeds, yogurt of combined B. cultures, flax seed meal, rice polish and raw wheat germ."[256] The USDA set its "Basic Four" foundation diet in 1956, but *Organic Gardening and Farming* ran recipes that were less rudimentary, such as those for Soya Muffins, Rye Bread, and Wheat Germ Cookies.[257] The magazine included an article stating that "original Americans lived on organic food," which was unlike the foods "low in protein and mineral content" produced by synthetic fertilizers.[258] Rodale also pointed out that hundreds of his readers claimed "wonderful improvements in their health due to eating organically grown foods."[259] Vitality, though, was difficult for chemists to measure, and the organic movement often had to use general descriptions of better health and well-being resulting from "vitalized" organic foods as evidence. Rodale himself had to tread carefully when making murky health claims about organic food. The FTC accused him of false and deceptive advertising for one of his books, *The Health Finder* (1954), though Rodale was eventually able to fight the case and win.[260]

Rodale's publishing company officially became Rodale Press in 1951 and actively released new titles. Rodale Press was instrumental in the diffusion of organic information. Thousands of visitors toured the Rodale Experimental Farm each year, including Lady Eve Balfour while she was on an American speaking circuit in 1951. The Organic Country Store at the farm sold seaweed and animal manure, phosphate, potash rock, peat moss, food shredders, and books. A survey in 1952 counted fourteen thousand organic farmers in the United States.[261] Rodale said that the tempo of the "organic farming revolution" was accelerating.[262] Organic farmer Philip Arena predicted that, since demand for organic produce was "getting greater and greater," the organic movement would thrive, as long as all growers continued to "serve the public fairly and justly."[263] Commemorating the tenth anniversary of *Organic Gardening*, Rodale felt that "exciting things are happening which we of the organic movement never dreamt would come to pass so soon."[264] He saw a "solidly established" organic movement that had become "a definite part of the life and lore of the American scene."[265] By late 1953, *Organic Gardening* decreed that the organic movement was still "growing by leaps and bounds, bringing like-minded people together from all over the world."[266] This group encompassed "an aroused citizenry, an ardent group of patriots, a conservation-and-health-minded type of American," in addition to farmers and gardeners. Rodale was convinced that, when the possibility of organiculture became apparent, it "strikes a person with the impact of a ton of bricks." He heralded the impending "organic revolution" that was "coming slowly but surely."[267] In 1954, *Organic Gardening and Farming* declared, "There is nothing static about the organic method."[268] Changes were certainly ahead, though much of the fervid rhetoric stayed constant.

Organic practitioner Joseph Cocannouer's *Weeds: Guardians of the Soil* (1950) and *Farming with Nature* (1954) shared an emphasis on "Nature's law of togetherness" and "co-operating with Nature" as the governing rules for agriculture.[269] He extolled "scientific compost making" as outlined by Albert Howard and promised that weeds could be helpful to the farmer. Cocannouer advised other farmers to build their pastures "Nature's way." He believed that adhering to Howard's method of scientific compost making resulted in a fertilizer that "ranks with Nature's best."[270] Dissenting from the customary war on weeds, he praised them as "Nature's true guardians of the soil" and said that weeds could be the farmer's friends when used intelligently.[271] Cocannouer declared that "in Nature farming the farmer accepts the blueprints of Nature as his guide."[272] He felt that applying outside materials to maintain soil fertility in heavily cropped land was imperative, because "man cannot wait on Nature's slow processes,"[273] but he did not seem to regard this kind of impatient intervention as incongruous with the "Nature farming" ideal of organic growers.

The *Wall Street Journal* in 1957 recognized "a flourishing cult of gardeners who shun chemicals entirely."[274] Malcolm Beck, who began operating his Texas farm organically that year, shunned chemicals because he cared most about "doing things Nature approves of."[275] He said that Nature had been building fertile topsoil "since the beginning of time" by mulching and composting the surface of the earth.[276] Compost worked so well because it was "Nature's way."[277] To many organic farmers, compost was "black gold." Ben Easey, an active supporter of the organic movement, asserted that organic gardeners and farmers had developed their techniques in response to the misuse of artificial fertilizers. Easey published *Practical Organic Gardening*, in which he discussed the critical role of making compost in organic gardening as "an art, a branch of gardening which deserves the same attention and skill as the old arts of brewing, baking and cheese-making, all of which apply biological principles."[278] Disbelievers, unenthralled by this "art," avowed that organic farming systems could not produce the astronomical yields that conventional agriculture did. To skeptics, organics were anathema and, furthermore, would contribute to global hunger. Organic farmer Hugh Corley denied these negative allegations in *Organic Small Farming* (1957). Corley agreed that "yields may be lower to start with, just as a drug addict may be in poor shape after he has given up his drugs, or as an underfed and overtired man may be unable to do much work." Yet, when "*real* fertility" was derived from organic methods, yields would climb and returns would improve. As an auxiliary bonus, this upgrade was "not bought at the expense of posterity."[279] The organic cohort often expressed this far-sighted vision.

J. I. Rodale was heartened to see the organic legion growing incrementally worldwide. Membership in the Soil Association, Britain's premiere organic agriculture organization, reached approximately thirty-five hundred by 1957.[280] Lawrence Hills, a horticulturist captivated by organic growing, established the Henry Doubleday Research Association (HDRA) in 1958. It began as a charitable research group to study the applications of comfrey, a plant introduced to Britain in the nineteenth century by Henry Doubleday. Early HDRA newsletters included tips on nutrition, health, and ways to grow plants organically. The HDRA would eventually change its name to Garden Organic and become the largest organic federation in Britain. Farmer Jorian Jenks, an officer of the Soil Association, felt that the organic approach was "a revolutionary body of ideas" emphasizing "wholeness," harmony between "Man and Nature," and the "cycle of nutrition." He argued that deteriorating human health could be remedied by the organic movement's embrace of biological wisdom. In *The Stuff Man's Made Of* (1959), Jenks wrote that the craze of artificiality was just "trying to play tricks on Nature."[281] Technology would not compensate for the deficiencies caused when ecology was neglected, so degenerative diseases were increasing in humans. The organic movement's "valuable pioneering work" could help craft an appreciative market for better-quality food.[282] Jenks had known and admired Albert Howard, although "the existing body of agricultural science" rejected Howard's Indore Process as "unproven and un-provable."[283] Jenks also appreciated that the organic movement was flexible enough to absorb new scientific discoveries. He believed "wholeheartedly in the organic case" himself, but he acknowledged that agricultural chemists were exceedingly cynical about organic farming's efficacy.[284] They were equally incredulous in the United States. The curricula of agricultural schools taught chemical weed control but ignored organics. North Carolina Agricultural Institute counseled students enrolled in 1960 that the need and demand for pest control operators—in households, home orchards, and flower gardens—were increasing rapidly, so courses addressed all aspects of pesticides, fungicides, and herbicides.[285] The consensus of the USDA, American Medical Association, and American Dietetic Association was that organic foods (and health foods in general) were gratuitous, more expensive, and apt to mislead people who were fooled into thinking that they might be cure-alls.[286] Consumers were wary of being swindled. Broad-based acceptance of organic food's virtues materialized only tentatively. Rodale was a pariah to the impervious establishment.

Still, at the Aware Inn on Sunset Boulevard, where Greta Garbo, Marlon Brando, Gloria Swanson, and other stars dined regularly, owner Jim Baker said in 1959 that the big selling point for his Hollywood restaurant was the organic food and drinks. As libations, he offered alfalfa-mint tea and dandelion root coffee.[287] Baker said that his two sons, who had eaten only organic food since birth and had never been sick, served as advertisements that "food as pure as nature made it" was healthier—even though it cost twice as much.[288] Rodale agreed that there were more than enough examples of organic foods' benefits. He produced the illustrated *Encyclopedia of Organic Gardening* (1959), a comprehensive A-to-Z guide that became a standard text; and he published another detailed book, *How to Grow Vegetables & Fruits by the Organic Method* (1961), which covered everything from laying out the garden to storing the produce. Both of these would be reissued in 1999, when *Publishers Weekly* would write of the "hefty" yet "timeless" volumes: "Though not a word has been changed in Rodale's manuals, four decades have seen a great shift toward this once controversial, now revered organic way."[289] Much of this great shift from reviled to revered took place in the 1960s.

In *The Complete Book of Food and Nutrition* (1961), Rodale outlined recommendations on healthy eating gleaned from the first decade of *Prevention* issues. The tome's thousand pages covered the properties—advantageous and dire—of individual foodstuffs. In the introduction, Rodale noted that the provender average Americans ate was undoubtedly responsible for "terrifying" rates of degenerative disease.[290] All processed foods contained preservatives and chemicals, and even "infinitesimal quantities" mounted up to dangerous, toxic dosages.[291] Rodale called for an awakening to the absolute necessity of returning to unprocessed food, avoiding foods poisoned with insecticides and chemicals, and fortifying diets with supplements.[292] Rodale asserted that there was much evidence available showing "the vital influence that organic foods have on health and resistance to disease."[293] However, acknowledging the lack of absolute proof that organic food was superior, he suggested that people test this theory by eating organically grown food for a few years and observing the difference in their health.[294] He urged readers to grow their own fruit and vegetables by the organic method whenever possible, or at least to purchase these products from organic growers.[295] Since all soil had been depleted of valuable trace minerals, natural supplements like brewer's yeast, bone meal, desiccated liver, and seaweed were also compulsory. He predicted that putting everyone in the country on a "really nourishing diet"—in which refined foods were forbidden while fresh organically grown produce was served raw at each meal—would cause all psychosomatic illnesses to disappear within a few months.[296] Rodale was not a medical doctor himself, but he staunchly alleged that physicians who ignored his warnings endangered their patients.

Rodale did have a "lust for ice cream," in which he occasionally indulged.[297] However, his fundamental advice was to consume foods "in as near their natural state as possible."[298] Some of his favorites for health were eggs, wheat germ, garlic, fresh fruit, vegetables, nuts, seeds, and raw foods in general; of course, organic comestibles were the crème de la crème. Rodale shared harsh words about the hot dogs, potato chips, candy bars, soft drinks, and other "empty calories" that most children ate. He felt that Americans could learn a great deal by studying "primitive peoples who eat a primitive, simple diet untouched by the avaricious hand of the factory."[299] This incorrigible opposition to industrial processing recurred throughout Rodale's work and struck a nerve with the public. Rodale continued to share information on the intricacies of nitrogen concentrations in organic crops, but he increasingly focused on uplifting, indelible messages that had more vivacity. His exuberant, magnetic, and polarizing energy would begin to draw assistance from some unlikely new friends in the 1960s, who would help to remove the stigma of organics.

CHAPTER TWO

A Noisy Spring

"Genius?" or "Fraud?"

Environmental angst was in the atmosphere in the early 1960s. Various national organizations promoted "wise use" resource conservation or wilderness-focused preservation. A handful of clairvoyants had already expressed alarm over industrial pollution and injurious chemicals in the mid-1940s. Well-known farmer and writer Louis Bromfield had counseled that the effects of the "indiscriminate use" of such sprays as DDT had not yet been properly observed and assessed.[1] The Audubon Society had initiated one of the first studies of how the unchecked use of DDT endangered bird life.[2] J. I. Rodale had warned about DDT and other pesticides that were saturating the land. Organic farmer John Hershey had pointed out that, while ten years earlier commercial fertilizer had been "the answer to a farm maiden's prayer," by 1947 he saw "an avalanche of public opinion against indiscriminate use of 'the soil poison.'"[3] It was scarcely an avalanche; the chemical industry bristled, but even in the 1950s there wasn't enough provocation to shake Americans from their chemical trance. A key turning point in awareness came with Rachel Carson's *Silent Spring* (1962), which blatantly charged that humans were poisoning the earth and were themselves in a full-blown "chemical war." It caused people to no longer be sanguine about the way food was produced. This chapter highlights the blossoming US organic movement during the 1960s and early 1970s, including the pivotal roles that environmentalists, counterculturists, homesteaders, and health seekers played within the development of the organic cause. Rodale's vision of improving individuals and the world shepherded the movement, but it never became a full-fledged revolution. I argue that American organicists never fought to overthrow the existing food edifice from its pinnacle; there was, instead, a less dramatic effort to advocate for organics as an alternative that could thrive concurrently.

THE "VIOLENT CROSSFIRE"

Rachel Carson wrote that all life was caught in the "violent crossfire" of a chemical-induced fusillade that was never extinguished.[4] The dilemma, Carson said, was "not only scientific but moral."[5] The evidence was incontrovertible that man had introduced radioactive by-products and carcinogens into his habitat. Notwithstanding damage already done, man had the power to eliminate the venom. Humility and remedial action—not arrogant blunders or reckless militancy—were needed to heal the mutilation. *Silent Spring* topped the best-seller charts, rallied bird lovers, and animated the populace's panic about invisible insecticides. Carson's admonitory tale instilled in Americans what later became known as the "precautionary principle," as she held up a stop sign to what seemed like a global menace. Untold numbers of people began to wonder if toxins in the air and water could trigger deleterious ailments. The agricultural chemical industry fought back vehemently, hoping to discredit Carson. The acrid public relations backlash noted that her scant "proof" about diseases was not ironclad. Hysteria increased, bolstered by both Carson's opponents and her supporters, inspiring apoplectic debates about whether or not commonly used chemicals were "Elixirs of Death." The jury of public opinion was equivocal, but pesticides no longer seemed safe.

Carson had been an early subscriber to *Organic Gardening and Farming* and echoed Rodale's opposition to DDT.[6] Salient similarities existed between the "balance of nature" and the "war against nature" rhetoric that imbued the work of both Rodale and Carson. Both suspected that the government and chemical industry were in cahoots. Both touched on personal health anxieties and censured the greed of chemical manufacturers. Both felt that humankind had to acknowledge noble "life forces" and learn to coexist with other creatures. The comparative obscurity of Rodale's *Pay Dirt* when it appeared nearly two decades earlier had been a matter of timing, style, and credentials. *Pay Dirt* predated the new tenor of "ecology" advocacy, lacked Carson's poetic eloquence, and did not have an author with scientific credentials. Carson's qualifications as a biologist bolstered *Silent Spring* as a high-profile indictment of pesticides—even as she called into question the nation's tendency to place blind faith in science. Her skill as a moving writer sparked deep introspection. She evoked the wounds to humans, wildlife, and the planet caused by "Rivers of Death." As an elegy for all the songbirds that were silenced and leaping fish that were killed by chemicals, Carson's book was touching; as an indictment of "biocides" it was relentless. In ways that

Rodale and his magazines never had, *Silent Spring* gained traction and penetrated the mainstream media.

Carson is credited with launching modern environmentalism, which seemed more personally relevant than older conservationist or preservationist approaches. Ecological sentience and furor about contaminants swelled in the 1960s, commencing a new wave of interest in organic gardening. Environmental values became part of the search for an enhanced standard of living.[7] Attempts to live lightly on the earth entailed a reaction against the throwaway mentality of a profligate, industrial, urbanizing society. Conscious consumers looked for more "natural" products to assuage their eco-guilt.[8] The organic movement got a makeover. Its unflagging anticorporate rhetoric dovetailed with the emerging discourse of environmentalists against the status quo. The number of subscriptions to *Organic Gardening and Farming* had arrived at 270,000 by 1961; after *Silent Spring* was released, readership escalated to 300,000.[9] Consternation over all forms of pollution gave the magazine new respectability. Rodale developed a larger following and acquired cultural capital in this climate. While the founding organicists' concerns for "healthy soil, healthy food and healthy people" persisted, the revamped organic movement differed from its earlier phases in that it included the core precept of environmental sustainability in its arsenal.[10] The USDA and agribusiness interests were still openly hostile to the upstart organic "zealots." In some circles, though, Rachel Carson and the counterculture had turned Rodale from a marginalized extremist "huckster" into an august visionary genius. Rodale became almost a heroic figure among tree-huggers who were perturbed about industrial effluence.

Silent Spring generated considerable publicity—and controversy. Three serialized excerpts were published in the *New Yorker*, so the American Chemical Society began attacking even before it was printed in its entirety. The National Agricultural Chemical Association spent $25,000 on advertisements and pamphlets touting the benefits of farm chemicals.[11] A *New York Times* editorial predicted that Carson would be accused of alarmism but felt that, if her message aroused enough public concern to convince the government to implement adequate pesticide controls, she would be "as deserving of the Nobel Prize as was the inventor of DDT." She posed a challenge to people who had become "mesmerized by the notion that chemists are the possessors of divine wisdom."[12] One of the primary accusations against Carson was her partiality; this was a deliberate strategy, since she felt that chemicals already had enough cheerleaders. She wanted to tip the scales back toward the side of restraint. The president of the Nutrition Foundation (largely funded by the food industry) pounced on the public frame of mind, "bordering on hysteria," caused by Carson's "one-sided" book; he said that she harped on the trickle of tragic accidents that pesticides had caused but overlooked the fact that the United States desperately needed agricultural chemicals in order to maintain an adequate food supply.[13]

The pandemonium instigated government action. The President's Science Advisory Committee began looking into Carson's claims and issued a report in 1963 that partly vindicated her book. Carson was invited to testify before a congressional subcommittee studying pesticide sprays.[14] She told a Senate Commerce Committee how low concentrations of chemical poisons multiplied as they progressed up the food chain. Discussing the sensitivity of marine organisms, she gave an example of shrimp being killed after an insecticide was applied to the surrounding area and rains washed lethal quantities into the water.[15] Many industrial and scientific leaders still doubted Carson's credibility. A committee of the Federal Council for Science and Technology began its own examination of pesticides in 1963. As people fixated on newfound fears, some scientists worried that a confused public would unwisely reject "valuable and necessary" chemicals. Although the United States was producing one billion pounds of pesticides per year, agricultural pests were said to be causing $15 billion worth of crop damage yearly. Farmers were intensely producing "high-cost-per-acre" crops that were susceptible to assaults from insects and disease. Consumers, for their part, were "accustomed to perfection and won't consider buying a wormy apple." The National Academy of Sciences conjectured that "the American people cannot be fed adequately" without chemical pesticides.[16] One member of the USDA commended DDT for saving over five million lives and preventing over one hundred million maladies, especially malaria, typhus, and dysentery. Although pesticides caused many accidental deaths, Fredrick J. Stare of the Harvard School of Public Health said that there had never been a single "medically documented death due to proper use of insecticides."[17] They were far more beneficial than hurtful. For the majority of farmers, weed-killers were a stalwart pillar of the agricultural house, not a frivolous embellishment. However, the refrain that this was agribusiness as usual did not allay the many fears articulated by many ordinary Americans.

The organic movement spoke up about the intricacy and diversity of nature. Organic farmers were at the forefront of groundbreaking research in managing farms as natural systems, demonstrating that crops could be

Organic row crops (Photo courtesy of Colleen Freda Burt)

grown successfully even when bereft of chemical inputs.[18] As public interest in organic living and communal farms mounted, Rodale actively endorsed and demonstrated organic farming techniques on his farm. Other pioneers of organic agriculture integrated holistic ecology into farming.[19] Organic farmers proudly began calling themselves stewards of the land. Rodale's *Our Poisoned Earth and Sky* (1964) expressed qualms about air and water quality, radiation, drugs and cosmetics, and other pollutants. Much of the book focused on the evils of processed food, additives, preservatives, and pesticide-reliant agriculture. Blaming chemical companies for the "poison in our food," Rodale directed his readers to write protest letters to the Food and Drug Administration (FDA) and to elected representatives. Until the government passed protective laws, he advised people to grow as much of their own food by organic conventions as possible or buy organically grown food.[20] Though critics liked to "ridicule the idea that natural organic fertilizers produce better food," Rodale noticed that auxiliary nutritional facts were coming to light proving how good soil, good food, and healthy people were all related.[21] More acolytes tuned in to Rodale's plangent missives. He initiated a newsletter called the *Environmental Action Bulletin* and renamed his publication *Compost Science* the *Journal of Waste Recycling*. Rachel Carson, who had breast cancer, passed away in 1964, but her name remained prominent, and environmentalism found a permanent place in the organic movement's conceptual repertoire.

WHEAT GERM, BROWN RICE, AND ORGANIC GYPSIES

At first glance, serene Rachel Carson seems far removed from Bert "Gypsy Boots" Bootzin (1914–2004), a hyperkinetic fitness and health food envoy with a cultish following. Bootzin was a recurring guest on *The Steve Allen Show*, a popular national comedy-variety show. Bootzin appeared on twenty-five episodes in the early 1960s, entertaining television audiences while exhorting them to eat mounds of organic fruits and vegetables. The long-haired Gypsy Boots would swing onto the stage with a rope, bearing organically grown food that he convinced Allen to try. He was a countercultural maverick who celebrated simplicity and chose to eat organic, vegetarian, unprocessed natural foods.[22] The star of Nat King Cole's hit song "Nature Boy," released in 1948, Bootzin had lived a bohemian life, frolicking and farming organically with his cohort of "Nature Boys" in the California desert. Celebrities sampled organic foods at the Health Hut he opened on Beverly Boulevard in 1958. He peddled organic produce door to door, offered fitness classes, wrote *Bare Feet and Good Things to Eat* (1965), and became a national healthy-eating icon. One obituary said that he "defined what it meant to live close to nature" decades before the nation became obsessed with "organic foods, yoga and exercise."[23] Bootzin helped make organic food seem like an essential tonic for aficionados who wanted a svelte, salubrious body.

Myriad observers have alluded to organic food as a former "hippie fad" when evaluating changes in the movement. However, organic food did not spring from the mutinous impulses of free-spirit activists who feasted on brown rice and granola while dressed in psychedelic garb. Organic farming was a groundswell that had sober roots in the 1940s, when the interconnections between soil, health, and civilization were primary concerns for agricultural pioneers. Yet organic food did resonate with the counterculture, and the movement thrived in this milieu. Organic farming, espousing ideals of sustainability and simplicity, entranced scores of people in the 1960s. Organic food in this era overlapped with health food, vegetarianism, homesteading, and environmental critiques of the nation's industrial food habits. Back-to-the-land buffs were keen to plant organic garden patches. One segment of young adults participated in an experimental social scene of intentional communes employing organic, macrobiotic diets. Fresh organic produce came from small-scale farmers and was mainly available through farmers' markets and natural food stores. Historian Doug Rossinow noted that cooperatives, which included food co-ops, gave shape to some anarchist sentiments. The goal was to run these stores "as democratically as possible, to eschew the profit motive, and to obtain and provide to the local hip population 'natural' food."[24] This new surge of co-op members and organic eaters simultaneously opposed the Vietnam War, the Man, and the Establishment. Riotous energy was pulsing through those who scoffed at the man the gray flannel suit as they scuttled toward Woodstock.

Organic food surfaced in the American psyche, as a key component of countercultural attraction to nutritious cuisine. This health revival was spurred to a certain degree by emerging environmental cognizance and a distaste for pesticides. "Natural" became a prevalent phrase on food labels, alternative food stores prospered, and consumers developed suspicions of food additives.[25] When the natural foods fad sprang up, the "health food store" was the principal outlet, but it sold little actual food, concentrating mainly on vitamins and nutritional supplements. Then "natural foods stores" opened, providing "whole, unadulterated, staple foods—organically produced if possible"—like "fresh produce, bulk grains, beans, nuts, cereals, and newly imported foods such as miso and tofu from Japan."[26] Natural foods stores relied on small farmers to obtain organic produce. One observer of the young adults who embraced organic foods during the 1960s said that "cheap, simple, and natural became their credo . . . and beans, brown rice, and granola became their manna."[27] Hippies famously wore beads and bell-bottoms, rejected middle-class values, extolled Eastern philosophies, tried herbal remedies, and enjoyed consciousness-raising diets.

Julia Child, the premier television cooking personality of the 1960s, dismissed organic foods; perhaps they appeared too precious or puerile to her unaffected sensibilities.[28] Organic provisions seemed draconian to Americans who were watching Child show off decadent, buttery French recipes (for example, sauce beurre blanc) on television, cooking beef Wellington and Swedish meatballs at home, or waiting on the orange stools at Howard Johnson's for the server to bring classic franks, macaroni and cheese, and ice cream sundaes. Meanwhile, brown rice, lentils, sunflower seeds, tofu, alfalfa sprouts, hummus, tabouli salad, and whole-grain bread were indeed common accompaniments to farm-fresh produce for the organic food congregation. Dessert was made from carob powder and dried dates instead of white sugar and milk chocolate. To those who were not disciples, "all-natural" meals appeared to consist of odd concoctions such as "marinated seaweed laced with blackstrap molasses and topped with a dollop of yogurt."[29] One unfavorable assessment later accused the counterculture of "proscriptive dietary yammering" about the stereotypical "brown rice, adzuki beans, loaves of bread that could anchor a tugboat, meatless chili, tea made out of crabgrass," and other "near-comestibles whose principal attraction . . . was that they were not what straight people were eating."[30] Legendary forager Euell Gibbons did not hide his esteem for wild, organic foods, which, he said, were not only edible but also a cut above "the devitalized days-old produce usually found on your grocer's shelves" that had been "sprayed with poisons."[31] In *Stalking the Wild Asparagus* (1962), he described a self-procured meal that incorporated wild fruit juices, snapping-turtle soup, chicken-fried frog's legs, water cress salad, boiled day-lily buds and cattail bloom spikes, golden muffins of cattail pollen with wild strawberry jam, blackberry cobbler, dandelion coffee, and candied calamus root. In *Stalking the Good Life* (1966), Gibbons explained that, although he preferred wild plants, he did believe that "the first organic gardener was born" when somebody decided to "deepen his relationship with nature" by domesticating wild plants in a way that was not possessive but "cooperative and mutually beneficial."[32] Gibbons also expressed his support for organics in a regular column he wrote for *Organic Gardening* magazine.

Paul Hawken—who later founded the Smith & Hawken gardening business—started Erewhon Trading Company in 1966 to sell organic foods. Within five years, the large Boston-based wholesaler was shipping "tons of organic rice each week," drawing more customers who recognized its benefits.[33] Rodale never pretended that organic food was a magic bullet for health, but *Rodale's System for Mental Power and Natural Health* (1966) offered a blueprint for becoming "more vital physically and more mentally alert."[34] Rodale discussed the remunerations of vitamins and exercise, the danger of foods with chemical additives, and even the correspondence between a good diet and safe driving. Rodale said that those who abided by *Prevention*'s natural diet, took their vitamins, ate right, did calisthenics, and walked an hour a day would not need any "drug crutches."[35] Different sorts of drug crutches may have been leaned upon at San Francisco's Human Be-In in 1967, where Timothy Leary invited people to "turn on, tune in, drop out." Tens of thousands of young people descended upon Haight-Ashbury during the "Summer of Love" in 1967. Ecology-minded, peace-and-love flower children chose to eat organic, natural, whole foods. The Grateful Dead performed a

Selling vegetables at the market (Photo courtesy of Colleen Freda Burt)

concert at Betty Nelson's Organic Raspberry Farm in Sultan, Washington, in September 1968. *Time* reported that the youth of the Woodstock nation were becoming vegetarians with "religious zeal" and were "in the vanguard of the flourishing organic-food movement."[36] Straight-laced Americans shuddered at the kaleidoscopic deluge of free food, free drugs, and free love. The organic movement was dancing on the edge of psychedelia, demonstrating that it had the capacity to be mind-altering in ways Rodale had never quite envisioned.

The *Whole Earth Catalog*, a canonical text for hippies and back-to-the-landers, espoused organic food, which was in keeping with the publication's ecological worldview. First published in 1968, the *Catalog* featured products and information related to "whole systems," gardening, geodesic domes, voluntary simplicity, "appropriate technology," personal computers, crafts, homes, communities, and yoga.[37] Stewart Brand, its creator, had been involved with Ken Kesey and the Merry Pranksters, communes, rock music, light shows, and the hallucinogenic drug scene. The *Whole Earth Catalog* reviewed tools like "a $4,900 Hewlett-Packard desktop calculator and a one-man sawmill."[38] Much like *Organic Gardening*, it offered resources for back-to-the-landers that were both high-tech and oldfangled. Rodale and Brand make for an interesting comparison: the former resembled a nineteenth-century man plunked down in the twentieth, while the latter conjured the ambiance of a twentieth-century man on the cusp of the twenty-first. Rodale was, according to his granddaughter, "not a hippie at all," but "more of a New York intellectual."[39] Brand, on the other hand, had his exploits with LSD and his status as an "Indian freak" fond of the peyote cults mentioned in Tom Wolfe's *The Electric Kool-Aid Acid Test* (1968). The fact that both Brand and Rodale produced defining documents of the convention-breaking 1960s reveals some of the organic movement's complexity.

RODALE THE LIFE CHANGER

One of the books Rodale published, *The Complete Book of Composting* (1960), was hardly a likely candidate to be reckoned life-changing for those who read it. In it, Rodale called compost "the heart of the organic concept" and said it was "a form of nature magic which puts Aladdin to shame."[40] Any enterprising gardener could tap into this alchemy by making a pile in the backyard of organic materials rich in nitrogen and carbon. The transformation into serviceable fertilizer was thrilling and electrifying (for Rodale, at least). He taught his readers the critical role of bacteria in making a compost heap. This was one of Rodale's topics that catered to a more limited audience—but Rodale was always reaching further. He dedicated the book "to all those who keep a love for the land in their hearts, minds and deeds."[41] Rodale also reiterated the paramount importance of maintaining "nature's equilibrium," a far more resonant theme. The mellifluous trilling of sweet birds seemed to waft up from organic gardens. This enchanting, land-loving approach to gardening was more compelling for Rodale's pupils than the hard-hearted rigidity of chemical gardening. Loyal adherent Eleanor Perényi had received her first copy of Rodale's magazine in 1945 from a friend, and she recalled it being "an inelegant little publication printed on cheap stock, with photographs strictly of the hand-held Kodak variety and a down-home prose style." She remembered the "bearded countenance" of Rodale that "glared forth from the editorial page like that of an Old Testament prophet." Perényi became a garden writer herself and had the opportunity to interview him for an article she was writing in the early 1960s. Upon arriving at his farm, she recalled, "my first sight of Rodale seemed to confirm the impression that he belonged in another century. With his neatly trimmed beard, three-piece city suit, and overcoat, he was an incongruously formal figure against the backdrop of rich Pennsylvania farmland."[42] Perényi later said that *Organic*

Gardening changed her life and was the only magazine she "continuously subscribed to for thirty-five years."[43]

Another admirer, Malcolm Beck, had started operating his family farm organically in 1957 and said his "first inspiration came from Rodale Press's little *Organic Gardening and Farming* magazine."[44] A friend gave him back issues selling the idea that plants grown in balanced soil, rich in organic matter, would be strong and healthy. Beck's other magazine—a "modern farm" one—was promoting the stance that noxious chemicals were needed to grow food and run a lucrative farm. Beck decided that farming could be "more fun, a lot more challenging, and even just as profitable if we followed the natural or organic laws, and the food we ate would be more healthful too."[45] He "really became a student of that organic magazine."[46] Beck purchased his second farm in 1968 and founded GardenVille, an organic composting business and retail horticultural supply house. He later acquired a reputation as "the grandfather of organics in Texas."[47] But Beck recalled that he had trouble when he first tried to impress a large independent grocery store owner with his produce, because "organic growing and pot-smoking hippies were thought to be on about the same level."[48] Some observers said that "a certain weirdness" clung to "the entire organic food culture."[49] The California Medical Association (CMA) felt that Rodale and others in the "misleading and costly cult" were deluded by "fantasies," like the assumption that chemical fertilizers removed the nutritional value of crops. Rather, the CMA said that organic farming was based on the "erroneous belief" that the quality of soil affected the quality of the crop.[50]

Erroneous or not, organic farming had gathered a "devoted following" by 1969. The *Wall Street Journal* saw more "ordinary housewives" willing to endure a "smelly pile of manure" in the yard in return for "unpolluted food." Organic growers devised "ingenious means" to combat pests without chemicals, and "because of the current uproar over the safety of pesticides and food additives, a lot of other people now take them seriously."[51] Rodale questioned the FDA's accepted levels of chemical compounds in foods, asking the *New York Times*, "How can the body cope with the sheer volume of chemical substances which trickle into it from a hundred different food sources each day?"[52] Betty Morales, proprietor of Organic-Ville in Los Angeles, said that her health food supermarket doubled its sales that year. She reiterated that organic food was more nutritious, more appetizing, and clearly a "superior product."[53] For many growers, organic was a "sincere philosophy," and the food was more expensive because costs for the farmer were higher than for those "doing it the commercial way."[54] Avid gardener Jeanie Darlington also described how subscribing to *Organic Gardening and Farming* changed her perspective. She had thought that organic gardening was "something weird old spinsters" did, but the magazine put her on the road to discovering the intricacies of blood meal, kelp meal, ground rock phosphate, and other "exotic sounding things."[55] She recalled that the publication would arrive each month with good ideas to help her. She soon wanted to instruct others in growing vegetables and flowers organically, because not only did the food taste better, but, most important, it was "better for your soul" to garden organically.[56] Darlington accused those who used chemical fertilizers of disregarding the fact that soil was a "living breathing thing." Poison sprays, she said, polluted the atmosphere and killed harmless insects and helpful predators, thus "destroying the balance of nature." Gardening organically, however, was about "working in harmony with nature."[57] Darlington published *Grow Your Own: An Introduction to Organic Farming* (1970) to share what she had learned. The market for organic guidebooks was expanding, along with the number of Rodale's protégés.

Farmer Samuel Ogden, a contributing editor to *Organic Gardening*, began growing vegetables without chemicals in the 1940s, and in 1971 Rodale Press published his *Step-by-Step to Organic Vegetable Growing*. For Ogden, the organic route meant studying "the whole cycle of life in the garden." The organic whole functioned "harmoniously in nature and as nature intended," though Ogden did add that this harmony had to be "carefully guided by the hand of man to his useful ends."[58] When Ogden's grandson, Shepherd Ogden, later wrote *Straight-Ahead Organic: A Step-by-Step Guide to Growing Great Vegetables in a Less-than-Perfect World* (1992), he built upon the advice of his grandfather. One of the advantages of organic gardening, the younger Ogden said, was that it allowed people to fine-tune their rapport with nature. He added that composting, an example of the cyclical interaction of the natural world, was still "the heart of modern organic gardening."[59] All the tender ministrations of organic farmers were meant to foster soil fecundity, with gentle succor trumping the arm twisting of chemical farmers.

HELEN AND SCOTT NEARING: LIVING THE ORGANIC GOOD LIFE

Helen and Scott Nearing had moved from New York City to a Vermont farm in 1931, yearning for "a simple, satisfying life on the land."[60] Over the next six decades, they became influential campaigners for organic gardening and homesteading. The Nearings believed that rural alternatives provided greater possibilities for a fulfilling life than urban environs. They rejected the strain and greed of the city, lambasting its complexity, tension, and artificiality. They explained, "We moved our center back to the land. There we raised the food we ate. We found it sufficient, delicious, and nourishing."[61] They worked to achieve economic, social, health-oriented, and ethical objectives. Their experiment was one of "sane living in an insane world."[62] They hoped to live a structured life of purposeful actions. Organic food and farming were integral to the Nearings' lifestyle. They believed in "fresh, vital food, organically produced."[63] On their farm in the Green Mountains, they set about building up the soil by composting. Among the handbooks on organic farming that they relied on were Rodale's *Pay Dirt* and *The Organic Front*, Albert Howard's *Agricultural Testament* and *The Soil and Health*, and Eve Balfour's *The Living Soil* (1943). They were adamant that fruits and vegetables grown in compost were healthier and more delectable. They also felt that organic gardening best expressed their compassion for nature and required minimal intervention.[64] They proposed that if other people created organized demand for organic food, this would extend its production and availability.[65]

The Nearings insisted on garden-fresh, unprocessed foods. They disparaged twentieth-century food habits that stemmed from large-scale factories and chemical fertilizers. They distinguished between "man's natural food" and the "denatured items displayed on the shelves of supermarkets."[66] While most American families depended unduly on convenient canned soup and frozen entrees, the Nearings lived year round on food raised during the brief Vermont growing season, including lettuce, cucumbers, squash, peppers, tomatoes, sweet peas, spinach, potatoes, beets, and cabbage. Eating "whole food" grown on their own farm enabled them to nurture a strong attachment to the earth and demonstrate a possible replacement for the dominant industrial lifestyle. They were also vegetarians for health and ethical reasons. Helen's reverence for all forms of life even compelled her to apologize to carrots before ingesting them.[67] In general, the Nearings ate very little and gravitated toward a monotonous diet, claiming that these food habits were simple, economic, and practical. By producing and consuming their own goods and services, they fashioned a subsistence homestead that was largely independent of the commodity markets. The garden was the basis of their home economy. They cut wood for fuel, put up their own buildings with local stone and wood, made implements, and bartered for other indispensable products. For Scott, an economist who had been ousted from his academic position because of antigovernment and antiwar political positions, home-steading was "an act of resistance to unrestrained capitalism."[68] The Nearings did not sugarcoat the amount of hard work homesteading necessitated. Still, while they persevered in working daily during specified hours in order to attain their goals, they were equally diligent about scheduling time for intellectual and creative pursuits.

The Nearings derived their income from lectures, writing, and maple sugar production. They were starkly set apart from their Vermont neighbors in several ways. The couple intentionally chose to live in an austere, frugal manner; they were not involuntarily poor. They opted to have no telephone or radio. Although they reveled in farm life, they had reservations about rural life. They never realized the elusive sense of kinship with the local community that they had hoped for, in part because they regularly looked down on their neighbors for consuming too many pies, cakes, doughnuts, and dead animals. The Nearings lamented that, even with open land at their disposal, nearby families would purchase canned or packaged food rather than raise it in a home garden.[69] These rustic Americans, in turn, were baffled by the Nearings' odd dietary habits and their disciplined, organized life. The Nearings did commend the "unpretentious" Vermonters and hosted an informal musical hour each Sunday morning for townspeople. They never locked their doors, and guests were always welcome, though most of those visitors came from the city. Ultimately, the Nearings felt that the nineteen-year Vermont experiment was a failure socially, although they deemed it a success in terms of individual health and happiness.

In 1952, the Nearings moved to Forest Farm in Harborside, Maine, where they persisted in their efforts at freeing themselves from "undue dependence on the Establishment."[70] By then, they were becoming renowned homesteaders and described their self-reliant lifestyle in *Living the Good Life* (1954). Like Henry David Thoreau, to whom they often alluded, they cherished simplicity, convenience, and harmony. The Nearings viewed Thoreau as the superlative homesteader. *Living the Good Life* was a back-to-the-land instruction book, much as *Walden* was a manual for deliberate living. The Nearings believed that, by following their example, others seeking the good life could learn the liberating art of "living in nature." Their new farm provided food, fuel, and shelter. They built compost piles, stone structures, and a yurt. Blueberries became their new cash crop. They worked out ways to store, dry, freeze, can, and preserve the food they raised organically. Due to the short

Organic blueberries (Photo courtesy of Colleen Freda Burt)

growing season in New England, they built a sun-heated greenhouse along with a garden to supply themselves with salad and other greens year round.[71] Since they refused to use animal products, they applied seaweed from the Atlantic Ocean as fertilizer. They said, "At all times we have in mind the basic principle of organic gardening: to put into the soil more fertility than crops or erosion take out."[72] The rhythms of planting, composting, harvesting, and eating were significant to their rituals.

The Nearings were resolute that "balanced, healthful living requires at-oneness with all aspects of nature."[73] Both Scott and Helen toiled on the farm, and their work was not divided by typical gender assignments. Helen did suggest that it was best for a couple—or an alliance of like-minded people—to tackle the work involved in homesteading. She took sole responsibility for cooking. However, in *Simple Food for the Good Life: An Alternative Cookbook* (1980), she expressed the opinion that "women need not hang over stoves and should not spend the major part of their time fooling with food and household work."[74] She favored recipes that used raw vegetables, straight from the garden, with minimal cooking. Her cookbook was directed at "frugal, abstemious folk who eat to nourish their bodies and leave self-indulgent delicacies to the gourmets."[75] From their sixty-year experiment, the couple concluded that it was indeed possible to craft a robust, ethical, self-contained economy.

The Nearings became exemplars for counterculturists in the 1960s and 1970s, due to their antiestablishment, organic, vegetarian, Spartan lifestyle. They were evangelical proponents of homesteading and wrote occasionally for *Organic Gardening*. When *Living the Good Life* was reissued in 1970 it became a best seller, poignantly appealing to a new generation of budding homesteaders and emergent community gardeners. Helen and Scott Nearing, living the "good life" on their Maine homestead, delighted these idealists. Forest Farm became a mecca for those who aspired to a simple existence, and the Nearings regarded themselves as missionaries. Thousands of visitors from around the world made the pilgrimage to the Maine coast each year to ask for advice and absorb inspiration from the lifestyle that the Nearings modeled and wrote about. Scott would die at age one hundred, in 1983. After his death, Helen would continue the no-frills life and still received a stream of visitors. Through her contagious and palpable energy, she stirred countless people to change their lives, slow down, eat a vegetarian diet, and farm organically.[76] Helen would die in 1995, at the age of ninety-one, and the nonprofit Good Life Center was established at Forest Farm to preserve the Nearings' legacy and promote sustainable living.

HARMONIOUS HOMESTEADS: ORGANICALLY BACK TO THE LAND

Homegrown food has long appealed to Americans eager to bond with the land and collect its bounty. Amateur gardeners have appreciated the opportunity to work outdoors, save money, and eat delicious, nutritious food. Homesteaders, acutely aware of where their meals come from, have articulated clear-cut connections between food and nature.[77] The insistence that accepting "Nature's terms" is enriching rather than limiting has been a leitmotif among homesteaders and organicists. When organic gardening and farming entered a fresh phase with the countercultural developments of the late 1960s and 1970s, Thoreau and the Nearings became idols. The allure of finding a way to "live deliberately" enveloped Americans. Those who sought a self-sufficient livelihood placed the garden and its results at the center of their days. Scores of young people "dropped out" from civilization, retreating to distant communes and rustic farms. According to some estimates, over thirty-five hundred utopian communes formed between 1965 and 1970, creating a reprieve from the dominion of industrial capitalism and the homo-geneity of manufactured foods.[78] Independent smallholders chose a more private yeoman model but also held to an antimaterialist creed.

New publications celebrated homesteading and rural ways of life. *Mother Earth News*, a spiritual descendent of Liberty Hyde Bailey's *Country Life in America*, was launched just before Earth Day in 1970. Other journals like *Futurist, Future's Conditional, Vegan*, and *Natural Living* advocated organic farming, health food, and "appropriate technology."[79] These sources joined *Organic Gardening and Farming* as beacons for the mingling of organic and counterculture philosophies. Organic farmer Samuel Ogden observed an "extraordinary change in the public point of view concerning the use of poisonous pesticides and herbicides" by the early 1970s. This recognition of dangers to humans and their surroundings had "induced a tremendous up-surge of interest in the kinds of food we eat, and in the manner in which they are grown." Ogden noticed a large demand for organically grown vegetables. More young people were leaving the city for the country, attempting to "re-turn to the soil as a way of life."[80] They were not likely to win over diehard Oscar Mayer hot dog eaters, but there was shared cognizance of a higher, greener purpose.

The Basic Book of Organically Grown Foods (1972)—written by the staff of *Organic Gardening and Farming*—noted that young people were "in revolt," expressing "vigorous dissatisfaction with the money-oriented, polluted, self-ish, unpleasant, technological society that has spawned them."[81] The edi-tors sympathized with this back-to-the-land crowd and went on to say that "natural, unpoisoned food" had become a major commitment for "young revolutionaries." Those who were gathering in communes or establishing permanent homesteads were "carrying the organic system to an intensity of fulfillment that older people just wouldn't be able to accomplish." The book said that some readers may have been "revolting in a mild way by boycotting synthetic foods and dangerous drugs," but these "longhaired young people" were "going much further by pulling up stakes completely and trying to live close to nature."[82] Among those "in revolt" were Pennsylvania homesteaders Tim and Grace Lefever, who farmed organically on sixty acres of land in the 1970s. The Lefevers frequently spoke to college, community, and church groups on the merits of organic food. They were steadfast about producing most of what they used, keeping material possessions to a minimum, and drawing on the sun to heat their home. They admitted, however, that the one modern convenience they found indispensable was their blender, utilized daily to make juice from edible plants like beet leaves, carrot tops, spinach, kale, and dandelions.[83] J. I. Rodale's son, Robert, saw the organic homestead as a testing ground for the "revolutionary anti-pollution and conservation methods" that were imperative for improving everyone's quality of living. He regarded organic gardeners and farmers as "members of that dwindling group of Americans who still have close, direct attachment to the soil and who have not forgotten what it is like to grow food and make the simple essentials of life."[84] He described the organic way of life as "sane living in a mad world"—a phrase he seems to have borrowed from the Nearings.

Homesteader Gene Logsdon also subsisted organically as a way to live sanely and pleasurably. For him, the main objective of modern homesteading in the 1970s was to gain independence and self-reliance. Logsdon asserted that the basic philosophies of the organic homesteader were "accommodate yourself to nature whenever possible" and "don't dominate nature when you don't have to."[85] He praised the virtues of compost. Logsdon admitted that organic farming was a more arduous way to raise food but believed that work on the organic homestead was creative and individualistic, something done out of love, not duty. In terms of labor, he emphasized that the organicist combined knowledge from "primitive" and "civilized" people. In a minority of cases, a good team of horses, fully in keeping with the spirit of organics, could be an asset to the homestead; however, a small tractor could be more sensible and economical at other times.[86] Two decades later, Logsdon still enjoyed farming his thirty-two acres in an ecological manner. Calling himself "the contrary farmer," he said that homesteaders and "cottage farmers" ought to separate themselves from the "capitalist/socialist economy."[87] However, like Louis Bromfield, he altered his hard-line organic stance over the years. Although his garden and orchard were what he called "100 percent organic," he no longer opposed applying a moderate amount of chemical fertilizer to fields as an economical way of maintaining fertility. In a rebuttal to those who critiqued him for not being "certified organic," Logsdon declared that "if a small amount of chemical fertilizer every fourth year on my crop fields makes me a cheater among the Chosen, that will prove in the long run to be the organic fraternity's problem, not mine."[88] He continued to criticize "modern society" for losing touch with hands-on farming techniques, and he pinpointed the garden as the only place urbanites could make close contact with "the basic realities of life."[89]

Organic homesteader Ralph Borsodi's influence was apparent at Deep Run Farm, a thirty-six-acre offshoot of the School of Living he had founded, which opened in 1976. Deep Run Farm operated a garden, a greenhouse, a kitchen, a bakery, and studios in York, Pennsylvania. Possessions were owned jointly; 75 percent of every person's individual income was shared; and each member contributed fifteen hours of labor per week to the commune. Its alternative school, open to the public, instructed nearly thirty students between the ages of five and eleven.[90] Deep Run Farm served as the administrative center of the School of Living. In spring 1979, the School of Homesteading and Organic Agriculture began there. It was a one-year program with a curriculum that included agriculture, food preservation, animal husbandry, aquaculture, crafts, mechanical skills, shelter building, conservation skills, survival training, forestry practices, and wild area projects. Director Arnold Greenburg likened it to a kibbutz, since members were mutually dependent on one another, producing most of their own food and developing many of their own energy sources."[91] The School of Living moved to Pennsylvania but was still operating decades later, and *Green Revolution* was published as a quarterly journal with a focus on cooperative living, land issues, monetary reform, permaculture, and alternative education. It exemplified the enduring links between organic growing and eating, homesteading, and "harmony with nature."

FROM DDT TO ECOLOGY

By the late 1960s, antipesticide activity had reached a zenith in the United States. *Time* magazine tagged 1969 as "the year of ecology" and indicated that, suddenly, "all sorts of Americans utter new words like ecosystem and eutrophication. Pollution may soon replace the Viet Nam war as the nation's major issue of protest."[92] Political activists at the People's Park protests in Berkeley that year wanted there to be an organic garden on vacant university land, not a parking lot. Joni Mitchell's "Big Yellow Taxi" memorably asked farmers to "put away that DDT now" so "the birds and the bees" could survive. When the Santa Barbara oil spill in 1969 killed thousands of creatures and Cleveland's oil-laden Cuyahoga River dramatically caught fire later that year, these were shocking visual manifestations of ecological crises. Environmental toxins, agricultural chemicals, and radioactive substances came under closer scrutiny. At the crest of this wave, the United States celebrated a new holiday—Earth Day—for the first time in 1970. Allen Ginsberg, Ralph Nader, Paul Ehrlich, and Barry Commoner were among the speakers at national rallies. Environmental mindfulness was said to be a thread that united the American people, cutting through "all ages and through all kinds of bags."[93] Congress authorized the creation of the Environmental Protection Agency (EPA), which could set tolerance levels for chemical residues. Momentum built for more legislation—but it was a divisive controversy.

Progressive Farmer maintained that DDT should not be singled out for attack, because it was "one of the most useful chemicals ever discovered."[94] From this perspective, DDT was a wonder drug—after all, it had spared millions from malaria. Entomology professor J. Gordon Edwards told an agricultural magazine in 1970 that the "barrage of anti-DDT propaganda" was "remarkably untruthful" and sensationalized. He called DDT a "great benefactor of mankind" and an "ally in our fight against death, disease and starvation."[95] Federal agencies and industry factions repeatedly said it was unnecessary to tremble about the possibility of accepted pesticide levels causing adverse effects on health. Another publication in 1970 by the farm chemicals industry expressed astonishment at how vociferously the "anti-pesticide cult" was conveying its misdirected concern about pesticides, when, really, "the most common type of food poisoning is spread by rodent feces."[96] Nobel Prize–winning plant geneticist Norman Borlaug denounced the "vicious, hysterical propaganda campaign" to ban insecticides. Without DDT, crop losses would soar, food prices would increase, and global famine would ensue.[97] Borlaug dismissed the short-sighted campaign against insecticides and fertilizers as "based on emotion, mini-truths, maybe truths and downright falsehoods." If the "full bellied philosophers, environmentalists and pseudoecologists" had their way, disaster would befall the world.[98] Blasé chemists were nonchalant about the fear of DDT. Activists, public interest groups, and citizens were not mollified; they amassed their own ammunition. The National Audubon Society president rebuked Borlaug for ignoring the ecological consequences of long-lasting pesticides. Furthermore, the great irony was that the very insects DDT was meant to target were, instead, developing immunity, becoming even more prevalent and dodgy.[99] Legions of environmentalists felt that irresponsible chemical use was far more liable to doom the world than "hysterical" organic farmers were. The USDA set up a monitoring program to determine the effects of routine pesticide use, and by 1972 the EPA had banned DDT. Both Carson and Rodale could take a chunk of the credit for this milestone, since both had helped infuse the nation with that "barrage of anti-DDT propaganda."

ORGANIC ODDITIES

Just as organic farmers couldn't shake their "unscientific" tag, other "odd duck" stereotypes came along with organics. When Jeff Cox started working at *Organic Gardening* during the 1970s, he had to conceal his affiliation with the magazine "just to get an interview with a plant scientist" at the USDA.[100] Intimately entwined with the chemical industry, the USDA was indisposed to consider the viability of organics. Cox remembered that Rodale Press would take clients and guests to a lunchroom called Fitness House that served "the most unpleasant food imaginable: unsalted buckwheat groats, sweet potatoes without butter, potatoes boiled in milk, musty-tasting sprouts." He said that "granola and groats became synonymous with organic food in many places in the 1970s." Cox also recalled eating "many an unpleasurable meal at back-to-the-land communes from Maine to California."[101] Even with various unpalatable options, sales of organic food boomed, reaching new outlets. *Life* magazine ran the cover story "Organic Food: New and Natural" in 1970, noting that "true devotees" of food grown organically had spawned a nationwide subindustry to accommodate their cravings.[102] Discussing health food stores of the era, Elaine Lipson said that they were "filled with character, community, and passion" and "helped seed a movement" that would grow far beyond anyone's expectations at the time.[103] Natural food stores flourished, and one economic analyst noted that they were "run by counterculture people who take lower incomes than their skill could demand elsewhere, in order to bring what they consider to be high-quality food to the people they wish to serve."[104] *The Organic Gardening Guide to Organic Living* (1970) described natural food stores in the San Francisco Bay area and mentioned that "the young mother in bell-bottom denims or the guy with hair down his back is a standard fixture in every store."[105] At the Oakland Food Mill, a purveyor of organic food, the *Guide* observed that there were "families on the Food Stamp plan . . . young mothers with babies strapped to their backs . . . elderly people . . . and, of course, there are many young people—in flamboyant hats and colorful long dresses—often buying foods in bulk to use in their communes."[106] *Life* magazine declared—inaccurately, as it turned out—in 1970 that organic foods were incompatible on a mass scale with a supermarket economy. At "small country-style stores" that were meeting the demand, food grown organically regularly cost at least fifty percent more, but "believers find it irresistible, and willingly endure the hassle and pay the prices to get it."[107] The price-blind "health nuts" received their share of ribbing. Gaynor

Organic vegetables at an indoor farm stand (Photo courtesy of Colleen Freda Burt)

Maddox, author of several books on how to eat well for less money, stressed in 1970 that the vitamin content of organically grown foods was "neither more nor less than the cheaper, mass-produced fruits and vegetables."[108] Humorist Art Buchwald's column cautioned that, when invited to dinner with the "organic food specialists," who eat "roots of moss and eucalyptus bark" instead of real food, you "can't walk on the lawn because that may be your dinner."[109] Still, with over seven hundred substantially sized stores selling organic produce, national news outlets opined that "it's no longer a fad, it's a movement." The Good Earth supermarket in New York doubled in size as it sold "fertile eggs, goat yogurt, dandelion coffee," and organic pizza. In fact, "hippie communes that subsist[ed] on organic food" were selling it to retailers to mitigate the scarcity.[110] More and more nonhippies were enthralled by organic food's potential.

Consumer demand for organically grown food exceeded the supply, but some food was sold as organic under false pretenses, so skepticism ran high. A UCLA nutrition scientist said in 1970 that "DDT and similar sprays have so permeated the life cycle" that growers could not guarantee toxin-free produce. Still, even the nonplussed knew that they preferred food grown "nature's way"; manifold how-to books on organic shopping and growing were available; and the market was swelling. Although it was difficult to regulate misleading claims, farmers growing for the Sun Circle cooperative in California in 1970 signed a statement swearing under penalty of perjury that they were not using synthetic fertilizers or toxic sprays on their "genuine organic produce." [111] Rodale launched a program in 1971 to create standards and verify organic practices. A seal reading "Organic Farmer: Certified by *Organic Gardening and Farming* magazine" was issued to growers who passed an on-farm inspection.[112] Rodale Press shouldered the costs in order to show that credible organic farmers existed, hoping that certification would raise confidence among consumers.[113] The number of participating farmers was small, but it was the first successful organic certification program in the United States, and it was a step beyond the informal, arbitrary networks that preceded it.

AN ANTIESTABLISHMENT GLAMOUR BUSINESS

In one issue of *Organic Gardening and Farming*, J. I. Rodale wrote, "Let's keep our chins up and help toward bringing America to an organic consciousness!"[114] Rodale's aplomb kept propelling the movement. By sheer dint of will, he challenged conventional agriculture's chemical stagnation. The intellectual milieu did shift in the direction of organic awareness. Significant attention to Rodale came when the *Whole Earth Catalog*, the landmark counterculture guidebook, glorified *Organic Gardening and Farming* as the nation's "most subversive" magazine. In the edition of the *Whole Earth Catalog* from spring 1970, Gurney Norman wrote:

> The thing to remember about organic gardening is that it's a movement, a national energy that since its beginnings early in the 1940's has grown into a force so potent by now that it contains serious political implications. . . . If I were a dictator determined to control the national press, *Organic Gardening* would be the first publication I'd squash, because it is the most subversive. I believe that organic gardeners are in the forefront of a serious effort to save the world by changing man's orientation to it, to move away from the collective, centrist, super-industrial state, toward a simpler, realer one-to-one relationship with the earth itself.[115]

The *Whole Earth Catalog* applauded *Organic Gardening* as one of the "anti-establishment heroes" in America. The *Catalog* recommended that "every young radical" should have a copy of *Walden, Organic Gardening,* and the *Cultivator's Handbook of Marijuana.*[116] Jerome Goldstein, who took over as the editor of *Organic Gardening and Farming* magazine, wrote in 1970 that, "in this post–Earth Day atmosphere, the simple ideas of J. I. Rodale's organic method have taken on a new aura of social significance."[117] Goldstein said that the idea behind organic foods was "basically right," but he still felt that it was "weird to find ourselves in the front lines of the ecology movement."[118] Rodale Press deemed itself the "communications center for environmental living ideas for the individual," and readership metrics undergirded this exultation. *Prevention,* which stressed "how the individual consumer can affect his environment by what he eats," had 725,000 subscribers. *Organic Gardening and Farming,* which developed "an organic way of life for readers, both in and out of the garden," had 500,000.[119] The circulation of *Prevention* doubled between 1968 and 1971, when it reached nearly one million. Rodale Press also published magazines on exercise, composting, and theater (another personal interest of Rodale's), though only *Prevention* and *Organic Gardening and Farming* were turning a profit.[120] As Americans embraced health foods, President Nixon and "a range of senators from Proxmire to Thurmond" were said to eat wheat germ—the most popular health food—for breakfast.[121]

Health-hunting Americans who were worried about how nutrition affected their well-being seized on organic food as an ally. The organic movement emphasized that a "natural" or "pure" organic diet was an elixir for physical vitality. When J. I. Rodale and his staff published *The Health Seeker* (1971), the thorough book covered everything from accidents, acne, alcoholism, and algae to warts, water softeners, and x-rays in an alphabetical format. In the entry "Chemicals in Food," Rodale noted that the country was "at last waking up to the danger of sprayed and processed foods," and that this would bring "salvation" from the perils.[122] He maintained that gardening by the organic method was the best way to obtain "the finest, most nutritious fruits and vegetables" that were needed for optimum health.[123] As organic foods seemed to bear more desirable qualities, these rich emotional associations compelled people to join the movement.

One of the best-known deputies for organic diets was Adelle Davis, who was called an "Earth Mother to the Foodists" by *Life* magazine as she was "singing the praises of proper nutrition." By 1971 she had been christened the "High Priestess" of natural foods. Discussing her "four spectacularly popular books on nutrition," Davis said that there were "fakes in the health foods business," peddling food as organic even when it wasn't. Still, she castigated the "hundreds of thousands of pounds of chemicals that destroy nutrients" in food.[124] Davis pushed people to acquire fruits and vegetables "grown on composted, mulched soils free from chemical fertilizers and insecticides," vouching that these would have "superb flavor and amazing keeping qualities."[125] In 1973, the *New York Times* dubbed her "chief showwoman for health foods" in a "rapidly growing 'organic nation' of health-food devotees." Though she was debunked by the "medical-scientific fraternity," her attractiveness to those spellbound by health food skyrocketed.[126] Rodale and the *Prevention* staff did not see eye to eye with her on everything, but they approved of Davis's *Let's Eat Right to Keep Fit* and complimented her *Let's Cook It Right* as "the best cookbook we know."[127] Both Davis and Rodale agreed wholeheartedly that they wanted chemicals expunged from the American dinner table.

For some consumers, organic food promised tangible gains, such as safety and nutrition. For others, the symbolic connotations—such as the indication of a "natural" lifestyle—were convincing. Some consumers were insouciant about pesticides or vitamins but still selected organic food based on taste, freshness, or favored brands.[128] Whatever the motive, some consumers confidently paid substantial prices for organically produced food. *Advertising Age* called organic food the fastest-growing sector of the food market.[129] Natural, organic, and other health foods were 1971's "glamour business," declared *Barron's National Business and Financial Weekly*. The "surge of interest in ecology and the back-to-nature trend" were responsible for catapulting health foods into the national scene and enabling them to command hefty retail prices.[130] Another reporter wrote that the "theory of organic living" at the heart of this change in eating was "a very radical idea." Consumers clamored for organic and natural foods, and this explosion indicated that people preferred food "the way nature serves it up to them," grown in nutrient-rich humus, even if it did have a few "bug spots."[131]

Regardless of bug spots, organic food was drawing more attention in print. The Ecological Food Society created *The Comprehensive Catalog of Organic Products* to help members order everything needed for "a total organic environment." The society said that organic food was "how good food used to taste" and promised that the prices of organic foods would not be more than "a few pennies above that of 'contaminated' products."[132] *The New York Times Natural Foods Cookbook* (1971) acclaimed the "nutritional benefits of the natural, fresh foods that Grandmother knew" and confirmed that demand for organic food far outstripped the current supply.[133] Its recipes, such as millet-stuffed peppers, goat cheese pancakes, and organic whole wheat bread, were contributed by "dedicated followers of the natural foods and organic gardening movements."[134] Alicia Laurel's *Living on the Earth* (1971) guided parents in making their own baby food from organically grown fruits and vegetables, since she felt that commercial baby products were unhealthy; and she sanctioned the Rodale books for organic gardening advice.[135]

Rodale Press was the unchallenged epicenter of organic expertise. Robert Rodale answered questions from those who were curious about the "organic health-food way of life" in a newspaper column in 1971. He suggested that the best way to get organic food was by growing one's own or sprouting seeds of organic alfalfa and mung beans indoors.[136] He also recommended Frances Moore Lappé's *Diet for a Small Planet* (1971), which was all the rage among the eco-attentive set. Lappé notoriously exposed the environmental ramifications of dietary choices. She discussed the health risks inherent in the American "high fat, high sugar, low fiber" diet, but her primary emphasis was on vegetarianism as a more democratic, ecologically sustainable food system that could alleviate world hunger. Urging the adoption of a meatless, unprocessed, "traditional diet," Lappé pointed out that "what's good for the earth turns out to be good for us too."[137] Ethnobiologist Charles Heiser agreed with Lappé's solution, explaining that "we could feed seven times as many people directly on grain as are fed when a given amount of grain is converted into meat."[138] He argued that the reduction of livestock should be considered as a potential solution for global hunger predicaments. There were many liaisons between organic and vegetarian food at the time; one example was a vegetarian restaurant serving organic cuisine twenty-four hours a day, called H.E.L.P. Unlimited, which opened in Los Angeles in 1971. The owner said it was meant to aid those who had eating or nutritional problems, so he also sold books and health food and offered classes in yoga, metaphysics, and cooking in the same spot.[139] Making similar connections was an intentional community known as The Farm, founded in Tennessee in 1971 by nonviolent earth-lovers eager to become vegetarian organic farmers. For this contingent, it seemed that enlightenment could arrive in an organic nirvana.

J. I. Rodale himself encouraged the formation of a dedicated group of "health vigilantes" that would band together to "picket supermarkets" or "enter them and break up sections that hold food with known harmful additives." Only by eating "unadulterated" organic food and vitamins could citizens feel secure, he told an interviewer.[140] Of course, a rogue band of supermarket vandals did not materialize; instead, those "health vigilantes" flocked

A farmers' market on Martha's Vineyard (Photo courtesy of Colleen Freda Burt)

to natural food stores. *Time* reported that sales at "organic food shops" had reached $200 million in 1971, and offerings there included "carrot cupcakes, sunflower-seed cookies and countless varieties of honey." Although many of the provisions could scarcely be distinguished from those in conventional markets, aficionados insisted that healthfulness and taste were hallmarks of organics. *Time*, though, thought that the most striking difference was price, since organic foods cost 25 to 50 percent more than regular foods. Again, this discrepancy was said to derive mainly from a supply shortage.[141] Veteran organic merchants were "overwhelmed," new stores kept opening to address the deficit, and food co-ops were "springing up all over the country." One Boston-based natural foods business, Erewhon Trading Company, was shipping "tons of organic rice each week."[142] Glamorous or not, these venturesome innovators were savvy enough to take advantage of alterations in American dietary currents.

Beatrice Hunter's *Natural Foods Primer* (1972) advised readers to look in health food stores or co-ops for foods grown organically. However, she noted that many large supermarket chains had started stocking organic food for interested customers and described this as a "heartening development."[143] Although Hunter acknowledged that the escalated cost of organics might put a strain on one's budget, she felt that so-called cheap food was actually more expensive if it led to ill health.[144] Bernice Kohn's *The Organic Living Book* (1972) agreed that organic foods were "the most wholesome, the most nutritious, and surely the best-tasting foods we can eat."[145] An item in *Time* in 1972, "Eating Organic," said that "health-food fans" did indeed live on "more than wheat germ alone." The reporter said that typical victuals included granola, skim milk, whole wheat bread, almond butter, berries, and spinach noodles.[146] Also that year, the second International Health Fair was held at Madison Square Garden. *Time* discussed this "nutritional circus" in which "visitors who wandered among the displays could pick up free vitamin-pill samples, munch organic foods or drink Swedish mineral water." However, *Time* put a damper on the trend when it asserted that there was "no reliable evidence that organically grown foods are any more nutritious than those produced by conventional means" and added that they were "sufficiently expensive to make eating them an affectation of the affluent."[147] Plenty of consumers preferred to save their money and forgo the unproven benefits of organic foods. Still, organic products suddenly carried expansive appeal, and newly established health food stores were doing brisk business among those who were more credulous in assuming that food grown without synthetic chemicals must be safer and healthier. *The Basic Book of Organically Grown Foods* (1972), written by the staff of *Organic Gardening and Farming*, explained that organic food was "ecological food," nurtured in a "natural system." Soil fertilized naturally produced richer food, yielding crucial vitamins and minerals. Biologically, organic foods provided "safer nutrition."[148] The editors professed that "the best way to health is proper nutrition and good nutrition comes from organically grown foods."[149] This dietary mantra, however, was not accepted universally.

Physician Alan Nittler castigated other doctors for ignoring how nutrition affected disease. In *A New Breed of Doctor* (1972), Nittler staunchly advised his patients to avoid processed, heated, or chemically treated foods, saying that "whole, organic, raw produce" should make up at least fifty percent of a diet.[150] However, he warned that organic food was being "prostituted" and mislabeled due to sudden demand, so consumers had to be cautious.[151] Nittler faced indictments of "quackery" and "faddism" from the medical establishment; both the California Medical Association and American Medical Association discredited him. Many doctors thought that organic food was a newfangled scam. In some circles, organic produce had a reputation for poor quality, jacked-up prices, and outright fraud.[152] Associations with whimsical "hippie food" and "health nuts" did not help establish its legitimacy. Yet Rodale was the consummate crusader. His cavalry soldiers—longtime readers of *Organic Gardening and Farming*, along with new recruits—were eager to fly the organiculturist's flag and fight for "more abundant and more perfect food."

RODALE AS PROPHET

As the organic movement gained steam, a flood of media sources focused on Rodale's role in popularizing organic farming. He became a well-known figure, emanating an air of sagacity, and acclamations turned up in the national press. In the early 1970s, Rodale told an audience, "Years ago they heaped violence and poured ridicule upon my head. I was called a cultist and a crackpot. . . . Now even the chemical people have become respectful towards me and my manure ideology. I am suddenly becoming a prophet here on earth, and a prophet with profits."[153] A Penthouse article in 1971 hailed "J. I. Rodale: Pollution Prophet" as the "belatedly honoured" man who had "acquired overnight respectability," overcoming the days when he was "widely regarded as an eccentric, if not an outright crackpot."[154] *Time* noted that ever since Rodale discovered organic farming he had "religiously followed his own advice to eat only pure foods, avoid refined white sugar and walk several miles a day." He looked and acted "like a much younger man."[155] *Smithsonian* called Rodale a prophet of the organic doctrine and the "elder statesman of health food votaries." While "still a rebel in his 72nd year," he zealously guarded his health and betrayed "few signs of aging." The article attributed the growth of the vitamin industry largely to Rodale's crusading.[156] In another extensive book, *My Own Technique of Eating for Health* (1971), Rodale elaborated on his personal diet of meat, fish, eggs, raw vegetables, and fruit. He did not eat anything that had "gone through a factory." He objected to milk, sugar, wheat, salt, and citrus fruit.[157] Rodale recalled that, before becoming health-conscious twenty-five years earlier, he had been eating "a typical modern diet," full of bread, cakes, starches, sweets, and no added vitamins or minerals. At the time, he weighed 205 pounds, did no walking, and was "very nervous" and angry. Now, at the age of seventy-one, he weighed 168 pounds, walked for at least a hour each day, and had become "wonderfully stabilized" emotionally.[158] Rodale may have seen himself as stable, but outsiders often felt that his daily routine bordered on fanaticism.

Health food advocates have historically been disparaged as faddists peddling bogus nostrums. Rodale was ridiculed for his excessive use of vitamins, which he ingested to compensate for the poor quality of supermarket food. He said that the supplements—up to seventy each day—were not drugs but were "merely food arranged in tablet form."[159] He felt that the regimen of taking vitamins and minerals, eschewing sugar, adhering to a low-salt diet, keeping his weight down, avoiding cigarettes and alcohol, and raising 80 percent of his food by the organic method was a deciding factor in giving him immunity to headaches, colds, and disease in general.[160] Mainstream media sources contended that dietary deficiencies were rare and counseled the public to beware of "food faddists," but Rodale pointed out that these other magazines were full of advertisements for the very products that he warned against, so readers ought to be wary of conflicting interests.[161] Certainly Rodale's eating habits may have been "abnormal," but he was genuinely committed to their verity. He was not selling sham vitamins or directly marketing organic food himself; rather, the profits he earned came from publishing information meant to help others. He steadfastly maintained his devotion to organic food and reasoned that it was patriotic to be health-conscious, because "a sick nation is a weak nation."[162] Rodale sought to reform the contemporary diet as well as the whole world through the organic way.[163] In doing so, he garnered both praise and mockery.

A cover story in the *New York Times Magazine* in 1971 proclaimed Rodale "Guru of the Organic Food Cult." The article dubbed him organic food's "foremost prophet," categorizing his faith in "salvation through ingestion" as a brand of "secular fundamentalism." Though Rodale looked "more like an apothecary than a revolutionary," he was described as "a prosperous health freak" with an "unorthodox, even anti-orthodox" cause. His "organic gospel" was rooted in "steadfast opposition to chemical fertilizers." At the time, Rodale was involved in scuffles with the American Medical Association (AMA) and the Federal Trade Commission (FTC) over his ostensibly misleading medical advice. Rodale acknowledged that his detractors scorned him as a "crackpot." He lacked unassailable proof for his testimonials, so the AMA reproached his health books as "quackery." Undaunted, Rodale proudly confessed to having been "a counterculturist for decades," even though he did not conform to all "organic-food orthodoxies." He denounced vegetarianism; he sometimes indulged in ice cream; he thought that cow's milk was unhealthy for people; and he admitted to having "an unorganic meal now and then."[164] Beyond Rodale's oddities, though, there was a social message.

According to the *Times*, beneath the "homely surface" of *Organic Gardening and Farming* "one can read an invitation to anarchy and parsimony, a disdain for big institutions and the products of technology."[165] The article pointed out that, for nearly two decades, Rodale's magazine had "struggled along on a hard core of cranky, generally conservative and often foreign-born gardeners as the main subscribers."[166] However, circulation rates and advertising rocketed upward in a newly ecology-aware nation. Readership climbed 40 percent in one year, reaching seven hundred thousand. The youth culture embraced it. Environmentalists enlarged Rodale's newfound prowess. Medical and agricultural experts still considered Rodale a charlatan, but he intrepidly confronted the medical powers-that-be; he could, at least, count on his trusty pupils and a handful of reputable scientists (for example, Barry Commoner) for substantiation.[167]

The Dick Cavett Show invited Rodale to be a guest for an episode in 1971, when the popular network show had a large national audience. Dick Cavett introduced Rodale to the audience in New York by saying, "My next guest used to be known as a food freak. Now that he's rich and famous . . . a lot more people are listening to him."[168] Even those who listened did not find him affable in every respect. One audience member recalled that Rodale boasted about his health, predicted that he would live to reach at least one hundred, and then "got down and started doing push-ups on the floor."[169] Unfortunately, after finishing his thirty-minute segment but while still sitting on the set as the rest of the show was taping, Rodale suffered a heart attack. He died that night (and the episode never aired). Many critics noted derisively that even the acclaimed organic health food guru couldn't stave off death at the relatively young age of seventy-three. Still, his granddaughter, Maria, later explained that Rodale "lived 20 years longer than any of his brothers and sisters, who all suffered from heart conditions."[170] Considering Rodale's family history, his organic lifestyle may indeed have extended his life.

Rodale left opprobrium and endorsements in his wake. Carlton Jackson's *J. I. Rodale: Apostle of Nonconformity* (1974) exploited the sensationalized hype surrounding Rodale's death. The back cover asked "Genius? Or Fraud?" in bold letters and broadcast "the uncensored critical biography of a professional iconoclast." The book called Rodale a "self-styled scourge of The Establishment." The front cover indicated that when he died, he was "still waging a personal Thirty Years' War that brought him from ridicule to triumph as the leader of the runaway organic farming and nutrition movements." Calling him a true "Renaissance Man," Jackson emphasized Rodale's preference for self-training over formal education and said that his disdain for authority often caused trouble. Jackson designated Rodale as "a prophet and a man ahead of his time but also a crank, a manure-pile worshiper, a humus huckster, and an apostle of dung."[171] Few people have earned all those epithets; and one must wonder whether Rodale would have even been insulted, considering that he had, in the past, referred to himself as a "cultist" in response to those who belittled him.

As indicated by all the nicknames applied to Rodale—describing his genius or inanity, his foresight or foolhardiness—he was a polarizing figure, neither entirely lovable nor wholly detestable. His marvelous peculiarity was part of his irrevocable charm but may have also occluded a more favorable reception for organics. Widespread debates fraught with drama over Rodale and his organic farming methods continued after his death. As Americans were experiencing mayhem related to the Vietnam War, the Civil Rights Movement, and other tumultuous protests, so, too, was the organic movement in a time of blustery transition, having just lost its most passionate champion. Organic farming was not yet a formidable competitor to the titan of industrial agriculture. There were many doubters and fence-sitters who suspected that the organic racket was some sort of scam. The organic movement was waiting in the wings, prepared for the main stage of American food culture—but with skeptics attempting to keep it in its less prominent role. At this critical juncture, compromises would be made to facilitate organic food's ability to hit the big time.

CHAPTER THREE

An Alternative Way to Live

After his death, J. I. Rodale's writings remained the foundation of the organic movement. The leadership of the inner sanctum passed to his son, Robert, a less colorful figure but one who vigorously promoted an entire organic way of life. Robert Rodale kept up the family company's messianic educational and research efforts to take the movement forward. He and his wife, Ardath, purchased a farm and conducted scientific studies on the viability of organic methods. Compost was still the emblematic "black gold" for high-minded growers, but other state-of-the-art elements were added to the organic repertoire. As president of Rodale Press, Robert Rodale upheld his father's long-standing policy of refusing to accept advertisements for alcohol, tobacco, chemical insecticides, or even coffee in his magazines.[1] He asserted that, while organic homesteading had financial and bodily health rewards, the primary purpose of this undertaking was to "live more in balance with the Earth." To be an organic gardener, though, one had to "reject the opinions of the experts and professors and stand up to occasional charges that you are a crackpot or faddist."[2] J. I. Rodale had coped with those charges all this life, and they were still being levied. Organic consumers carrying the "eccentric" label faced scorn in their endeavors.

Although mounting patronage did much to legitimize the organic movement, it was chiefly a fringe ensemble up through the 1970s. A gardening column for the *New York Times* in 1972 by Kenneth Beeson, a Cornell University professor of soil science, said that the "militant" organic "cult" had "no valid evidence." Supporting these "extremists" would limit agricultural output, causing "widespread malnutrition and even starvation."[3] Organic farming was not just silly but also frightening to conventional agriculture. Robert Rodale's *Sane Living in a Mad World: A Guide to the Organic Way of Life* (1972) noted continuing opposition but expressed hope that more people would start thinking like organic gardeners and farmers, because the organic way was "the *only* all-embracing ecological program." He felt that "we organic people hold in our hands the key to the survival of America as a viable society."[4] Other voices were chiming in to suggest that organic food could be the antidote to environmental poisons bombarding human bodies. This chapter examines the complex ambience of organics, including prominent opponents and idealistic proponents, during the 1970s and 1980s, when the organic cadre faced convoluted challenges. These decades saw fervent health concerns; skepticism about organics; resurges in homesteading, Rodale Press, and agrarian advertisements; a farm crisis; newfangled organic specialty stores; an uptick in organic businesses; and the first organic regulations. Both producers and consumers propelled the American organic movement until it was about to reap great rewards, almost—though not quite—seizing a mainstream role. To eliminate the things holding it back, the movement had to make accommodations, some of which would cause serious trouble when denunciations of selling out would surface in subsequent decades.

NUTRITION AND PSEUDOSCIENCE

By the 1970s, organics were a noteworthy aspect of the wide-ranging American health food movement. In some circles, organic food carried the aura of an all-natural elixir. The National Health Food Society pronounced in 1971 that organically grown foods were "healthful and nutritious because we leave Mother Nature alone to do the work that she does best!"[5] The 1970s saw a true mutation in healthy eating. Social critic Christopher Lasch attributed the newfound adoration of health to an apolitical preoccupation with the self that was prevalent in "the culture of narcissism."[6] Building on this self-absorbed foundation, organic foods attracted more followers that were eager to soak up the perceived personal health benefits of organic tonics. The *Organic Gardening Guide to Organic Living* (1970) noted that dozens of restaurants in the Los Angeles area were already serving organic food in gourmet style. One of these, The Source on Sunset Boulevard, was run by James Baker—known as Father Yod—who was the leader of a spiritual cult residing in a Hollywood Hills mansion.[7] The restaurant became a destination for celebrities and wayward souls intrigued by organic vegetarian food and the "enlightened" longhaired servers. The Source earned recognition as one of the most prosperous restaurants in Los Angeles.[8] With a similarly quirky-but-healthy attitude, a Jamaica Tourist Board advertisement in 1971 promised to feed visitors plenty of organic fruits and vegetables, implying that organic produce was essential to fully experiencing a natural vacation on the beaches of that "virginal" island.[9]

Health was a tremendous part of why the organic appeal was growing. By 1972, over seven hundred thousand subscribers received *Organic Gardening*, and the National Farmers Organization was introducing a marketing program for organic foods. But a page-one headline in the *Modesto Bee* blared, "The Organic Living Fad Can Cost You a Bundle." Purchases in organic food stores had quadrupled in the past two years, reaching $400 million. The article warned that "the high pressure promoters, the deceivers, the gypsters are moving in," and the danger of being "swindled" was growing daily."[10] The staff of *Organic Gardening* bristled; they urged health-conscious readers not to overlook "one of the most important reasons of all for eating organic food. It tastes better."[11] Pointing out that the excellence of French food started on the farm, the staff pressed Americans to demand the superior flavor of organic food, which would bring "greater pleasure for our palates," create better national health, and "ultimately revolutionize the entire system of food production."[12] They admitted that the prices of organically grown foods would never be as low as those for commercially produced foods. However, many people were indeed willing to pay more for the "quality, variety, and flavor" of organic foods, and *Organic Gardening* advised that "you're getting exactly what you pay for."[13] Foods with the organic label commanded a high price, as the "wholeness" of organics enticed Americans inclined to splurge. Still, some organic ventures found that people were deterred by the unusual appearance—the cosmetic imperfections—of organic produce. The Goodnews, Sunshine, Fruit and Vegetable Co. in Sacramento pitched a consumer education project to teach that organic carrots only looked like "short, squat Bugs Bunny types" because they were grown without sprays and chemicals.[14] Along with dubious aesthetics, the dearth of irrefutable nutritional studies also plagued the movement. *Life* magazine asked, "What's So Great about Health Foods?" in a piece in 1972 that raised doubts about organic trustworthiness. One letter from the president of the Lehigh Valley Committee against Health Fraud, published in response to the article, said, "The promoters of 'organic faddism' are seducing federal and state agencies into certifying 'genuine' worthless products." The letter bashed this "consumer deception."[15] The *Los Angeles Times* ran an article that year titled "Organic Foods: Skepticism" in which a professor of food science reiterated that chemicals in food were indispensable.[16] Fredrick J. Stare, chairman of the department of nutrition at Harvard's School of Public Health and an indefatigable champion of insecticides, questioned the rage for organic foods, which, he assured people, had "no added nutritional value over foods grown with chemical fertilizer."[17] Some nutritionists saw the organic craze as "a harmless search for nutritional peace of mind," whereas others dismissed the "organic food cult" as "nonsense" and not entirely benign.[18]

The New York attorney general conducted a consumer hearing in 1972 to clarify the reigning puzzlement about organic foods. Professional nutritionists testified that some organically grown foods were "overpriced" and "lacking in the nutritional values they claim to offer." Tests had shown traces of DDT and chlorinated pesticides on organically labeled products. One doctor shrugged that consumers were free to "waste their money" on something with "no acceptable medical benefits," but another thought that organic foods were actually a "public-health nutrition threat."[19] Nutritionists were clearly contemptuous of organic foods, but the reason that they were so caustic is less discernible—after all, even if organics were not *superior*, they were not necessarily *harmful*. Some may have feared that their own credibility would be questioned by colleagues if they endorsed an "unscientific" doctrine; others may have been under the sway of chemical companies that wanted to stymie the movement. Whatever the causes, there was increasing resistance.

Along with scientists, an entrenched agribusiness system spurned the scattered organic craze. Earl Butz, the US secretary of agriculture with the same mentality of "get big or get out" that had governed the USDA for decades, scoffed at the organic inclination. Butz infamously debunked the organic farming vogue of the early 1970s, insisting that its widespread adoption would cause fifty million people to starve. According to Butz, chemicals and antibiotics were required to produce "adequate amounts of safe and wholesome food."[20] Butz and others assumed that organic farming was a pseudo-scientific hobby, only plausible on an amateur scale, if at all. Hilda White, a professor of home economics, concurred in a *Food Technology* article in 1972 that if up-to-the-minute agricultural technology were discarded in favor of organic farming, "the worldwide problems of hunger, malnutrition, and famine would be multiplied immeasurably."[21] Those who praised the abundance of American food habitually attributed it to the "miracle" of agricultural chemicals. Agribusiness and Congress seemed to be working hand in hand. The USDA did not officially recognize organic farming, treating it with hostility or apathy.[22] Although the scare talk about chemicals had led to a ban on DDT, in a column in 1972 for the *Dallas Morning News*, Murray

Cox expressed the prevailing supposition of most "agricultural authorities" that "total production would undoubtedly drop disastrously" with organic farming. Cox allowed that organic farming might work in some gardens, but America was not ready to go organic in the larger "cotton or corn patch."[23] Technocracy was still supreme in the capital-intensive "fencerow to fencerow" regime.

HOT PROPERTY OR HOGWASH?

Farmer Earl Lawrence started off with herbicides, insecticides, and other "modern methods," but after switching to "100-percent organic" on his new large-scale Virginia farm in 1971, he was convinced that, "by working with nature," he could grow crops without chemicals. Organic farming, he said, was a self-sustaining "holistic system."[24] The holistically minded Robert Rodale often espoused these types of broader social and environmental messages in his organic evangelism. His biggest contributions seem to have been expanding the family empire and reframing the organic food movement into one addressing global concerns. He was conscious of the need to "welcome and hold the young converts to the organic gospel according to the Rodales, while comforting the older faithful."[25] Introducing *The Basic Book of Organically Grown Foods* (1972), Robert Rodale pointed out that "the word 'organic' is a hot property these days. It's appearing on more and more foods each year."[26] He announced that the organic code was the "only one way to make America more natural, more reasonable in its burden on the ecosphere."[27] The book, written by the staff of Rodale's *Organic Gardening* magazine, urged people to start their own organic plots that would demonstrate the "cleanliness" and spirituality of "nature's design for life on this planet." Compost was at the base of the organic procedure. Artificial chemical fertilizers, which had no part in organics, symbolized "unnatural" gardening and farming.[28] The book avowed that paying for organic foods was an act of dissent that would "encourage change in American agricultural methods."[29] The authors added: "By wanting to buy organically grown foods raised by a family farmer who is not supposed to be able to make a living on the land, you are helping to reverse a trend that has driven people off the land and made farming an old man's profession. By buying organic foods at a mama-and-papa neighborhood store that is not supposed to be able to compete with supermarket chains, you are helping to change the make-up of America."[30]

There were many others who wanted to help reverse the "unnatural" drift too, albeit in small ways, by showing how kindhearted organic farming was. An advertisement in 1972 for the Good Earth natural foods supermarket said that its organic corn was grown in "rich composted soil by dedicated organic farmers," whose "tender loving care" made the corn nutritious and delicious.[31] Catharine Osgood Foster's step-by-step instruction book, *The Organic Gardener* (1972), was said to be based on her four decades of experience "planting and harvesting with profound respect for the wholeness of nature."[32] More officially, the International Federation of Organic Agriculture Movements (IFOAM), founded in 1972, defined organic agriculture as "a holistic production management system that avoids use of synthetic fertilizers, pesticides and genetically modified organisms, minimizes pollution of air, soil and water, and optimizes the health and productivity of interdependent communities of plants, animals and people."[33] In the early years, people assumed that organic practitioners operated according to a different logic than large agribusiness firms. *The Basic Book of Organically Grown Foods* professed that "growing food organically is a subversive activity."[34] Many organic farmers had strong personal convictions. Yet it was already transparent that others were going organic in order to supply a profitable market. The authors were optimistic that organic foods could be "a real force in America."[35] However, before rigid inspection practices were solidified, some unscrupulous merchants couldn't resist the temptation to mark ordinary food as organic. A *New York Times* article in 1972 warned: "Organic Foods: Spotting the Real Thing Can Be Tricky."[36] Three major supermarkets—Safeway, Boys Market, and Market Basket Stores—faced a $40 million class-action suit in 1972 for selling generic food as "organically grown."[37] Critics accused the organic industry of capitalizing on consumers' insecurities or falsely labeling products. As organic food became a "mass market idea," it would need government assistance and "a foolproof certification program" to ward off cheating and deception.[38]

In 1972 the Maine Organic Farmers and Gardeners Association (MOFGA) used Rodale Organic Garden certification guidelines to certify twenty-seven farms, and they published a directory.[39] Three years later, MOFGA had five hundred members spread across every Maine county.[40] Also responding to concerns about erratic standards, a union of farmers founded California Certified Organic Farmers (CCOF) in 1973. Building on the program Rodale started, it offered third-party certification of organic practices. Its goal was to combat fraud and ease consumer confusion. CCOF perceived itself as a grassroots organization and disagreed with the idea of universal standards, because these might smooth the path for agribusiness capital to engulf smaller operations.[41] CCOF originally had fifty-four grower members and ran its operations out of its president's home.[42] Mark Lipson, the CCOF's first paid staff member, and Bob Scowcroft, who became the first executive director, would both later be instrumental in steering the passage of California's— and then the nation's—organic foods act.[43] In the meantime, other regional associations followed suit. The nonprofit Tilth Association formed in 1974 to promote organic agriculture in the Pacific Northwest. Regional chapters of Tilth educated people about organic food and farming through newsletters, conferences, and workshops. Other private organizations began developing certification criteria in order to strengthen legitimate product claims.[44] These certification programs were decentralized, and there was disagreement from state to state about what "organic" meant. Organic chef Jeff Cox remembered "a one-page flyer called 'Organic Gardening in a Nutshell,' distributed by the thousands in the 1970s."[45] Industry enforcement was not strict; the federal government kept its distance; there was much ambiguity over the definition of organic food; and fraudulent labels were not uncommon.[46]

Notwithstanding a recession, soaring prices, and the absence of a nation-wide code for "organically grown," the *New York Times* noticed in 1974 that "a sturdy core of middle-class consumers" continued to pay high prices for what they considered more purifying, nutritious food.[47] The Department of Consumer Affairs protested that "no single food should be termed an 'organic food,' because all foods are organic."[48] Members at the American Association for the Advancement of Science meeting in 1974 went further and assailed the organic "nonsense."[49] One doctor blamed "pseudoscientists" for unwarranted public distress about a poisoned food supply. Dr. Thomas Jukes, professor of medical physics at UC Berkeley, stated outright that the "organic food myth" was "counterproductive to human welfare," because it did not facilitate the production of food at "maximum efficiency." He favored "regular food," which cost less and was "more sanitary."[50] Jukes's subsequent article in the *Journal of the American Medical Association* swore that the fear of chemical residues was "actually based on a state of mind, not on tangible evidence." Contaminants present in food were "not known to have any injurious effect."[51] The *American Journal of Clinical Nutrition* ratified that nutritionists and dietitians needed to counteract "misinformation" about organically grown foods, vegetarianism, and the Zen Macrobiotic Diet—all deemed dangerous examples of "food faddism."[52] There was no substantiation for claims of nutritional superiority or finer taste, yet Americans were "paying from 30 to over 100% more for organically grown groceries." Distrust of the nation's regular food supply was misguided, and the organic farming technique had the "disadvantage of possible *Salmonella* contamination that can result in food poisoning," admonished the journal.[53]

Edward Rynearson, Mayo Clinic emeritus professor of medicine, published a piece in *Nutrition Review* in 1974 expressing his concerns about "food faddism" and "quackery."[54] He said that J. I. Rodale, the "man who gave the term 'organic food' to the English language," had "used his own interest in organic farming to finance his innate desire to publish," and Rynearson felt that this indicated a prurient preoccupation with profit. Rodale's word was "regarded as gospel by some," yet he had "no scientific training," and some of his beliefs "could be harmful."[55] The recompenses that organic farming and gardening claimed had not been authenticated but were spread by "extraordinarily popular magazine articles." Certainly, most physicians and nutritionists preferred homegrown fruits and vegetables, but Rynearson insisted that "blanket indictments of everything having to do with 'the establishment'" were not going to change the fact that most Americans had to rely on supermarkets. "Food cultists" were mistaking Rodale's "fuzzy thinking" for valid information, though it was truly just "humus for hogwash."[56] This medical expert was not the only one who said that the organic movement was harboring underlying coarse—almost lascivious—motives.

The American Dietetic Association issued a "position paper" in 1975 flatly denying claims that organic foods had "superior nutritional value" or "miraculous curative powers."[57] Not every consumer heeded these alerts, but they cast a penumbra of misgivings on organics. Still, some families felt that insufficient supply—not a barrage of mendacious claims—was the primary glitch with organics. Price-conscious families were grumbling about inflation in even ordinary grocery store food prices. The manager of one health food store noticed that his customers were bargain hunting and would give up meats so they could afford a surplus of healthy produce. Customers were still paying for kelp, carrot juice, goat's milk ice cream, and desiccated liver, because they had no interest in commercial foods anymore. One customer flatly stated, "When it's your money or your life, health foods are still a bargain."[58] One group of housewives in Long Island preferred to pay the $2 membership fee to join a cooperative for natural and organic foods that year. Buying directly from a mail-order health food company usually saved them money, and they also loved how it tasted. One member said that she was "not a health food nut," but the flavor difference in the co-op's organic peanut butter—

which actually cost more than the mass-produced jars on the shelf—was "so dramatic it's worth it."[59] Flavor became another selling point for organics.

A turning point for organic food took place not in co-ops but in eateries, where the movement toward gentrified organic food began in the 1970s. J. I. Rodale was one of the first idols for Jesse Ziff Cool, who opened an organic restaurant in Palo Alto in 1976, when organic ingredients were not yet easy to come by. Food scholar Julie Guthman observed that California was "a center for both the counterculture and the yuppie explosion that put organic food on the proverbial map."[60] It was there that organic sales took off "when growers started to sell 'through the back door' to celebrity chefs and their restaurants."[61] Chef Alice Waters helped forge the connection between these two points on the organic continuum. Inspired by her visits to France, Waters opened a café in 1971 in Berkeley. Chez Panisse served fresh, local, seasonal ingredients. The restaurant linked healthy countercuisine to succulent haute cuisine.[62] At the time, Waters said that she and her friends were "reacting against the uniformity and blandness of the food of the day" and soon discovered that "the best-tasting food came from local farmers, ranchers, foragers, and fishermen who were committed to sound and sustainable practices."[63] In 1977, Waters bought 160 acres and planned an organic garden to reap auxiliary crops for the restaurant.[64] Consumers began to see her organic produce as a precious specialty item on the menu, and other tasteful restaurants followed suit. Organic salad mix became an elite commodity.[65] Waters continued to embrace organic farming, local food, and slow food throughout her career. Thomas McNamee, in his biography of Waters three decades later, said that she "transformed the way many Americans eat and the way they think about food. Her insistence on the freshest ingredients, used only at the peak of their growing season, nearly always grown locally and organically," would become "a ruling principle in the best American restaurants and for many home cooks."[66] The Berkeley neighborhood in which Chez Panisse was located would acquire the moniker of "Gourmet Ghetto," but restaurants that highlighted local, seasonal, and organic produce snowballed there and around the nation.

"NATURE PROVIDES": HOMESTEADERS AND AGRARIANISM

The burgeoning band of organic foodies ran the gamut of social positions. Seemingly removed from the fancy farm-to-table café patrons or the quirky co-op delegates were the ardent small-scale homesteaders, growing their own organic vegetables in backyard gardens. Most kept a bucket next to the kitchen sink where all food scraps were deposited, which were then emptied into the outdoor compost heap. A common composting routine was to layer nitrogenous matter, carbon-rich materials, granular lime, and manure from backyard livestock. As the piles were turned periodically and decomposed, they morphed into sterling organic tilth that would replenish soil nutrients. Aside from Rodale's publications, there were scant forums for homesteaders to collaborate on compost (or other topics). In 1969, Jerome Belanger placed a classified advertisement in *Organic Gardening and Farming* announcing the inception of a newsletter for homesteaders. Within a few months, he had several hundred subscribers to *Countryside*, at $1 per year. Belanger bought a country journal, *Small Stock Magazine*, and started *Dairy Goat Guide*; and then in 1973 he rolled the two magazines and the newsletter into the bimonthly *Countryside and Small Stock Journal*. Soon there were ten thousand subscribers; it catered to bona fide and aspiring homesteaders. This periodical was an information exchange for practical small-scale farming.[67] *Countryside and Small Stock Journal* published articles on making cheese, pressing cider, raising poultry, cooking from scratch, preserving fruit, and organic gardening. The magazine advocated an exemplary assortment of organic ideas and attitudes in its philosophy:

> A reverence for nature and a preference for country life; a desire for maximum personal self-reliance and creative leisure; a concern for family nurture and community cohesion; a certain hostility toward luxury; a belief that the primary reward of work should be well-being rather than money; a certain nostalgia for the supposed simplicities of the past and an anxiety about the technological and bureaucratic complexities of the present and the future; and a taste for the plain and functional. *Countryside* reflects and supports the simple life, and calls its practitioners *homesteaders*.[68]

Belanger ran his own small organic farm on an experimental homestead. He felt that organic farming was both a philosophy and a management system; organic farmers were opposed not to progress, but to the misuse of technology.[69] Belanger and his wife tried spinning wool, tanning rabbits, and making cheese, butter, and sausages. As more people asked them where to buy homestead tools, they started the Countryside General Store, which sold items like hog scrapers, kerosene lamps, and cast-iron cookware.[70]

Also embarking on an illustrative homesteading adventure were Sue and Steve Robishaw, who began subscribing to *Organic Gardening and Farming* and *Mother Earth News* in the 1970s. After moving onto eighty acres in Michigan's Upper Peninsula, they found that "nature provides what we really need quite generously."[71] They ate what they could gather in the woods and grow in the garden. The Robishaws thought that those who created homes "in harmony with the earth" were "homesteading heroes."[72] Homesteaders Bob and Lee Light left New Jersey for Vermont in 1972, also seeking rapport with nature. They started to raise 80 percent of their own food organically while selling milk, butter, and eggs at the end of their dirt lane. They bartered with neighbors and traded work with friends, trying to find "an alternative way to live."[73] In a parallel vein, John Seymour's *Complete Book of Self-Sufficiency* (1976) described the "true homesteader" as one who was striving for a higher standard of living, growing fresh, organic food, achieving bodily health and peace of mind, accomplishing difficult but satisfying tasks, and husbanding the land without disturbing its "natural balance."[74] Seymour's title homed in on exactly what dedicated back-to-the-landers circumventing dominant economic institutions sought: "ways to live simply but well on the land." In the late 1970s, these "long-haired refugees from the urban middle class" were "raising the battle cry of 'self-sufficiency,'" according to media coverage. As they helped to repopulate rural areas, these metropolitan expatriates were enthusiastically growing their own food with hoes, organic fertilizers, and nonchemical pesticides.[75] Some of the most avid supporters of organics were home gardeners, homesteaders, and commune-dwellers, who also shared many of the tenets of agrarianism.

Agrarian philosophy has acclaimed the rural world for possessing intrinsic visual and metaphysical superiority over the moral decrepitude of urban situations. The American sense of self (to the extent that such a thing exists) has been intertwined with a wistful agrarian aesthetic for centuries. The agrarian ideal is predicated on the symbolic weight of natural landscapes and private land ownership. In the United States, farms are the quintessential representations of an idyllic countryside. J. Hector St. John de Crèvecoeur (1735–1813), a Frenchman who settled in New York State as a farmer and writer, helped inspire American democratic agrarianism. In *Letters from an American Farmer* (1782), he wrote of how "we are all tillers of the earth," and he praised "good substantial independent American farmers."[76] In the eighteenth century, individual small-scale farming developed into the dominant mode of national agricultural production and was economically vital.[77] The farmer became the heroic heart of the nation. Thomas Jefferson, who maintained that "those who labor in the earth are the chosen people of God," is also renowned for his agrarian philosophy.[78] Jeffersonian agrarians celebrated farmers for their rectitude, political virtue, and centrality to democratic society. Other writers in the agrarian genre have defended the honorable yeoman farmer as the best model for mankind.

Agrarian visions of "the good life" were inseparable from those of the iconic traditional farmer; an organic family farmer was customarily cast in the starring role of this earthy drama. The benefits of contact with nature and the virtues of austerity were rudiments of the agrarian mythology. Agrarianism has been an evolving collection of ideas and rhetorical strategies, but all strains clutched the idea that the family-owned, family-operated farm was the chief repository of the favorable qualities necessary to decent society. Cultural geographer Yi-Fu Tuan analyzed the immense body of literature that sentimentalized farmers, promoted "the elevation and beauty of country living," and subscribed to ideas about "the virtue of living and working close to the soil."[79] Tuan noted that "work on the farm has always been hard," but "it is this gritty character that makes farm life seem virtuous and good."[80] Ironically, Tuan pointed out that most of this literature was written by "members of the leisured class" who knew little about "the hardships of manual labor."[81] Still, organic farming handbooks have often echoed ancient texts like the *Tao Te Ching*, which "speaks nostalgically of a small and sparsely settled country where the people live on fresh food, have simple but beautiful clothing, comfortable homes, and pleasurable rustic tasks."[82] The Country Life movement in the early twentieth century espoused much of the agrarian canon. In the same vein, agrarians have argued that farmers were more likely than other citizens to demonstrate the frugality, discipline, self-reliance, and respect for order that were crucial for a well-functioning republic.[83]

The organic movement has attached ethical undertones to enduring agrarian convictions, including the Jeffersonian paradigm of virtuous American democracy rooted in an agricultural past. Organic farmer Karl Schwenke expressed the agrarian belief that renewing the nation's "agricultural heritage" would require cutting back the scale of agricultural ventures. In *Successful Small-Scale Farming: An Organic Approach* (1979), he encouraged the adoption of "tried-and-true farm practices" that organic growers cherished, such as the "age-old method" of composting.[84] Since agribusiness was subsidized by tax dollars, undersized farms would have a rough time competing on the wholesale market, but organics had their own unique selling points. The

An idyllic American farm (Photo courtesy of Colleen Freda Burt)

small-scale organic operator could "find his way into the consumer's pocketbook through his taste buds."[85] A contemporary New Agrarian contingent has lauded small farms, resolving that these were more ecologically, morally, and socially sound than large ones. New Agrarians valued embedded connections between land and people. This worldview was posited as being in stark contrast to the mechanistic, reductionist slant of industrial agriculture—another clause in the story of small organic and big conventional, good and evil.

Farmer and writer Wendell Berry became a preeminent spokesperson for agrarianism and small-scale organic farming after he retreated from New York City to his 125-acre Kentucky farm in 1964. While continuing to teach at the University of Kentucky, he wrote for *Organic Gardening and Farming* and other Rodale publications (in addition to his poetry, fiction, and nonfiction works). For decades, Berry insisted that small family farms attached people to the land much more intimately and democratically than the industrial system did.[86] The multinational economic structure, he asserted, did not foster the same love and knowledge of terrain that traditional farmers possessed. Berry believed that farmers enjoyed a meaningful sense of place, because only familiarity could truly bond a person to land.[87] Like Jefferson, Borsodi, Rodale, and others before him, Berry sponsored the opinion that as many people as possible should share in land ownership.[88] However, he lamented that small, independent American farmers were being forced off the land by absentee owners, corporations, and machines.[89] Berry's disapproval of truant owners was equivalent to the criticism leveled against irresponsible tenant farmers by Rodale in *Pay Dirt*. Berry encouraged local small producers and local consumers to revolt intellectually against global industrial corporations.[90] He framed the larger social struggle in terms of family farms versus factory farms. Berry also claimed that cities preyed on the countryside, extracting resources and energy from their victims while destroying the principle of self-sufficiency. As a grassroots dissenter, Berry outlined a desire to overthrow the multinational economy and rebuild sustainable local economies. Berry's unabashed antiestablishment opposition to consumer capitalism echoed the outlook of legions of back-to-the-land supporters who attempted—at least partially—to remove themselves from its ubiquity.

Berry was a prominent supporter of organic farming, stating that a person growing an organic garden was "improving a piece of the world."[91] He also cautioned that the organic approach should not be an end in itself. He defined an organic farm not by its use of certain methods or avoidance of substances; rather, its structure had to imitate a natural system and hold the integrity of an organism.[92] Pointing out that organic farming was originally attractive "both as a way of conserving nature and as a strategy of survival for small farmers," he became dismayed at the emergence of huge organic monocultures.[93] Berry asserted that consumers who demanded organic food had expectations for "good, fresh, trustworthy food," and a global corporation could not produce such food.[94] Like Rodale, he predicted with acuity the transformative potential of organic products. Berry proclaimed that when concerns about food quality and purity grew extensive enough, consumer demand for organics would rise and change agriculture.[95] Critics pinpointed Berry for naïveté; his reliance on horses seemed to place him among the ranks of Luddites. Secretary of Agriculture Earl Butz called Berry's *The Unsettling of America* (1977) a "fantasy" that exhibited a "nostalgic longing to turn the agricultural clock back."[96] Butz decried all agrarian devotees for ignoring the fact that "our productive modern agriculture has freed millions of us from virtual serfdom on the land."[97] Organic detractor Alex A. Avery later characterized Berry's poetic view of rural, small-town life as indicative of the organic movement's elitist, antitechnology "wish-dreams." Avery impugned the "myth of the organic utopia" as "a romanticized glorification of the agrarian economy of 1840 that bears no resemblance to historical reality."[98] "Organic fantasies" like Berry's impeded the acceptance of agricultural biotechnology, which, Avery felt, was more environmentally friendly and less costly to society.

Agrarianism has been criticized for not recognizing the fluid boundaries between the city and the countryside, discounting indispensable rural-urban relationships. Other critics have interpreted agrarians as excessively unrealistic or reactionary and have pointed out that isolated communities were often susceptible to provincialism, not progressivism. Insofar as agrarian ideology was based on the infallibility of the family farm, it reinforced quixotic notions; in truth, small and large farms were equally capable of contributing to environmental degradation and social injustices. In many respects, as the prestige and relevance that this profession once held waned, agrarianism has lost its cachet. Notwithstanding these social alterations, there are pervasive tendencies in some quarters to put farmers on a pedestal. For some Americans, the farmer is still a long-suffering paragon of integrity.

MAKING THE NEWS

Japanese farmer Masanobu Fukuoka, who managed rice fields and orange groves on the hillsides near his home, was uniquely influential in the organic movements. Fukuoka's *The One Straw Revolution* was published in Japan in 1975 and then in the United States by Rodale Press in 1978. He practiced what he called "do-nothing" farming, based on the idea that "nature, left alone, is in perfect balance."[99] This scheme, he said, completely contradicted neoteric agricultural techniques. Fukuoka criticized agricultural authorities who focused only on au courant machinery to achieve greater yields. He did not use the term "organic" or make compost, but he utilized no machines, fertilizers, or chemicals. Fukuoka felt that the principles of organic farming popular in the West did not differ from "those of the traditional Oriental agriculture practiced in China, Korea, and Japan for many centuries."[100] To grow vegetables in a semiwild way, Fukuoka would toss out seeds on a vacant lot or riverbank. He controlled weeds by spreading straw on the crops and was rewarded with high yields on his land. As Fukuoka's fame swelled in organically and environmentally minded circles, students arrived from around the world to live and work with him.

Fukuoka believed that the human diet should be adjusted to the "natural cycle." He urged simplicity in lifestyle, disparaging meat and imported food as

"luxuries." He said that a "simple local diet"—such as brown rice and vegetables—would allow people to live "simply and directly."[101] Western nutritional
science served only to isolate human beings from nature.[102] He sold his rice
and fruit to natural food stores and reasoned that, since this kind of food could
be produced with the least expense and effort, it should be sold at the cheapest
price. Fukuoka warned that, "if natural foods are expensive, they become luxury foods and only rich people are able to afford them."[103] But opulence was
increasingly associated with organic food. Fukuoka could not shake organic
food loose from its luxury status. In the 1970s, Barbra Streisand "stuffed the
fridge with organic fruits," and plenty of other stars did too.[104] Organic foods
were slammed as much for their frivolity as for their fallaciousness.

Vocal critics Fredrick J. Stare and Elizabeth M. Whelan, a demographer
and medical writer, implicated magazines such as *Prevention* and *Organic
Gardening and Farming* for perpetuating "scare stories" about chemical additives in food.[105] They launched caustic criticism at nutrition writer (and
organic fan) Adelle Davis, whom the White House Conference on Food, Nutrition, and Health had proclaimed "the most damaging single source of false
nutrition information in the country."[106] In *Panic in the Pantry* (1975), Stare
and Whelan sought to prove that the "back-to-nature mania" and the proliferation of health food stores were "a hoax" perpetuated by opportunists
intent on taking advantage of nervous, gullible consumers.[107] They called J. I.
Rodale the "founding father" of "Healthfoodland" and noted that he and his
associates had reaped over $9 million in 1970 alone from advocacy of "natu-
ral living."[108] Many companies were hopping on the "back-to-nature band-
wagon" and exploiting "natural food myths."[109] Food fraud was stemming
from fuzzy definitions for organic and natural food and the presence of an
"unsuspecting health-oriented consumer population."[110] Stare and Whelan
denied that organic food was nutritionally superior or that processed food
was inherently unhealthy. Rather, they asserted that food additives were safe
and played an important role in keeping the nation's food "plentiful, fresh,
and attractive."[111] They were primarily disturbed that the fascination with
natural-organic products could threaten America's "imperiled food supply,"
and they thought that Rodale had been a shyster.[112]

According to *Newsweek* in 1977, wacky theories about organic and natural
foods were turning Americans into "nutritional hypochondriacs" but yielding nearly $900 million in annual sales. Experts concurred that organic foods
were "simply a fetish," differentiated mainly by being unnecessarily expensive.[113] Undeterred, the organic movement found all the proof it needed in

personal experiences. By 1976, there were more than eight hundred thousand subscribers to *Organic Gardening and Farming*. The magazine dropped the *and Farming* for good in 1978, suggesting a recognition of futility with respect to reaching substantial agriculturalists. Only the *Organic Gardening* version survived, indicating that it was intended mainly for home gardeners. Other media sources, however, continued to use both names when referring to the magazine, and estimations of it were mixed. A *New York Times* article in 1979 noted that Rodale Press "never did have pretensions about being orthodox." Although the magazine lost money for the first sixteen years, it had more than a million subscribers while 2.25 million readers swore by *Prevention*. The company had annual revenues of $60 million.[114] Still, the "higher mission" of Rodale Press was "to make the world a healthier place to live in." Ideally, all people would eat organic foods, become self-sufficient, and farm organically, but Rodale Press did not expect an "overnight revolution" to that effect.[115] Robert Rodale said that his father had "decided to do his missionary work through publishing." Rodale Press channeled a large percentage of returns into research and hoped to "make the news," not just report on it.[116]

Robert Rodale coined the term "regenerative agriculture" to describe his vision of enhancing soil quality with organic agriculture. The Soil and Health Foundation established by J. I. Rodale was renamed The Rodale Institute in the 1980s, becoming a nonprofit organization dedicated to regenerative organic agriculture. The Rodale Institute Farming System Trial (FST), a long-running experiment comparing organic and conventional farming side by side, debuted in 1981. The institute also inaugurated the first wholesale price index of certified organic foods, an online tool that helped organic farmers determine an appropriate premium to charge for their products. This index compared organic prices to conventional prices in selected produce, herb, dairy, and grain markets across the country and was updated weekly. The Rodale Institute's motto—"Healthy Soil, Healthy Food, Healthy People"—harked back to the very truism *Organic Farming and Gardening* was founded on. The Rodale Institute kept engaging with farmers, the food industry, and consumer groups as it researched and promoted organic farming.

ORGANIC ADVERTISEMENTS: SELLING THE FARM

There was a time when simple advertisements for organic food ran only in alternative publications. A small notice in the *Organic Gardening* issue in July

1944 advised those who desired to purchase sunflower seeds grown organically to contact J. I. Rodale at once, so he could personally arrange such transactions between readers. A text ad in the issue of *Bio-Dyamics* from summer 1954 offered four pounds of organic oatmeal for $1 plus postage. *Mothering* magazine, initially a home-based periodical, featured a classified notice in the back of an issue in 1980 that quietly announced "The 6th Annual Natural Organic Farmers Association Conference and Celebration of Life," to be held that year in New Hampshire. Another hand-drawn *Mothering* advertisement from 1983 offered a cookbook titled *Organic Cooking for (Not-So-Organic) Mothers.* These low-budget promotions indicated an organic movement that was still on the fringes, unfamiliar to the general public. As the target audience for organic food evolved, promotional campaigns altered as well. Consumers were recipients of these missives but were also active in interpreting them and constructing subtexts. Advertising transfers cultural meanings onto consumer goods; it shapes collective values and also reflects them. Organic industry advertisements sold products as well as connotations. The industry attempted to correlate its merchandise with health, purity, harmony with the earth, and the "balance of nature." Organic advertisements relied on the assumption that people would purchase the product as well as its integrity, making an investment in the "good life." Buying organic was expected to make one feel virtuous, so advertisements depended on this aura of righteous wholesomeness.

Organic food advertisements reflected cultural discernments that were affiliated with environmentalism, which has historically propagated a firm division between "nature" and "culture." This distinction was derived from an Enlightenment dualism that partitioned ideal, sublime nature from corrupt, human society. Ever since forests were cleared and "tamed" to create farms, cultivated land has been ideologically opposed to uninhabited "wild" land.[117] Tension between environmentalists and farmers has historically stemmed from assertions by wilderness-lovers that all agriculture causes undue degradation to the innocent earth. Yet the organic movement promoted itself as an exception to that rule. Many followers have classified the organic approach as ecologically unblemished, as gardening "*with* nature rather than against it."[118] Organic agriculturists tended to privilege "natural" growing, placing this in opposition to "artificial" fertilization. The organic movement's rhetoric depended on solid distinctions between nature and artifice, agrarian and industrial, and agriculture and agribusiness. Organic farmers were said to be in tune with nature, working to preserve the stability of life. It followed, then, that organic food companies claimed to embody these same characteristics.

Recurring themes in the iconography of organic advertising expressed and perpetuated culturally resonant ideals, capitalizing on positive associations. The language of organic advertisements transmitted chastity. A key strategy in organic food advertising was the marketing of nostalgic agrarianism. Sentimental images conveyed the powerful myth that all organic products stemmed from self-sufficient family farms. Yet, even in 1972, one small dairy farmer noted that keeping corporate money out of agriculture was becoming increasingly difficult.[119] Mechanization and efficiency were the guiding principles. On actual farms in the United States, the sovereign yeoman with a few cows in the barn capitulated to the monolithic enterprise of agribusiness and feedlots. Droves of small farms disappeared each year in the 1970s, due to new nonfarm employment opportunities and legislation that nurtured commercialization and consolidation. The remaining farms owned superfluous acreage; they relied on vertical integration and technology to increase productivity and meet global demand.[120] Tax policies encouraged business-oriented farmers to expand; farmers borrowed to buy more expensive machines. Many family farms incorporated, becoming legal business entities rather than kinship operations.[121] Federal efforts to save smaller farms by enforcing size limitations and residency requirements faced staunch resistance from superfarms (often under absentee ownership), which felt that the restrictions were unrealistic and uneconomic. One geographer averred in 1975 that the supremacy of large-scale agricultural operations made a "reconsideration of the image of the American farm" compulsory.[122] This applied doubly to organic farms.

Wholesome rusticity was indelibly woven into organic food advertisements. Scrutinizing the gap between advertisements and reality revealed examples of "greenwashing" or "farmwashing"—companies gratuitously feigning eco-friendliness or crouching behind a "family farm" doppelgänger. Santa Cruz Organic, which was founded in 1972, presented an illustration of the family farm myth. The company wanted people to know that its founder pressed his first batch of apple juice by hand and sold it as one of the first packaged organic products.[123] However, Santa Cruz Organic became the world's most successful organic juice brand, bought fruit from hundreds of orchards throughout California and Arizona, and was owned by Smucker Quality Beverages. One Santa Cruz Organic juice advertisement showed a young, tan woman in overalls and a sun hat, drinking a glass of juice behind teeming baskets of lemons and apricots; the corresponding text stated: "Our juices taste the way nature intended—wholesome and delicious as if you picked the fruit from the orchard and juiced it yourself." A white middle-class farm girl did not leisurely pick all that fruit and juice it on a whim one summer afternoon, though organic consumers might have preferred to make that assumption. Garden of Eatin'—founded as a health food company in the 1970s—also showcased its own agrarian spirit. One advertisement for Garden of Eatin' organic tortilla chips depicted a solitary farmer harvesting his corn. Presumably the viewer was supposed to believe that the ingredients for all twenty varieties of chips that the company made were drawn from the "organic corn heritage" of diminutive farms and sovereign farmers, not a corporate entity. Comparable marketing techniques for other organic products suggested the quaint atmosphere of independent farmers who were in tune with nature, even as giant organic corporations began to displace those small-scale farms. By the mid-1980s, there were only 2.2 million total farms in the United States (down from an all-time high of 6.8 million in 1935), and it seemed that a handful of conglomerates were controlling food production.[124] With an upsurge of large corporations in the organic landscape, the lines between organic and industrial agriculture blurred, and the organic label was no longer the darling of family-food lovers.

THE NOT-SO-ORGANIC USDA

Most farmers in the early 1980s found themselves facing heavy debt loads, compounded by poor harvests, falling land values, and declining American exports. Corporate ownership of farms exacerbated this crunch on profits. For some farmers, organics seemed like a promising avenue. The USDA released *Report and Recommendations on Organic Farming* by its Study Team on Organic Farming in 1980, at a time when little research or published information was available to assist organic farms. The report noted that demand for organically grown food was still limited, but the USDA was receiving an increasing number of requests for information on organic farming. Some organic farmers felt neglected by the USDA extension service and land-grant universities, which had long directed research toward high-production chemical agriculture. Many said that they were stung by the knowledge gap and had "no one to turn to for help on technical problems."[125] According to the Study Team, the lack of certification programs and a "poor understanding of certification standards by consumers" were obstacles to marketing organically grown products.[126] The *Report* outlined some benefits of organic farming, the primary one being that the production costs of organic farmers were considerably lower than those of conventional systems, due to the exclusion of energy-intensive agrichemicals. Although acreage was moderated on organic farms, the slackened input costs meant that net farm income was comparable. The Study Team noted organic farming's potential to curtail soil erosion, boost water permeation, and minimize "pollution hazards caused by excessive fertilization" on conventional farms. It tentatively stated that "reduced exposure to chemical pesticides may also enhance human and animal health." Since geopolitical instability contributed to the uncertainty of obtaining petroleum supplies used for agrichemicals, organic farming was seen to offer "a measure of personal independence to the American farmer" and make the American food supply more sustainable.[127] These Study Team conclusions, at least, seemed auspicious for organic farmers.

Over thirty-eight thousand copies of the *Report* were distributed, and it looked to be, by most accounts, realistic and objective. The USDA received hundreds of calls and two thousand letters in response; all but three were positive. Even nonorganic farmers were attentive to possible relief from astronomical energy prices. At the University of Nebraska's Organic Agriculture Field Day in 1981, 110 of 150 attendees were conventional farmers interested in learning how organic farming practices could lower their production costs. Shortly after John Block became secretary of agriculture in 1981, farmers requested that an organic agricultural advisory board be formed at the USDA, though that never materialized. According to Daniel Colaciccio, the economist who served as chairman of the Study Team on Organic Farming, the data showed that organic farmers used "significantly less energy" for crops by substituting organic wastes and legumes in rotation for nitrogen fertilizers. However, organic wastes had limited availability, and he did not believe that they would be a feasible substitute for all the synthetic fertilizers currently used. Furthermore, organic farmers used more fuel than nonorganic ones, since they took ancillary trips to spread organic wastes over the fields. However, organic yields were often higher than conventional yields during drought years.[128] Though the jury was still out, the Study Team recommended that research and educational programs be developed and implemented to address the specific necessities and vexing tribulations of organic farmers.

One step in that direction was the proposed Organic Farming Act that reached Congress in 1982. Intriguingly, at an agricultural subcommittee hearing in the House of Representatives, the USDA itself resisted the bill. The proposed act (H.R. 5618) would have created a network of volunteers providing information and advice on organic agriculture, with a "special emphasis on family farms." It would have required the USDA to identify the problems and needs of organic farmers, establish six pilot projects for "holistic research," and disseminate scientific findings gleaned from its studies. Jim Weaver, a representative from Oregon and chairman of the Subcommittee on Forests, Farms, and Energy, was chief sponsor of the bill. He opened the hearing by saying that it was motivated in part by skyrocketing energy costs, the health hazards of heavy pesticide use, environmental degradation, and the soil depletion associated with conventional farming. Organic farmers, according to Weaver, could use less energy and provide affordable food without destroying land and water. Dr. Terry Kinney, administrator of the USDA Agricultural Research Service, spoke against the bill at the House hearing, saying that it would put too much of a strain on the USDA's research and extension program budget. Kinney predicted that most American farmers would continue to rely heavily on conventional farming methods, so the USDA did not feel that legislation amplifying organic farming was necessary at that time. His stinginess was hard for Weaver to swallow, since the proposed bill requested only $3 million (less than 1 percent of the USDA's $430 million research budget). Weaver asked if the USDA was intentionally quashing research on nonchemical agricultural techniques; Kinney intransigently rebuffed the accusation.

Representative George Brown Jr. from California acknowledged that organic farming was "polarizing," was disturbing to the agrichemical industry, and seemed "faddish" to some farmers. Brown had seen a "counter reaction against organic farming" setting in and asked if there had been any deliberate efforts by the USDA to downgrade or suppress the Study Team report from 1980. Kinney again denied purposeful sabotage by the USDA; he said that research should focus on "systems of production and not organic farming versus conventional farming." But the battle lines were already drawn—and the pro-organic voices were not loud enough yet. Dr. Garth Youngberg, the USDA organic program's solitary employee, estimated that there were forty thousand organic farmers in the United States at the time. He admitted that there had been cases of chemical companies cutting off funding to universities that reported positive research on organic farming. Even as the lone organic coordinator, Youngberg had been directed to devote part of his time to other activities; meanwhile, "a couple hundred" USDA scientists were working in the chemical field.[129] The priorities were clear.

Richard Harwood, director of the Rodale Research Center, also presented data from on-farm and plot studies at the H.R. 5618 hearing. He focused on the ways that organic farming was advantageous to farmers economically, because "we are in really tough straits," and environmental issues had to "take a side light." In his testimony, Harwood said that Rodale Press's readership was seventy thousand, of which "about 20 percent are pure organic. They call themselves organic," while "another 40 percent call themselves partially organic." The USDA, he said, ought to direct its research at conversion methodology to meet the information needs of more farmers interested in becoming fully organic. Harwood felt that the Organic Farming Act of 1982 had the "potential for major impact on mainstream as well as Third World agriculture." He knew that organic agriculture, by decreasing fertilizer and biocide inputs, would "incur the wrath of commercial interests in those products." However, ignoring the organic option would be "a major disservice to American agriculture." Chairman Weaver commended Harwood on his "outstanding" testimony and for the "excellent work" Rodale Press was doing.[130] Rosemarie West, president of the National Nutritional Foods Association, then testified about the "alarming and growing trend" of hybrid crop varieties being planted in monocultures that only responded well to "heavy doses of expensive chemicals" in conventional farming. Seed companies had been "placed under the wing of chemical giants like ITT, Monsanto, Purex, Sandoz, Union Carbide, Ciba-Geigy, and Upjohn," so, "naturally, there is a corporate bias to conduct research and promote seeds which enhance sales of their chemical products." By describing these threats to the viability of organic farming, West hoped to convince the subcommittee to support the proposed Organic Farming Act. But the USDA and Weaver's colleagues remained divided; in the end, the House defeated H.R. 5618 by a vote of 198 against and 189 for. Representative Joseph Skeen of New Mexico said that the measure was "an ill-advised move to study the principles of organic agriculture that have been studied and studied since the beginning of time." In essence, opponents said that allocating the research funds would be a waste of money.[131]

The belittling of organics did not abate. Fredrick J. Stare and Elizabeth M. Whelan pursued their denigration of dietary gimmicks with *The One-Hundred-Percent Natural, Purely Organic, Cholesterol-Free, Megavitamin, Low-Carbohydrate Nutrition Hoax* (1983). Again, they criticized "health hustlers" and lamented how much money was wasted on overpriced natural or organic products.[132] They said that *Prevention* magazine, which then had a circulation of over three million, regularly discussed "poisons" in food and the yearning for a "100 percent natural way of life."[133] Stare and Whelan felt that this "propaganda" was "nonsense" and forecast that discarding modern agricultural technology in favor of organic farming would transform the cost of ordinary food into "a luxury for most families." They feared that this would multiply worldwide "problems of hunger, malnutrition, and famine."[134] Contrary to the principles of "Robert Rodale and his organic-gardening cult," Stare and Whelan said that there was no way to change the nutritional content of food by the manner in which it was grown. Consumers were getting ripped off when they paid twice as much for an organically grown apple that was "essentially the same as any other apple."[135] Chemical additives were beneficial, providing consumers with better products at lower prices. Because poisonous chemicals and artificial additives were present in "extremely small amounts" in the food supply, Stare and Whelan insisted that they were perfectly safe. Another denunciation of "nutritional quackery" and "health food faddism" came from diet book author Dale Atrens, who made a point of dismissing organic food's allegedly superlative nutritional quality. Atrens said that a health food store could "present any nonsense with the appropriate incantation of *natural, holistic, organic,* and so forth, and it will be swallowed faster than alfalfa pills."[136] He flatly stated that the purportedly superior flavor of organically grown products was "a fiction" and "a simple prejudice supported by no data at all."[137] He further claimed that, since organically grown plants were not sprayed, they were inevitably *more* susceptible to damage caused by insects and plant diseases; this meant that organics were also more liable to be high in natural carcinogens and natural pesticides.[138] Organic farmers were besieged by a rigorous slate of critiques, but they steadily ignored the vitriol.

Robin Ostfeld and Lou Johns started an organic vegetable farm in the Finger Lakes region of New York in 1987. Spreading manure and rotating crops were more work than using herbicides and chemical fertilizers, but the couple said that being certified organic after a stringent review process by the Natural Organic Farmers' Association of New York was worth it. Consumers were willing to pay higher prices, and the farmers felt that it was important to "raise healthy crops without poisoning the land or people."[139] In *Rushall: The Story of an Organic Farm* (1987), veteran organic farmer Barry Wookey wrote, "'Going organic' is really a philosophy of life as much as a system of farming." Nobody should embark upon organic farming, he believed, without accepting that "it involves a lifetime's commitment."[140] Bob and Connie Gregson became prototypical organic homesteaders when they moved to a flower and nut farm on an island near Seattle in 1988. They said that they were "determined to drop out of corporate careers for a better lifestyle."[141] They commenced selling their organic fruit and vegetables at a self-service farm stand along the driveway and drew subscriptions for a Community Supported Agriculture program. Though the work was sometimes tedious and frustrating, they discovered it to be "glorious" and "immensely rewarding," a true "labor of love."[142] They felt that general culture disregarded the "mystical bond between people and the good earth" but ascertained that this link was "rekindled on the small organic farm."[143] Enthused by their fruitful feat, they wrote a handbook for others who wanted to make a "reasonable, community-oriented, non-exploitative, earth-friendly, and aesthetically pleasing living" as small-scale organic family farmers.[144] While organic homesteading was still a low-profile pastime in the 1980s, organic food hoopla was mushrooming.

As organic growing progressed—even without adequate USDA funding—there seemed to be changes in the type of farmers converting to organic methods and their motivations. Richard Harwood said that a mailer in January 1982 had drawn ten thousand new readers to *Organic Gardening*, but the "concern to us is that our readership is changing, and larger farmers now are becoming more interested in what we are doing."[145] Studies by Julie Guthman and others demonstrated that agribusiness firms increasingly appropriated organic commodity chains throughout the 1980s. Rent-driven land assessments helped replicate past practices of overexploiting land and labor, thereby causing the "paradox of organic farming." Price competition also undercut the economic survival of those who did wish to pursue a socially responsible form of organic farming.[146] While some producers began organic farming as a way of life, others saw it as primarily an economic enterprise, particularly when organic foods could be marketed with premium prices.

NEW LEADERS

Rodale Press remained the vanguard for organic information, but a number of venerable organic food companies emerged in these decades of growth; one was Paul Keene's Walnut Acres. Keene left his job teaching college math-

ematics to study homesteading at Ralph Borsodi's School of Living and ecological agriculture at Ehrenfried Pfeiffer's Kimberton Farms School in the
1940s. J. I. Rodale asked for his assistance in starting *Organic Gardening*; instead, Keene and his wife purchased Walnut Acres farm in central Pennsylvania in 1946.[147] They were inspired by both Sir Albert Howard and Mohandas
Gandhi to live simply, spread health, and "enrich the earth and its people."
They began their mission by farming one hundred acres without electricity,
tractors, pesticides, or chemical fertilizers.[148] Initially, Keene said, they were
considered "kooks," but after one newspaper lauded their apple butter, they
started receiving orders.[149] One of the first organic farms in the country became the nation's first organic food marketer, hawking its eggs, vegetables,
grains, and condiments through an unassuming direct mail catalog. Keene's
columns in the catalog shared his reflections on rural life, natural farming,
and "the oneness of all life."[150] Keene wrote of his attempt to "cooperate with
nature and lean upon it."[151] The 360-acre farm grew its grains and vegetables
without chemicals or poisonous sprays, and Keene felt that organic farmers
"give more than they take," by actually feeding the soil.[152] A column in 1984
noted that "we are careful in defining the word *organic*, and we use it only
when we feel certain about it. . . . We want people to know what they are
putting into their bodies."[153] The Walnut Acres "oasis" grew to five hundred
acres and into an employee-owned business earning $5 million per year that
was selling three hundred organic products by the late 1980s.[154]

When Organic Gardening profiled this "legend in the organic food industry" in 1991, Walnut Acres had a retail store, grain mill, peanut-butter
room, commercial kitchen, and packaging center for its cereals, baked goods,
dried fruits, flours, and other wares. Crops were fertilized with manure from
the farm's own organic beef and chicken farms. Field rotations and legume
mixes reinforced good tilth. Keene said, "People trust us because we were
the first in the field and we wanted to do it right."[155] Two decades later, the
catalog and many of its products had been phased out; the Hain Celestial
Group—a natural foods titan—had purchased Walnut Acres; and the company obtained most of its ingredients from other suppliers, not the original
farm. The recipes for its certified organic juices, soups, salsas, pasta sauces,
and fruit squeezies were developed by professional chefs. Walnut Acres Organic products, like "Incredible Vegetable" juice, were sold at supermarkets
nationwide, with the tagline "Live Pure" and a cute red farmhouse on the
logo. The website said: "True to our beginnings, we make organic foods and
beverages that nourish your body and invigorate your soul."[156] Organic food

companies like Walnut Acres vigilantly assured consumers that, despite its appearance, it ran according to organic principles.

Frank Ford, who founded Arrowhead Mills in 1960 to create a larger market for organically grown wheat, shared a similar story of becoming prosperous after staring very small. Arrowhead Mills was part of what Ford called "a counter-movement, the organic revolution," a response to the synthetic fertilizers and chemical pesticides that were polluting the soil. As early as the 1970s, Ford recognized the need for a distribution system that would bring truckloads of his stock to major cities. He recalled that "there were other visionaries at this time who saw this same need, and together, we began to 'plot' the natural food revolution."[157] Arrowhead Mills succeeded; its organic products became available throughout the nation; and it, too, was later purchased by the Hain Celestial Group. Arrowhead Mills sold organic whole-grain flours, rice, beans, cereals, and nut butters, along with mixes for organic chocolate cake, stuffing, oatmeal raisin cookies, pizza crust, and more—all flaunted as "Deliciously Wholesome Choices." Despite its accelerated growth, Arrowhead Mills maintained that it upheld "the principles it was founded on" and marketed "products that are true to our heritage and organic roots." Its slogan was "From America's Heartland to Your Table."[158] After retiring, Ford said that he continued to feast on organic foods "almost exclusively."[159] Adherence to linchpin organic commandments was meant to fend off the accusations that an organic food company had betrayed its pedigree.

The documentary *The Story of Grimmway Farms* told the "classic American success story" of a family business built on "honesty, faith, and people."[160] Brothers Rodney and Robert Grimm first set up a roadside produce stand near their grandfather's chicken farm in California's San Joaquin Valley. This became the foundation for Grimmway Farms, which, during the 1970s, relocated to another part of California, focused on baby carrots, and later expanded into the world's largest grower of carrots. Eventually, they would process and ship millions of shredded, crinkle-cut, petite, matchstick, and other fresh, peeled carrots internationally and domestically. The Grimmway Farms organic division, Cal-Organic Farms, started in 1983 with a quarter acre of lettuce. It eventually grew dozens of other vegetables on thousands of certified organic acres, including yellow baby carrots and bunches of purple, yellow, and orange carrots. The Cal-Organic tagline was "Healthy by Choice." Grimmway Farms's website said that the Grimm family "still insists on walking the fields," assuring high-quality products.[161]

Arrowhead Mills organic pancake and waffle mix (Photo courtesy of Colleen Freda Burt)

Organic tea pacesetter Celestial Seasonings told a corresponding narrative about how it safeguarded core values of "beauty and truth" despite intensive growth since its inception in 1969. Founder Morris Siegel recalled harvesting herbs by hand in the Rocky Mountains, drying them on screen doors, and using an old Singer sewing machine to create the muslin bags of tea he sold to local health food stores.[162] Celestial Seasonings became known in the 1970s for funky, artistic designs and inspirational sayings on its distinctive packages. Consumers could admire the peaceful pagoda, verdant mountains, and icy waterfall on the Goji Berry Pomegranate Green Tea box, or the Buddha curled up in purple flower petals and dancers formed from clouds on the Sweet Coconut Thai Chai box. The cheerful overtones of Siegel's innovative, colorful packaging were meant to elicit an upbeat mood in buyers making their tea selection. Kraft, Inc., purchased Celestial Seasonings in 1984 and then sold it to Lipton, Inc. As his endeavor became a national success, Siegel claimed that "even though we haven't used screen doors and muslin bags for many years, we still make your teas with the same love and fervor."[163] Whimsical boxes of Chocolate Raspberry Bliss, Mango Darjeeling Organic, and seasonal Sugar Cookie Sleigh Ride were among more than one hundred flavors (though not all were organic). Celestial Seasonings also added organic coffee, spice blends, cider, instant drink mixes, and bottled organic kombucha energy shots to the line of green, black, red, white, herbal, wellness, dessert, and organic teas. It was the largest specialty tea manufacturer in the United States and spread into international markets. The production plant in Boulder, Colorado—with a gallery of original artwork, free samples, the Celestial Café, and a gift shop—was open to visitors. Celestial Seasonings advertised that it was still "a company with a conscience," quenching the thirst of consumers looking for unique, natural beverages.[164] Dispositions toward health and purity were visible in the marketing approaches of nearly all lucrative, pioneering organic businesses.

These years saw unprecedented interest in organic food, despite premium charges and ongoing uncertainties. The rising number of health food stores, from five hundred in 1965 to in excess of three thousand in 1972, indicated a "health-food explosion."[165] The nonprofit Way of Life Co-Op opened in Pleasantville, New York, in 1971, because "members anxious to avoid chemical fertilizers, pesticides, sprays, additives and preservatives" wanted a source for natural and organic foods.[166] Eden Foods started as a co-op and deli in Ann Arbor, Michigan, and claimed that it was "one of very few places in the U.S.A. where you could get natural, organic, macrobiotic food." By 1972, it

Celestial Seasonings tea (Photo courtesy of Colleen Freda Burt)

had created a brand, had opened a warehouse, and was heading down the path toward being a purveyor of organic miso, soba noodles, and shoyu soy sauce (among other items).[167] In 1974, organic boosters called for a "consumer revolution" to convince farmers that a market existed for organic crops. To achieve this, buyers were exhorted to ask for organic produce every time they shopped.[168] More comprehensive grocers were established to accommodate demand, such as Bread & Circus in Brookline, Massachusetts, in 1975 and Mrs. Gooch's Natural Foods Market in West Los Angeles in 1977. As these specialized organic outlets appeared, some conventional supermarkets were also creating organic food sections. A *Newsweek* cover story in the summer of 1975 affirmed the expanding enchantment with organic foods as part of "The New Wave" in food. The National Nutritional Foods Association listed 8,850 retail health food units by 1982, with total industry sales of $1.93 billion (compared to "sales in excess of $9 to $10 billion" at major supermarket chains like Safeway and Kroger). The association's president, Rosemarie West, said, "Organically grown products continue to be specialized food items," not yet in the mainstream. Consumers were voluntarily paying higher retail prices, though, because they knew organic farmers had used "environmentally sound" practices that ensured the "nutritional integrity" of crops.[169]

A number of "healthy" retail chains crafted distinctive shopping atmospheres. One of the most efficacious in doing so, Whole Foods Market, would become the largest merchant of organic and natural foods in the world. Influenced by people like biodynamics founder Rudolf Steiner and nutrition writer Adelle Davis, CEO John Mackey opened Safer Way Natural Foods in Austin in 1978, a "quirky granola den" using local farmers as suppliers. The fledgling shop sold "brown rice, beans, nuts, unbleached flour, raw milk, and organic produce."[170] Mackey added other products and began to expand. In 1980 Safer Way and Clarksville Natural Grocery merged as Whole Foods Market, one of the first natural foods supermarkets in the United States. *Time* magazine noted that this original store served "vegetarians, macrobiotic dieters and those seeming oddballs who took supplements such as ginkgo biloba and Echinacea. Like other mom-and-pop organic shops that dotted the country, the store was friendly, cozy, intensely concerned with its products' purity and expensive."[171] That bout of coziness didn't last, but it was part of the Whole Foods charisma and lore.

Organic yogurt producer Stonyfield Farm also had a tale of humble beginnings. Gary Hirshberg, who became the president and CEO, recalled that, in the 1970s, many dismissed organic food as a "fringy fad." Stonyfield Farm started out in 1983 as Samuel Kaymen's organic dairy, with just seven cows; Hirshberg joined up a few months later. While Hirshberg was committed to both the food and the politics of the organic movement, he also believed that organics would have to accommodate supermarkets in order to "gain traction and grow beyond our original small enclave of activists." This belief caused friction with others "who seemed more interested in fighting culture wars than seizing new commercial opportunities."[172] The key challenge to winning acceptance was taste, and Hirshberg decided that his organic yogurt would have to be "delectable" to gain customers. Fortunately, he said, "what began as a philosophical fondness for dishes like brown rice and seaweed eventually matured into a tasty cuisine that attracted talented chefs."[173] Hirshberg found that paying extra for top-quality organic ingredients was worthwhile, because his customers gladly paid more for superior products. Stonyfield's slogan became "You just can't fake this stuff." Twenty-five years later, Stonyfield had grown into the world's largest organic yogurt maker, with $300 million in annual sales.

New organic ventures kept cropping up. Another organic frontrunner, Earthbound Farm, proffered a familiar storyline: it began as a roadside organic raspberry stand in 1984 that, according to founders Drew and Myra Goodman, was a "labor of love." At the time, the Goodmans said, organic farming was still known as "hippie farming." Choosing organic produce often

Stonyfield organic yogurt (Photo courtesy of Colleen Freda Burt)

meant a sacrifice in quality for consumers, and "organic wasn't on the radar" for most people.[174] The Goodmans claimed to have "started a salad revolution" in California's Carmel Valley by selling their packaged, prewashed salad mixes to restaurants and supermarkets. They wanted to bring the benefits of organic food to as many people as possible and did not remain backyard gardeners for long. Earthbound Farm became the world's largest grower of organic produce, with thousands of employees. Managing forty thousand organic acres in California, Arizona, Mexico, Canada, Chile, and New Zealand,

Earthbound Farm broccoli and cauliflower (Photo courtesy of Colleen Freda Burt)

it sold more than seventy-seven different bagged fruit and vegetable products and reaped annual sales of $360 million.[175] Earthbound Farm was a fore-runner in demonstrating how organic food could move through an efficient industrial system. In subsequent decades, it regularly offered information about the importance of organic food, such as an activity book for children, a cookbook—*Food to Live By: The Earthbound Farm Organic Cookbook* (2006) by Myra Goodman, and a *Pocket Guide to Choosing Organic* (2008). Myra insisted that she and Drew still felt a "personal commitment to everyone who buys an Earthbound Farm product."[176] The company's advertisements high-lighted longevity in the organic market as proof of Earthbound's unadulter-ated dedication to the chaste values of family farming. These self-effacing stories became de rigueur for organic companies.

Rachel Berliner and her husband, Andy, started Amy's Kitchen in 1987, the year their daughter, Amy, was born. Berliner had grown up eating organic foods and wanted to make all-natural vegetarian foods for busy parents who didn't have time to cook from scratch. Armed with organic ingredients, the couple was ready to take on mass-produced freezer staples like Banquet beef enchiladas and Stouffer's Lean Cuisine glazed chicken. They began, in their own house and barn, to make a line of frozen "comfort food"—for exam-ple, vegetable potpies and macaroni and cheese—which Amy, as a toddler, loved.[177] They hardly could have guessed that one day they would be earning millions in annual sales. The Berliners added frozen pizzas, burritos, and lasagna, then canned soups and salsas, and eventually packaged snacks like spinach tofu wraps and desserts like chocolate pound cake. Amy's would remain one of the last independently owned organic companies in the coming decades (along with Eden Foods). Though dwarfed by huge food companies like Heinz and General Mills, Amy's Kitchen and other organic trailblazers flourished, due to a growing demand for food positioned at the intersection of health, taste, and convenience. It was higher-income consumers who were chiefly allowing the growth in organic products, since they willingly paid the sector for the benefits that it proclaimed.

POISON APPLES

During the 1980s, consumers were bombarded with self-described health foods. Though health jargon became ensconced in the national consciousness, this fixation did not necessarily improve actual diets or general physical well-being, nor did it drastically reduce dietary-related diseases. In 1980, the USDA first published its complete *Dietary Guidelines for Americans*. After decades of massive confusion about nutritional principles, people realized that they were paying a stiff penalty for their eating habits, as evidenced by dietary links to diabetes, dental decay, and mental retardation.[178] Extensive government promotion of dietary goals and guidelines began to target diseases and illnesses. The central premise was to "eat a variety of foods; maintain ideal weight; eat foods with adequate starch and fiber; avoid too much sugar; avoid too much sodium; avoid too much fat, saturated fat, and cholesterol; and to drink alcohol in moderation." This prescription was built on "a remarkable consensus among scientific and nutrition experts."[179] But legislative struggles in the 1980s did not indicate any kind of consensus about organic food's health remunerations. The USDA Study Team on Organic Farming acknowledged in 1980 that many organic farmers perceived organically produced foods as more healthful than analogous conventional products. However, nutritionists and other scientists had examined the evidence, and, in each situation, the authority involved "denied the validity of claims for nutritional superiority made by others for organic foods."[180] The Study Team reported that it had uncovered no conclusive proof that pesticide residues in foods caused cancer, birth deformities, or other health problems.[181]

In the 1980s, despite pervasive interest in health and exercise, the Centers for Disease Control and Prevention indicated that even more Americans had become overweight or obese. Some critics blamed the heavily advertised packaged-food industry for promoting foods high in fat, carbohydrates, sodium, and calories. Others faulted automobiles and technological gadgets for underwriting a decline in exercise frequency.[182] The *Shopper's Guide to Natural Foods* (1987) noted that an increasingly health-conscious population had created a market for organic rice. However, of all the rice Americans ate, less than 2 percent was brown, and only 0.3 percent was organically farmed, so organic brown rice had unquestionably not yet found its way into the daily lives of Americans.[183] Other unprocessed whole grains, such as quinoa, kamut, and millet, seemed even more foreign to the public. The *Shopper's Guide* focused on consumer clout, reiterating the philosophical and political authority of shopping. Selecting produce was "the equivalent of casting a vote for the type of world you wish to live in."[184] Organic fruits and vegetables were worth the adjuvant cost, because, "in addition to sparing your body some poisons, you are supporting a grower who is raising food in a way that enhances both the soil and the environment."[185] The manager of one organic food co-op told a reporter in 1983 that the organic oatmeal he sold was free of chemicals but was "slower to cook and a bit more bitter, gritty and nasty to some taste."[186] This humble admission of inferiority did not deter devoted organicists. A plethora of consumer guides averred that buying organic food was a potent course of action, carrying persuasive power that would convince politicians and businesses to shift toward a better society.

Health claims were essentially illegal in food labeling and marketing. However, the food industry petitioned and pressured the Food and Drug Administration (FDA) to approve a number of qualified food-specific health claims. Capitalizing on a study asserting the benefits of oat bran during an oat bran craze in the 1980s, the Quaker Oats Company and other food producers were allowed to flaunt the benefits of oatmeal. The commercialization of healthy eating commenced when thousands of low-fat, fat-free, sugar-free, and high-fiber products were launched in the 1980s.[187] Americans held certain health notions sacred: at first glance, smoothies were healthier than milkshakes, and muffins were healthier than cupcakes (even if they contained the same ingredients). Fruits and vegetables were always supposed to be good for you—and organic food was too. The organic label did indicate that a product was grown or processed without forbidden pesticides or hormones, but it was emphatically *not* a health claim. Levels of sugar, sodium, fat, and calories were not addressed. Yet studies indicated that consumers continued to think organic foods were healthier than nonorganic ones.[188]

Fear-based marketing and hyperbolic press coverage of food safety incidents contributed to the popularity of organics. While naysayers often implied that organic food buyers had succumbed to hysteria, fretful consumers saw themselves as entirely rational and pragmatic. They weighed the risks of future illness and took actions to ward off those perils.[189] A defining moment for organic food's healthy connotations came with the Alar shock in 1989. The plant growth regulator Alar, or daminozide, had been available for decades and was habitually used to treat apples. A Natural Resources Defense Council (NRDC) report on Alar's carcinogenic effects in mice led to a dramatic CBS News broadcast of *60 Minutes*. The government's top pesticide controller told astounded Americans that Alar posed an unacceptable cancer risk.[190] Overnight, parents stopped feeding their children apples. Other news conferences followed, as every major television show, newspaper, and newsweekly covered the story. Meryl Streep, speaking on behalf of the NRDC, urged Americans to support organic farms.[191] Sales of organic food catapulted. Skeptics pointed out that the NRDC report was never published in a peer-reviewed scientific journal. The Environmental Protection Agency (EPA), the FDA, and the USDA all said that risk estimates were inflated.[192] Still, the media blitz had direct results, and Alar was removed from the market.

Stories about lurking chemicals pushed organic food onto American radar screens. Even with all the eye rolling going on, organics were a cause célèbre. By the 1980s, *Organic Gardening* was the largest gardening magazine in the world, with a circulation reaching 1.3 million.[193] Many gardeners and farmers credited the magazine for having a personal impact on them. For this corps, compost was indeed "gold in the earth," and the "vigorous and growing movement" of organiculture was "here to stay."[194] Organic food's visibility had ratcheted up. The organic lifestyle finally resonated with a substantial segment of the country. A cornucopia of organic cottage industries had sprouted, and mammoth institutions were becoming key distributors of organic food to the masses. The environmental cognoscenti doted on exquisite organic possibilities. However, as the organic movement gained momentum, it also had to make a complicated pivot; intricate organic precepts were disputed, scruples were tested, and the very definition of "organic" was histrionically debated.

CHAPTER FOUR

Leaders, Land Lovers, Locavores, Labels, Laws, and a Little Lunacy

In dedicated circles, organic food was always the cream of the crop, exemplifying purity and harmony. Protecting the integrity of "organic" in the lexicon and maintaining a positive, noble ambience were the lifeblood of the organic movement. For the organic imprimatur to be trustworthy and marketable to a wide swath of consumers, however, it had to meet stringent expectations. Before the existence of a nationwide certification process, even fervent users of organic food had nagging doubts about the truth of its claims. Vague labels and sporadic dishonesty abetted distrust. Cognizant of this, and hoping to stave off the dwindling confidence bedeviling the movement, J. I. Rodale had been an early champion of authorized labels for organic food. In the wake of the Alar apples mayhem, the phenomenal organic food wave in the 1990s reflected consumers' increasing sensitivity to food safety.[1] The organic cohort capitalized on this and besieged the USDA with petitions for legislation. Bob Scowcroft cofounded the Organic Farming Research Foundation (OFRF) in 1990 to help fund organic farming initiatives and agitate for a national organic law. Calling J. I. Rodale and Walnut Acres the first generation of organic activists, Scowcroft said that *his* generation would take the organic vision and put it into practice.[2] Bitter squabbles about what that prophecy entailed—and what kind of practices it stipulated on the continuum of sustainability—would divide the movement.

This chapter highlights how interwoven threads in the blossoming organic movement—the Rodales, homesteading, environmentalism, government regulations, and corporate co-optation—merged into a glittery tapestry in the 1990s and after. It argues that, just as in previous decades, the organic core had to make compromises that caused enduring schisms between itself and the periphery. In 1952, J. I. Rodale had voiced that "it may be necessary for the organic movement to become interested in politics."[3] Yet little dynamism in the organic movement was ever directed at taking radical steps toward revamping the entire agro-food paradigm; instead, it mainly focused on benefits to individual farmers and consumers.

At times, the movement failed to petition stridently enough for deep policy reforms that could have weaned American agriculture off its unremitting diet of toxic chemicals and lethal insecticides. Laxity in regulations was a repercussion of striving to reach a broader audience; still, the movement retained subversive elements.

THE OFPA, THE RODALES, AND NEW LEADERS

When the Organic Food Production Act of 1990 (OFPA) passed, it was a watershed for the organic movement—but it was also nearly a debacle. The OFPA required the USDA to develop consistent, uniform standards for organic agricultural production. This seemed to be a well-intentioned attempt to bolster public trust in legitimate organic products that sported an authoritative seal. Synthetic chemicals and fertilizers, genetic engineering (GE), sewage sludge, and radiation would be precluded from USDA-certified organic food. But organic sticklers were leery of the laws, which were far from draconian. There were quarrels over every detail. Several organic pioneers expressed frustration with the loose ends. They were alarmed that tussles over the legal definition of "organic" would make consumers even more dubious of the label. According to the Congressional Research Service, the OFPA passed with "widespread support" from the organic industry, state departments of agriculture, farm groups, and consumer groups.[4] Yet the ramifications were formidable. The Demeter Association, which certified biodynamic products, warned that the USDA's course of action risked "undermining the basic principles upon which organic farming is based."[5] During the tumult, questions about priorities in the organic movement were reinvigorated.

The OFPA established unswerving national standards for selling organically produced foods. The USDA suddenly owned the word "organic" and regulated its appearance on fresh and processed food. The coveted green USDA Organic seal began materializing more regularly in the marketplace. From one perspective, the legislation was a godsend; from another, it opened the door for corporate hijackers. Farmers had to pay to be certified as "organic" (something that previously was free and informal). Farmers who had been amalgamating organic and conventional techniques had to decide if they would go organic all the way to obtain certification. Others that *had* been full-fledged organic opted to bow out of the expensive red-tape tangle, forgoing advantages that might have tagged along with bearing the seal.

The OFPA established the legal basis for the National Organic Program (NOP) and set up the National Organic Standards Board (NOSB). The NOSB members were responsible for developing proposed criteria and advising the secretary of agriculture on implementing the NOP. The NOSB included fifteen representatives from the organic community: four farmers/growers; three environmentalists/resource conservationists; three consumer/public interest advocates; two handlers/processors; one retailer; one scientist; and one USDA-accredited certifying agent. These members naturally had sundry concerns in advancing their recommendations on crops, livestock, compliance, accreditation, and certification. The NOSB meetings were open to public comments, allowing space for considerable debate.[6] Passage of the OFPA brought more mainstream funding to nascent organic endeavors, and J. I. Rodale's dreams of an organic gold rush were finally realized. Preserving the unadulterated nuggets of organic ideals, though, presented a conundrum for those votaries who feared that they were being hidden behind a gilded façade.

With lavish optimism, Robert Rodale had envisioned global cooperation among all nations on organic standards. He was scheduled to deliver the opening address at the first International Conference on Agriculture for the 21st Century in October 1990.[7] A month before the meeting, however, he died in a car accident while visiting Moscow, where he had hoped to start a complementary organic farming magazine.[8] Robert's wife, Ardath Rodale, became chairman of Rodale Institute and CEO of Rodale Press after his death. Robert's son, Anthony Rodale, was named vice chairman of the Rodale Institute (and, later, chairman of the board of directors). Rodale Press remained a lucrative family-run business, even though *Organic Gardening* struggled to retain readers and advertisers, and circulation declined to eight hundred thousand.[9] John Haberern, Rodale Institute's president, reiterated that Rodale Press's philosophy was established on "fundamental respect for the soil."[10] By 1992, when annual revenues of Rodale Press were $350 million, some "longtime devotees" questioned whether the company had become "more gray than green, more willing to consult customer data bases than its conscience."[11] Still, editor-in-chief Mike McGrath defended the company's conscience that year:

OG has the largest paid circulation of any gardening magazine in the world! That's some pretty hot compost, eh? And I firmly believe that *OG* is number one *because* we're organic, not despite it. . . . One thing that has remained unchanged over the years is our unyielding commitment to the organic philosophy. Fifty-plus years of pointing out that maybe it isn't the best possible idea to spray poison all over your food before you eat it.[12]

Unyielding commitment or not, *Organic Gardening*'s circulation fell still further, dropping below 660,000 by 1998; and ad pages dropped nearly 20 percent. Renovations ensued. Maria Rodale, taking the helm of a new Organic Living unit, restated that *Organic Gardening* was "the flagship magazine and the soul of the company." The new game plan was to "attract a wider audience of women interested in organic issues," even if they were not gardeners themselves.[13]

Throughout the organic story, certain prominent "movement intellectuals" have been vocal in expressing what organic farming has meant to producers, consumers, and the general public. Organic veterans with an aura of hard-boiled world-weariness have seemed supremely credible when commenting on the movement's trajectory. Along with members of the Rodale family, Helen and Scott Nearing, and Wendell Berry (discussed previously), contemporary "experts" have included Eliot Coleman, Joel Salatin, David Mas Masumoto, and Michael Ableman. All four were farmers themselves who led with their actions, but they were also visionary gurus who publicly aired appraisals and broached disputes in the movement. Their discursive strategies acutely affected how organic farming has been represented and understood in American culture.

Maine farmer Eliot Coleman has been one conspicuous ambassador for the organic movement. Coleman was a quintessential back-to-the-lander who quit his job as a college Spanish teacher and moved his family from New Jersey to coastal Maine with $5,000 in savings in 1968. He began working eighteen hours a day to produce chemical-free peas, sweet corn, and potatoes on his truck farm.[14] The land Coleman tended in Harborside was adjacent to Scott and Helen Nearings's homestead. When the Nearings were alive, they taught him a wide range of economic survival skills. He later managed to gross $100,000 per year, despite farming only one and a half acres. Like Liberty Hyde Bailey, Louis Bromfield, and others preceding him, Coleman felt that underlining the economic potential of farming was crucial for drawing young people to farming.[15] The Nearings's greenhouse also inspired Coleman to devise a way to eat garden-fresh, chemical-free food all year long, despite the snowy Maine winters.[16] His secret was low-energy cold frames and unheated greenhouses. Over the years, Coleman steadfastly believed in the merits and rewards of the small farm. He sought agricultural techniques that were "in harmony with the natural world."[17] The key to successful organic food production, for Coleman, was to produce quality compost and enhance natural processes. The optimal organic farming system was a crop-friendly ecosystem that mimicked the biology of the natural world.[18] Coleman observed that pests did not bother healthy organic plants, so pesticides and other additions were unnecessary. Coleman's Four Season Farm was recognized as a national model of small-scale sustainable agriculture.

In *Four-Season Harvest* (1992), Coleman explained that his home garden had been organic for thirty years, because organic methods were simpler, worked better, and implied a "partnership with nature."[19] Like Rodale, he said that compost was the trick for fertile soil. Echoing Rachel Carson, he wrote that chemicals "were conceived in an age of hubris by minds that ignored the marvelous balances of the natural system."[20] Though Coleman disapproved of the "takeover" of organic labels by "industrial food giants," he remained convinced that family farmers were "the last refuge protecting the values of the early organic pioneers against the onslaught of the industrial organic hucksters."[21] Coleman's wife, Barbara Damrosch, was also a sagacious gardener and a collaborator in Four Season Farm. Damrosch's *The Garden Primer* has been a popular resource for gardeners since it was first published in 1986. Damrosch said, "I take my cues from the way nature gardens, and also from the gardens of the past."[22] She issued a revised edition of the book in 2008 that carried a "100% Organic" symbol on the cover. Damrosch referred to J. I. Rodale's *How to Grow Vegetables & Fruits by the Organic Method* as her "bible."[23] Together, Coleman and Damrosch have earnestly tended their farm and garden, lectured and written a great deal, helped publicize organic growing, and served as mentors to a new generation of farmers.

Joel Salatin—who might be dubbed a celebrity farmer—also garnered a good deal of attention at his environmentally conscious, "family-friendly" Polyface Farm in Virginia. The precocious Salatin manages 550 acres without chemicals and sells most of his eggs, broilers, cattle, hogs, turkeys, and rabbits directly to adoring consumers. Salatin's grandfather was an early aficionado of J. I. Rodale. Salatin said that Rodale's *Complete Book of Composting* "put the final nail in the excuse coffin of the naysayers who still believed chemical-based fertilizer was the answer to soil fertility."[24] Like Rodale, Salatin envisaged the soil as a living organism. He cited Sir Albert Howard, Louis Bromfield, John Muir, Wendell Berry, Charles Walters Jr., Allan Nation, and Paul Hawken as role models for his ecological perspective. Salatin critiqued the industrial paradigm as too rigid and simplistic, preferring to approach farming from a "nonmechanical" worldview.[25] He allowed that growth was not inherently bad but said that he favored small farms and believed that "huge conglomerate agriculture could not be family friendly."[26] The opinionated Salatin accused the industrial food system of "unabashed greedy pride" for destroying soil and disrespecting "the inherent uniqueness of the living world."[27] In his antiestablishment spirit, Salatin snubbed government subsidies for the "diversified, grass-based, beyond organic, direct marketing farm," on which he honored "nature's template" and "the pigness of the pig."[28]

Salatin was an insider to the organic certification process and also became an outspoken dissenter. He realized that food integrity could not be "bureaucratically regulated." He saw farmers flock to a "premium-priced niche" without true convictions for what it involved and then watched the "corporate empire" join the organic movement and adulterate it further.[29] Salatin had always farmed organically, but he said that organic was a "noncomprehensive term" that did not "speak to some of the larger variables," such as the abhorrent prospect of organic feedlot beef. Instead of using the word "organic," he invented other terms, such as "Pigaerator Pork" and "Pastured Chicken," to eliminate hardening of the categories.[30] Salatin maintained that "organic by neglect was far different than organic by design" and rebuffed blanket approval for farmers appropriating the label.[31] His own ingenuity, offbeat quips, and ecological obduracy were enough to make him an icon. In 2005, *Time* magazine featured Salatin as "High Priest of the Pasture," due to his penchant for evangelizing in the realm of organic and natural farming.[32] The *New York Times* admired Salatin, a "philosophizing organic farmer," as an agricultural hero whose free-ranging livestock provided a counterpoint to villainous industrial feedlots full of "cruelly crammed cattle."[33] The *Atlantic* hailed Polyface as the "Mecca of Sustainable Agriculture" in 2011. Polyface Inc. was earning over $2 million in revenues that year—rather impressive for a setup that used pig power to aerate the compost applied as a natural fertilizer on the farm. Salatin's folksy persona, self-identification as a "Christian-libertarian-environmentalist-lunatic" farmer, and refusal to be "Wall Streetified" made him a colorful organic envoy.[34]

Less comical and more erudite than Salatin was third-generation Japanese peach grower David Mas Masumoto, who converted his California orchards to organic when he took over the family farm in the late 1980s. Within a few years, he was peddling his fruit to Chez Panisse, where a single peach would be served to diners, unadorned, on a dessert plate. His endangered Sun Crest heritage peach variety was nominated for Slow Foods USA's Ark of Taste, an honor reserved for products threatened with gastro-extinction.[35] Masumoto's *Epitaph for a Peach* (1995) lyrically described his efforts to rescue the Sun Crest from becoming obsolete. Fruit brokers had spurned the Sun Crest, which turned amber gold when ripe instead of bright red and was far more fragile than the omnipresent commercial peach varieties bred for long-distance trucking and long-term storage. Masumoto affectionately described its natural sweetness—free from the taint of herbicides or pesticides—as the way peaches used to taste.[36] Renowned chef Dan Barber reminisced that the first Sun Crest peach he ever bit into was "the best peach of my life."[37] Masumoto also grew other stone fruits and grapes on his eighty acres, but he disagreed with the "genocide" that other farmers performed when they created "a legion of new weapons" to combat weeds. In doing so, they were creating sterile soil and contaminating the water beneath their farm. Instead, by "allowing nature to take over" the farm, Masumoto said, "everything grows voraciously," including weeds. He was comfortable with chaos, though, and did not feel that he could harvest juicy, luscious fruit in a barren landscape.[38]

Masumoto's "non-cultivation" philosophy harked back to the "do-nothing" methods that Masanobu Fukuoka used in the 1970s, and Masumoto frequently alluded to his own Japanese ancestors as traditional organic farmers who knew how to work with nature.[39] This literary farmer has written several other books. In *Wisdom of the Last Farmer: Harvesting Legacies from the Land* (2009) he described the difficulties of farming organically and surviving financially, without resorting to fast-killing chemical sprays if worm outbreaks occur. Masumoto said that organic farmers wanted to grow "life-giving food with life-enhancing methods." The challenges included exhausting work like weeding by hand and constantly monitoring the crops to head off insects. However, he felt recompensed by organic fruit consumers who clamored for "authentic flavors" and appreciated the tastes and aromas that could not be mass-produced.[40] He was proud of having saved "heirloom peaches and nectarines whose nectar explodes on the palate" before they vanished.[41] Masumoto has been featured in national magazines and television programs; he has written regular newspaper columns and has served as a keynote speaker at annual culinary and agricultural conferences.

Organic farmer Michael Ableman has been another leading speaker and writer on organic matters. In California, Ableman managed Fairview Gardens, a twelve-acre organic farm that became an exemplar for small-scale, urban agriculture. Chef Alice Waters christened it "a storybook farm set right in the middle of generic suburban sprawl."[42] Ableman remembered that "nature seduced me and I fell in love with the little farm on Fairview Avenue."[43] When he first started selling food directly to consumers, he never used the word "organic," because it was "considered a bit weird, practiced by long-haired people with bare feet, who weren't sophisticated enough to get the techno-chemical thing straight."[44] However, Ableman started a successful Community Supported Agriculture (CSA) program, conducted many educational programs, and helped Fairview Gardens become the nonprofit Center for Urban Agriculture. Ableman later moved to British Columbia with his family and began farming on Salt Spring Island. One year, on a quest to find farms that were "helping to put a face back onto our food," he visited Coleman in Maine, Salatin in Virginia, and numerous other small growers.[45] Ableman believed that farmers possessed a sense of rootedness and a relationship to natural cycles that other Americans longed for.[46] He referred to growing and eating food as "sacred acts." These sentiments were similar to those of the voluminous homesteaders, small-scale farmers, and agrarian advocates for whom he has served as an exemplar in articulating the dogma of organic agriculture.

AGRICULTURAL NOSTALGIA:
SMALL FARMS, HOMESTEADERS, AND AGRI-TOURISTS

Organic homesteading and small-scale farming are akin to other manifestations of the organic movement in that they are largely personal acts. People who felt alienated by urban life and went off in search of sanity expected superior lives for themselves, not social upheaval. Collectively, though, homesteaders like Helen and Scott Nearing always believed that it was "not only a movement for individual betterment"; it denoted "social change and improvement as well."[47] Organic farmer Scott Chaskey had a similar philosophy; his Quail Hill Farm in New York was inspired by a joint desire among residents to encourage sound land stewardship. The organic CSA program started growing vegetables, berries, and apples for over two hundred families. It also supplied restaurants, food pantries, and a local school.[48] Chaskey recorded the yearlong challenges and rewards of his small farm in *This Common Ground: Seasons on an Organic Farm* (2005). In communicating his distaste for the obliterating effects of plows on land, Chaskey claimed to favor "the holistic approach to farming," which was a familiar agrarian mind-set.[49] Advancing comparable sentiments, small-farm advocate John Ikerd noted that consumers demanded organic food because "the philosophical roots of organics" were in "stewardship and community, in caring for the earth and its people."[50]

J. I. Rodale extended anticorporate impulses in defense of natural farming methods in *Pay Dirt*, and these have recurred in the organic movement. Heart-rending, nostalgic representations of farm life have abounded among those beguiled by agrarianism. In response, detractors have asserted that nostalgia for prototypical bucolic farms was untenable and inaccurate, demonstrating a yearning for a time and place that never existed. Organic food critic Thomas DeGregori has accused organic enthusiasts of having their heads in the clouds and of holding "antiscience views," romanticizing the past, and "imbuing the lifeways of prior times with an array of virtues that they simply did not have."[51] Organic farmers have commonly been stereotyped as backward and anachronistic for refusing to accept modern pesticides. More neutral observers have often designated organic agriculture as "the oldest form of agriculture on earth."[52] The organic approach, though, was both ancient and modern, seasoned and fresh. It was not merely neglectful farming that ignored bugs. Lynda Brown, a writer on organic living, has said that organic farming used "the best of the old with the best of the new."[53] Even organic farmers who claimed to employ "Nature" as their paradigm tapped into veteran as well as inventive techniques. More substances have been added to the organic canon each decade. Organic farming has blended tradition with innovation, simplicity with intricacy, and technophobia with avant-garde techniques. Prince Charles once said that he was "astonished at just how many other farmers still look at organic farming as some kind of drop-out option for superannuated hippies." He felt that organic farming combined "the traditional wisdom of sound rotational farming practice with much of the best that modern technology can provide."[54] Mary-Howell Martens, who ran a large-scale organic farm in western New York, concurred, saying that organic farming was "not a case of using nothing. Modern organic farming is a synthesis of traditional methods with cutting-edge science."[55] Rather than coveting a golden age of "arcadian bliss," organic farming has aimed for "gentler, more intelligent, more scientific methods."[56] As such, organic farming guides have united veneration for the past with novel recommendations for the future.

Journalist Samuel Fromartz noted that "critics often portray organic farming as a pre-industrial anachronism practiced by aging hippies, romantics, Luddites, and quacks who are incapable of feeding the world."[57] Conjectures about "hippies" spellbound by organic food have lingered but have also been amended. When Karl Schwenke published *Successful Small-Scale Farming: An Organic Approach* in 1979, he said, "An 'organic' farmer was synonymous with a 'lonely hippie troublemaker.'" But in his preface to the reprint edition in 1991, Schwenke noted with irony that, by then, the organic farmer was "classed somewhere between a high-priced elitist and an opportunist liar."[58] In *The Organic Garden Book* (1993), Geoff Hamilton described two camps: "those who think that organic methods of cultivation are the sole remaining way to save the planet and, at the other extreme, those who think that organic gardening is the refuge of bearded loonies in kaftans and sandals who live in grubby communes on brown rice and sunflower seeds."[59] Though he placed himself in neither faction, Hamilton admitted that organic gardening did have "more than its fair share of eccentrics."[60] Eccentricity is not easy to gauge, but when Jim Minick and his wife started an organic blueberry farm in Virginia in 1995 they soon found that they had become "prophets of a new religion"—the organic one—and that their farm was a "house of worship."[61] They sold berries at the farmers' market and encouraged people to visit the farm to pick their own, though most customers preferred to leave the back-bending labor of gathering to the farmers.

Despite unglamorous daily tasks, many people who took up organic gardening were unafraid of the hard work. Joan Dye Gussow, a nutritionist and self-proclaimed "suburban homesteader," retreated from Manhattan in the mid-1990s, hunting for sustainability and "vegetable self-reliance."[62] Along the banks of the Hudson River in upstate New York, she began producing enough of her family's vegetables to last throughout the year. She feasted on her own organic peppers, eggplant, zucchini, beans, onions, spinach, leeks, garlic, blueberries, currants, and raspberries. Like the Nearings, she referred to this as an experiment in relearning dependence on the land. Though Gussow described herself as "absurdly healthy," she was attracted to fresh, seasonal food primarily for environmental reasons. She shunned genetic engineering and long-distance food transportation. She advocated seasonal limitations on local food, saying that we should all "adjust our choices and our appetites to what Nature will provide in a given year."[63] Still, she did not

Flowers and vegetables at a farm stand (Photo courtesy of Colleen Freda Burt)

eschew hedonism, confirming that reeducating one's taste buds to crave seasonal food was "a delicious adventure."[64]

Homesteaders John Ivanko and Lisa Kivirist, also channeling the Nearings, moved from fast-track advertising agency jobs in downtown Chicago to a small farm in southwestern Wisconsin in 1996 as part of their own quest for the "good life." Armed with Rodale's *All-New Encyclopedia of Organic Gardening* and "a vision of living closer to the land," they grew organic crops, baked bread in a sun oven, bartered their chickens' multicolored eggs with neighbors, managed a bed and breakfast, and stayed connected to others through "Earth-friendly technology."[65] They promoted the advantages of this lifestyle through their "Rural Renaissance Network." Home gardening met about seventy percent of their food needs. Ivanko and Kivirist described how the farm enabled them to live "more ecologically, more independently, and with a greater sense of community."[66] Their language was akin to that of other organic homesteaders as they told of a "desire for living authentically," celebrated "a life simpler in design yet richer in meaning," and claimed that "Nature is our model."[67] The 5.5-acre farmstead began selling a seasonal selection of organic vegetables, fruits, and herbs directly to customers. The couple's motives for growing organically included health, safety, ecological diversity, soil conservation, and an emphasis on "respect and care."[68] Their farm and B&B, Inn Serendipity, were powered entirely by renewable wind and sun energy. The property included a solar-heated straw bale greenhouse for growing papayas, earned multiple awards for being a top eco-destination, and operated as a carbon-negative business and homestead.[69] Ivanko and Kivirist used the term "farmsteadtarian" to describe people like themselves who prepared "healthy meals with ingredients sourced as close as possible from a farm, ranch or artisan food purveyor." Eating crops from their own garden, grown in soil fertilized with their own compost and green manure, was a way to "reclaim sanity."[70]

Organic growers have often been creative agri-preneurs, innovating in order to make a living. Organic farmers Jennifer Megyes and Kyle Jones found when they began operating Fat Rooster Farm in 1998 that, to some fellow Vermonters, "'organic' meant a certain moral posturing, a zealousness, a lot of starry-eyed, pie-in-the-sky, highfalutin, tree-hugging, nature-loving, pious, finger-wagging rhetoric."[71] Other local farmers were skeptical of the barter system that the couple proposed in lieu of cash payments.[72] Still, customers were intrigued by their twenty-eight varieties of heirloom tomatoes, so these sold briskly at the farmers' market. Megyes and Jones then established a CSA program that raised herbs, vegetables, flowers, maple syrup, eggs, lamb, duck, and veal. Also successful with unique tomatoes was Keith Stewart, who left his small New York City apartment shortly after turning forty and became an organic farmer. *It's a Long Road to a Tomato* (2006) recounted Stewart's yearning "to live on a piece of land, closer to nature" as the proprietor of a farm in the Hudson Valley.[73] His diversified organic farm was "swimming against the current" of industrial agriculture, chemicals, and cheap food.[74] He believed that a small farm was a place where one could develop an "ecological consciousness" and live in some measure of "harmony with one's surroundings."[75] Still, Stewart purposefully disabused others of idyllic notions that the farm was a precious haven. Small-scale organic agriculture entailed taxing physical work. However, he worked full-time on his eighty-eight acres and regarded this as "enlivening."[76] He soon realized that being a small organic grower hawking vegetables and herbs to restaurants and directly to the public at New York City's Greenmarket had become fashionable and profitable. Just as small farms were depicted as constituents of the country's heritage, organic food itself seemed infused with integrity.

The actual and imagined charms of organic homesteading continued to lure converts. People interested in experiencing the small organic farm lifestyle have used the register managed by World-Wide Opportunities on Organic Farms (WWOOF), which has helped potential volunteers find farmers willing to provide room and board in exchange for makeshift labor. The Maine Organic Farmers and Gardeners Association (MOFGA) has organized the Common Ground Country Fair each year to educate fairgoers about the vibrancy of small farms and homesteads. MOFGA's Journeyperson Program has provided opportunities for prospective farmers to develop the requisite skills to farm independently. The Midwest Organic and Sustainable Education Service (MOSES) and Renewing the Countryside, both nonprofit organizations, have managed workshops and social networking activities for their Young Organic Stewards project to educate and empower emerging organic farmers. Agri-tourism, a branch of eco-tourism, became a buoyant business sector that included activities like harvest festivals, cheese making and handspinning workshops, and overnight stays on farms. Agri-tourism was well liked among those eager to bask in a farm setting but not quite ready to make a commitment. For example, a two-night stay in an "elegantly rustic" tent at Kinnikinnick Farm, a working organic farm in northern Illinois, cost about $565 per tent. Guests cooked their own soup or stew on an open fire for supper; during the day they could help harvest crops, gather eggs, or tend the garden.[77] At Weatherbury Farm in Pennsylvania, where the owners raised grass-fed beef and sheep and grew organic grains on one hundred acres, overnight guests were invited to help with chores and watch the farm's daily operations. Children received activity books about farming and could help bottle-feed baby animals. Most guests, though, spent their "haycation" days relaxing in the peaceful setting, not subjecting themselves to the toil of a farmer's life.[78]

Each gardener or homesteader has expended varying degrees of effort, and those without a green thumb have sought shortcuts. In *The Lazy Environmentalist* (2007), Josh Dorfman applauded that "these days you don't need tools and soil in order to grow organic herbs, flowers, fruits, and vegetables. All you need is a glass of water and a Garden-in-a-bag made by Potting Shed Creations. Pour some water and the accompanying seeds into the bag and presto! You've got yourself your very own organic garden."[79] The USDA-certified organic products from Potting Shed Creations were featured in magazines from *In Style, Martha Stewart Living, Bon Appétit,* and *Dwell* to *Prevention, Cooking with Paula Deen,* and *Country Living Gardener.* But if the Garden-in-a-Bag was even too much work, an Estonian company manufactured the Click & Grow flowerpot, which needed only batteries and water.

The sensors and microprocessor in the electronic planter helped seedlings grow without any other intervention.[80]

Back-to-the-landers not averse to perspiration frequently have had to rely on moonlighting in full- or part-time nonfarm work to supplement their incomes. At Trout Gulch, a modern-day commune in Aptos, California, the eighteen residents grew organic vegetables and fruit trees, used composting toilets, lived in tree houses and thatch huts, and ran a film production company called Encyclopedia Pictura. The members of this "hillside neighborhood" said that they valued "DIY skills, long term thinking, experiential education, and friendship," yet they managed to combine this traditional earthiness with state-of-the-art technology for their livelihood. Trout Gulch served as another template of organic homesteaders who were not "stuck in the past."[81] In fact, many organic farmers were consummate enviro-techies, using all manner of gadgets and gizmos to facilitate their undertakings. Alex Schimp, a nineteen-year-old programmer from a farming family, developed an iPhone and iPod Touch application to help certified organic farmers organize their crop records while out in the field. Farmers who had purchased the app, Seed to Harvest, said that one main advantage was that they did not need to take paper notes in the field and then enter them on a computer that night—it simplified everything.[82] Overall, most homesteaders and small farmers have persisted in placing a high premium on personal sovereignty, unpretentiousness, domestic tasks, and bonds with the natural world. These characteristics are comparable to those habitually attributed to small family farmers, particularly organic ones, who have been seen as environmental archetypes.

ENVIRONMENTALISM AND ORGANICS

Nature lovers may have cherished how organic farming supported the fungal dynamics underlying plant health, but it was hard to find billions of microscopic soil organisms endearing. A more charismatic cause could be found on a box of EnviroKidz Organic Amazon Frosted Flakes, where a kinkajou— an exotic rainforest mammal—dangled by its tail from a branch, while another kinkajou cozied up to a bowl of cereal placed amid the lush foliage. Boxes of organic Penguin Puffs, Orangutan-O's, Koala Crisp, and Gorilla Munch cereals also displayed appealing images of animals in natural settings. The products announced that 1 percent of sales were contributed to assist endangered species, habitat conservation, and environmental education for children. EnviroKidz donation recipients included the World Wildlife Fund, Amazon Conservation Team, Australian Koala Foundation, and Dian Fossey Gorilla Foundation. Nature's Path, the company that owned EnviroKidz, named environmental sustainability as one of its primary goals, and all the products it made were USDA-certified organic. Like many organic companies, EnviroKidz used the ideal of harmony with nature to market its food.

Environmental benefits have been part of the multifaceted network of rationales for growing and eating organic food. Studies have shown that consumers regarded organic products as safer, more natural, and less hurtful to the environment than those produced conventionally.[83] Some organic companies have used sustainably sourced ingredients or donated money to conservation leagues that protected endangered species, capitalizing on associations between organic farms and biodiversity.[84] Organic consumers have been willing to pay more for food grown in a way that they believed safeguarded the environment. The organic movement has considerably intersected with the broader environmental movement in American culture. For some families, saving the earth has seemed as painless as starting each day by pouring organic milk over a delicious bowl of organic Peanut Butter Panda Puffs.

Perceptions of nature as static, pure, and unsullied have long prevailed in the popular imagination. Just as J. I. Rodale reinforced clichés of organic agriculture as "natural" farming, descriptions of organic agriculture have reiterated that it was holistic, ecological, and environmentally scrupulous. The reverse portrayal was of conventional agriculture that was addicted to chemicals and hooked on fossil fuel. The organic philosophy viewed humans as "part of nature, not separate nor dominating or controlling it."[85] While industrial farming was thought to be a "reductionist" and confrontational line of attack, organic farming was said to use a "whole system" methodology.[86] Making compost was integral to this system of natural cycles, and some organic gardeners not only had a penchant for manure but even referred to composting as an "art form."[87] Rodale told his readers in 1945 that making compost was "an art rather than a science," and mechanically following rules would neither yield the best results nor be enjoyable.[88] Organic farmer Charles Dowding agreed that "compost heaps and bins are magical means of turning garden waste into something of great value."[89] Dowding began growing organic vegetables in the 1980s, using "simple, natural practices." The farmer, he said, should ignore chemical ideas and instead cultivate an approach "based on Life," and he thought that spreading good compost would encourage this respect for life.[90] While Dowding admitted that some unnatural conditions were required, because "nature does not do vegetable gardens," he still believed that he was gardening "the natural way."[91] Francis Blake's guide to organic farming also said that it aimed to be "in harmony rather than in conflict with natural systems."[92] Organic farming was a "holistic" philosophy of life, because it was "concerned with the wholeness, the interconnectedness of life."[93] Blake advised that an organic system, "striving to be in co-operation with nature," had to be suited to the conditions in which it operated.[94] Organic farms were supposed to be balanced, ecologically diverse, and mindful of their bioregions.

Like many organic farmers, the authors of *Taste Life! The Organic Choice* (1998) stressed that the organic model was "an integrative world view" that replaced domination with cooperation.[95] A study in 1998 concluded that organic producers organized their farms and entire lifestyles around nature. It said that the organic farmers meticulously worked with nature to manage ecosystems, while the conventional farmers merely turned out commodities.[96] Such a blanket assessment could certainly be challenged, since many nonorganic farmers have felt that they, too, were in touch with nature. Bob Flowerdew's *The Organic Gardening Bible* (1998) acknowledged that organic gardening necessitated cooperating with nature but was also "enticing her." This was not accomplished by releasing the reins and "letting nature have her way." Rather, "we must guide and channel her."[97] This guidance, though, did not preclude "harmony." Flowerdew blamed the chemical mode for displacing the "harmony and closeness to nature" of "traditional" gardeners and farmers during the last century.[98] Organic gardening was more sustainable, ecologically sound, and environmentally benign than the "artificial regime." To obtain maximum nutrition from a small space, he said that home gardeners should concentrate on organic carrots, spinach, chard, peas, onions, potatoes, broccoli, Brussels sprouts, and kale. Instead of using harmful pesticides as a crutch, Flowerdew said that organic gardeners could apply "wit and cunning" to outsmart pests and diseases.[99] Organic farmers have tried to be shrewd while still epitomizing symbiosis.

In *Maria Rodale's Organic Gardening: Your Seasonal Companion to Creating a Beautiful and Delicious Garden* (1998), Maria Rodale described how "delightful" and "fun" organic gardening could be. She assured readers that "you can create the garden of your dreams without resorting to anything toxic or ugly."[100] She dedicated the book to her grandfather, J. I., and father,

Robert. Maria Rodale recalled a conversation with Bob Hofstetter, who began gardening for the Rodale Organic Farm in 1970. He told her that J. I. Rodale "wanted to see organic farming as part of mainstream agriculture. He wanted to see this as part of society." Maria said that her grandfather taught her "to see gardening organically as a sacred responsibility."[101] She explained that, more than anything else, compost was identified with organic gardening and was "partly responsible for giving organic gardening its questionable and 'icky' reputation."[102] However, the Rodale Organic Method was committed to the use of compost, which was easy and fundamental to providing soil with excellent nutrients.[103] The purpose of Maria's book was to show readers how to "make the world a better place by creating an organic Eden in your own backyard."[104] Maria Rodale encouraged the general public to explore eco-minded organic avenues.

Boosters of small organic farms have long insisted on their intrinsic superiority to gargantuan, industrial outfits. The bifurcation between small-scale/artisanal/fecund and large-scale/industrial/desolate has been predicated on assumptions that organic was always good and conventional was always bad. Evoking this populist sentiment, organic farmer Raoul Adamchak contrasted the goal of conventional farming ("high yields and inexpensive food") to the goal of organic farming ("health of the soil, the crop, the farmer, the environment, and the consumer").[105] This ironclad distinction could be problematic, though, particularly since farms that sparingly used nonorganic inputs might still be environmentally friendly, while a "corporate industrialized organic farm" might not be.[106] The boundaries between conventional and organic farming have constantly been in flux, and as growers converted from one method to another, they did not necessarily experience an upheaval in their personal or political stance. Within the organic movement, there was a continuum of approaches. Just as organic farming operations have varied in size, some organic practitioners were rigid purists, while others were more flexible.[107]

Studies have found that organic farmers were motivated by multifarious reasons, including apprehension about chemicals in food, personal health, price premiums, and concern for the soil.[108] Aspirations to get in tune with nature were not driving all organic farmers, although some stalwart organicists refused to admit that small organic family farmers might have crass motives too. *Organic Living* (2000) author Lynda Brown stated that organic farmers worked "with nature rather than against it" and shared "the same basic holistic aims and beliefs, based on respect for all living organisms."[109]

The simple message of the "organic way," she said, was to "respect nature, and nature will be your best friend." Brown referred to organic growers as "guardians of the environment." It was their partiality for "cooperation at all levels, rather than destruction or domination," that made the most sense.[110] Similarly, the authors of *Living Organic* (2001) likened the organic gardener to a holistic therapist, working "alongside nature rather than in opposition to it."[111] Organic growers were said to be punctilious custodians of the earth, wreaking far less havoc on the environment than conventional farmers.

The Food and Agriculture Organization of the United Nations World Health Organization stated that organic production systems were aimed at "achieving optimal agro-ecosystems" that were "socially, ecologically and economically sustainable."[112] Likewise, the USDA Organic seal was a declaration about an agricultural system meant to enhance "ecological balance." The National Organic Standards defined organic agriculture as a production system that responded to "site-specific conditions by integrating cultural, biological, and mechanical practices that foster cycling of resources, promote ecological balance, and conserve biodiversity."[113] Key production rules that certified organic producers had to follow included "abstaining from use of certain crop chemicals and animal drugs," using "ecologically based pest and nutrient management," and following a sustainable organic system plan.[114] The final organic legislation emphasized ecological caretaking and agricultural diversity more than human health, social justice, or living wages for farmworkers. Organic farming was perceived as a way of using nature prudently, relying on self-regulating biological processes. In *Eat More Dirt* (2003), organic landscaper Ellen Sandbeck scorned chemical fertilizers as "heroin for plants," creating "a quick rush, then a sudden drop into weakness and dependency." On the other hand, organic fertilizer was "a food, not a drug."[115] Also using the drug theme, the Rodale Institute offered workshops such as Help Your Garden Kick Its Chemical Dependency—a 12 Step Program.[116] Organic farmers were often thought to be performing a true "labor of love," not browbeating the earth into submission.

The definition of organic agriculture has always been contested terrain. Despite the binary of industrial-conventional-artificial agriculture and sustainable-alternative-natural agriculture in popular discourse, most farms have fallen somewhere in between these ends of the spectrum. A farm need not be small to exemplify organic ideals. A study of organic farmers in 2004 demonstrated no significant differences in the attitudes of large broad-acre farmers as opposed to small horticultural farmers with respect to motivations for organic farming. The study authors argued that growth in the number of organic farms had *not* deradicalized the organic industry, since the values propelling organic farmers were shared equally by long-standing and newer members of the business.[117] Notwithstanding size or tenure, there were some conjoint characteristics among organic farmers. *The Gaia Book of Organic Gardening* (2005) admitted that "organic gardeners go on a lot about compost," because it was clearly the best organic matter for soil.[118] Though composting was a simple process, it seemed "like magic."[119] The book advised organic gardeners to "make peace not war,"[120] harness natural processes, and "learn to love your weeds," because "your garden is not a battleground."[121] Longtime organic farmer Adrian Myers, who ran an extensive garden and orchard, also believed that organic agriculture did not attempt to battle nature. At the heart of the organic tack was the "view of Nature as self-organizing, self-sustaining, self-regenerating and self-regulating."[122] Myers argued in *Organic Futures: The Case for Organic Farming* (2005) that organic husbandry was the standard in terms of sustainability, because conventional agriculture was fundamentally flawed.[123] One advantage of organic production was that it required less fossil energy per unit of food produced. It followed, then, that importing organic food when it could easily be grown locally violated "the whole ethos of organic and sustainable farming."[124] Myers, like many organic farmers, felt that nature was the supreme model for humans.

Consumer guides have echoed the sentiments of organic farmers themselves. *The Organic Food Guide* (2004) said that "balance and prevention" were central to the philosophy of organic farming.[125] Organic farmers, it explained, "don't believe in conquering nature; rather, they strive to coexist with it."[126] *The Organic Food Handbook* (2006) asserted that organic farmers worked more closely with nature than anyone else. They cultivated "a down-to-earth sensibility along with a spiritual perspective about nature's greater intelligence."[127] *The Organic Cook's Bible* (2006) also made it clear that "nature's way" of growing vegetables was toxin-free. Rather, when your vegetables were grown organically, it was a weighty announcement: "you are assured that your food is wholesome, that you are supporting an environmentally conscious farmer, that you are helping protect all the creatures that make up the farm's ecosystem, and that you are protecting the land itself through wise and sustainable practices."[128] The Sustainable Agriculture Network (SAN) asserted in a report in 2007 that "switching to organic farming requires a major philosophical shift."[129] While acknowledging that many farmers converted to organic production for economic reasons, SAN stated that profit was rarely the sole argument for farming organically. Organic farmers used nature as a model for the agricultural system and considered the farm as an "integrated entity, with all parts interconnected." Organic farms included crop rotations, cover crops, green and animal manures, and biological controls, instead of synthetic pesticides and fertilizers.[130] Along the same lines, the authors of *Grow Organic* (2007) lamented that humans had lost the ability to "garden in harmony with Mother Nature, instead of fighting her." They prescribed organic gardening as the best way to "reconnect with our gardening roots," by using "nature's arsenal" rather than the quick chemical fix.[131] They also confirmed that "Mother Nature" was an ally, so properly managed organic gardens required very little human interference.

Wendy Johnson, who gardened organically at the San Francisco Zen Center's Green Gulch Farm, said that she did so because organic gardening was rooted in "local stewardship," encouraged protection of land and water resources, worked "in harmony with natural ecosystems to sustain diversity," and developed "real health in the garden and in the wider community."[132] Comparably, an article in *O, the Oprah Magazine*, in 2009 persuaded readers that vegetable gardening at home was not backbreaking labor and did not upset the "balance of nature." The author, avid gardener Michele Owens, accentuated that it was "easy to grow a flood of beautiful food" and noted that gardeners were not bullying nature: "Push a seed into the earth and it wants to grow."[133] Owens, too, called the process of composting "magical," just as J. I. Rodale and Albert Howard had. Betty Louise, talk radio host and organic farming fan, affirmed that an organic life was one that flowed with nature, allowing people to "get in tune with the rhythms of Mother Earth."[134] Another straightforward summary of these sentiments came from Seeds of Change, advertising its organic seeds as ones that would sprout "deliciously good food that's good for the planet too." As organic farmers have aligned themselves with environmental well-being, they have envisioned organic gardens as part of the ecosystem, almost cultivating themselves, free of human wrangling.

SAVING WILDLIFE OR (NOT) FEEDING THE WORLD?

For farmers motivated by consideration for the environment, a major argument on behalf of the organic method was that it provided benefits like enhanced air, water, and soil quality.[135] Fewer chemicals ended up in rivers and streams when farmers did not use toxic pesticides. Some studies showed that organic fertilizers enriched soil fertility and crop quality.[136] Others found that organic farms increased biodiversity by using less pesticide and incorporating wildlife-friendly practices.[137] Organic farms tended to nurture more plant and animal species than conventional farms.[138] However, numerous groups have challenged the claims that organic production methods are more salubrious for the environment.[139] Both sides of the dispute have produced compelling evidence. Many controversies over substantiation—or the lack thereof—have raged. The Natural Resources Defense Council stated unequivocally that organic food was better for the environment, because it eliminated the massive quantities of venomous pesticides and fertilizers used in conventional farming.[140] Meanwhile, other experts demonstrated that organic farming was *not* always environmentally superior. This polarized clash over organic agriculture's ecological integrity has been paramount to its legitimacy. The quest for tangible proof of environmental benefits has affected the degree to which the organic movement has obtained acceptance and approbation.

Some detractors have viewed the biggest cost of organic farming as its lack of productivity; using more land for cultivation required encroaching on wildlife habitat. Some also said that relying on plows in place of herbicides increased soil erosion.[141] Critical assessments have pointed out that, if organic farms were less productive and ate up more land, they would leave less collective wilderness. Soil scientist Norman Adams asserted that "lower-yielding organic farming methods take up more land for food production and put yet more pressure on dwindling wildlife habitats."[142] An article in *Nature* magazine in 2001 contended that organic agriculture used land inefficiently, leading to decreased yields. The author also argued that organic farmers caused damage to nesting birds, worms, and invertebrates because of frequent mechanical weeding. Conventional agriculture, on the other hand, was more environmentally friendly and could match organic performance while using only 50 to 70 percent of the farmland.[143] Some experts have predicted that insufficient yields from organic farming would contribute to world hunger; others have countered that the greatest cause of world hunger was inefficient distribution, not lack of food. Developmental economist Thomas DeGregori stated in 2004 that the issue of "how we will feed nine billion people in less than half a century from now" could not be seriously addressed by those who sought "refuge from modernity" in organic food.[144] The question of world hunger has long been an unacknowledged question when considering organic farming's feasibility.

In contrast to the antiorganic doomsayers, journalist Christopher Cook played on Frances Moore Lappé's legacy with his *Diet for a Dead Planet* (2004), which was full of dire warnings about pesticides, ecological degradation, and the "toxic cornucopia of poison-laminated harvests."[145] He cautioned that "we are steadily farming and eating our way to oblivion."[146] The solution, he said, was a subsidy system that would promote "diversified, small-scale organic farming" and expand food security "to make healthy and sustainable food economically viable."[147] Though Cook had great hope for the "organic revolution," he hesitated in giving it his full support, both because large corporations had become involved and because organic foods were chiefly "pricey boutique items."[148] Anna Lappé, the daughter of Frances Moore Lappé, had a more buoyant tone about organics in *Grub: Ideas for an Urban Organic Kitchen* (2006). The younger Lappé discussed how, in the past thirty years, organic food had "moved out of the patchouli-scented aisles of food co-ops" and into "the Wal-Marts, Costcos, and Sam's Clubs of the new millennium." Organic food had become "haute cuisine," and vegetarianism, once "more associated with yurt dwellers than Golden Arches connoisseurs," had become "pedestrian."[149] The environmental repercussions of dietary preferences, however, had not diminished. Like her mother, the younger Lappé advised that choosing wholesome food would significantly improve the health of humans, the planet, farmers, and farmworkers, all at once.[150] Rodale Institute CEO Timothy LaSalle went even further in an interview in 2008 with Anna Lappé, saying that organic farming could actually reduce global warming. LaSalle argued, "Those who say we can't feed the world with organic farming are perpetuating a myth of falsity. With the onset of peak oil, we will not be able to feed the planet with conventional chemical-based agriculture." He also termed organic farmers "climate change heroes," because they took carbon out of the air by nourishing the biology of the soil.[151] LaSalle proposed that farmers be paid for their "positive, soil-carbon impact" instead of for commodity crop yields.[152] He said that treating farmland with respect and relying on renewable resources instead of external inputs could be a way out of ecological crises.

On the other hand, Dennis T. Avery, a vocal opponent of organic farming, denounced organic farming as an "environmental disaster." If adopted as a global food production system, he said, it could force an additional five to ten million square miles of wild land to be plowed. Avery was adamant that the careful use of farm chemicals to minimize crop losses was more beneficial for wildlife populations. He blamed naïve fears of chemicals and technology, along with "faith in going back to nature," for blinding those infatuated with organic farming to the positive effects of high-yield agriculture. Organic farming, he said, was "an imminent danger to the world's wildlife and a hazard to the health of its own consumers."[153] Alex A. Avery elaborated on his father's arguments in *The Truth about Organic Foods* (2006), which displayed organic farming as a great threat to natural ecosystems and biodiversity. Both members of the father-son Avery team were listed as "Agriculture/Biotechnology Experts" at the Hudson Institute, a "nonpartisan" think tank that received funding from agribusiness giants and biotechnology lobby groups (for example, Monsanto and DuPont).[154] Their research may not have been entirely nonpartisan, but it was echoed by other sources. The younger Avery hailed herbicide-tolerant crops developed through biotechnology as far more cost-effective and eco-friendly than organic farming.[155] The USDA and the International Federation of Organic Agriculture Movements (IFOAM) firmly excluded genetically modified organisms from the definition of organic agriculture. However, *Tomorrow's Table* (2008), written jointly by a plant genetic scientist and an organic farmer, posed the unusual suggestion that combining organic farming with the judicious use of GE was the "key to helping feed the growing population in an ecologically balanced manner."[156] The authors argued that integrating GE plants into organic farming systems would protect the environment and help mitigate crop losses to disease.

The land-use requirements of organic agricultural techniques have been a major point of contention. There has been an ongoing need for more independent analyses of organic farming and gardening. The National Parks Foundation, the Environmental Protection Agency (EPA), and SafeLawns .org sponsored one venture in 2007 designed to determine whether a healthier, hardier lawn would germinate from toxic-free care. The two-year project maintained a four-acre section of the National Mall organically. Compost and mulch were applied to the soil, and the area was later reopened to public foot traffic so it could be tested by daily use. Environmental coalitions hoped that assessments of the organic renovation could prove that chemical fertilizers and pesticides were not necessary to create resilient lawns. Another study based on experimental plots at Iowa State University deduced after nine years that organic crop production systems did show greater yields, profitability, and soil quality over conventional ones. The most salient differences were in soil and water quality. The organic plots reduced soil runoff and cycled nutrients more efficiently. The study was touted as the "largest randomized, replicated comparison of organic and conventional crops in the nation."[157] Researchers at the University of Michigan indicated in 2007 that organic farming could double or triple yields in developing countries. In industrialized nations, yields were nearly equal on organic and conventional farms. One of the Michigan study's principal investigators asserted that the fears of organic agriculture causing people to starve were "ridiculous." The findings revealed that organic farming was "less environmentally harmful" yet could "potentially produce more than enough food."[158]

Analogously, the Wisconsin Integrated Cropping Systems Trials concluded in 2008 that organic corn-soybean systems were 90 percent as productive as nearby conventional farms, while organic forage crop yields were actually the same as conventional yields.[159] Science writer Rob Johnston spoke to many of these results in his exposé "Great Organic Myths," claiming that a study of organic tomatoes showed that they used twice the energy even though their yield was only 75 percent that of conventional tomato crops. Addressing sustainability, he pointed out that organic potatoes may use less energy for fertilizer production, but they used more fossil fuel for plowing. He explained that organic dairy production was a major source of greenhouse gas emissions for several reasons, such as that organically reared cows burped "twice as much methane as conventionally reared cattle." Johnston cited studies showing that organic milk required more land for production and contributed more to acid rain. He also tried to shatter the false sense of security that some people felt in assuming that organic farmers did not use any pesticides; in truth, "organic" pesticides could be safety hazards too.[160]

When profiling organic cherry farmers, writer Katherine Gustafson was surprised to learn that some used fermented bacteria, an organic pesticide made by Dow Chemical. This flew in the face of the misconception she had that organic meant "you just sprinkle your happy wishes over your fields and watch protective rainbows of joy appear over each of your tender seedlings."[161] In fact, some pesticides approved for use on organic crops might have been more detrimental than synthetic chemicals. Potentially hazardous bacteria in organic fertilizers have also been a cause for concern, compared to government-monitored conventional pesticides that might have been safer.[162] Horticultural scientist Jeff Gillman pointed out that certain synthetic herbicides, when used properly, were safe for the environment while not all "natural" inputs were guaranteed to be desirable. Gillman stated that organic growing was usually more beneficial for the earth, but the permitted practices were not risk-free.[163] The National Organic Standards Board (NOSB) provided a list of allowed and prohibited substances that applied to organic food production. Ingredients like nonorganic baking soda were permitted in organic bread. Monosodium glutamate (a flavoring) and carrageenan (a seaweed for thickening) were allowed in organic products, which was offensive to some organic foodies. Products like iron phosphate slug and snail baits were sanctioned for organic gardening. Most synthetic substances were prohibited from organic products, while nonsynthetic ones were usually allowed, but there were exceptions. The NOSB had the authority to add or remove materials from the national list. Public policy sentinel Jim Hightower was irate when he saw that the NOSB's list of allowable nonorganic ingredients had grown from 77 in 2002 to 245 in 2009.[164] The leeway was largely due to lobbying by corporate behemoths like General Mills, Dean Foods, Campbell's Soup, Whole Foods Market, and Earthbound Farm. Again, the exalted criterion for "organic" seemed to be waning.

Amid all the abstruse research, the quarrel persisted between half-truths and hazy corroboration. Executives from the CropLife Association wrote to Michelle Obama in 2009, commending her on "recognizing the importance of agriculture in America" by starting a White House organic garden; however, they encouraged her to consider "crop protection technologies." The letter respectfully pointed out the value of conventional agriculture for "feeding the ever-increasing population" and ensuring a "safe and economical food supply."[165] Without specifically mentioning the "O" word, the letter implied that organic farming lacked practicality. A chief executive of the National Corn Growers Association, Rick Tolman, told the *New York Times* in 2009 that his organization felt that there was "a place for organic" but did not reckon that humans could "feed ourselves and the world" that way.[166] Advocates of conventional agriculture continued to verbalize this position. *Nature* published a new analysis of the existing science in 2012, stating that chemical fertilizers were necessary in agriculture to produce "the bulk of the globe's diet." According to the study's lead author, organic yields were "significantly lower" for most crops.[167] *Time* magazine's Ecocentric blog sided with the study by stating that "organic farming may not be as good for the planet as we think" and suggested that GE crops might be the utmost solution.[168] An organic activist volleyed back, pointing out that "yield is not the same as efficiency." Lower chemical input costs might offset "modest yield penalties" on organic farms, and the "environmentally sound production practices" of organic agriculture would always have advantages.[169] The proprietors of a thirteen-hundred-acre legume and grain farm added fodder to the discussion by reporting that, after converting from synthetic pesticide and herbicide inputs to organic methods, they did *not* experience a decrease in yields. Rather, they were able to maximize yields *and* profits while "refocusing their farming practices on long-term responsibility."[170] A piece in the *Atlantic* said that all the examples and counterexamples missed the point: "To assume that the best farming practice is the one that produces the highest yield is like observing that a Lamborghini outraces a bicycle, and thus should be the world's only vehicle." Economic, social, and environmental factors all deserved consideration.[171] There was no end in sight to the scientific and philosophical wrangling on this divisive issue.

Since the 1930s, US federal farm policy has combined price supports with supply management. The goal of government intervention has been to provide farm income assistance.[172] The organic movement has rarely had commanding allies in the political realm; the USDA itself was often an adversary that seemed to be in collusion with the agribusiness and biotech industry. Organic farmers, for their part, did not demand incentives for being eco-friendly. The organic movement never stipulated that chemical-based agriculture ought to pay for externalities—for example, pollution, soil erosion, and resource extraction—that society at large absorbed. Geographer Leslie Duram has pointed out that organic farms should not be held to a higher standard of "ecological integrity and social change" than other farms, unless given adequate monetary support. She said that organic farmers could not be expected to "step in and rescue our rural natural resources, save the family farm, and improve social relationships within agriculture."[173] Such expectations would certainly be unfair and make organic farming decrees even more tedious. However, the director of the Rodale Research Center once told Congress that, although organic farming could solve many problems, "we are not asking to transform U.S. agriculture into an organic model."[174] By not asking for a complete overhaul, organic leaders may have seemed too nonchalant and may have abetted their own disenfranchisement.

Farm policies have long mandated that farmers squeeze as much as possible from the soil, thereby spurring encroachment on environmentally sensitive lands, flood-prone areas, and wildlife habitat.[175] Farm and food policies have upheld the overproduction of certain crops and have generated artificially low prices. US farm bills have allocated eight times more in subsidies for commodity soybeans, corn, rice, wheat, and cotton than what was given for edible fruits, nuts, and vegetables.[176] Corn crops grown for animal feed, ethanol, and high-fructose corn syrup have received billions in cash entitlements. Subsidy benefits have flowed disproportionately to colossal farms, funding consolidation in growing, food processing, and transportation.[177] Economic incentives for maximum per-acre yield have often impeded the survival of small and moderate farms. Financial backing slanted toward the high production of commodity and biotech crops on maximum acreage has not favored farms growing organic produce. Conventional food prices have not reflected the unmeasured cost of the toll that pesticides and toxins take on humans and land. Instead of keeping the cost of natural resources artificially low through subsidies, the government could have encouraged conservation and conscientious production. A shift in farm policy priorities could have included inducements to reward organic farming systems and promote ecological management. Pesticides and chemical fertilizers could have been taxed more heavily than friendlier organic inputs. Fees for organic certification could have been defrayed or even refunded. Government policies could have catalyzed sustainable agriculture by providing "green payments" as reparations to organic farmers who were providing civic goods (such as improving soil quality over time). Some USDA conservation programs have compensated farmers for being good wardens of the land, but organic practitioners have said these were perfunctory. Attempts to implement innovative organic alternatives have too often been met with insouciance. A formidable program of institutional aid for organic farmers could have translated into more organic farmland.

ORGANIC, LOCAL, VEGETARIAN, AND OTHER ECO-LABELS

For environmentalists, the fact that organic foods transported long distances have left footprints on nature as large their conventional counterparts has been problematic. As a corollary to the environmental question, the debate over whether organic or local fare was more sustainable has been confounding. Predilections for "local" and "organic" food have often gone hand in hand, but consumers seeking eco-credibility were uncertain about which of the two they should lean toward. In terms of traceability, "USDA Organic" carried a precise definition, but "local food" was a cloudy term. Assessments of "food miles" became common for comparisons. "Locavores" paid homage to local food as an enriching way to build a sense of community because it reconnects growers and eaters who felt alienated in the global food infrastructure. Many aimed to eat mindfully, with knowing the farm from which their food came. Organic farmer Frederick Kirschenmann, a proponent of producing and acquiring organic food locally, placed food at "the heart of any community," because people in a regional "foodshed" were "much more connected to their food source."[178] As locavores investigated the derivation of their food, many took stabs at home gardening, and some delved into homesteading themselves.

The locavore movement was highlighted in *Coming Home to Eat* (2002), in which ethnobotanist Gary Paul Nabhan documented a year of eating locally (defined as obtaining food within a 250-mile radius of his Arizona home). He combined home gardening and foraging with purchases from the vicinity. While castigating biotechnology, he celebrated the "sensual plea-sure of food."[179] Nabhan concluded that native foods were healthy, good for the land, and "good for our souls."[180] Inspired by this passion, more than one thousand locavores pledged in 2005 to eat only products from within 100 miles of their home. They inaugurated Locavores.com to discuss their "100-mile diet" endeavors. One cover of *Ode* magazine that year proclaimed that "Local Is the New Organic." Bloggers who wanted to attempt local eat-ing launched their own site, EatLocalChallenge.com, to sway others; people could vow to eat from a 100-, 150-, or 250-mile radius. Also related was the "eco-gastronomic" Slow Food organization, which rejected "fast life" and in-sisted that food should be "good, clean, and fair." According to some surveys, 80 to 90 percent of American consumers preferred buying food from small, local farms to any other options, including organics.[181] Local food became a riveting issue, either paired with organic food advocacy or contrasted to it.

Media sources fluctuated in their advice on navigating the culinary pal-ette. The Sierra Club addressed the rift between organic and local in a short film, *The True Cost of Food* (2005). It saluted organic farms for enriching the soil with natural ingredients, not pollutants. However, it said that organic farms that shipped their food around the world negated the idea of sustain-ability. The film advised consumers to get to know the farmer growing their food so as to feel comfortable with the choices they made. A Sierra Club list in 2006 on how to eat responsibly placed "buy organic" near the top, because organic farmers were generally better guardians of the environment. The caveat, though, was that consumers should be wary of "multinational food conglomerates moving into organics," since their products traveled long distances. The list also included advice to "support local farmers," "eschew meat-centered meals," and "cut back on processed, packaged foods."[182] For those troubled about the overuse of fossil fuels, organic black bean enchiladas packaged in California and shipped to Delaware in a refrigerated truck missed the point. Cindy Burke's *To Buy or Not to Buy Organic* (2007) noted that "organics are actually starting to smell like yesterday's news, while local, sustainable food is becoming the fresh choice for ethical eaters."[183] Local food has gained fans, and the *New Oxford American Dictionary* chose "locavore" as its 2007 word of the year. In March of that year, *Time* featured the headline "Forget Organic. Eat Local" on its cover, with a photo of an apple. In the accompanying story, author John Cloud weighed the decision between an organic apple from faraway California and a nonorganic one from his home state. While he preferred a locally grown organic apple, Cloud contended that "for food purists, 'local' is the new 'organic,' the new ideal that promises healthier bodies and a healthier planet."[184] In the end, when posed as an either-or choice, he came down in the camp of local food, because it made him "feel more rooted," it tasted better, and it seemed safer.[185] In a survey in 2008 by the National Restaurant Association, 81 percent of chefs named locally grown produce as a "hot" trend, while only 75 percent named organic produce.[186] Farm-to-table menus gained momentum as restaurants made an effort to procure ingredients nearby.

A wave of published accounts about other experiments to survive on local food included Barbara Kingsolver's *Animal, Vegetable, Miracle: A Year of Food Life* (2007); Alisa Smith and J. B. MacKinnon's *Plenty: One Man, One Woman, and a Raucous Year of Eating Locally* (2007); and Doug Fine's *Farewell, My Subaru: An Epic Adventure in Local Living* (2008). The staff of *Sunset* magazine began blogging about their "One Block Diet" project in 2008, setting out to raise everything they needed for a series of seasonal feasts. They tried raising chickens, keeping bees, pressing grapes, and brewing beer at home.[187] Erin Byers Murray and her husband gave a less gourmet version of local eating a shot, recording it all in *Body + Soul*. They felt more physically and ecologically pure after a month of shopping at the farmers' market. Though they did succumb to the lure of popsicles, potato chips, and out-of-season produce again when the trial was over, Murray said that they had trained themselves to "always look for local, pesticide-free options before buying anything else."[188] Amy Cotler also conjured up tips on the basics of eating locally in *The Locavore Way: Discover and Enjoy the Pleasures of Locally Grown Food* (2009).

Leda Meredith was already spending extra money to buy organic and decided to go further, devoting one year to eating locally (which she defined as within a 250-mile radius of her Brooklyn home). Meredith then wrote *The*

Locavore's Handbook: The Busy Person's Guide to Eating Local on a Budget (2010), which promised to help other people reclaim their food, understand their own feeding rhythms, and palliate their environmental impact. She also discussed "numerous attempts" by conventional agricultural corporations to "discredit the local and organic food movement." Although "the old guard" was mighty, Meredith assured readers that "small changes" did make a difference.[189] Choosing to make big changes and grow her own food, Annie Spiegelman began her about-face from "a girl raised and hardened on the streets of New York City" into a California master gardener with "lots of trial and error and a plethora of dead plants."[190] A decade later, she was writing an organic gardening column for the *Pacific Sun* newspaper and sharing her environmentally friendly horticulture tips in *Talking Dirt: The Dirt Diva's Down-to-Earth Guide to Organic Gardening* (2010). Spiegelman characterized true organic gardening, with no need for synthetic fertilizers or petrochemicals, as a way to beat "the Man." The "Dirt Diva" advised novices to peek at *Organic Gardening* magazine for inspiration and said that they would be "working alongside Mother Nature, not against her" if they created sustainable gardens.[191] She, like many other enthusiasts, saw the goals of the organic and local food movements as intertwined. Katherine Gustafson's *Locavore U.S.A.: How a Local-Food Economy Is Changing One Community* (2012) explained that nearly all member-farmers of the Western Montana Growers Co-Operative were certified organic by the USDA, but some used the alternative organic "Montana Homegrown" classification, which melded a local perspective with organic standards.[192]

Critics have said that local foodists were mistaken in grandiose claims about being at the pinnacle of dietary sustainability. A *Boston Globe Magazine* article in 2009 averred that local food was "not greener food," in part because shipping was only "a small portion of the total carbon footprint of any foodstuff." Megafarms were more efficient and less resource-intensive, so the "warm and fuzzy" delusion of saving the world with local food was misguided.[193] Not all calculations of food miles have taken the energy used to produce and harvest food, such as with farm machinery or by hand, into consideration. Some studies have found weak verification for the diminished environmental impacts of local food. Due to varying agricultural effects in different parts of the world, global sourcing could be a superior environmental option for particular foods.[194] Supermarkets and food processors could be more discriminating about the source of their goods, taking account of fluctuating environmental burdens.[195] There have been many complicating factors in determining how to make environmental improvements in one's diet, pointing toward a case-by-case assessment as the best approach.

This context sensitivity also applied to the environmental impact of packaging, processing, shipping, refrigeration, and cooking. Economies of scale have affected the efficiency of shipping products from farms to stores. For individuals, transporting food home, storing it, and cooking it could be consequential. Few consumers who diligently shopped at the farmers' market and remembered to bring their reusable bags considered that the decision to boil or roast their organic baby purple potatoes was another weighty decision. Studies have suggested that, for certain foods, the ecological setbacks from car-based shopping and ensuing methods of home cooking were greater than those derived from transport. Some provisions have required high energy usage to prepare, giving them a bigger environmental "cookprint." Large proportions of grocery products have been wasted in the home, and every pound of wasted food that enters a landfill gives rise to greenhouse gases.[196] Lundberg Family Farms has sold individual microwaveable portions of organic short grain brown rice, which obviously used far more packaging than bulk bags of conventional rice. An economic geographer and policy analyst husband-wife team cowrote *The Locavore's Dilemma: In Praise of the 10,000 Mile Diet* (2012), arguing that local food was an imprudent marketing fad. The provocative book called food miles a "worthless measure" and "misleading distraction" when assessing the overall environmental impact of food production. The authors reckoned that consumers' own transportation choices and food waste were far more relevant. They felt that the efficient modern food supply chain was the most economical and sustainable system.[197] They said that locavores shooting down "modernity" and threatening rebellion against agribusiness were extremists, a "menace" to be viewed with "conspiratorial alarm."[198] A definitive answer to the eco-shopping riddle has not yet been supplied. Still, most locavores and organicists have maintained that their food preferences are good for the planet.

Organic food and local food are more paramours than adversaries, but they are not the only potentially "righteous" options in the ecological Catch-22. Several studies have indicated that consumers could help the environment most by simply eating less meat.[199] Meat products have had the greatest environmental impact of any foods, followed by dairy products.[200] Studies have showed that legumes are "a more energy-efficient way of providing edible protein than red meat."[201] Overall, animal protein sources are

Nearly organic beef (Photo courtesy of Colleen Freda Burt)

more detrimental to the environment than vegetable proteins. Carnivorous consumers may find that opting for organic instead of conventional meat helped alleviate their eco-remorse. Once nominally associated with vegetarian diets, the organic food movement began promoting organic meat as an environmentally friendly surrogate for feedlot meat. The farmer-owned Organic Prairie co-operative plugged its "Healthful, Wholesome & Humanely Raised Organic beef, pork, chicken & turkey," saying its "ecologically efficient" method of pasture-based feeding meant "less fossil-fuel consumption, less erosion, less air and water pollution and greater soil fertility." Organic Prairie told potential customers that its organic production standards reflected the brand's "deep convictions in our role as stewards of the earth."[202] Applegate Farms, whose organic meats were widely sold in supermarkets, pledged that its animals received "space, fresh air, and a healthy diet"—not hormones, antibiotics, or artificial growth promoters. Organic practices, according to Applegate Farms, "preserve the environment."[203] This "sustainable meat" rhetoric elided the extent to which the act of raising *all* domesticated animals required production practices that were more wasteful than those for plant-based food. Peter Singer, professor of bioethics and animal rights advocate, has argued that meat-eating Americans could reduce their personal contribution to global warming more effectively by switching to a vegan diet than by swapping their family car for a fuel-efficient hybrid.[204] In *The Way We Eat: Why Our Food Choices Matter* (2006), Singer and Jim Mason argued that, despite the availability of organically produced animal products, the vegan diet was still "far more environmentally-friendly than the standard American diet."[205] The international Vegan Organic Network promoted plant-based "veganic agriculture" as a way to protect animals, improve soil life, and reduce farming's ecological footprint. This was viewed by some as the ultimate organic technique. Farms identified as "veganic" used only plant-based fertilizers, in part because, even on organic farms, animal waste could contain traces of antibiotics, hormones, or pesticides.

Eco-labels like "veganic" and "organic" furnished consumers with information that typically remained murky, buried in the chasm that separated farmers from the retail channels in which their goods were sold. The organic seal was meant to be the crème de la crème of labels, but it caused mystification and faced competition. Certified labels implied superior characteristics and conveniently allowed consumers to make selections that buttressed their social values. A survey in 2011 found that the labels that consumers liked most (in order) were "100 percent natural," "USDA Certified Organic," and

"Grown in the USA."[206] Aside from these, credence labels have included "Fair Trade Certified" coffee, tea, and chocolate; "Bird Friendly" coffee; "Rainforest Alliance Certified" coffee, chocolate, cocoa, bananas, and oranges; "American Humane Certified" bison, chicken, cows, pigs, sheep, and turkeys; and "Animal Welfare Approved" chickens, cows, ducks, geese, pigs, rabbits, sheep, and turkeys. For eggs to be USDA-certified organic they had to come from laying hens that had year-round access to the outdoors and were not confined in cages. That outdoor space could be in a pasture or in an enclosed concrete patio, because the rules don't specify every detail. Eggs could also be "cage-free," "free-range," or "Omega-3 enriched" without being organic. It's not surprising that consumers were confused.

Motley agencies have offered similar—sometimes overlapping—certifications. One of these, the nonprofit organization Naturally Grown, created a "Certified Naturally Grown" label as a proxy to avoid high certification fees. It materialized on produce from small-scale farmers who used organic practices but were not officially certified. Naturally Grown's standards were based on USDA Organic Standards, but its requirements were more affordable. This grassroots program was said to undergird "small farms at the heart of the organic movement." Naturally Grown insisted that it did not want to discredit the USDA Organic Program; rather, the label was formulated to impel people to purchase organic food from small, diversified farmers. The organization claimed that "the Organic label was not grown with government control and high licensing fees, it was grown with sweat, idealism, and farmers helping farmers to improve and stick to those ideals."[207] Because it was not affiliated with the USDA, Naturally Grown said that it could actually maintain more rigorous standards and not succumb to industry pressure to "water down" regulations.

Ayrshire Farm in Virginia, which specialized in rare and endangered breeds of livestock and heirloom produce, proudly displayed its distinction badges on its home page: USDA Certified Organic; Certified Humane Raised & Handled® (for its meats); Virginia's Finest (a state agriculture program); Food Alliance Certified (pertaining to social and environmental responsibility); and Predator Friendly (recognizing wildlife stewardship).[208] Ayrshire Farm's high-end heritage beef certainly seemed like an irreproachable luxury, but it was easy to get lost in the warren of labels and seals. Untangling the question of what to eat in order to stay inimitably aligned with environmental principles has been far from straightforward. "Greenwashing," or painting an eco-sheen on nominally green products, has been prevalent among untold numbers of organic and "natural" brands. Consumers concerned about saving the environment continued to juggle organic, local, vegetarian, and other "earth-friendly" options. Without unequivocal evidence to solve the quandary, many people have not seemed to mind munching on apparently eco-friendly foods like the tasty chocolate cereal—made with organic cocoa, molasses, and brown rice flour—in boxes of Envirokidz Koala Crisp.

PASSING THE LAWS: INTENSIFIED CORPORATE POWER

At the time the OFPA was passed, organic packaged and refined food businesses were scattered and undersized. Soon, titanic corporations—from General Mills, Pepsi, Kraft, and Dole, to ConAgra and Cargill—experimented with centralizing organics. The organic sphere mushroomed from modest farms and mom-and-pop shops into a decidedly profitable section of the international import and export system. It was a mixed blessing. As the organic produce sector planted deep roots in US retail markets, *Vegetarian Times* attributed the pace of this growth to "increasingly sophisticated organic growers" who, attuned to market demands, upgraded the appearance, quality, availability, and selection of organic fruits and vegetables. Despite pervasive high prices, Americans seemed "increasingly willing to pay the difference to make a difference."[209] However, as agribusiness firms appropriated lucrative parts of organic commodity chains, many were abandoning the sustainable agronomic practices traditionally associated with organics.[210] After struggling for decades, the organic farming industry became one of the most rapidly proliferating segments of US agriculture. As organic farming became ensconced in the industrial capitalist system, critics said that this caused socially progressive initiatives to fall off the farmers' agendas.[211] Some questioned whether the industry was truly practicing responsible agriculture. They alleged that agricultural intensification threatened to erode stringent regulatory standards. Whereas organic farming was once thought to challenge dominant systems of food provision, it instead became "formalized, institutionalized and integrated within conventional food systems."[212] The meteoric growth entailed a hard-nosed victory in terms of grasping a more extensive audience, but it was also a purported defeat with respect to the corporate takeover of the cause. This eclipse became canonized as the "conventionalization thesis." With conventionalization, organic agriculture was said to "resemble in structure and ideology the mainstream food sector it was established in opposition to."[213] Subsequent scholarship asserted that the stunning growth of organic food production and consumption from a small niche market into a multi-billion-dollar global industry indicated corporate usurpation.[214] The saga of organics became a narrative of declension.

Food policy watchdog Jim Hightower said that, instead of viewing the organic certification program as "an assurance of integrity," agribusiness giants viewed it as "a marketing tool."[215] Lofty goals, it seemed, had dwindled. Capital was concentrated among large producers that had superseded and subsumed their predecessors. Conventionalization was not unique to organics, but the process drew frequent exposure from industry insiders and onlookers. The climate shift struck one observer as so sweeping that it had become "easy to forget how outrageous the organic worldview appeared only a few decades ago."[216] The power struggle between grassroots organics and supersized organics was waged both in the legislative arena, where large-scale organics appeared to win, and in the national media, where grassroots organics appeared to win. The industry seemed bifurcated between big, mass-production operations and small, artisan-style ventures. There was polarization between large organic farms, frequently categorized as superficial, and small organic farms, more often presumed to be implacably striving to recapture marginalized values.[217] The conventionalization thesis has loomed large within the organic movement, but scrutinizing the dynamics of this rationalization reveals that it has been something of a cliché—and not a terribly useful one.

Consumers and farmers wanted greater assurance about organics, and government certification established its veracity. The toilsome process required a USDA agent to parse all aspects of a farm, including an annual production plan and five years of office records pertaining to the organic undertaking. Longtime organicists found the formalized regulations to be piecemeal and reductionist, not holistic. It was difficult to codify a comprehensive morality of organic farming. Technical lists of acceptable and prohibited inputs were easier to mandate. The protracted process for establishing federal organic standards involved a tug-of-war that, in the end, largely fomented industry growth through agribusiness. Purists felt that the OFPA left out philosophical codes that they had associated with the organic movement.

Organic campaigner Fred Kirschenmann pointed out that, in the 1970s, nobody predicted that the USDA would one day buttress organic agriculture, but "it happened because we changed the trend."[218] Yet Kirschenmann, who served on the NOSB, then bemoaned that hundreds of citizens' letters demanded guarantees of organic food safety—not soil health or a "balanced ecology"—indicating what he felt were flawed priorities.[219] Kirschenmann later charged the USDA with facilitating the "hijacking of organic agriculture," because it refused to acknowledge that "elegant ecological systems" with closed nutrient cycles were far "more organic" than input substitution systems that met the minimum requirements.[220] Michael Sligh, a founding member of the NOSB, cautioned that if the process to institutionalize the word "organic" proved to be "too onerous or false, the soul of organics will be lost." In that case, "those who love organics" would have to either "reclaim the word and concept" or "find new words and concepts."[221] Sligh also felt that "family-size" grassroots operations were more aligned with organic axioms and a "balanced ecological system" than well-developed farms.[222] The sense of cohesion from the movement's early collective identity was crumbling. Organic practitioners did not have to "genuinely love the soil" or treat the soil as a "living organism," as J. I. Rodale had advised. A rift between "passionate" and "profiteering" organics seemed to manifest itself.

Many organic farmers and food processors were making straightforward financial decisions and did not subscribe to a social or political philosophy. *Time* reported that, although the switch to organic could be difficult and expensive for dairy farmers, consumer demand for organic dairy products grew so rapidly, and the price premium was so enticing, that more farmers—even some who "once dismissed organic farming as a bunch of New Age nonsense"—wanted to join up.[223] Accusations circulated that scores of organic farmers were economically driven, cashing in solely to pursue revenues. Mark Lipson, writing in 1997 for the Organic Farming Research Foundation (OFRF), examined the "dual personality" of organic farming. While the "small-o definition of organic" was prescriptive and provided "the agronomic identity of organic farming," the "capital-O definition of Organic" was "essentially prohibitive, constituting the legal standard for production labeled as 'Organically Produced.'" Lipson said that the small-o identity was "first fully articulated by J. I. Rodale and others in the 1940s." This agroecological approach prescribed "high levels of soil organic matter, reliance on ecological processes for pest and disease management, closure of energy and material flows within the production operation, and reduction of external inputs." Meanwhile, the capital-O identity stemmed from "the appearance of commercial markets for 'Organically Grown' foods." It mainly emphasized forbidden synthetic materials and acceptable substances.[224] Competing definitions and interpretations of "organic" abounded.

In 1998, the USDA solicited public feedback on its first draft of the national organic standards. The proposal would have allowed irradiation, genetically engineered seeds, and the use of sewage sludge–based fertilizers for crops defined as organic. All were anathema to organic advocates. The USDA received over 275,000 outraged comments, which was the largest negative response in the agency's history.[225] A network of organic retailers, consumer organizations, and trade associations orchestrated the lobbying campaign. Some observers noted that the volume and source of the comments already reflected "the highly organized and coordinated nature of the organic and natural food industry" at that point.[226] Groups involved in rallying complaints included the Organic Trade Association, Mothers for Natural Law, California Certified Organic Farmers, Pure Food Campaign/Save Organic Standards, and Bio-Dynamic Farming and Gardening Association. Foes of the draft felt that the watered-down standards in the "insidious proposal" were "an insult to organic farming."[227] The vehement protest caused the rules to be rewritten so as to exclude the practices considered the most abhorrent.

Despite the modifications, federal organic standards did not advance a socially just food system. There were chinks in the organic armor. One observer of organic and sustainable agriculture movements saw that industrial farmers could be distinguished from a smaller "constellation of 'movement' farmers committed to a deeper, more ideological notion of sustainability."[228] Several presenters at the International Federation of Organic Agriculture Movements (IFOAM) conference in 2000 expressed concern over the changing nature of the organic food market. One speaker noted that organic agriculture had grown from "a small and decentralized holistic foods movement to a diversified industry," and, as more "mainstream" actors entered the market, the challenge to organic "pioneers" amplified.[229] Another speaker predicted that small family operations would be "increasingly marginalized from mainstream organic markets," and minor health food stores would be "either absorbed as parts of national retail chains or themselves marginalized as small players" in the burgeoning industry.[230]

Farmers and others who regarded these pernicious developments as co-optation or "selling out" sparked a backlash against "Big Organic" or "Shallow Organic," favoring what they baptized as "Small Organic," "Deep Organic," "Organic Plus," or "Beyond Organic." Some farmers sought an entirely new vocabulary to define themselves. Michael Pollan's New York Times piece in 2001 helped raise awareness about the "organic-industrial complex," in which organic food had attracted attention from "the very agribusiness corporations to which the organic movement once presented a radical alternative and an often scalding critique." Pollan, who was becoming move vocal in the organic movement, worried that the word "organic" was being emptied of its meaning. He also said that competition between small farmers and powerhouses had opened a gulf between "Big and Little Organic" and "convinced many of the movement's founders that the time has come to move 'beyond organic'—to raise the bar on American agriculture yet again."[231] Farmers who just barely met the rules for compliance seemed to be organic in name only, not in moral fiber. Brian Halweil, a researcher at the Worldwatch Institute, also predicted the development of two complementary markets for organic products: the "industrial organic stream," servicing major supermarkets and food manufacturers; and the "local and regional organic stream," which sustained strong connections to consumers.[232] William Lockeretz likewise delineated two coalitions of organic consumers: a larger group that welcomed the convenience of processed organic foods available in mainstream stores, and a smaller clan that adhered to "a more all-inclusive notion of 'organic.'"[233] It was assumed that the smaller coterie had a more "authentic" organic proclivity.

When the National Organic Program was finalized in 2001, the USDA acknowledged that national standards might "change the composition of the organic industry." The imposition of the rules could discourage some small organic farms from entering the industry and cause others to exit, "resulting in a higher concentration of larger firms." On the other hand, the USDA suggested that it might be easier for small outfits to comply with livestock standards prohibiting confinement production systems and requiring 100 percent organic feed.[234] Many reviewers had requested that the NOSB proscribe certification of "factory farms," which used customs and materials inconsistent with the OFPA. However, there was no "clear, enforceable definition" of these, so the final rule did not have that exclusion.[235] The USDA implemented its National Organic Standards, a uniform set of standards that replaced the patchwork of state standards, in October 2002. The final regulations governed the production, handling, and processing of organically grown agricultural products. Any farm selling over $5,000 worth of produce was not allowed to refer to its products or growing methods as "organic" unless certified. This worked well for larger farmer operations but put some small, diversified organic producers in a quandary. Certification was expensive and required a lengthy paper trail for each crop. Also, the transition period to reach full organic status was often stressful for producers and could

A certified organic farm (Photo courtesy of Colleen Freda Burt)

occasion an interim reduction of crop yields, during which time the farmer had to forgo adequate compensation from premium prices that didn't arrive until official certification was achieved.[236] The USDA imprimatur of organic approval did not guarantee the compassionate treatment of fruit-pickers, and organic agribusinesses did not ameliorate the arduous working conditions of agricultural laborers, many of whom were undocumented migrants. One dairy, Green Valley Organics, publicized that its employees were paid a living wage and received health care benefits, that its creamery was powered by solar energy, and that its Certified Humane cows "lived the good life" on over seventeen hundred acres of green organic grass.[237] Yet those were company decisions, above and beyond what was mandated; not all organic farms had self-imposed policies akin to those standards. Clearly, there were loopholes in what initially seemed to be an enormous success for organics.

THE DYNAMICS OF CO-OPTATION

Those dismayed by the menace of massive organic monocultures contended that the agribusiness phenomenon negated the loftier mission of the grassroots movement. From this perspective, the industry seized humble organic farming ideals and commodified them. The powers-that-be also engaged in rhetorical capture, mimicking agro-ecological discourse and defiling the very word "organic." Organic food, sopped up by the industrial marketplace, displayed similarities to other cultural inclinations. Historian Warren Belasco analyzed how the clash between the counterculture and the food industry in the 1960s led to a "countercuisine." The organic paradigm, a major element of this, imagined "a radically decentralized infrastructure" comprising "communal farms, co-operative groceries, and hip restaurants."[238] But unmitigated growth brought challenges, gentrification, and unrelenting attention from mass marketers. Including himself as one of the "counterculture missionaries" who wanted to apply dietary amendments to revolutionary ends, Belasco concluded that "we failed to change the world—or even ourselves—very much."[239] In the same vein, Randal Beeman and James Pritchard scrutinized how "permanent agriculture," a reformist-utopian ideology of ecological farming, was co-opted and adulterated by conventional agriculture.[240] The agricultural establishment—including the USDA—adopted the terminology of "conservation" but ignored the holistic social and ecological worldview that was meant to inspire fundamental refurbishments. The remnants of permanent agriculture evolved into the concept of "sustainable agriculture," and organic farming was one component of that broadly defined notion.[241] Beeman and Pritchard asserted that co-optation did increase the legitimacy of many sustainable agriculture techniques, but "the establishment" only "focused on short-term profitability rather than long-term ecological integrity, land health, or any substantial social reform."[242] Comparably, Karen and Michael Iacobbo discussed how, as vegetarianism seeped into the mainstream, suppliers scrambled to meet the demand for products free from animal ingredients. However, the vegetarian movement began to be defined as simply a *diet* or *practice*, not as the "community of *purpose*" that it was meant to be.[243] Much of the general population regarded it as "a taste option, rather than a dedicated dietary choice."[244] For some, eating vegetarian was less political and more personal; the same could be said for eating organic. No world-changing results emanated from all the new organic groupies.

The prevailing "conventionalization" thesis was that external bodies sought to appropriate, swallow, and benefit from elements of a countercultural philosophy without sincere dedication to the movement's ethics.[245] The organic campaign could be read as a cultural resistance movement that, due to its success, was subjected to what Max Weber called the "routinization of charisma." Weber evaluated the procedure whereby a "pure" form of charismatic domination waned and turned into an "institution." It was then displaced by other structures, or it fused with them. As the antagonistic forces of charisma and tradition merged, charisma became "a part of everyday life."[246] A common assertion became that the organic movement had turned into an institutionalized part of everyday life and, along the line, had misplaced its charisma. It was not living up to the mesmerism embedded in its name. Rapacious capitalists had seized control, tainted the recipe, and pilfered the profits. As one observer noted, "Today you can buy organic food without adjusting your lifestyle."[247] As soon as the organic movement went from purity to paycheck, it seemed to lose some of its leverage. There was concern that the explosion of the sector could potentially jeopardize its ultimate success. The normative theme of these cautionary tales was that the gallant organic movement had been betrayed and ought to be rescued from corruption.[248]

These dystopian sentiments about organics had matching diagnoses. The organic movement was "a victim of its own hard-won success," according to Daniel Imhoff, and it was "lurching toward mass production, long-distance transport, and even fast food."[249] The Organization for Economic Co-Operation and Development (OECD) asserted in 2003 that organic agriculture was "no longer limited to those farmers for whom organic production is a holistic life-style"; rather, it had "extended into the mainstream of the agri-food chain as an economic opportunity to satisfy a niche market at premium prices."[250] The organic innovators and high-minded early adopters were being shuffled under the rug. Julie Guthman's *Agrarian Dreams* (2004) argued that, in California, organic farming had "replicated what it set out to oppose" and had fallen short of addressing social justice.[251] Kregg Hetherington discussed how government certification was a vital step in making organic farms economically plausible, but he thought that bureaucratization also "removed the element of trust between producer and consumer, the 'bond' that had always been fundamental to organic farming."[252] Evidence that a "bond" had always existed was thin, but this was emblematic of the poignant stories that many organicists believed.

Maine farmer Eliot Coleman asserted that organic farming was analogous to other ideas that diverged from "the orthodoxy of the moment." The orthodoxy, he said, "first tries to denounce it, then tries to minimize its importance, and finally tries to co-opt it."[253] In 2005, Coleman bewailed the state of organics: "Longtime members of the so-called organic movement find themselves at odds with some of their organic-industry colleagues. A movement that was based on the simple goals of regenerating soil and growing food for local communities has become an industry requiring a vast bureaucracy of organicrats to inspect, police, advise, and manage a comparatively small handful of folks who are actually doing the work of organic farming."[254] Coleman differentiated "deep-organic farmers," who mimicked the "elegance of nature's systems," from "shallow-organic farmers," who looked for "quick-fix inputs."[255] Although organics remained peripheral in terms of total agricultural production and food sales, organic food systems resembled their conventional counterparts.[256]

Similarly, nutritionist Joan Dye Gussow lamented how organic was becoming what "some of us hoped it would be an alternative to." She referred to "veterans of *Organic Gardening*'s earlier battles" with skeptics and held that "when we said organic, we meant local, healthful, and just."[257] Organic farmer Malcolm Beck discussed how the word "organic" was "beginning to get screwed up." Though the national organic certification rules were helpful to some niche farmers, he said, "I don't think Nature necessarily approves of all the rules."[258] Farmer Keith Stewart said that the word "organic" "lost some of its luster soon after it received the federal and corporate embrace."[259] Due to this tarnish, farmers who chose not to participate in the National Organic Program (NOP) were opting for "words like *natural, biological, regenerative, eco-local,* and *sustainable* to describe what they do."[260] Though Stewart himself decided to stay with the federal program, he was increasingly uneasy with it. Other organic farmers felt they, too, were at loggerheads with the NOP. Jane Goodall's *Harvest for Hope* (2005) distinguished between deep organic, which meant trying to "grow the most delicious, nutritious food possible while assuring the health of the planet," and shallow organic, which merely meant meeting certification standards "within the industrial paradigm."[261] Despite all the corporate muscle, Goodall did believe that the organic certification movement was protecting consumers and the environment from the injuries caused by chemical agriculture. However, she said that farmers' markets, CSA programs, and co-operatives were "the purest expression of the original vision of the organic movement."[262] Leslie Duram, in *Good Growing: Why Organic Farming Works* (2005), also saw a conflict "between the market-driven success of organic products and the grassroots ethical concerns of organic farming."[263]

Many foot soldiers who had been stigmatized as oddballs were circumspect about the transformation of organics from an antiestablishment subculture into a multinational, routine presence. In a Sierra Club article in 2006 on how to "eat green," the author wrote, "Not too many years ago, natural and organic food were smiled on as the quirks of cranks and hypochondriacs. . . . Today natural foods have become so mainstream that some of us former eccentrics are feeling uncomfortably normal."[264] The *Washington Post* also printed the customary bashing: "What passes for organic farming today has strayed far from what the shaggy utopians who got the movement going back in the '60s and '70s had in mind. . . . If these pioneers dreamed of revolutionizing the nation's food supply, they surely didn't intend for organic to become a luxury item, a high-end lifestyle choice."[265] Agricultural economist John Ikerd agreed that the trends transforming organic food production into an exploitative process were "based on the principles of industry rather than nature" and directly contradicted the historic credo of organic farming.[266] Ikerd drew an analogy between "deep organic" and "deep ecology." Deep organic, he said, espoused the biological and spiritual roots of organic farming, with a compulsory philosophical commitment to farming as a "self-renewing, regenerative process, based on nature's principles of production." Ikerd contrasted this to the standardization, specialization, and consolidation driving the newer extraction-oriented organic approach.[267] Cliques were materializing in the movement.

The uptick in organic labels struck many consumers as a gimmick. When Wal-Mart announced that it would expand its organic offerings and "democratize" organic food by selling organic products for just 10 percent more than their conventional equivalents—compared to the customary premiums of 20 to 30 percent—Michael Pollan fretted that sales at lower-than-average prices would hasten the globalization of organic food. Pollan insisted in *The Omnivore's Dilemma* (2006) that because the organic movement was "conceived as a critique of industrial values," then industrialization would "cost organic its soul."[268] As national retailers began to take organic food seriously, Pollan predicted that the vast expansion of organic farmland required to stock Wal-Mart would indeed be an "unambiguous good for the world's environment," meaning "substantially less pesticide and chemical fertilizer being applied to the land—somewhere." However, he expected the chain to source its organic food from cut-rate global suppliers. Pollan said that trying to sell organic food for only 10 percent more than conventional meant that Wal-Mart would bring cold-blooded efficiency and economies of scale to a food production scheme that was "supposed to mimic the logic of natural systems rather than that of the factory." This, Pollan thought, would fail to "advance the ideal of sustainability that once upon a time animated the organic movement."[269] The plan would "give up, right from the start, on the idea, once enshrined in the organic movement, that food should be priced not high or low but responsibly."[270] None of these dirges ever mentioned which organic founder had enshrined these sacred pricing notions or when. Some observers championed Wal-Mart's move as a way to introduce more low-income Americans to organic food; others grieved that this democratic accessibility entailed a loss of prestige for organic certification and possibly meant diminished quality for the organic niche.

Ken Roseboro, in *The Organic Food Handbook* (2006), discussed how organics were once derided as a counterculture craze that "created images of granola-crunching hippies or wilted and bruised produce sold in natural food stores."[271] Those days were gone, though, and people were choosing organic food for "a simple reason: common sense."[272] At the time, an evocative advertisement for Kashi Organic Promise cereal illuminated the newfound panache of organics: "Stop letting the macramé sandal crowd hog all the good food." Kashi announced to stylish consumers that the organic label was not something reserved for the "free love," "tie-dye crowd." It was no longer the purview of bohemian communes. Notably, Kashi, founded as an independent natural foods company, became a subsidiary of the Kellogg Company, a worldwide leading producer of cereal and convenience foods, further contributing to the mainstream positioning of Kashi products. According to USDA estimates, certified organic cropland more than doubled between 1990 and 2002, and then doubled again between 2002 and 2005.[273] Total organic product sales also doubled during that time.[274] Not everyone celebrated this surge. Critics worried that the real costs of growing food would not be reflected in prices at the cash register, and the bona fide benefits of organics would be disregarded. Cindy Burke, in *To Buy or Not to Buy Organic* (2007), affirmed that "many consumers are beginning to understand that some foods are *more organic* than others" and are seeking surrogates for big-business organics.[275] *The Organic Food Shopper's Guide* (2008) warned that "the term *organic* will become meaningless" as more compromises are made and small farmers are left out.[276] Caveat emptor: being organic was not tantamount to being categorically trustworthy.

Organic farmers were underserved by the public agricultural research system for decades. As the *New York Times* noted in 2007, cheerleaders for industrialized agriculture "often viewed organics with suspicion, if not outright disdain."[277] Despite the discernible infiltration of organics into middle-of-

Daily farming operations (Photo courtesy of Colleen Freda Burt)

the-road retail channels, only 3 percent of food purchases in the United States were organic products in 2008. Less than 1 percent of US farmland was certified organic.[278] Large-scale corporate agriculture reigned, pushing organics to the "alternative" subsector. Agricultural research was still unduly weighted toward chemicals and biotechnology. According to some evaluations, the USDA's National Organic Program remained underfunded and seemed to be a low priority.[279] Organic farmers had to rely more on self-help, and many felt isolated. One organic farmer pointed out that "there are substantial economic forces vested in maintaining the status quo."[280] Overall, though, the organic food and farming movement openly transitioned from marginal to mainstream. More universities acknowledged the need for research into organic agriculture methods. Washington State University started allowing students to major in organic agriculture systems and obtain hands-on experience at WSU's certified organic teaching farm, which was funded in part with grants from the National Science Foundation, Earthbound Farm, and Pacific Natural Foods.[281] WSU also offered an online organic agriculture certificate, meant to prepare undergraduates for farming or food industry management professions. Several other universities began offering degree programs or certificates as well. The University of Florida at Gainesville initiated a public-private partnership with organic farmers in the Center for Organic Agriculture. It began working to facilitate research programs, disseminate scientific information on organic production throughout the state, respond to consumers' questions, and increase the market share of organic food and fiber.[282] The USDA announced in 2009 that it would grant $50 million in new funding to stimulate organic food production, create a division within the agency dedicated to organic agriculture, and plant a six-acre organic "People's Garden" at its headquarters. Still, as organics acquired endorsements in majority culture, its insurgent potential might have been undermined. Accusatory headlines continued to blare "Has 'Organic' Been Oversized?," "Multinational Food Corporations Thank You for Buying 'Organic,'" and "Is Organic Labeling a Victim of Its Own Success?"[283] The Organic Center published a white paper, "The Organic Watergate," censuring the USDA for allowing the corporate influence in the National Organic Program that had led to the NOSB's favoring of agribusiness.[284] It was undeniably big businesses that had taken the lead in advancing the organic movement.

DIVIDED CONSCIOUSNESS

The ascendancy of "organic agribusiness" reflected the extent to which large vendors apparently suppressed subversive facets of the movement. But this, like the conventionalization thesis, was a bit too simplistic. Despite the specter of almighty "Big Ag," its supremacy over organics was not merely a clampdown on the avant-garde. Even as the grassroots organic model seemed to be under siege, a "contradictory consciousness" was visible.[285] Ostensibly docile groups have sometimes shared complicity in their own subsidiary position. As cultural critic Raymond Williams argued, all alternative or oppositional initiatives were actually tied to the hegemonic. Williams reasoned that some ideas, though clearly affected and possibly cramped by a hegemonic ceiling, still contained independent and original elements.[286] Unconventional meanings and values could be "accommodated and tolerated within a particular effective and dominant culture."[287] Alternative forms of culture do exist, though there is always an attempt to incorporate them into the norm. The process of incorporation is essential to understanding the forces involved in the continual making and remaking of organics. Mainstream culture tolerated the emergent meanings and values of organic farming and adopted some of them. The relationship was incessantly renewed and altered.[288] The organic movement is an example of counterhegemony, and its ideology has been in perpetual flux. J. I. Rodale embodied this byzantine state. He preferred small-scale husbandry by assiduous farmers, but he also hoped that organic farms would take over the world. Despite his fondness for small farms, he helped precipitate the organic invasion of the United States. In 1947, Rodale conveyed to staunch *Organic Gardening* readers how important it was for them to "tell as many people as possible about the 'goodness' inherent in organic gardening."[289] He zeroed in on the keys to success for the youthful movement. Even the nonconformist Gypsy Boots took full advantage of mass media to access millions in his TV audience. Many organic entrepreneurs have followed Rodale's example in being starry-eyed and idealistic, yet still practical and profit-minded. Divided consciousness has appeared time and again in the history of the organic movement. Unfettered purity has been rare in any social movement, and organics were no exception. Perhaps it was agrarian pretension to think that organic farmers should not have tried too hard to sell their corn, lest they lose credibility as "tree-hugging, nature-loving" romantics.

The organic movement was designed not to supplant conventional agriculture but to provide a deviating route. Still, the organic minions were not always doe-eyed and delicate when facing chemical agribusiness. Though the charismatic brilliance of organics dimmed, the movement retained unorthodox and oppositional elements. Passion and peculiarity could be diluted and packaged but not obliterated. In 2008, organic farmers Casey Gustowarow and Daniel Bowman Simon campaigned around the United States, gathering signatures for a petition asking President Barack Obama to plant an organic garden at the White House. These "ex–Peace Corps buddies" drove a school bus modified to hold an herb and vegetable garden on the roof, carrying on the lineage of somewhat bizarre flag-bearers for organic food.[290] When the petition request was victorious, Gustowarow and Simon became the primary White House Organic Farm Project farmers.[291] The history of organic food and farming reflects intricate political, cultural, and discursive struggles like these.

The "conventionalized" organic disposition did not obviate iconoclastic practitioners who made deliberate choices to buck the system. So-called shallow versions of organic production still left room for "deeper" paths to coexist. Seasonal organic blueberry stands and door-to-door milk sales persevered alongside the magnitude of global supermarket chains. "Routinization" impinged on the organic movement's transgressiveness, but an abundance

Farmers' market (Photo courtesy of Colleen Freda Burt)

of quixotic venues offering organic products continued to be differentiated spaces, brimming with foibles and whimsicality. When a mysteriously "green" bakery opened in the East Village of New York in 2005, customers were first told that the establishment had no name. It was built entirely from recycled and ecologically sound materials. The wait staff, clad in hemp, served organic muffins, scones, and coffee from behind a recycled denim and bamboo countertop. It became known by the code name "Birdbath." Eventually word leaked out that the bakery's owner, Maury Rubin of the well-liked City Bakery, had not publicized the name because he wanted to draw attention to its small-scale sustainable construction and organic products.[292] Rubin's goal had been to create a top-to-bottom green bakery that would showcase eco-friendly materials. He said that he hoped to encourage people to link their organic food with the organic materials in the place they were eating. The walls were assembled from wheat and sunflower seeds. Floors were made of cork. The paint used came from milk and beets. The bakery was acclaimed as "a political statement, an architectural pioneer, and a bit of performance art, all wrapped in one."[293] Birdbath Neighborhood Green Bakery served organic food, was powered by wind, gave a discount to anybody arriving on bicycle or skateboard, and delivered food from its main kitchen on bicycle-powered rickshaws.[294]

Another example of a "deeper" initiative was INNA Jam, established in 2010 to make small batches of fresh single-varietal jam in recyclable glass jars. INNA Jam (yes, it is a pun) only used organic sugar and fruit from organic farmers within 150 miles of its Emeryville, California, kitchen to make the seasonal jams. Even the famous Jalapeño jam was made from local jalapeños only available from July to November; other flavors included ouachita blackberry and satsuma plum. INNA Jam was delivered via bicycles (in the Bay Area) or packaged in renewable, compostable vegetable starch packing peanuts for shipping.[295] These quirky, aberrant endeavors were emblematic of the organic movement's idiosyncrasies. One got the feeling that J. I. Rodale, Gypsy Boots, zealous organic admirers, and even some of the most punitive critics—those who had thrown up their hands at the juggernaut of "Big Bad Organics"—would all have approved.

CHAPTER FIVE

Individual Organic Optimization

Health Hopes and Fears

Kimberly Rider, author of *The Healthy Home Workbook* (2006), thought that buying organic food at the farmers' market was a "life-affirming" step toward a natural, nontoxic lifestyle.[1] To create a truly healthy home, Rider advised consumers to patronize local farmers, bake bread from scratch, start an organic herb garden, and grow organic vegetables.[2] To take a smaller step in the same direction, the Rodale Health blog recommended that people choose Leaping Lemurs Organic Cereal from EnviroKidz instead of Lucky Charms from General Mills—not just because it had eco-appeal but because it was lower in sugar content, sweetened with mineral-rich molasses, and free from genetically engineered (GE) ingredients.[3] In sum, it was healthier. There is a broad perception that all organic foods are more nourishing than all conventional foods. Despite the dearth of unambiguous proof, organic food seems like a guilt-free health boost. The health properties of organics, or at least their façade of clean living attributes, have long been one of the foremost selling points. Some consumers are leery of medical experts, disregard cryptic labels, and dismiss mercurial nutritional advice. Others are constantly perplexed about exactly what constitutes the healthiest diet. Yet interest in the relationship between organic food and health is sky-high, and all kinds of "health foods" are enduringly popular.

Federal organic standards do not mention nutrition, and reputable organic businesses tend to (or ought to) avoid making vague health claims. *New York Times* food writer Mark Bittman has reminded consumers that the word "organic" is "not synonymous with 'safe,' 'healthy,' 'fair' or even necessarily 'good.'"[4] However, organic sustenance is the sine qua non of a healthy diet for a multitude of consumers. "Organic" is famously shorthand for "wholesome," "safe," and "nutritious." Organic foods are supposed to preclude extraneous, dodgy ingredients. Part of the organic allure—real or imagined—is its contribution to physical robustness and, ultimately, the "salvation" that J. I. Rodale augured. Rodale felt that organic food was "an essential way to help make the world and us healthier and happier."[5] There has been a long-standing quest to attain health through organic food, whether from backyard gardens or big businesses. Organic foods are riveting for both selfish and selfless reasons; they seem to deliver a package of benefits. This chapter focuses on how those health-related motivations have played out in American culture since the 1990s. It reveals how the organic movement has been a collective undertaking, but individuals have always been expected to bear the burden—and monetary costs—of acquiring organic food that might improve their own well-being.

HEALTH CLAIMS AND CHEMICAL INTOLERANCE

In its early incarnations, organic food had links with quirky natural food shops, environmental activism, and a degree of dietary austerity. Organic meats were rare; organic lettuce might be wilted; and some organic bread was unpalatable; but a dedicated coterie felt virtuous in making their purchases. Organic corporations targeted what food journalist Michael Pollan called "the true natural"—a committed, socially conscious consumer. Then, industry players saw that the future lay with a substantially larger ensemble of affluent "health seekers" who were "more interested in their own health than that of the planet." Pollan pointed out that this posed a marketing challenge, because the health case for organic food was more problematic than its environmental justification.[6] Still, an assemblage of people commenced buying organic for perceived health benefits. Natural food stores increased in size and presence during the 1990s. Organic farmer Nicolas Lampkin noted that, as bigger supermarket chains were selling organic produce, they were eclipsing local, "alternative" outlets. These, in turn, were "making organic produce available to a much wider range of people, many of whom are likely to be less committed."[7] The profile of the average organic shopper changed during the 1990s. The caricature of ascetics eating spoonfuls of organic barley grass powder began to dissipate as organic foods refurbished their image. They went from "unattractive, worthy products for the 'sandals brigade' to highly aspirational products beloved on the basis of taste—and health."[8] New shoppers for natural and organic products were still amenable to making ecology a factor in their grocery decisions, but they tended to be upper-income, wellness-conscious individuals. Beef became one of the organic system's fastest-growing segments. Given the mounting assortment of health foods catering to mainstream consumers, many people no longer felt that it was essential to sacrifice flavor or freshness for nutrition.

Healthy humans and a healthy natural world cannot be detached, but in some ways the organic movement has been situated within an isolated sphere of "toxic anxiety." The zenith of organic food's popularity may have been nurtured in part by what sociologist Andrew Szasz called the "inverted quarantine" phenomenon: an individualistic attempt to barricade one's self from looming noxious threats.[9] A desire to protect one's own body from harm has motivated this organic consumer. Health angst is largely self-centered, and studies have indicated that organic foods are most often procured because of their presumed personal health benefits. Egocentric values, such as forebodings about bodily hazards or food safety, have been shown to predict organic food purchases to a finer extent than altruistic motives, such as compassion for environmental or animal welfare. Maria Rodale's hard line was that "anyone who cares about the environment should be a supporter of organic food and farming." Still, though she did believe it was important to "save the polar bear or other rare species," organic farming was more about saving humans: "If we are going to stay here, we need to go organic."[10]

Agitation about private wellness has been the strongest predictor of favorable attitudes toward buying organic foods and has been a significant predictor of purchase frequency.[11] As with the health food movement at large, sometimes the most effective impetus for elevating organics has been trepidation about illness or death. Poisoning scares and marketing based on fear have contributed to the magnetism of organic foods. Among organic farmers, the desire to improve family health has been one of the main reasons cited for switching over from conventional farming.[12] Self-interested intentions have trumped magnanimous ethical causes in the pursuit of organic fitness. A plethora of consumers have quietly consented to fork out more cash for organic food in order to avoid health menaces. This was in line with the movement's overall individualization emphasis. Few organic advocates ever insisted that government subsidies to organic farmers, which could have lowered prices and reduced health risks for everyone, were crucial.

Diverse practices have long existed among participants in the health food movement, which, from the start, was a diffuse collection of groups and businesses that followed miscellaneous food philosophies thought to augment health. Formal organization was limited, though communication centers or "network nodes" did exist. Gathering points included health foods stores, organic farms, offbeat restaurants, and co-operatives.[13] Spokespeople who disseminated health food information in media venues extended the reach of these physical entities. Messages about what constituted a healthy diet came from medical professionals, personal acquaintances, and media sources. Each of these authorities may have defined healthy eating in different and even contradictory ways.[14] Developments in both research and taste have reworked American health habits. Nutritional criteria have varied over time, depending on culturally and historically specific standards.[15] Consumption patterns have also responded to fluctuations in price, disposable income, and food assistance programs.[16] A variety of discourses on healthy eating have affected everyday food customs. In one study, researchers identified three distinct discourses: "cultural/traditional" healthy eating discourses drawn from family and community members; "mainstream" healthy eating discourses focusing on monitoring food and nutrient intake, often competing with cultural notions; and "complementary/ethical" healthy eating discourses encompassing issues of morality and sustainability, including rationales for vegetarian, local, natural, and organic foods. While the discourses have competed, they coexist and have contributed simultaneously to everyday food decisions; all three have played a role in the organic movement.[17] Achieving optimal dietary vigor has entailed making personal modifications but—to true believers—has involved cultural and political transformations as well. Organic food is one way that health-seekers have sought to enrich the quality of their lives. The healthy eating trifecta—"cultural/traditional," "mainstream," and "complementary/ethical"—is visible in the marketing language of nearly all organic companies.

Precursors to the organic label came with the Nutrition Labeling and Education Act (NLEA) in 1990, which mandated the now-standard Nutrition Facts label for packaged foods. Food, nutrition, and health marketing began on an unprecedented scale in the 1990s.[18] Product labels that bore health implications proliferated. One of the main goals of health food activists was to coerce the food industry into offering healthier foods. Manufacturers responded by marketing a host of products with enticing labels—"low-calorie," "low-sodium," and "whole-grain"—while reaping enormous benefits for themselves.[19] The food industry enthusiastically embraced the concept of "functional foods." Also known as "nutraceuticals," these foods and beverages provided health benefits exceeding basic nutrition.[20] Functional foods blurred the demarcation between food and medicine. Marketers first developed products for people who were ill or had specific health-related medical conditions. Next were products that enhanced individual health and could possibly prevent diseases. Vitamins, minerals, protein, and other isolated ingredients were added to make functional properties extrinsic. Furthermore, myriad ordinary foodstuffs—for example, tomatoes, soy, and whole grains—were marketed on the basis of their intrinsic, health-promoting assets.[21] Some of the contentions seemed to be gimmicks: the "whole grain" ingredient in a sugary cereal bearing the official Whole Grains Council stamp may have been pesticide-laden corn. Still, producers formulated and marketed products according to a gamut of health propositions. This spectrum included organic, vegetarian, and reduced-fat items, as well as everyday foods said to bear built-in nutritional advantages.[22] Disney even jumped into the value-added label game, adding a "Mickey Check" to nutritious foods that were "Good for you—Fun too!" Industry observers have noted that the central premise of the functional foods revolution was that the risk of disease could be curtailed by diet, so it thrived on nervousness.[23] Anxious consumers would choose a conspicuously labeled "value-added" food with the expectation that it would reduce high cholesterol, stimulate healthy blood pressure, or help them lose weight.

Organic foods certainly seemed to have this kind of additional value. *Time* reported that a "parade of food scares" was "propelling more shoppers to go organic" in 2002. With sales of natural and organic foods mushrooming at 18 percent per year, "the industry no longer figures its prime market is Birkenstock-wearing proles hankering for tofu and lentils. It's courting health-conscious consumers of every stripe."[24] The market for "natural" foods has always been even larger than that for "organic." The Federal Trade Commission (FTC) has attempted to establish a definition of "natural" but has concluded that it was unable to do so. Rather, the FTC said that it would abide by a "reasonable basis" standard to determine whether an advertisement was deceitful; the word "natural" has indeed been challenged. In 2006, the Center for Science in the Public Interest confronted the use of a "100% natural" label for a soft drink that contained high-fructose corn syrup (HFCS), asserting that this was deceptive in terms of consumer expectations. Those expectations were hefty. Consumers have often hypothesized that organic sugar was healthy and natural, while they demonized HFCS and other sweeteners. However, research has shown no nutritional difference between HFCS, sugar cane syrup, and table sugar (organic or not); all were sources of "empty" calories and none was actually good for you. After the Corn Refiners Association successfully petitioned the Food and Drug Administration (FDA) in 2008, manufacturers of foods with HFCS were again allowed to make "natural" claims.[25] The FDA never set regulations governing the use of phrases like "lightly sweetened" or "low sugar" on products; efforts to mandate a "natural" label encountered even more hindrances. Ironically, a survey by the Shelton Group advertising agency indicated that Americans preferred the word "natural" over the term "organic" when choosing a green product, thinking that organic was more of an "unregulated marketing buzzword," indicating only that it was pricier.[26] In fact, "natural" was the word that had no legal consequences and was not strictly policed. Only organic foods were certifiably produced without synthetic chemicals, genetically modified organisms (GMOs), radiation, or sewage sludge, but puzzled shoppers sometimes fallaciously believed that "natural" products met these requirements too. Organically raised animals could not be injected with growth hormones or antibiotics and could not be confined without outdoor access, but "natural" meat did not need to meet those standards.

Fears about chemicals have convinced more people to participate in organic gardening themselves. Garden experts and radio show hosts Elizabeth and Crow Miller have averred that making compost was "akin to making bread or beer"—easy enough for anybody to try.[27] The nonprofit Kitchen Gardeners International more than doubled its membership between 2007 and 2009, while national seed manufacturer Burpee saw increased sales of vegetable and herb seeds.[28] The New York Botanical Garden hosted the exhibition "Edible Garden" during the summer of 2009, which included compost demonstrations, seed-saving instructions, and celebrity chef appearances. The events inspired people to grow, prepare, and eat garden-fresh produce under the mantra "Buy Local, Cook Global" and verified the revival of home-grown food. Robert Kenner's film *Food, Inc.*, released in 2009, tackled the grim scandals of industrialized food, mechanized agriculture, and consumer health through interviews with farmer Joel Salatin, Stonyfield Farm CEO Gary Hirshberg, and other venerable organic spokespeople. The film exposed the indignities of contamination, animal cruelty, and abysmal ethics that—like Upton Sinclair's *The Jungle* during the Progressive era—shocked viewers (and gave them a stomachache). In a survey by the International Food Information Council, 63 percent of Americans indicated that they read the Nutrition Facts panel when deciding to purchase or eat a food or beverage, while 51 percent checked the ingredients list, and 13 percent looked for the "organic" label on packaging.[29] Still, savvy Americans may have been gardening or reading labels more, but they were not necessarily heeding nutritional guidelines.

Michael Pollan referred to the national eating disorder as "orthorexia," an unhealthy obsession with healthy eating. Ironically, the American population—preoccupied with nutrition—was markedly unhealthy.[30] The food industry, nutrition science, and journalism all stood to gain from confusion about what to eat, so Pollan indicted the "Nutritional Industrial Complex"— an assemblage of "scientists and food marketers only too eager to exploit every shift in the nutritional consensus"—for this insidious bewilderment.[31] Like Weston A. Price and J. I. Rodale, Pollan traced most chronic diseases to the industrialization of food. His advice was to eat "well-grown food from healthy soils." He acknowledged that it would be simpler to say "eat organic," but since some "exceptional farmers" were not certified organic, he concluded that "organic is important, but it's not the last word on how to grow food well."[32] Furthermore, Pollan warned people not to erroneously assume that the organic label automatically signified healthfulness, especially when the food was processed and transported long distances.[33]

As people's fascination with upgrading their diets rose, there was inconsistency between this enthrallment and collective health statistics. The USDA's assessment of major patterns in food consumption between 1970 and 2005 noted that most Americans were not meeting federal dietary recommendations for certain food groups and that the US obesity rate among adults had doubled during that period. Notwithstanding all the Rodale health and fitness publications, Americans were consuming heaps of high-fat, high-carbohydrate foods and beverages and scant nutrient-dense foods and beverages. Consumers were eating more refined grains but not enough whole grains. They were eating more fruits and vegetables but less than the prescribed amounts. Americans tended to eat more meat, eggs, and nuts than necessary; they needed to scale back on added sugars, sweeteners, fats, and oils.[34] Nutritionists generally assented that everybody adhering to the Standard American Diet (SAD) ought to eat more fruits and vegetables, whether these were organic or not, to achieve better health. Fewer than 5 percent of adults were eating the recommended daily amount of fruits and vegetables.[35] Exhaustive, captivating health claims on products have not always lead to healthier diets. Still, organic labels flourished in a climate of optimism about newfangled healthy promises and pessimism about standard food.

Organic companies have, at times, purposely reinforced the belief that their food was healthier than nonorganic victuals. Eden Foods, bearing the tagline "Pure and Purifying," advertised that its organic whole grains provided "supreme quality for assured rejuvenation of your well-being." Earthbound Farm's *Pocket Guide to Choosing Organic* (2008) counseled people to choose organic food because it was more "nutritious and delicious," and it kept "potentially dangerous chemicals out of our bodies." Earthbound Farm's activity book proclaimed that children could "find out why Organic is the healthiest choice for you, our planet, and earthworms, too!" Some product labels have combined functional and organic propositions. For example, Horizon Organic Dairy said that it supported brain health with organic milk enhanced by DHA Omega-3 fatty acids and supported digestive health with low-fat, vitamin-fortified, probiotic organic vanilla yogurt. Alive and Radiant Foods made chocolate-covered "Kale Krunch" snacks that were certified organic, raw, gluten-free, vegan, and "anti-oxidant rich." Stacking claims on top of one another has been even more likely to attract organic health-seekers.

While probiotics and antioxidants may be compelling, the absence of frightening chemicals is the essence of what makes organic food healthier for most consumers. Pesticides have been assaulted for causing a variety of health problems, including cancer, hormone disruption, brain and nervous system toxicity, and skin, eye, and lung irritation.[36] Synthetic chemicals classified as endocrine disruptors (for example, Polychlorinated Biphenyls, or PCBs; bisphenol-A, or BPA, found in some plastics and cans; phthalates, found in some beauty products, toys, and detergents; DDT and dioxin, which, though banned in the United States, are still present in human bodies; and some other fertilizers and pesticides) are particularly troubling, because even tiny doses could have potent effects. The Food Quality Protection Act (FQPA) of 1996 required dramatic reductions in pesticide use to ensure that consumers were protected. However, the pesticide industry, along with farm and agribusiness interests, opposed changes to the criterion, which remained inadequate. The Environmental Protection Agency (EPA) dragged its feet to make improvements. Pesticide use actually increased.[37] Risks from neurotoxins, particularly organophosphate (OP) insecticides, also rose.

According to the World Health Organization, millions of instances of pesticide poisoning occur each year in farmworkers from direct and chronic exposure. Acute pesticide poisoning cases account for significant morbidity and mortality among agricultural workers worldwide.[38] Numerous pesticides on the market today could be treacherous for humans, and conventional fruits and vegetables—even when peeled or washed—may still provide unsafe exposure levels to consumers. The Centers for Disease Control and

Prevention's biomonitoring program has detected pesticides in 96 percent of Americans. The Environmental Working Group (EWG), a nonprofit watchdog, argues that there is "widespread pesticide contamination on popular fruits and vegetables." Government monitoring may be insufficient to assure the safety of conventional crops. Although 99 percent of food samples comply with federal pesticide residue restrictions, "legal" may not be "safe." The USDA and FDA both collect statistics on pesticides in the food supply; the EWG believes that both should set more austere tolerance levels to adequately protect children eating produce. While recommending an all-organic diet as the easiest way to reduce pesticide exposure, the organization recognizes that organic food might be inaccessible or expensive. The EWG compiles a "Dirty Dozen" list of the most menacing produce—such as apples, bell peppers, celery, peaches, lettuce, grapes, and strawberries—and a "Clean 15" list of those that have the least toxic contaminants. Since the twelve most contaminated fruits and vegetables present the majority of health risks, it is best to select safer substitutes for these. EWG advises people to be choosy about their intake of conventional produce.[39] Tests have shown that even organic foods are never completely pesticide-free, due to contaminant levels present in air and water. Cross-pollination is a tricky issue; there are cases in which an organic farm has sued a neighboring conventional farm for trespass, because pesticides have drifted onto the organic farm, rendering its tainted crops inedible in the organic market. Certain inorganic products can legally be included in foods labeled as organic. Even so, over four hundred chemicals regularly used in conventional farming are banned on organic crops. None of the three hundred synthetic food additives permitted by the FDA in conventional foods are allowed in products that are certified organic.[40] The rules and lists shuffle often, but, overall, the pesticide standards for organic foods are undeniably higher than for nonorganic ones. The discrepancy, again, highlights how organics are primarily an option for some individuals to select, not a surrogate to raise the bar on the entire food supply.

GMOS AND FOOD SCARES

Vermont college student Tom Stearns started out growing and selling just twenty-eight varieties of organic seeds in his own shed during his spare time. Less than ten years later, though he continued to look like a hippie farmer molded by the back-to-the-land counterculture, he had crafted a multimillion-dollar business out of his hobby. Stearns's High Mowing Organic Seeds met escalating consumer demand for organic seeds by cultivating six hundred heirloom varieties. Stearns served as an evangelist throughout the state for "safe seeds," genetically diverse agriculture, and healthy organic food.[41] Many consumers buy organic food because they deliberately want to not only eschew toxic pesticides and excess chemicals, but also shun injected hormones, antibiotics, and the prospect of animal cloning. The Quinn Popcorn company advertises that its organic microwave popcorn—packaged in compostable, chemical-free paper—is made from non-GMO corn, non-GMO canola oil, and Parmesan derived from non-rBGH milk; essentially, it has no coatings, chemicals, or "other scary stuff."[42] Health food purveyors have long positioned themselves to assuage uneasiness by providing "safe" choices. Buzz about pesticide use, mad cow disease, and genetically engineered foods inspired major supermarket chains to ramp up their organic offerings. Polls suggest that food frights are an important factor in organic growth.[43] In the wake of an alarming report about an *E. coli* outbreak or some other kind of outbreak, organic sales tend to soar. Since gene-altered crops produce their own toxic insecticides, they can withstand being repeatedly doused with weed-killers. With unknown considerations surrounding GE foods, a health-conscious corps prefers to avoid them and has pegged "Frankenfoods" as public enemy number 1.

The USDA has largely been love-struck with hybrid crops, which are closely allied to the profit interests of the biotechnology industry. Monsanto, a Fortune 500 multinational corporation that stands as the bête noir of organics, is a global leader in producing patented plant biotechnology traits, crop protection chemicals (for example the Roundup brand), and GE seeds. Shortly after the Organic Foods Production Act (OFPA) passed, organic food stakeholders met their nemesis: the first biotechnology food products, used for making cheese, gained FDA approval. The FDA announced that the FlavrSavr tomato was as safe as conventional tomatoes, so special labels were not needed on GE foods.[44] Agribusiness embraced genetically modified organisms (GMOs), while organicists saw them as abhorrent. The war between organic growing and genetic engineering would go on for decades, and they would be held up as polar opposite food production methods. Some members of the organic movement have inculpated Monsanto for "undue influence over lawmakers, regulators and the food supply."[45] Monsanto seems to garner legislative favoritism and backdoor deals from this collusion, such as the Monsanto Protection Act of 2013, a temporary rider that allowed it to circumvent federal restrictions on planting unapproved GE crops. Powerful biotech corporations have advertised their goal of "feeding the world" but have aggressively promoted their pesticides and have strong-armed farmers in both first- and third-world countries to purchase seeds for GE crops. Over 90 percent of the soybeans and 80 percent of the cotton planted in the United States are genetically engineered.[46] Despite distressingly lax parameters, keeping the scourge of GMOs out of organic crops is a sacred cow for the organic movement. There has long been a consensus that organic standards should exclude GMOs, since their safety is still unknown. Genes of *Bacillus thuringiensis* (Bt) are commonly used as pesticides in GE crops, and studies have showed that Bt is partially responsible for causing the Colony Collapse Disorder, which has killed swarms of honeybees. Food in many other nations must be labeled if it contains GE material, whereas the United States has no such law. A national coalition consisting of over four hundred organizations began the "Just Label It" campaign in 2012 to petition the FDA to require mandatory labeling, asserting that people had a right to know what they were eating. Over one million people signed on within the first 180 days.[47]

A flurry of lawsuits escalated the rancor. When the USDA deregulated "Roundup Ready" (GE) alfalfa, increasing the potential that organic farms could suffer from irreversible contamination, the organic movement created a unified front of opposition and set a lawsuit in motion (filed by the Center for Food Safety and Earthjustice) on the decision. Monsanto was prepared to fight back. In Vermont, a popular legislative bill requiring mandatory labels on genetically engineered food stalled after Monsanto threatened to sue the state if the bill passed.[48] Monsanto spent millions trying to block a California law that would have required labeling of GE foods; along with DuPont and Dow Chemical—two other massive developers of biotech crops—it launched a publicity battle to combat public sentiment against the chemical regime. Unfazed, other states have created ballot initiatives for GE food labeling measures. In the meantime, over 80 percent of nonorganic food on supermarket shelves contains GE ingredients, and only the USDA Organic label or a newer label from the Non-GMO Project verifies that there is no genetic tinkering involved.

The chemical industry has bitterly retorted that pesticide residues do not jeopardize human health and that organic panic is unwarranted. Opponents seem to begrudge organics for reasons that are not always straightforward. Antagonists groaned that the creation of the organic label itself might have given some consumers the impression that all conventional foods were unsuitable for ingestion. Organic farming critic Alex A. Avery censured the organic industry for "scaremongering" tactics that frighten consumers into thinking that organic food was the only safe option. He professed that pesticide residues on crops—both synthetic *and* natural—were miniscule and rendered no threat to humans.[49] In spite of assurances like these, food scares and distaste for anything "artificial" helped organics enter the mainstream. The Weston A. Price Foundation is one group that has actively endorsed organic foods as the antithesis of artificiality and buoyed the "traditional" foods of "our ancestors" that were displaced by the "so-called civilized diet."[50] Founded in 1999 to promote the research Price conducted in the 1930s—the findings that influenced J. I. Rodale—the organization has taught consumers to buy organically raised meats and produce, stressing that these are richer in nutrients and free from most toxic residues.[51] The foundation's opposition to prevailing technology and processed foods has correlated with its ongoing support for organic and biodynamic farming. Overall, the entire organic movement has remained oriented toward praising acts of individual salvation, not mobilizing for social revolution.

BIG (BUT NOT-SO-BAD?) ORGANICS

When Nell Newman, daughter of Paul Newman, started Newman's Own Organics as a detachment of her father's food company, her pretzels, popcorn, chocolate cups, and Fig Newmans—organic versions of the iconic cookies—were instant hits. With a folksy aura, each Newman's Own Organics package featured an American Gothic "Pa" Newman and daughter Nell in proper costume. The organic Ginger Snaps and organic Oatmeal Chocolate Chip cookies were labeled "Family Recipe Cookies." Like other early organic food companies, Newman's Own Organics had an idiosyncratic personality that was not easy to uphold once it achieved broad-spectrum popularity. Some consumers began to assume that all snacks with the Newman name were organic, but most products in the original Newman's Own line were not. In fact, some of the Newman's Own Organics were not even certified organic, compounding the confusion. Throughout the decades, many organic companies like Newman's Own Organics have worked sedulously to make the healthy ambience of their brands stand out on increasingly crowded shelves.

Health food stores once dominated the market for organic products to a far greater extent than supermarkets. In 1991, only 7 percent of organic products were sold in conventional supermarkets, while 68 percent were sold in health and natural food stores.[52] In *Profitable Organic Farming* (1995), Jon Newton said that most organic farmers wanted to sell their products in their local towns and were "apprehensive about the power and ruthlessness of the supermarket buyers." However, supermarkets were the main sources of food procurement, so organic food would have to be sold there to reach a larger portion of the population and reach a significant percentage of the food market.[53] As esteem for organic food grew, major retailers in the United States—for example, Wal-Mart, Kmart, and Target—added organic products. The allotment of organic foods sold at these outlets instead of smaller stores jumped from 1 percent in 1998 to 13 percent in 1999.[54] By 2000, more organic food was purchased in conventional supermarkets than in any other venue. Organic food was the fastest-growing fraction of food sales in North America. United Natural Foods (UNF) was the largest distributor of organic food in the United States, and Whole Foods Market was the largest single buyer.[55] Although organic food accounted for only 1 percent of the total food industry, its speedy progression attracted attention from mainstream food producers, handlers, and retailers.[56]

Industrial food giants who controlled the bulk of grocery sales ascertained the budding profitability of organic food and soon manufactured the majority of organic products in the retail market. "Big box" retailers like Costco, Sam's Club, and BJ's Wholesale Club accounted for over $600 million in organic sales in 2005.[57] National supermarket chains rolled out organic private label product lines with more affordable prices. Safeway launched its version of organic packaged goods, "O Organics," in 2005, and three years later this was the biggest organic brand in the country. Publix began selling USDA-certified organic ketchup, mustard, and more in its GreenWise Market Organic line, advertising that you can "enjoy the benefits of organics even as a condiment."[58] Established independent organic companies met head-on competition from this upsurge in lower-cost store brands. Buyouts and acquisitions of small, pioneering organic companies by hefty corporations occurred regularly. Samuel Fromartz's *Organic, Inc.* (2006) discussed the growth of organic food businesses and said that "the organic food industry is littered with founders who built companies, then cashed out to mainstream food giants."[59] Daniel Imhoff noted that Wall Street mergers and consolidations were "undermining the community orientation of the movement's origins."[60] Both wariness and exuberance from the public greeted these organic leaps into the mainstream.

Some high-profile businesses that capitalized on organic food—like Horizon Organic and Cascadian Farm—have been the target of hostile critiques. Others—like Stonyfield Farm and Organic Valley—have been more successful at convincing the public that "Big Organic" can still be beautiful. Some fall in the middle of positive and negative perceptions. One example is the Hain Pure Food Company, which health food advocate Dr. Harold Hain founded in 1926 to market his natural carrot and celery juices. He expanded the offerings to the point where, by 1970, his successors were selling $5 million worth of saffleflower products. The company sought to provide "wholesome and delicious products in their natural pure form."[61] In 1998, Hain Pure Foods commenced an alliance with H. J. Heinz, which came to own approximately 20 percent of the company. In 2000, the Celestial Seasonings tea company merged with the Hain Food Group, generating the Hain Celestial Group. The Hain Celestial Group turned into the category leader of the natural-foods business in North America and Europe by buying up dozens of smaller companies. In 2004, CEO Irwin Simon explained that the Hain mission still entailed "changing the way the world eats" and also included providing "a healthy way of life." Its business strategy, meanwhile, was to "enhance mainstream products for mass appeal" and meet consumer desire.[62] In 2007, Simon noted that "the natural and organic sector has moved into mainstream acceptance," helping sales of Hain's "better for you" products to soar. Consumers' heightened appreciation for sustainability, environmental responsibility, functional foods, and healthful solutions boded well for the company.[63]

By 2010, Hain Celestial Group owned heaps of widely recognized natural, organic, and specialty brands. These included Arrowhead Mills (grains, nut butters), Celestial Seasonings (tea), Walnut Acres Organic (juices, sauces, soups), Earth's Best Organic (baby and kids' food), Garden of Eatin' (chips), Health Valley (soups, cereals, baked products), Spectrum Naturals (oils), Imagine Foods (soups), Soy Dream (soy milk), Rice Dream (rice milk), DeBoles (pasta), MaraNatha (nut butters), SunSpire (chocolates), Avalon Organics (personal care), and JĀSÖN (body care). Even astute organic consumers often do not realize that many of their favorite brands actually all belong to the same owner. Obscure ownership configurations may lead consumers to believe that they are purchasing organic food from small grassroots companies. Hain markets nearly two thousand organic products, making it the largest single organic supplier in the country, and its stock is traded on the NASDAQ market. Still, the company emphasizes its initiatives that extend "wholesome eating" to everyone, use sustainable packaging, and encourage conversion to organic agriculture. It participates in the Non-GMO Project, is a founding member of the Whole Grains Council, and does not permit trans fats or high-fructose corn syrup in its products.[64] Hain has extended its distribution channels through partnerships: McDonald's offered a McVeggie Burger that was cobranded with Yves Veggie Cuisine; Delta Airlines began serving Earth's Best Organic Applesauce; and JetBlue Airways chose Terra Blues as its official chip. In 2011, Hain also purchased Danival, a French organic producer, and GG UniqueFiber, a Norwegian natural foods company; and the company was attracting billionaire investors.[65] Even while reaping revenues in the organic kingdom, the Hain Celestial Group has trumpeted that it supports family farms, makes a positive impact on people's health, and keeps millions of pounds of chemical pesticides from being dumped in the soil each year.

Stonyfield Farm, whose beginnings were discussed in an earlier chapter, was another "Big Organic" health food success story. When CEO Gary Hirshberg sold Stonyfield to the multinational consumer-products giant Groupe Danone Corporation for $125 million, some critics grumbled, but he asserted that the deal was a "win-win" situation for organic producers and consumers. Hirshberg's family made $35 million in the deal, yet he put a spin on jabs about selling out by saying that Danone's buying power would help Stonyfield's core values spread even further.[66] Though criticized for abandoning his progressive social business stance, Hirshberg resolved that Stonyfield Farm was still "here to change the world."[67] Nutrition professor Marion Nestle was skeptical, saying, "Stonyfield may be organic, but it is Big Yogurt."[68] Still, Hirshberg continued to describe himself as an "eco-entrepreneur," the "CE-Yo" of a company that aimed to be both sustainable and profitable.

A Stonyfield Farm print advertising campaign in 2000 used celebrities like filmmaker Ken Burns and restaurateur Rick Bayless to broadcast environmental messages tied to Stonyfield's "Yogurt on a Mission" tagline. Hirshberg stamped this concept "ad-tivism," combining advertising and activism.[69] Though there was plenty of sugar in the yogurts, many of the spots launched in a national advertising campaign in 2003 focused on health. Another Stonyfield strategy was to cultivate rustic, pastoral images of itself. The yogurt ingredients were listed as "Our Family Recipe," even though some included organic annatto extract and zinc gluconate (rarely household pantry staples). Stonyfield professed, "We want you to feel good inside." Cartons and lids were used as minibillboards for relevant social and environmental

Stonyfield YoKids, YoBaby, and yogurt (Photo courtesy of Colleen Freda Burt)

messages, including information about Stonyfield's pledge for organic family farming and its vow to give 10 percent of each year's profit to environmental causes.[70] In an article in 2007, the Sierra Club gave Stonyfield a seal of approval for the company's labors to reduce its carbon footprint, such as investing in an anaerobic manure digester and reducing the amount of plastic used in its cups. By remaining true to "save-the-planet values," the company built customer allegiance.[71]

Stonyfield Farm is a well-articulated brand with healthy connotations that has gained a cult-like following. Lids for Stonyfield's Oikos organic Greek yogurts have given reasons why "buying organic is worth it," and in 2011 a Stonyfield blog post included advice on how to reuse the lids as Christmas ornaments that would "jazz up your tree."[72] Stonyfield created a website in 2012, iWillKnowMyFood.com, that aimed to foster a "food awakening" in people and teach them that "each bite matters—to you, your family, farmers, animals and the planet."[73] The site included a virtual tour of Stonyfield Farm and a sweepstakes to win a "farm-to-fridge adventure" and refrigerator makeover. A typical advertisement for its organic yogurt catered to eco-friendly proclivities by promising: "You're supporting farmers committed to protecting the environment." Stonyfield's YoBaby yogurt packages were made from plant materials and had codes that could be redeemed for rewards, like a donation to the Organic Farming Research Foundation (OFRF), a one-quarter-ton carbon offset from NativEnergy, or a YoBaby bib. The @Stonyfield Twitter account had nearly 44,000 followers in 2014, and over 330,000 people "liked" the Stonyfield Farm Facebook page. Stonyfield expanded its customer base by forging emotional connections, making its label an invitation to a healthy lifestyle.

Hirshberg also created O'Naturals, a fast-food restaurant chain offering convenient, healthy meals that started with outlets in New England in 2001 and subsequently opened franchises in other locations. It was the same year that Eric Schlosser's *Fast Food Nation: The Dark Side of the All-American Meal*, an exposé of unsanitary and unappetizing assembly-line meals, was published to much critical acclaim. Hirshberg's restaurants proclaimed a "revolution in fast food." O'Naturals did not serve ingredients with additives, preservatives, or "multiple syllable stuff that you find in processed foods." Organic mixed greens, organic beef, organic tofu, and organic ranch dressing were used in tossed salads, flatbread sandwiches, soups, pizza, and noodle dishes. The Caesar salad included organic romaine, flatbread croutons, grated Parmesan, and vegan dressing. Kids could have organic mac 'n' cheese, hormone-free mini turkey sandwiches, or organic apple juice. O'Naturals said, "Organic and natural foods are better for you and the planet too."[74] With this venture, Hirshberg seemed to bridge the dichotomy that organic food advocates often posed between "fast food" as an unmitigated evil and "real food"—meaning local, healthy, and organic—as its hallowed opposite. O'Naturals later changed its name to Stonyfield Café and added sweet-n-tart organic soft serve frozen yogurt to the menu but assured fans that it was "the same 'green,' all-natural, organic restaurant you love."[75] Though Stonyfield struck some people as too pervasive, Hirshberg maintained that thousands of organic dairy farmers would be out of businesses if it were not for support from his company.

Another organic powerhouse self-styled as a "family farm"—Cascadian Farm—sells organic cereals, granola bars, frozen fruits and vegetables, fruit spreads, and juice concentrates that are perceived as healthy alternatives to conventional foods. When Cascadian Farm founder Gene Kahn started his twenty-acre berry farm in 1971, he was a steadfast subscriber to *Organic Gardening and Farming* magazine. Kahn believed in market populism over health asceticism and felt that, even if the masses wanted saccharine organic confections, organic businesses should provide them.[76] Cascadian Farm commenced contracting with other organic growers and morphed quickly

Cascadian Farm organic cereal (Photo courtesy of Colleen Freda Burt)

Cascadian Farm: open to visitors (Photo courtesy of Lisa Powell)

into a successful grower, marketer, and distributor of organic products. The company became a miniconglomerate, and Kahn regarded this as an opening to bring high-quality organic food to even more people. Cascadian Farm became part of Small Planet Foods in 1998; General Mills purchased Small Planet Foods in 2000. Michael Pollan used the "organic empire" of Cascadian Farm to illustrate the progression of corporate routinization on what began as a "communal hippie farm." Pollan expressed his disapproval by saying that "in the eyes of General Mills, organic is not a revolution so much as a market niche."[77] Cascadian Farm, however, saw its growth as universally good. When the company redesigned its products in 2008, a new series of advertisements featured the Cascadian Farm logo across an image of crops in the foreground and mountains in the background. Beneath pictures of the granola bars and cereal boxes was the proclamation "organic goodness from farm to table." One advertisement showed rolling farmland at dawn and the words: "This is the place that inspires our farmers . . . to make our organic granolas so incredibly delicious." The original roadside stand was "still home to the organic values we've always believed in."[78] Cascadian Farm even invited members of the public to visit its "Home Farm" in Washington's Upper Skagit Valley for a dish of fresh berries.

These kinds of promotional efforts at crafting fealty by organic companies are frequently successful. Tenaciously loyal organic consumers tend to forge intense relationships with the brands they feel connected to. According to a survey by the Natural Marketing Institute, many consumers perceive brands such as Cascadian Farm, Horizon Organic, and Stonyfield Farm as small, authentic, and even artisanal cottage industries, even though larger corporations own these companies and their products are not handcrafted in small batches.[79] Newman's Own Organics, the Hain Celestial Group, Arrowhead Mills, Celestial Seasonings, Stonyfield Farm, Cascadian Farm, Earthbound Farm, and other major organic players have all done their utmost to distinguish themselves as corporations that retain the crux of healthy, wholesome organic attributes.

Wendell Berry's notable statement that "eating is an agricultural act" illustrates how food consumption cannot be separated from how and where it is grown.[80] For Marx, the labor power of a producer initially bestowed the value of a commodity. As money became the sign of worth, it replaced labor's clout with an apparently autonomous value for the commodity. This illusion of sovereign value gave rise to commodity fetishism, in which the significance of labor was disavowed.[81] Rather, the commodity was animated by its assessed monetary worth, indicated through a price tag. Commodity fetishism usually entails an erasure of the marks of production. However, organic food is fetishized precisely because it elucidates production circumstances. It is regarded as a specialty or craft object, not a mass-market commodity. Instead of making the worker's labor invisible, the organic certification system pulls back the curtain on production methods. The organic label is meant to demystify how food is grown. In this sense, it is an attempt at transparency, distinguishing it from unmarked food. Organics might have languished without escalating consumer sentience and the demand for an identifiable label.

LITTLE BODIES

The squeezable plastic Peter Rabbit Organics pouches of pea, spinach, and apple puree—adorned with illustrations of Beatrix Potter's iconic bunny alongside the USDA Organic seal—seem innocuous enough. One must assume, though, that a parent gamely pays $2.50 for one serving because he or she has deemed the glass jar of Gerber nonorganic mashed peas that sells for 87 cents to be intrinsically inferior. Nobody wants to take chances with a baby's health. Even ten years after the Alar episode, an Environmental Working Group report upbraided the government for not doing its job to shield children from pesticides. Organic activists have agreed that the EPA did not deliver on its promise to "fully protect infants and children from damaging pesticide exposures."[82] Other reports have surfaced linking pesticides in food to neuro-behavioral problems, such as allergies, autism, and ADHD. The US Centers for Disease Control points to food as one of the main sources of pesticide exposure for American children. Concentrations of pesticide residues are six times higher in blood samples of children eating conventionally farmed fruits and vegetables, compared with those eating organic.[83] Parents have been a bull's-eye for organic food marketers, though uncertainty about pesticides is revived regularly. *Baby Talk* magazine addressed the question in an article in 2000 but offered divergent perspectives. One professor of pediatrics believed that parents should feed their infants only organic food, because babies' small size left them more susceptible to pesticides, while the chairman of the American Academy of Pediatrics' Committee on Nutrition maintained that the amount of pesticides in processed baby foods was far too low to be a threat. The article concluded that there was "no solid evidence" that conventional food posed a risk, but parents might want to offer organic food "for a change of pace."[84] Most likely, though, organic foods have been chosen as a kind of health insurance policy to allay parental disquiet about babies' less-developed immune systems rather than for variety's sake.

Nielsen Homescan data has disclosed that parents of young children are more likely than childless people to purchase organic food.[85] Hyatt hotel chains offer healthy three-course organic meals for kids, created by chef Alice Waters. At M Café in Los Angeles—known for "contemporary macrobiotic cuisine"—the menu for kids includes a "Mini Macro Burger with Organic Fries" (and soy cheese, pickles, and macro ketchup on a mini whole grain bun). Olivia's Organics has kid-friendly packaging on its celery, spinach, butternut squash, and salad blends. Annie's organic bunny-shaped fruit snacks are popular in kids' lunchboxes. The organic kids menu at Terrapin Restaurant in Rhinebeck, New York, includes mahi-mahi crispy fish sticks and chicken nuggets. Celebrity magazines have reported that actress Denise Richards treats her children to organic frozen yogurt with chocolate covered goji berries at Malibu's SunLife Organics.[86] Though McDonald's has not yet indicated that it will make organic Happy Meals, large chains could be headed in that direction. Children may not know the difference when they are eating organically, but, of course, their parents do.

Reports have showed that organic baby foods have become increasingly vital to parents looking for guarantees about nutrition and food safety.[87] Not *all* mothers are terribly perturbed about chemicals, though. Both the American Academy of Pediatrics (AAP) and the American Dietetic Association have assured parents that they should feel perfectly safe feeding their babies nonorganic food and formula. The bottom line, according to *Parenting* magazine, is that "buying organics for your baby is more of an environmental choice than a health one."[88] Yet, since pesticides affect the bodies and brains of children more so than those of adults, parents often choose organic products for infants even before buying these for themselves. *Organically Raised: Conscious Cooking for Babies and Toddlers* (2010) advised that incorporating organic eating into your lifestyle may demand more thought, time, and commitment, but "your efforts will reward your baby with more taste, vitality, and well-being."[89] A recent ad for Horizon read: "Behind every child who finishes the day strong there's a mom who chooses Horizon Organic Milk." Unmistakably, the industry's message has been that choosy moms ought to choose organic.

A mélange of organic food companies cater to parents' protective impulse. The German company Sunval began making organic baby food as

Organic baby food (Photo courtesy of Colleen Freda Burt)

early as 1950 under the Bio Bambini label, with raw materials coming from organic-certified farms. Bio Bambini pledges that "our baby food is produced with respect and love for nature." The products, made in Germany, include upscale purees of parsnip and potato, pumpkin with potatoes and fennel, pear and apple muesli, wholemeal noodles and ham, and ratatouille, perhaps insinuating that babies have fairly sophisticated palates.[90] Many other companies have followed suit. Plum Organics makes lustrously decorated pouches of blueberry oats and quinoa "Mish Mash" purees, boxes of apple carrot "Fiddlesticks" (fruit and grain snacks), and "Teensy Fruits" soft fruit snacks. Plum Organics claims that introducing babies to these "delightful tastes and pure ingredients" will lead to a lifetime of healthy eating.[91] Earth's Best Organic baby food offers whole grain dinner blends for infants akin to those healthy entrées popularized by the counterculture, like vegetable beef pilaf, rice, and lentils, and plum banana brown rice. Apple & Eve Sesame Street Organics juice boxes are less exotic but costar recognizable characters for tots, in Elmo's Punch, Big Bird's Apple, and Bert & Ernie's Berry. Sesame Street figures also greet children on packages of Earth's Best Organic cereals, mini waffles, cookies, smoothies, and pizzas. Several of these products—like Elmo's organic cheese ravioli—contain evaporated cane syrup (from sugar cane), whereas Ella's Kitchen staunchly declares that it will never add sugar or salt to its organic baby food—not even to its Yum Yummy Apple + Ginger Baby Cookies. Ella's Kitchen says that "yummy 100% organic food" is better because it has "no nasty additives" and contains higher levels of vitamin C and essential minerals.[92] One advertisement for Stonyfield Farm's YoBaby yogurt told parents that organic food can "drastically reduce pesticide content in a child's body," echoing that it is "especially good for babies."

Some parents may resist organic food on the grounds of price. An ad for Earthbound Farm, known for its organic salad mixes, urged people to start gardens of their own, declaring that "with each delicious bite, you can take comfort in knowing you're protecting your family's health. And that's priceless." The text might have made consumers feel embarrassed for quibbling about the higher price tag of organic arugula, because it implied that, considering how organic food could safeguard the health of one's children, a few extra dollars ought to be inconsequential. This "your child is worth it" provocation emerged in marketing for other baby products as well, like bumGenius organic cloth diapers, Aveeno Baby Organic Harvest diaper rash cream, Vermont Soap organic aloe baby bars, and Dolphin Organics baby bubble bath. The corn-based beach toys from Zoë b Organic were biodegradable, made in the United States, and free of BPA or phthalates. Parents were encouraged to protect their "bundle of joy" from the "ill health effects" of synthetic chemicals by using the Miessence certified organic baby line. These "nurturing products" might even "give your baby a head start in life."[93] Avalon Organics said that using its baby shampoo "lets you rest easy knowing you are treating your baby's delicate skin and hair with the utmost care."[94] And Nature's Baby Organics also said that "you can rest easy" knowing that its organic products have been formulated with the finest and purest ingredients for a baby's sensitive skin.[95] The description for Nature's Baby organic baby oil began: "Would you put petroleum on your baby's skin? Of course not. But most baby oils are made with mineral oil, a petroleum by-product. Instead, try our nourishing Organic Baby Oil. . . . This 95% certified organic oil is made with skin-soothing organic moisturizers—Organic Olive Oil, Jojoba Oil, Tamanu Oil & Sunflower Oil to feed and protect skin."[96] BabyGanics also described its bath and body care products as nontoxic, safe, made with "natural plant-based ingredients," "gentle on baby's skin," and "earth safe, people safe and picky mother-in-law safe." Parents do need to be careful when observing the line between natural and organic; despite what the brand name suggested, BabyGanics products were not certified organic and did not bear the USDA seal.[97]

Happy Baby: The Organic Guide to Baby's First 24 Months (2009) reiterated that babies were "more vulnerable" to pesticides, so parents should serve them organic foods.[98] The Happy Family line of organic baby and toddler foods was endorsed by renowned pediatrician Dr. Robert W. Sears, who co-wrote the book. Happy Family sold Happy Yogis organic freeze-dried banana mango yogurt snacks; Happy Bellies organic multigrain baby cereal with DHA, pre- and probiotics, and choline in a BPA-free canister; and Happy Baby organic sweet potato puffs in BPA- and PVC-free recyclable packaging. The Happy Times (Tagline: "Organic Superfoods") Yummy Yogis caramel yogurt apple bits box said that they had no artificial ingredients, no preservatives, no trans fats, and no GMOs—just "100% goodness" and "an added boost of nature's best nutrition." The Happy Melts yogurt snacks were made with organic milk, organic sugar, organic fruit, and pre- and probiotics for digestive health. Happy Tot organic meals were fruit and vegetable mixes fortified with antioxidants, nutrients, and Salba (a "super grain"). Happy Family clearly embraced the concept of functional ingredients and descriptive labels in its organic baby blends. Also combining health claims with social consciousness was Little Duck Organics, founded by a father who snubbed

Happy Baby organic snacks (Photo courtesy of Colleen Freda Burt)

the extra sugar and GMOs he saw in baby snacks. Instead, he created a company selling "awesome treats" like organic freeze-dried fruit snacks, and Little Duck Organics teamed up with 1% for Humanity to help fight hunger and malnutrition worldwide.[99] Stonyfield Farm YoBaby ads stated that organic yogurt was "a simple, everyday way to feed your little one pure, healthy food" and cited studies showing that organic fruits and vegetables were "more nutritious than their nonorganic counterparts." Again, it was an alternative, not a replacement: the organic baby food segment has been more successful in cementing a not-in-my-baby mentality among "enlightened" parents willing to buy organics than in removing unsafe elements from all baby food.

ORGANIC DESSERTS

Whether for children or adults, industrially processed organic foods once seemed like a contradiction in terms, beyond the realm of possibility. In

1972, Robert Rodale explained that, by his designation, organically grown food was not refined, chemically treated, or extensively altered. He said that there could be no such thing as organically produced white bread, because refining the wheat would destroy its organic quality.[100] Soon, however, not only was organic white bread being sold, but so were organic donuts, organic jelly beans, organic soda pop, and organic snow cone syrup—other products that would have seemed oxymoronic in days of yore, had anybody possessed the temerity to conceive of them. Organic gummy bears would have once looked absurd. Industry observer William Lockeretz discussed the early days, when "organic farming proponents stressed the importance of a wholesome diet based on a variety of whole or minimally processed foods." Since then, he had seen "a growing number of organic products that no doubt would have shocked the pioneers," labeled organic without regard for nutritional implications.[101] Packaged organic brownies, cinnamon rolls, marshmallows, and other delicacies the Rodales would have been aghast at filled out the supermarket shelves. Consumers could stock their pantries with overrefined snacks depleted of "wholeness" but still wearing the USDA Organic seal.

Nutrition professor Joan Dye Gussow pointed out that the OFPA had focused too narrowly on the process of organic production but not enough on the product. Gussow tackled the ironic question of if an organic Twinkie can be certified and concluded that, for better or worse, it could indeed. While developing national standards, a segment of the organic food industry was "working toward a parallel food supply where a certified organic Twinkie or its equivalent would not be beyond imagining." Although the rest of the organic community might be appalled by the idea of organic "junk food," these objections—that organic foods should be "healthy" or "wholesome"—were far more difficult to quantify.[102] Gussow felt that, originally, the word "organic" carried "an implicit environmental, social, economic, and nutritional wholesomeness." But, under a strict legal definition outlining growing and processing methods, the term no longer had "a conscience."[103] It also seemed progressively distant from actual organic farmers.

The proliferation of organic "junk" food illustrates a plane of cognitive dissonance—or what Antonio Gramsci termed "contradictory consciousness"—in American health acuity. Some consumers rationalize that the organic label negates any qualms about indulging in sugar-laden sweets. There are people who eat organic salad every day but never exercise. Some people trick themselves into thinking that nothing organic can hurt their diet; the organic label skews judgment and dissolves scruples. Jovial brand cookies made from organic einkorn flour (an ancient wheat) seemed virtuous enough; the recycled cardboard carton said that they were "crafted in small batches by passionate Italian artisan bakers" and contained three grams of protein per serving (never mind that organic cane sugar was the second ingredient listed). An organic Peanut Butter Classics cookie by Liz Lovely was touted on the package as "dairy-free, egg-free, no trans fat, low sodium, certified vegan," containing fair trade certified ingredients, and "certified organic by Vermont Organic Farmers." However, one single cookie still had 420 calories, 24 grams of fat, and 28 grams of sugar. Comparably, when the Bernod Group introduced its Spun City brand of certified organic cotton candy in 2008, it advertised that this "deliciously decadent" vegan treat contained no chemicals, cholesterol, sodium, artificial colors, or artificial flavors. The cotton candy was still pure sugar, albeit disguised as "organic evaporated cane juice," a sweetener derived from sugar cane syrup that was not juice at all.

Inclusion of organic ingredients does not transmogrify every nutrient-deficient saccharine product into a healthy one. Fats, oils, and sweets should be eaten sparingly whether one is svelte or pudgy; choosing organic fudge over nonorganic cauliflower just because it's organic is obviously not a sage choice. Nutritional perceptions and reality are notoriously disengaged and often paradoxical. Gramsci believed that the coexistence of contradictory views was not simply self-deception; rather, it signified how individuals made choices between concurrent conceptions of the world.[104] Indeed, many consumers could defend purchasing items like FruitaBü Organic Smooshed Fruit Twirl Roll-Ups and Rawzins Organic Chocolate Covered Raisins as a lesser evil—or even as downright saintly—in an ominous atmosphere of noxious foods. Noting this inherent partiality, one study even warned that "eating organic food may make you fatter," because when people envisioned that a food was more nutritious they let their guard down in terms of counting calories.[105] Making sensible choices when you don't have all the answers and feel bombarded by muddled labels is difficult.

Organic "SuperChocolate" bars from Fearless Chocolate are crafted in a low-temperature environment to preserve "maximum nutrition," and the organic 70 percent cacao "SuperFruit" variety is "infused with ultra-super-food organic Açai plus Maqui berry for a super-duper healthy fruity zing."[106] The chocolate organic sandwich cookies made by Late July Organic Snacks—affixed with both the USDA Organic seal and Jane Goodall's seal for ethically produced products—are advertised as a "good source of whole grains," "good source of calcium," "good for the earth," and "good for all." It is difficult for some people to imagine that organic foods like these could *not* be more nutritious—yet there are still those who jeer at that suggestion, viewing the organic label as a device to extract money from the credulous. Beyond that, organic "junk food" seems to have undermined the potential of organic food to be a gastro-groundbreaker. Meanwhile, organic dairies have encountered their own regulatory debates and public relations issues.

SOUR MILK

Organic milk differed from other organic products in that it began as a crossover product, appealing even to people who had not sampled any other organic foods. Since organic dairy products were often the first organic foods a consumer experimented with, they were considered a gateway to supplementary organic sectors. The rise of organic milk consumption was attributed to a "not-in-my-body" politics that arose in response to controversy over artificial growth hormones. Organic milk was unique, according to one sociologist, because the clamor for it came "without the significant social and political organizing—the food co-ops, the consumer-farmer coalitions—that created the organic food system over the last few decades."[107] Consumer interest in organic milk has burgeoned since the mid-1990s, largely due to the increasing use of recombinant Bovine Growth Hormone (rBGH) or recombinant Bovine Somatotropin (rBST) in conventional dairies. All cows produce natural growth hormones; however, conventional cows are commonly injected with a genetically engineered growth hormone to increase milk production by about a gallon per day. The Monsanto Corporation produced the artificial hormone under the commercial name Posilac, and in 1993 the FDA concluded that it did not pose a threat to human health. Sponsors of rBST insisted that it was safe and effective. Organic dairies did not use the artificial growth hormone, and some milk cartons featured a label promising that the milk came from cows not treated with rBST. In 2003, Monsanto sued Oakhurst, a small Maine dairy, for stating on its label that the milk came from cows receiving no rBST. Monsanto alleged that this implicitly disparaged milk coming from cows given the synthetic hormone. Instead of going to trial, Oakhurst agreed to add a disclaimer to its label: "FDA states: No significant difference in milk from cows treated with artificial growth hormones."

In 2005, the Center for Global Food Safety, an industry group funded by agribusinesses, launched an aggressive "Milk is Milk" campaign to persuade consumers that there was no difference between milk produced by cows injected with genetically engineered hormones and organic or "natural" milk. The campaign also attempted to stop organic farmers and retailers from labeling their milk as "hormone-free," asserting that this was bogus, since all milk contained hormones. Brands advertising that they did not use artificial growth hormones were forced to include a small proviso that milk from non-rBST cows was not significantly different. However, demand for organic milk was strongly correlated to the fact that regulations excluded rBST. Consumers spoke up. McDonald's announced in 2007 that it would switch to organic milk for its coffee and hot chocolate drinks in the United Kingdom, and consumption grew 22 percent in the next two years.[108] Wal-Mart determined in 2008 that, due to a lack of consumer patronage, its store-brand milk would no longer be sourced from dairies treating cows with the artificial hormone. Monsanto decided to sell off its beleaguered Posilac business in 2008. By 2009, Dannon and General Mills also declared that they would phase out the use of rBST milk, in accordance with consumer preferences. Speculation about cancer risks and other health hazards from the use of synthetic hormones is still a major reason that consumers choose organic milk.

The "Happy Cows" advertising campaign by Real California Milk, featuring cheerful talking cows, bolstered the illusion that dairies treated their cows kindly. This expectation might be double for organic dairies.[109] Many organic consumers speciously believe that all organic milk flows from contented cows grazing tranquilly among the silos and barns on small family farms. The majority of organic dairy farms do embrace humane animal husbandry as they follow legal and ethical standards. Not all organic livestock is happy, though. When the USDA Organic Standards in 2001 required "access to pasture for ruminants," this law caused heated discussions. Some hardliners felt that it did not give adequate details on stocking rate, feed expectations, or confinement. A dairy hoping to circumvent the higher costs and labor requirements of producing organic milk could meet protocol with a loose interpretation of "access" or "pasture." Certification agencies construed the requirements differently, permitting some suspect activity. There were factory farm dairies, certified as organic, that confined thousands of cows to feedlots and gave them grain and hay (albeit organic), rather than granting meaningful access to grass from pasture. Organic factory farms could be organic in letter but violate the spirit of organic standards. Some were skirting regulations. Even while plagued by these disputes, the organic dairy industry was tremendously profitable, with sales in excess of $15 billion by 2006 and frequent market shortages.[110] Assurance of top commodity prices has been a lifeline for many organic dairy farmers. Overall sales of organic milk and cream comprise approximately 6 percent of retail milk sales. Conventional channels sell the majority of organic milk products; the two main US suppliers, providing approximately 75 percent of branded organic milk, are Horizon Organic and Organic Valley, two dairies with divergent story lines.[111]

Horizon Organic, founded in 1991, is the nation's largest organic food brand in any category. The company calls itself a pioneer in organic dairy farming and land stewardship. Horizon's founders joined other industry leaders in helping to develop the National Organic Standards and the USDA Organic seal.[112] Horizon garners over $200 million in annual sales and is the leading brand of certified organic milk in both the United States and the United Kingdom. Dean Foods, a $13-billion food and beverage company that is the largest milk distributor in the United States, owns WhiteWave Foods, which, in turn, is the parent company of Horizon Organic.[113] When Charles Marcy, president and CEO of Horizon Organic, addressed the IFOAM Organic World Congress in 2002 about organic sales and marketing, he said that one of the creeds of good organic retailing was to "capitalize on the authenticity and commitment of the brand." In all retail formats, from natural food stores to supermarkets, an organic brand should position itself "as something that mainstream consumers would naturally and logically want to incorporate into their lifestyles."[114] Horizon has adhered to these strategies and catered to the majority. Its recognizable national advertising campaign features a fun flying cow mascot, publicizes the company's obligation to organic family farms, and emphasizes personal benefits to the consumer. Horizon tells consumers that organic means "No antibiotics. No added, artificial hormones. No junk you'd rather avoid. Just creamy, wholesome milk the way the cows intended." However, much of Horizon's organic milk is produced at industrial-size dairies and confined animal feeding operations (CAFOs) with thousands of cows, which has made it a magnet for vilification.

The Organic Consumers Association (OCA) led a boycott of Horizon Organic in 2006, indicting its dairies for violating federal laws that govern organic foods. Critics charged that Horizon used milk from cows confined indoors. Horizon defended itself by saying that the company complied with USDA requirements and also adhered to its own "Standards of Care" guidelines. While admitting that it sourced some milk from large farms, Horizon said that the greater portion came from "small family farms."[115] The OCA disagreed. More skirmishes occurred in 2009, when Dean Foods announced that it would begin marketing products under the Horizon brand name that were *not* certified organic. Instead, it would use a stand-in "natural dairy" label (and create its own definition for "natural"). A Dean spokesperson said that the nonorganic Horizon would be "easier on the pocketbook," since nonorganic products would cost less. The Cornucopia Institute, a farm policy watchdog group, responded that Dean Foods had "chosen to profiteer" and had "declared war on the organic industry" by pilfering organic consumers. Ironically, the Cornucopia Institute was a shareholder of Dean Foods, which controlled five dozen dairy brands; yet Cornucopia wanted to police the industry on behalf of organic consumers, in the spirit of shareholder activism.[116] Horizon's nonorganic Little Blends toddler yogurts and Milk Breakers boxes did not last long; Horizon went back to all-organic products. At the same time, though, Dean Foods switched the soybeans in most of WhiteWave's Silk soymilks from all-organic to "natural" (conventional) soybeans, without lowering the price or publicizing the change. One of the Silk varieties remained organic, but this, too, alarmed organic food advocates and seemed a bit sneaky, especially considering the rampant perplexity about enigmatic natural and organic labels.

In addition to milk, Horizon sells cheese, butter, cottage cheese, cream cheese, yogurt, Tuberz yogurt tubes, eggs, and holiday eggnog. Horizon maintains a "Healthy Families" community on its website and a "Toolbox for Moms" on its Facebook page; both promise to provide coupons, recipes, news, and advice for "busy moms like you." The Horizon "About Us" page has said, "We were the first company to supply organic milk nationwide, and we're proud to be America's number-one organic dairy brand today."[117] Dean Foods/WhiteWave had also owned the Organic Cow of Vermont, which was promoted as "New England's original organic milk" and advertised alongside images of children frolicking in autumn foliage, even though its milk was not produced exclusively at farms in New England. In 2011, after sharing Horizon's milk supply for over a decade, the Organic Cow officially changed its packaging label over to Horizon Organic and dissolved into the colossus.[118]

Horizon's major competitor is the Organic Valley Family of Farms, the largest US organic products co-op. Seven Wisconsin farmers organized the Cooperative Regions of Organic Producer Pools (CROPP) in 1988, when farmland values were at a historic low. The co-operative's goal was to serve small family farmers and improve rural community health. The farmers' milk, cheese, and butter were marketed under the Organic Valley brand, which capped production to guarantee each farmer a reliable income. Organic Valley CEO George Siemon, one of the original founders, said that there were few voices advocating "farming in harmony with nature" at the time, but J. I. Rodale was "an inspiration to all the early pioneers of today's organic movement."[119] Siemon's family had operated an organic farm since 1977, and, for his new title, he cleverly preferred "C-E-I-E-I-O."[120] More than twelve hundred farmers in thirty-four states had joined the co-operative by 2007, when it reported revenues of over $400 million. Organic Valley dairy products are available throughout the nation, and its certified-organic meat products are sold under the Organic Prairie label.[121] The Organic Valley logo features a red barn set on a picturesque field of crops in neat rows. Milk cartons have carried personal statements from farmer-owners. In 2008, Organic Valley embarked on a kid-oriented advertising campaign that announced, "The Future Is Organic." The accompanying text on one ad read, "Choosing organic today helps ensure a healthy tomorrow." Organic Valley's single-serving milks, deli-sliced cheeses, and cheese sticks were said to be "great for growing bodies" because "they come from our family farms, where the cows eat grass and they're never treated with antibiotics, synthetic hormones or pesticides." An accompanying activity booklet, distributed at state fairs and other events in 2009, asked children to look at drawings of an Organic Valley farm and find "a cow happy to be outside eating green grass," "an organic carrot in soil made rich by earthworms and compost," "a piglet rolling in the shaded dirt," "corn growing without chemicals," and additional cute items. An adult-oriented brochure in 2009 urged consumers to choose organic because of quality ("safe, wholesome food—produced in harmony with nature"); environment ("keeping our air and water safe from pollution"); and family farms ("a viable means to sustain their farms and strengthen our rural communities"). When the Rodale Institute partnered with the Organic Valley dairy cooperative and the Nature's Path organic food brand in 2009 for an "Organic Heroes" promotion, it hoped to convince conventional farmers that farming organically could be an act of heroism. Advertisements encouraged each consumer to "Be a hero. Eat Organic!" Overall, Organic Valley pitches a sentimental connection between consumers and their organic milk producers, but it has not escaped unscathed from criticism.

Another milk controversy arose when the Cornucopia Institute charged in 2005 that all CAFOs should be outlawed by organic regulations. Cornu-

Organic Valley dairy products (Photo courtesy of Colleen Freda Burt)

copia accused both Horizon Organic and Organic Valley of violations of the organic grazing laws at facilities with no functional pasture. They also filed a formal complaint in 2006 with the USDA's National Organic Program against Aurora Organic Dairy of Colorado for livestock management improprieties. Aurora was a $100 million enterprise that managed over five thousand cows and provided private-label organic milk to chains from Wild Oats and Trader Joe's to Safeway, Wal-Mart, and Target. Cornucopia charged that Aurora's cattle grazed in feedlots rather than pasture and that Aurora obtained its cattle from a noncertified organic source. The USDA launched an investigation and found fourteen "willful" violations of federal organic law. Aurora had to meet certain conditions but was not fined and remained in business as an organic dairy.[122] The dairy eventually agreed to pay consumers $7.5 million in a class-action lawsuit for fraudulent marketing claims regarding its organic milk.[123] Another formal complaint from the Cornucopia Institute in 2011 led to a USDA investigation of Shamrock Farms, a supersized organic dairy in Arizona. Chastising the treatment of Shamrock's overconfined cows, Cornucopia said that the dairy was in "flagrant violation of the law" and was "masquerading as organic." The USDA moved to revoke the organic certification for Shamrock Farms after discovering inadequate, overgrazed pasture that did not meet federal regulations.[124] Still, faultfinders have reproached the USDA for lax oversight, repeatedly letting other "organic" factory dairies off the hook, and the organic movement continues to strive for a full-scale crackdown on the unchaste farms. The rancor over organic milk persists.

PROOF IN THE ORGANIC BROWN RICE PUDDING

J. I. Rodale was always adamant that organically raised vegetables contained the most vitamins and minerals.[125] There continued to be many who devotedly announced the connections between organic food and health. The mantra of "pay your organic farmer now, or pay your doctor later" is heard time and again in organic circles. Bob Flowerdew's *The Organic Gardening Bible* (1998) said that "anything grown organically at home of a good variety will always carry more nutritive value than store-bought produce."[126] Well-known physician Andrew Weil, director of the Program in Integrative Medicine at the University of Arizona and a board member of the Organic Center, has been a longtime ally of organic food for health. He has opined that choosing organic was a way of getting "the nutritional benefits nature provides," and that organic food was "a cornerstone on which to structure a lifestyle that will promote and maintain health."[127] Elaine Lipson, in *The Organic Foods Sourcebook* (2001), concluded that the overarching query—"Is Organic Food More Nutritious?"—was ill-advised. Organic was not a health fact but, rather, "a claim about a food production system."[128] Still, organic food could be "more wholesome." Lipson expounded: "Greater nutritional value in the entire category of organic foods may not be provable. But all things being equal, that organic carrot will more likely have been grown in conditions that nourish both soil and humans without potential harm, and that may reveal to us, if we are willing, a joyous connection to the earth and to those who grow our food."[129] Lipson is not alone in fealty to organic food's advantages for mind, body, and soul.

One innovative organization that united organic food and health was Organic Athlete, which associated "the founding precepts of organic agriculture with an Olympic spirit." Founded in 2003, it espoused health, exercise, ecological stewardship, and "a better world through sport."[130] Organic Athlete organized "Tour d'Organics" for the public, an annual series of bicycle rides to organic farms. The diet that Organic Athlete endorsed was organic and vegan for environmental, ethical, and health reasons. Organic foods, assumed to be free from pesticides and other toxic chemicals, were preferable because they had "consistently higher amounts of essential vitamins, minerals, and other nutrients compared to their conventionally grown counterparts."[131] The group members shared training tips, recipes, nutrition advice, and news. Athletes formed local chapters to train together and plan events that would educate people about organic, plant-based nutrition.

Several studies have indicated that organic food does have more nutrients, vitamins, minerals, flavonoids, or antioxidants than conventional food.[132] The Organic Center, a nonprofit organization founded in 2002, is dedicated to presenting peer-reviewed scientific data on how organic products benefit human and environmental health. It specifically aims to publish "credible scientific studies" that advance the organic cause. The Organic Center urges consumers to seek out organic produce because of its higher antioxidant, vitamin, and mineral levels and its lower levels of pesticides and mycotoxins, both of which may pose health risks or cause food poisoning. The Organic Center's *Core Truths* (2006) included research on why organic food often tastes better, why organic food drastically mollifies pesticide exposure, and why organic farms typically use less energy.[133] The University of California at Davis released the results of its Long-Term Research on Agricultural Systems project in 2007, demonstrating that tomatoes grown organically had "consistently higher levels of vitamin C and other antioxidants, including flavonoids," which are associated with reduced risk of heart disease and certain cancers.[134] Some research shows that this elevated antioxidant content in organic plants is correlated with the lower amount of available nitrogen common in organic cultivation, when manure is used instead of synthetic fertilizer.[135]

As a personal experiment, pediatrician Alan Greene spent three years eating nothing but organic foods and documenting it. At home it was easy, but when snacking on the road or dining out he found it exceptionally challenging. The all-organic standard was still "far off the beaten food grid," he said, and he resorted to carrying organic backpacking food with him. At the end of three years, though, Greene reported feeling more energetic and was rarely ill, despite his ongoing exposure to sick children.[136] Along with personal anecdotes, some organic advocates have issued reports that organic food helps protect against obesity.[137] An extensive report in 2008 confirmed the nutritional preeminence of organic produce, chiefly with respect to polyphenols and antioxidants.[138] These findings may be blemished by pointing out that the Organic Center's board of directors included Dr. Andrew Weil, Dr. Alan Greene, restaurateur Nora Pouillon, and "green lifestyle expert" Sara Snow, but also high-ranked executives from Whole Foods Market, Dean Foods, WhiteWave Foods, Organic Valley, Sambazon, United Natural Foods, and Earthbound Farm—all corporations that stood to gain financially from the advancement of organic foods.

With researchers propounding a hodgepodge of messages, carte blanche approval for organics is hard to come by. The hunt for hard proof is hindered by significant disparities in individual farm practices and crop strains. Some studies categorically dispute the legitimacy of organics' claim to nutritional preeminence. Organic food critic Thomas DeGregori has stated that "there is no scientifically verifiable evidence conferring any nutritional benefit to organic produce," regardless of the "antimodernist" preference for "eating closer to nature."[139] Detractors tend to highlight the weak health claims of organic agriculture and also call attention to food safety issues concomitant with the use of manure and compost.[140] In 2000, the ABC news show *20/20* aired an episode in which correspondent John Stossel stated that organic produce could actually be more harmful than conventional produce, citing findings of bacteria on certain samples. Environmental nonprofit federations challenged the allegation and uncovered that Stossel had fabricated his findings; Stossel later offered an on-air apology. Alex A. Avery asserted in 2006 that organic foods had more risks than conventional foods. He attributed the greater likelihood of food-borne illnesses and fungal toxins to organic farmers' heavy reliance on animal manure for fertilizer.[141]

The American Council on Science and Health (ACSH) published a report in 2008 stating that the Organic Center's evidence of nutritional superiority for organic crops was based on unscientific comparisons and irrelevant data. The ACSH said that "a consumer who buys organic food thinking that it is more nutritious is wasting a considerable amount of money."[142] Notably, the ACSH is a nonprofit consumer education consortium that has been funded in part by donations from Monsanto, Archer Daniels Midland, ISK Biotech Corporation, and Exxon, so it can hardly be unbiased. Still, a systematic review of studies on organic foods published in academic journals between 1958 and 2008 found "no evidence of a difference in nutrient quality between organically and conventionally produced foodstuffs."[143] Rob Johnston's "Great Organic Myths" also scoffed at health-related claims for organics and, instead, mentioned several studies showing that organic chicken flocks had higher rates of food-poisoning bacterium, Salmonella, and parasites.[144] Another study, funded by the United Kingdom's Food Standards Agency, created an uproar among organic boosters in 2009 when it declared that organic food did not offer any noteworthy nutritional benefits compared with conventionally produced food. The Organic Center, the Rodale Institute, and the Soil Association criticized the study's failure to take pesticide residue and other germane criteria into account. Stonyfield Farm CEO Gary Hirshberg also called the study misleading and flawed for omitting the recognition that "organic farming's avoidance of chemicals offers health benefits beyond nutrition."[145] But inordinate numbers of people still viewed organic food as flawed. Stanley Feldman, professor of anaesthetics at London University, thought favoritism for organics was "illogical" and that "zealots of the cult of organic food" were using "unscientific scare tactics."[146] Feldman said that "one should smell a rat" when proponents promised that organics were on the side of "nature" or were the way to "purity and truth."[147]

Political commentator Mischa Popoff impugned the entire organic industry for insufficient field testing to ensure that farmers were actually steering clear of toxic pesticides and synthetic fertilizer. Popoff, who grew up on an organic farm, said that the lack of accountability had created a culture of fraud and cheating. Popoff also accused organic activists of "fanciful thinking" and unfounded fears for rejecting genetically modified seeds. He lambasted organic farms as inept and antitechnological for shunning disease-resistant crop varieties. He said that the "romantic view" of organicists was "imperiling the very sustainability of our food supply."[148] Popoff's book, *Is It Organic?* (2010), was subtitled *The Inside Story of Who Destroyed the Organic Industry, Turned It into a Socialist Movement and Made Million$ in the Process, and a Comprehensive History of Farming, Warfare and Western Civilization from 1645 to the Present.* He called Jordan Rubin's "Beyond-Organic" weight loss plan—based on organic foods—the latest "scam of the organic biz," since there was no scientific research on "Beyond-Organic" food's nutritional superiority. Popoff said that the "Big Organic food boondoggle" relied on unproven evidence and sounded like "self-righteous missionary zeal couched in a get-rich scheme."[149] Popoff thought that organic food was a false god. The Cornucopia Institute, for its part, described Popoff as a "conservative ideologue" who—like Dennis and Alex Avery—was making unsubstantiated contentions because he felt that the organic industry had "a socialist/liberal agenda."[150]

None of the disbelievers have furnished the organic movement's coup de grâce, but conflicting studies and bad publicity do fuel the feeling that organics are a rip-off. Factors keeping a tight rein on organic food selection include complacency, a lack of trust, and a shortage of perceived value.[151] Consumers who spurn organic food may not believe that perilous consequences from pesticide residues will ever be manifested. Some are on the fence or even fear contagion from organic food. Organic Italian olives were blamed for a spate of botulism in 2011, causing all jars and cans of Bio Gaudiano olives to be recalled.[152] Organic frozen berries were condemned for an outbreak of hepatitis A virus in 2013. These incidents—disconcerting to those who expected top-notch organic products to be pristine—reinvigorated rabble-rousers who claimed that using manure to fertilize crops just invited toxins. While the USDA Organic label itself does not purport to confer nutritional merit, the industry built around it dreads the possibility of a backlash that would curtail the organic market share. Without more scientifically substantiated evidence on health attributes, the organic movement could lose traction. People will only pay price premiums if they have faith in organic food's advantages, and sizable skepticism in the scientific domain could temper sales.

ORGANIC DETOX

We each approach organic food (and our own health) differently. One man may be vigilant about buying organic milk and produce, but if his neighbor has a cherry pie cooling on the windowsill and offers him a slice à la mode, does he pause to ask if the fruit and ice cream are organic? Another woman may spurn "unsanitary" compost-based organic farming methods, but if a coworker offers her a handful of organic potato chips, does she decline due to fear of contamination? Some hard-nosed organivores attach a reflexive moral judgment to their decision to avoid pesticides; more lenient patrons pick and choose when they will or will not eat organics according to convenience or price. Some consumers drive their SUVs to the farmers' market for fresh organic vegetables and see no irony in that. Celebrity diet sites have reported that Nicole Kidman's secret for a "perfect body" and youthful skin is that she eats only organic food.[153] However, actress Gwyneth Paltrow admitted that she used organic beauty products but also received high-tech laser treatments from her facialist.[154] The organic chili for sale at the Super Bowl in Indianapolis in 2012 was the first organic concession item ever offered at a Super Bowl—but much of the other food sold there was far from healthy. These contradictions and paradoxes are woven throughout the motivations for organics. What is clear is that Americans do want options—and they want comprehensible labels. Though the hodgepodge of monikers confuses some shoppers, at least those labels are being scrutinized. Technically, the word "organic" indicates something "carbon-based"; in a different sense, many people still use it as a synonym for either "gradual" or "intuitive." But since "organic" became a movement and an official legally sanctioned label, the buzzword cannot be bandied about quite so casually.

One lifestyle guide, *Organic Bath: Creating a Natural, Healthy Haven* (2007), told each consumer that using organic merchandise was "the best way to create an idyllic retreat" and transform a bath into a true haven.[155] The miniature waterproof book, designed to fit in a soap dish, promised that "using organic products for staying clean and serene can help slow brain waves, lower blood pressure, enhance visual tracking, relieve cold and flu symptoms, prime you for falling asleep, or get you in the mood for love."[156] Organic oaths of nobility like these don't seem baseless to the faithful, who rave about how organic food nurtures the body and the soul. Grassroots gardening campaigner Heather Flores called organic food "a gateway drug to an ecological consciousness," because "when you eat organically, your body chemistry changes and you become more attuned to the subtle harmonies of nature."[157] J. I. Rodale's declarations were never quite so exalted—it was physical health more than communion with the natural world that he promised—but he, too, felt that going organic was life-changing. Though other motivations for consumption coexist, health-minded narcissism has fostered organic food's trajectory.[158] The "Digital Detox" personal wellness retreat at Orr Hot Springs resort in California, started in 2012, offered a four-day package for a baseline cost of $600 per person that promised "peace and quiet," "creative bliss," complete disconnection from technology, accommodations in an eco-yurt, yoga classes, guided hikes, art and writing workshops, "guaranteed Aha moments and epiphanies," and, of course, daily organic meals.[159]

Actress Salma Hayek was known for using organic juice detox "cleanses" to uphold her health—and her hourglass figure.[160] Australian supermodel Abbey Lee Kershaw included organic Amazing Grass Green SuperFood on her list of beauty and style obsessions in *Marie Claire* in April 2012.[161] The Amazing Grass company grew organic alfalfa and cereal grasses on a Kansas farm and added health boosters like açaí, yerba mate, and chia seeds to its SuperFood varieties. Gwyneth Paltrow has lauded Organic Avenue's "Almond Mylk" and "Cacao Smoothie" for fasting and detoxing. Organic Avenue founder Denise Mari said that the company's raw, vegan, organic juices and smoothies were meant to help people include "clean, beautiful, living foods" in their diet; the concoctions yielded "vibrant health" and "a more youthful appearance and glow." Organic Avenue's Green Powder included antioxidants and phytonutrients that had been "electrically charged to energize, optimize, and revitalize the body."[162] Guarantees of health seem to be compounded when they come from organic companies.

RODALE EMPIRE

Fortune Magazine listed Rodale Inc., the new name for Rodale Press, as one of the "100 Best Companies to Work for in America" in 1999. The company's cafeterias served its employees "as many organic products as possible," because, as the executive chef said, J. I. Rodale established "a commitment to healthy living throughout the organization."[163] Rodale Inc. had an inviting attitude and a reputation for stability, but the business experienced turbulence in 2000, when several high-level publishing executives resigned. By then, annual revenues were $500 million, and *Prevention* was the world's biggest health magazine, with over three million subscribers.[164] Rodale Inc. was also publishing *Men's Health, Women's Health, Runner's World, Backpacker, Bicycling, Best Life,* and other magazines; though none focused exclusively on organics, all seemed in line with the company's mission to make the whole world healthier.

The Rodale Institute began operating a 333-acre organic experimental farm near Kutztown, Pennsylvania, which drew twenty-five thousand visitors each year. It included an organic demonstration garden, apple orchards, a composting site, and fields for scientific trials. Programs were geared toward farmers, agricultural professionals, children, and the general public. Most of the farm's acreage was devoted to grains. The wheat was sent to an organic pretzel maker; the white corn went to taco and tortilla chip producers; soybeans were sold to tofu or oil manufacturers; oats, rye, yellow corn, and hay ended up at organic livestock farms. The produce was sold to local grocery and health food stores. Orchard visitors picked apples each fall, and the farm made cider and apple butter. The Rodale Institute claimed that the results of its Farming Systems Trial had proved that organic management increased soil quality, reduced greenhouse gas emissions and groundwater pollution, and competed economically with conventional systems. The institute's mission was to "improve the health and well-being of people and the planet" through organic leadership.[165]

J. I. Rodale's ambitious objective of all-encompassing improvement reappeared when Rodale Inc. began publishing *Organic Style*, a lifestyle monthly that focused on "the art of living in balance." The new magazine was a blend of environmental consciousness and lighthearted diversions, presenting organic living in a stylish spread. Maria Rodale said that she launched it in 2001 "to seduce people into doing the right thing rather than scaring them."[166] The target for the glossy magazine was sophisticated, well-educated women between the ages of eighteen and forty-nine. *Organic Style*'s articles editor said that it was directed at women who were "intelligent, compassionate, and alive to life and all its pleasures." The primary interest of its readers was health. Stories also addressed food, travel, fashion, yoga, home, and gardening.[167] Promising potential subscribers that they could "have it all" without needing to "settle for less," the magazine was to be a "partner in your quest for health and well-being, authenticity and the search for balance."[168] However, *Organic Style* struggled financially from its inception, due partly to its lack of a focus or stable voice, and suspended publication in 2005.[169]

The organic life force continued in other Rodale business ventures. The Rodale Institute commenced an online Transitioning to Organic course, designed to help farmers who were ready to embrace organic certification understand the National Organic Standards. The program highlighted environmental, economic, and community advantages of organic agriculture. Ardath Rodale was cochairman of the Rodale Institute board and then "chief inspiration officer" of Rodale Inc. until her death in 2009. Maria Rodale succeeded her mother as chairman of the board and then as Rodale Inc.'s CEO.[170] *Organic Gardening*'s advertising revenue increased that year, and, finding itself "sitting on top of a tsunami of veg-growing popularity," the magazine expanded its food and cooking coverage.[171] The content changes were expected to attract more ads for food and health products. After a decade of decline, circulation jumped to 275,000 in 2010, a 28 percent rise over three years. More Americans were drawn toward healthier, environmentally conscious lifestyles, and the publication unveiled a new layout and editorial content meant to "help people truly bring the garden to their table." Editor-in-chief Ethne Clarke said that *Organic Gardening* had originated as "the prophetic voice of organic horticulture 67 years ago" and was "more relevant now than it has ever been."[172]

Despite the rustic "family farm" atmosphere and the Rodale Institute's relative insularity, Rodale Inc. had become a global multimedia company reaching a substantial audience. Its tagline was "Live Your Whole Life," and the press specialized in healthy lifestyles. Among Rodale Inc.'s best-selling books were Al Gore's *An Inconvenient Truth*, Alicia Silverstone's *The Kind Diet*, Martha Stewart's *The Martha Rules*, and titles within *The Biggest Loser*, *The South Beach Diet*, *The Abs Diet*, and the *Eat This, Not That!* franchises. Other publications pertained to fitness, environmentalism, wellness, home improvement, and, of course, organic gardening. Rodale Inc. has released digital books, digital magazine editions, mobile websites, content channels for YouTube's original programming initiative, and more than fifty apps for iPad, iPhone, and Android platforms.[173] Rodale Inc. epitomized business prowess, not promotion of organics; still, the company wrote its own history in *Our Roots Grow Deep: The Story of Rodale* (2009). Advertisements for the book announced:

Get inspired by the trailblazing story of the first family of the organic movement. With a corporate mission to inspire and enable people to improve their lives and the world around them, the Rodale family has kept the organic spirit alive for more than 75 years. Now, for the first time ever, their rich history of environmental responsibility and self-reliance is revealed. . . . You'll be inspired by the Rodale journey, from a family vision and passion for health and wellness to the largest independent book publisher in the United States that lives its mission and helps readers do the same.

While more publishing energy was directed at general healthy living than specifically at organic gardening, the Rodales were still the "first family" of organics, though none of the other family members has ever made as much of a commotion as J. I. Rodale. More than any other member of the family, Maria Rodale has carried the torch as a preeminent organic lifestyle expert. Posts at her "Maria's Farm Country Kitchen" online blog have ranged from political to homey to meditative. She reflected, "My grandfather's books were eccentric, funny, crazy, and brilliant. He got into trouble for the stuff he said, but I was shocked at how much of it was finally proven to be true."[174] J. I. Rodale's original definition for organic farming may have been short on style, but it emanated an expansive forecast for the movement. Organic farming and gardening meant "bringing nature back into balance," and Rodale was part of a movement attempting to "bring farming back to a more sensible and natural basis."[175] He felt that a "sacred trust" was placed in the organic farmer, who had been given the tasks of preserving soil fertility, producing food that would "impart health to the people who consume it," and passing on this "precious heritage" to subsequent generations.[176] Once accused of being a crackpot and con artist, J. I. Rodale was still eyed with suspicion by some, but he was also revered by many who shared this purpose and helped turn the small publishing business he had started into an empire.

Those who were besotted with organics kept spreading the gospel. *Organic Gardening* magazine—referred to as *OG* until it was finally phased out, replaced by *Rodale's Organic Life* magazine, in 2015—established a steady presence on blogs, Google+, Facebook, and Pinterest. Active organic-themed Twitter accounts included the official *Organic Gardening* account @ogmag ("Living lightly from the ground up"); Organic Authority @OrganicAuthorit (the account of a website "devoted to delicious foodie culture & healthy living"); Organic Guru @organicguru (the account of June Stoyer, host of the *The Organic View* radio show); @HelgeHellberg ("organic food advocate" and host of *An Organic Conversation*, another radio show); @TheOrganic View ("educating the world, two ears at a time"); and Organic Nation TV

@OrganicNation ("Exploring America's sustainable food network"). A niche dating site for "people who love the organic lifestyle," called OrganicMatch .com, launched in 2012, intimating that a shared infatuation with organic food might spark enough ardor to be the foundation of a lifelong relationship. The only requirement to join and browse profiles was that you "love organic food, are environmentally conscious, get off on green or just simply love the great outdoors."[177] The site could, at least, bring more organically inclined children into the world.

As a testament to the trendiness of gardening, the Brooklyn Botanic Garden opened an exhibit celebrating urban gardens in 2012, with displays of vertical gardens, container gardens, and ornamental edibles. Even Williams-Sonoma, a high-end purveyor of kitchenware and home furnishings, launched the Agrarian line of garden tools and supplies in 2012, to connect the "virtues of the homegrown and homemade to your everyday table."[178] The "essentials" for gardening, beekeeping, cheese making, and home canning ranged from $659 chicken coops and $339 beehives to $140 heritage watering cans and $70 vintage hand trowels. These designer supplies indicated that even those who had absolutely no economic *need* to grow their own food might still do so for health or delectation. Some people just want to buy the *idea* of homesteading; for them, the Williams-Sonoma catalog also sold organic heirloom beans and organic grains (already harvested, ready for cooking). Some gardeners do feel that they only attain therapeutic benefits with solemn sweat, while others prefer to avoid slogging through compost. Actress Jennifer Aniston had a chicken coop and vegetable garden installed at her $21 million Bel Air mansion in 2013, somewhat muddling the definition of "homestead." The summer Wanderlust festival in 2013—"a four-day celebration of yoga, music, and nature" designed to "create community around mindful living"—conjoined yoga classes, live musical performances, inspiring lectures, hiking, bike tours, wine tasting, and organic food in outdoorsy settings.[179] It exemplified the cardinal role organic food has historically played in the quest of people seeking health, balance, harmony, communion with nature, personal awareness, and fulfillment.

J. I. Rodale predicted that conscientious consumers would be willing to accept higher price points for what they divined as nutritional benefits, and he urged farmers to take advantage of this. At first, Rodale was an oddity and lost money on his attempts to disseminate information on organics. However, he turned a profit when organic food became fashionable, and profit was something he supported from the movement's genesis. With his typical buoyancy, Rodale declared in 1949 that the field of organic farming was "wide open for money-making opportunities" to reach the "health conscious public."[180] Organic farmer Leonard Dodge also told fellow organic farmers in 1950 that "we owe it to ourselves and to the world to sell the organic concept."[181] The way these pioneers sold the concept was as a healthy standby, not as a complete replacement for the standard American diet. It's another example of how the organic movement pushed the individualization of responsibility. The notion that organic food may be a holy grail for personal welfare has been a controversial but far-reaching aspect of the movement. Throughout the decades, though, each expectant organic eater has had to take the reins for his or her own revitalization.

CHAPTER SIX

Organic Consumers
Voting with Dollars and Forging Identities

At Bacchanalia, one of Atlanta's top restaurants, gourmands can dine on an organic five-course prix fixe meal that includes two appetizers, an entrée, a cheese course, and a dessert for $85. At Café Gratitude in Los Angeles, health-conscious ethicureans can order an organic, vegan, gluten-free blueberry scone for $4.50. Patrons of Binny's Beverage Depot in Chicago can splurge on a bottle of Koval's organic aged apple brandy for $32.99. Chicago residents can have a large box brimming with fresh fruits and vegetables delivered to their home from Door-to-Door Organics for $55. Any shopper trying to avoid pesticides can buy a one-pound bag of organic carrots for 99 cents (on sale at Shaw's supermarket), four organic mangoes for $5 (on sale at Kroger's), or half a gallon of organic milk for $3.39 (on sale at Hannaford's). All these options accommodate eaters from every social stratum. But cultural pervasiveness does not indicate destabilizing resistance to the conventional "foodopoly."

Reveling in the organic heyday, renowned primatologist Jane Goodall acclaimed consumer power by noting that organic food had indeed become universally available, thanks to people all over the world who had insisted on it.[1] Goodall optimistically predicted that if everyone would make ethical food choices and request organics, then "we can, collectively, change the way our food is grown and prepared."[2] Within the discourse about consumption in the organic movement, the ethos of buying and eating organic food has been concocted as a politically effective act. The lexicon has also situated it as a statement of social position and a marker of "green" identity. This chapter inspects contemporary organic food consumption, including demographics, guiding moralities, fear factors, shopping landscapes, gentrification, marketing dictums, media messages, identity construction, and market projections. It elaborates on praise that has bolstered organic revenues and critiques that have beleaguered the organic food fraternity. Unraveling the key conflicts and oppositions of organic consumption provides insight into how the movement's mutinous munching has affected independent resolutions and personal identities but has not been world shattering.

WHO BUYS ORGANICS? AND WHY?

"Organic" is an intangible feature that requires impartial third-party verification to bestow trustworthiness and consistency. Suspicion of fraud always hovers. Since consumers cannot visually distinguish organic from standard foods, they must take a gamble on the organic label. Why do they bank on it? Food derived from organic farms may dispense public goods. It may offer personal remunerations, some of which are more immediate than others. Consumers have steadily gained keener awareness of the USDA Organic logo, but its tactile efficacy is murky. Unverifiable benefits may provide merely a psychological stimulus to organic buffs. Under the "halo effect," certain attributes of organic foods radiate to such an extent that they affect how people perceive other characteristics. A person recognizing organic potato chips as more eco-friendly might automatically think they are also more nutritious or delicious.

The Organic Foods Production Act did not have stipulations on food safety or nutrition. Still, a study conducted by the National Center for Public Policy (NCPP) in 2000 revealed that a majority of consumers felt that a USDA Certified Organic seal insinuated a positive difference over foods without the seal—that organic foods were safer, healthier, and better for the environment. The NCPP was concerned that the seal would mislead consumers, because it was really "only an accreditation of production methods used by farmers and not an assurance of food safety, quality, nutrition, or health."[3] A study by the Hartman Group in 2000 backed up this assumption, showing that the top motivators for organic food and beverage purchases were, in order, health and nutrition, taste, food safety, environment, and availability.[4] According to the Organization for Economic Co-Operation and Development in 2003, the main motivating factors for buying organics were the opinion that it entailed benefits to health and the environment, the judgment that it had higher levels of food quality and taste, and the belief that it assisted small-scale local producers and communities.[5] Marketers seldom have misgivings about abetting these motives, which can spark backlashes. The organic movement's main problem is that masses of people still have reservations about the denotation, connotations, and accuracy of the label.

Very few people buy organic food in every instance. Most natural and organic food consumers also add a mishmash of nonorganic products to their carts.[6] The Natural Marketing Institute (NMI) reported in 2005 that 90 percent of US consumers had heard of organic foods, but only 30 percent used organic products. The NMI divided consumers into Devoteds (9.2 percent), who were "committed, zealous and have high organic usage and spending rates"; Temperates (16.7 percent), who were "pragmatists, with moderate attitudes"; Dabblers (3.8 percent), who were noncommittal and for whom organic usage was "more about hipness than health"; and Reluctants (70.3 percent), who had "some level of belief in the benefits of organic usage" but were not using organic products. "Devoteds" and "Temperates" together represented 90 percent of all organic spending.[7] A global overview of the organic market in 2006 asserted that the attributes of organic products likely to influence consumers, from most to least important, were health (low chemical residues and high nutritional worth), environment (environmentally friendly production and processing), taste, animal welfare, minimal processing, novelty, and fashion. On the other hand, the elements most likely to restrict the consumption of organics were high price, limited availability, skepticism about credibility of product claims, poor appearance, nonawareness of organic, and contentment with existing products.[8]

Attempting to gauge consumers' willingness to pay for foods with certain credence attributes is not simple. A study in 2006 found that a perceived health benefit from reduced pesticides was the primary motivating factor for organic food, and taste was a close second. Willingness to pay was intrinsic to quality perception and rose with added differentiation, such as fair trade certification and first-class ingredients. One limitation of this model was that it did not account for deviations on the basis of mood, emotion, or key components of marketing—such as ambiance of the shop and limited-time promotions—which also sway consumers.[9] Gender disparities have repercussions as well. A case study in 2008 showed that women had more favorable attitudes toward organic foods, but men were more inclined to pay markups.[10] Some studies have suggested that consumers do not see organic food as a moral imperative, so they rarely feel guilty for selecting conventional food. However, other studies have indicated that choosing organic food does evoke upbeat feelings. Consumers may experience organic food choice as a "morally right thing to do," which provides an "internal reward" that affects intentions to purchase organic food.[11]

According to the International Food Information Council (IFIC), the most important factor in Americans' decisions to buy all foods and beverages (not just organic) is taste, which is followed by price, healthfulness, and convenience.[12] Organic promoters do vigorously present exceptional taste as the foremost incentive for purchasing organic fruits and vegetables. Chef Jeff Cox, in *The Organic Cook's Bible* (2006), explained that ingredients for "the perfect dish" should be organic, because these tasted better and because, for the cook, "organic produce sets the standard of quality." Organic foods grown in rich soil received all the nutrients needed to develop "maximum flavor nuances." Also, Cox pronounced, organic food had "come to be appreciated for its richness of flavor, its freshness, and its purity."[13] *The Organic Food Shopper's Guide* (2008) assured consumers that organic food tasted better and contained "the maximum amount of flavor."[14] Organic chef Jesse Ziff Cool, in the cookbook *Simply Organic* (2008), said that organic products had more flavor, and this great taste was "the reason why many chefs—even those not active in the organic movement—are purchasing organic products."[15] Dr. Charles Benbrook, the chief scientist of the Organic Center, included the assertion that "organic food delivers more intense flavors" on his list "Top 12 Reasons to Go Organic." Benbrook attributed this to "higher levels of flavor-enhancing nutrients" and "lower concentrations of water and sugars" in organic fruits and vegetables.[16] Even the fast food chain Chipotle, which had been increasing its use of organic pinto beans and black beans, maintained: "We believe *food* raised *organically* benefits people and the environment, and we know it *tastes better.*"[17] Customers who had honed their palates would presumably also discern the transcendent piquancy.

While some research augments the certainty about unsurpassed organic delectability, inferences about organic food overall are complicated by diverse farm management practices, which lead to considerable variations in organic crops. Taste is a highly subjective consideration, and preconceived notions about organics can trigger foregone conclusions. One study published in the *Journal of Food Science* showed that consumers favored organic bread over conventional bread under blind conditions. However, when the identity of the samples was divulged and the survey group received information about the health and environment benefits of organic food, they liked the organic bread even more.[18] Convictions about taste superiority may be ascribed partly to the halo effect (or "flavoritism") activated by the organic label. Another explanation could be confirmation bias: our proclivity to esteem information propping up existing creeds. People may postulate that an organic bite is more flavorful and succulent before even ingesting it. A similarly murky idea is that of *terroir*—the romantic but wooly belief that climate, topography, and geology affect the flavor compounds of food (or wine). While individual motivations for going organic wax and wane, in the end the features that mitigate hassles and lighten wallets often override olfactory verdicts. If consumers need to expend prodigious effort locating food with favorable traits, and if these products come at greater monetary cost, then price and convenience often trump ethics and scrumptiousness. Overall, consumers purchase organic food for reasons both selfish and noble, both scientific and instinctive, both mundane and radical.

TRUE NATURALS, LOHASIANS, AND SHOPPING LOCALES

The desire to emanate a certain self-image can affect food determinations, so choosing organic food is a communicative act. Symbolic meanings influence all buying decisions and help disclose social identities.[19] Since organic goods can be symbolic *and* practical, they are not merely evidence of conspicuous consumption. Organic foods defy narrow categories in that they are utilitarian goods with real-world purposes; hedonic goods bringing subjective pleasure; and positional goods hauling status-signaling power. Still, people do use consumption to display prestige or flaunt ideologies. Marketers have long recognized particular demographic clusters as prime consumers of organic products. The Hartman Group distinguished a coterie of "True Naturals" who encompassed the core of the demand for organic food.[20] Self-identifying as a "green" consumer is a positive factor in predicting a person's intention to purchase organic food.[21] Analogously, ethical self-identity positively forecasts attitudes and intention to buy organic produce.[22] Studies have found that the more people are sensitized to environmental and animal rights issues, the more liable they are to have favorable attitudes toward organic food.[23]

A cohort known by the acronym LOHAS—Lifestyles of Health and Sustainability—has been said to make conscientious purchasing and investment decisions based on social and cultural values. According to a *Newsweek* report in 2006, LOHAS members, or "Lohasians," were "dedicated to personal and planetary health." Their interests included organic food, yoga, feng shui, meditation, eco-tourism, recycling, green building, and fuel-efficient cars. They engaged in the "devotional consumption" of products affiliated with health, the environment, social justice, sustainable living, and "metrospirituality." They shopped at eco-conscious stores like Whole Foods, Anthropologie, and Patagonia. *Newsweek* said, "If you have a yoga mat and 'singing bowls,' if you chant or do polarity therapy or energy healing, if you consume goji berries or biodynamic organic wines, you just might be a Lohasian."[24] This assemblage collectively spent nearly $300 billion annually on products perceived as fitting their principles.[25] Advertisers reached them through magazines like *Body & Soul, Vegetarian Times, Yoga Journal, Plenty,* and *Mother Jones.* The Lohasian preference for products with certain attributes has been an influential force in the ethical food explosion, helping to make organics the fastest-growing segment of the food industry. Taglines like "Food to Live By" for Earthbound Farm organic produce, "Goodness from the Ground Up" for Seeds of Change frozen organic entrées, and "Making a World of Difference" and "Every Sip Counts" for Horizon Organic milk reveal ethical overtones and play to the LOHAS vibe.

Organic guidebooks have recognized that Lohasians want serenity without scruples, a form of stylish conscientiousness. In a somewhat hyperbolic vein, *Organic Body Care Recipes* (2007) instructed readers on how to make organic personal care products that would lead to "skin, hair, and nails that sing with vitality, vibrance, and inner wellness."[26] Author Stephanie Tourles, an aesthetician and holistic skin care specialist, claimed that the natural approach to beauty began with a "whole-foods" diet. She advocated eating things "in their whole, natural, preferably organic, unprocessed state"[27] Her recipes included parsley and peppermint astringent, fennel soother, coconut and vanilla brown sugar body buff, and aloe and calendula cleansing cream. Reminiscent of Euell Gibbons's *Stalking the Wild Asparagus* (1962), Tourles said that the required ingredients could be obtained by growing herbs from seed or by foraging for wild herbs. Lohasians lean toward these kinds of books and products. They prioritize health and sustainability to such an extent that they are often trend predictors in that realm.

Another grouping, dubbed "New Luxury" consumers, involves middle-market shoppers primarily interested in selectively "trading up" for products and services. "New Luxury" items possess "higher levels of quality, taste, and aspiration" than other goods in the category but are not prohibitively expensive.[28] Those who "trade up" in food seek out organic foods, exotic ingredients, and premium desserts—like Bora Bora wild pomegranate pecan bars, Navitas Naturals organic cacao nibs, and Organicville caramel swirl ice cream. These may be self-indulgent enjoyments, but many sybarites think of them as a medium for relaxation, personal reward, or revitalization. New Luxuries promise physical rejuvenation, emotional uplift, or comfort. They are based on strong emotional engagements.[29] Consumers align themselves with brands that they have an affinity for and that match their own individual style.[30] New Luxury shoppers are also apt to favor organic brands with distinctive personalities. One prototype is Dagoba Organic chocolate, which prints convoluted stories on the outside and inside of its wrappers expounding on how the company transmutes "exceptional cacao into edible gold" in its "constant quest for chocolate perfection." Another illustration is 479° Popcorn, named for the precise popping temperature at which its popcorn is made "the artisan way—by hand in small batches."[31] Its heirloom organic kernels come from a small California family farm; frilly flavors include fleur de sel caramel, madras curry coconut & cashews, and black truffle and white cheddar. The catchy description for Pimentòn de La Vera relays how the paprika pods are grown near a Spanish monastery garden, smoked over oak wood, and milled with heavy stone wheels; it adds: "If you feel a sudden urge to take up flamenco dancing halfway through the box, we suggest that you act on it." Pristine organic ingredients and attention to detail make 479° Popcorn a "treasured indulgence."[32]

Those who want to learn more about products in their shopping baskets eagerly embrace elaborate narratives authored by New Luxury companies, such as Trader Joe's.[33] Trader Joe's is a quirky grocery chain that people interested in obtaining organic products are fond of. It draws a higher-than-average concentration of organics consumers.[34] Joe Coulombe founded his first Trader Joe's store in Pasadena, California, in 1967, with the mission of making difficult-to-find epicurean items more accessible to American consumers. His target shoppers were well educated and budget-conscious. He sold boutique wines and gourmet foods but maintained low pricing.[35] Trader Joe's touts itself as a "different kind of grocery store," where "shopping for food is actually fun," and value is taken seriously.[36] In some ways, it emulates mom-and-pop specialty groceries and swanky organic food shops. The three hundred stores are apt to be smaller than other supermarkets and offer a limited selection of high-quality products.

Trader Joe's gives some shoppers the illusion that it is a healthy, noncorporate store. Foods sold under the house brand are free of artificial preservatives, MSG, trans fats, and genetically modified ingredients. Trader Joe's is considered a "New Luxury" player based not on extravagant prices but on tasty, unusual products that appeal to middle-market customers who pine for adventure, discovery, and fun in their shopping experience.[37] *Fearless Flyer*, the store's monthly newsletter, has ornate descriptions of products, ingredient sources, and business practices that save shoppers "serious money." Alongside anecdotes and cartoons, the bulletin proclaims, "We've always felt that the purchasing and consumption of food should be a social experience; that's one reason why we run small, funky, often odd-shaped neighborhood stores."[38] By 2005 Trader Joe's commanded $2 billion in revenues, despite using no broadcast advertising, and average store productivity per square foot was two to three times the industry average.[39] Trader Joe's often packages products in innovative ways, with superfluous explanations. Offerings include private-label organic dried tomato halves, organic honey sticks, organic steak sauce, frozen organic foursome vegetable blend, and Get Thee to a Bunnery organic hamburger buns. The store obtains organic mango fruit spread from Canadian fruit growers, organic mild cheddar from Wisconsin, and organic fair trade breakfast blend from "small mountain cooperatives at the base of the Andes."[40] New Luxury consumers, many of whom gravitate toward organic foods, appreciate these kinds of novel, engaging narratives.

While these consumer blocs (True Naturals, Lohasians, New Luxury, and so on) do overlap, shoppers may have dissimilar priorities in mind when visiting alternative locales. The location in which organic food is sold—a Piggly Wiggly or a Target Supercenter, a pick-your-own farm or a gas station—affects its meanings. Various retail venues have a propensity for drawing identifiable consumer clusters. Landscapes of food shopping possess elements of what Raymond Williams called the dominant, residual, and emergent. The supermarket is presently the dominant constituent but exists in proximity with residual spaces, such as farmers' markets, and with emergent sites, such as websites offering home delivery.[41] Many Americans have embarked on a rekindled search for "authentic" goods within the world marketplace. Feeling alienated, people have wanted food to bond them to distinct places, and they assumed these foods would be of outstanding quality. There have been rehabilitated efforts to connect rootless consumers with the sources of their food. Farmers' markets have flourished along with interest in local, organic, place-based, and "traditional" foods. Farmers' markets sell not just produce but also culturally rich values, like "authenticity," "simplicity," and "heritage."[42] In the 1940s, Louis Bromfield recognized that his market stand at Malabar Farm was a differentiated consumer site: "There is no point in the country roadside market attempting to compete with the chain stores on a basis of price and the chain store customer is quite frankly not the kind of customer we seek but rather those who want freshness and high quality and are willing to pay for it."[43]

Organic farmers tend to rely more heavily on direct marketing to consumers, through farmers' markets or Community Supported Agriculture (CSA), than conventional farmers do.[44] Organic farmers participate widely in farmers' markets, and the demand for organic products is strong. The number of farmers' markets in the nation has grown, yet produce sold at these sites represents only 2 percent of US sales.[45] Farmers' market managers have noticed that their consumers seek "freshness, high quality, fair pricing, pleasant social interaction with farmers and market shoppers, and locally grown foods."[46] Competent organic farmers also satisfy customer desires for specialty crops and stellar customer service. Managers have reported that customers with the strongest insistence on organically grown products are most likely to exhibit interest in social and environmental issues.[47] A study in 2006 found that customers at direct markets were mainly interested in taste, quality, and natural or organic foods. Brick-and-mortar grocery shoppers, meanwhile, gave higher importance scores to health measures, ease of preparation, convenient packaging, and product brand.[48] Farmers' markets are an accessible, flexible sales outlet for farmers. Surveys have showed that patrons particularly appreciate the freshness, quality, and traceability of farmers' market products, along with the sociability of shopping there.[49]

Organic farming was, for a time, seen as an economically viable way to keep family-owned outfits afloat. Some farmers suspected that they could benefit from lower input costs and reap premium "farm-gate" prices. Ironically, when "organic" became an official USDA designation, inordinate numbers of diminutive farms that were already organic in practice could not afford the expense of paying inspectors to have their small holdings certified in name. Large-scale commercial composting equipment made shoveling manure heaps by hand passé. Organic farms, though, were still welcomed as small, sustainable examples of the nation's agricultural legacy. Consumers progressively became more eager to prop up family farms. Elizabeth Henderson of Rose Valley Farm asserted the ubiquitous judgment that farming was "an art as well as a business" and was "practiced more creatively by family farms than by big corporations."[50] The poignant resonance of the family farm intensified even as the number of working farms dropped each year.

The average size, yields per acre, and productivity of farms mushroomed throughout the twentieth century. The number of farms steadily declined from 6.4 million in 1910 to under two million farms in 2004, while average farm size more than doubled during that same period.[51] Production became concentrated on a small number of specialized operations. The distinction between corporate and family farms is not always clear, as obscure ownership arrangements interfere with simplistic definitions. The USDA categorizes small farms as "farms with less than $250,000 gross receipts annually on which day-to-day labor and management are provided by the farmer and/or the farm family that owns the production owns, or leases, the productive assets." While this does encompass a majority of all US farms, the net income of those small farms is below the US poverty line.[52] Massive corporations produce 95 percent of American food and virtually monopolize sales.[53] The poetic American family farm reverie disguises the true trends of large-scale farming and agribusiness.[54] Agriculture is primarily a utilitarian activity designed for feeding people, but it also has an aesthetic dimension, evoking images like Grant Wood's folksy *American Gothic*. Perceptions have altered since the attitude of "get big or get out" has taken over farming. Visions of old-fashioned hayrides and innocent country pastures have been upended. Nonetheless, many Americans who sanctify small family farms are distressed about their impending extinction, caused by what is perceived as the monolithic "Big Ag" monster.

Though organic gardening has lost most of its rebellious connotations, some participants still feel that it entails defiance against industrialization. Agrarians regard small organic farms as a necessary element for establishing a sustainable food system, built on close ties between farmers and consumers. Alternative forms of agriculture and food production—including farmers' markets, roadside stands, and CSAs—capitalize on the quest for more profound social connections.[55] Organic and local food initiatives, such as urban community gardens and "guerrilla gardening," are sometimes meant to resist power structures and open an "alternative economy," detached from corporate or governmental meddling.[56] These projects have become popular responses to salient concerns in regions worried about their ability to regularly obtain fresh, nutritious food. In many urban areas, residents have turned vacant lots into public gardens, generating access to organic vegetables within city limits. The grassroots group Food Not Lawns hopes to increase personal and community empowerment by encouraging people to grow organic gardens. It hypes organic vegetable gardening as the radical first step toward a "healthier, more self-reliant, and ultimately more ecologically sane life."[57] Similarly, the author of a how-to book on growing organic crops in pots has called urban gardening an act that "challenges the domination of supermarket culture." The guide also says that gardening organically is all about "working with nature," not adhering to a scientific process.[58] Red Root Farm, an organic farm in Alabama, gives its CSA subscribers a recycled cotton bag full of fresh produce each week. With an emphasis on sustainability, the farm explains that it is "part of a growing network of resistance to genetically modified foods and use of harmful chemical pesticides." The five-acre farm uses cover cropping, composting, and other methods that blunt its environmental footprint and "help to create harmony in the natural world." The owners view their choice to farm as a larger act of "resistance to an often-dehumanizing mass culture that focuses only on consumerism and selfishness."[59] In these contexts, buying organic food may be viewed as a deliberate social statement.

WHOLE FOODS MARKET

Whole Foods Market, whose birth was discussed in an earlier chapter, was the first national certified organic grocer, obtaining this voluntary certification from Quality Assurance International (QAI), one of the major USDA-accredited organic product certifying agencies. Whole Foods capitalized on the rise of ethical consumerism, or belief-driven buying, by highlighting organic, natural, and eco-friendly products. The store's slogan was "Whole Foods, Whole People, Whole Planet." Pleas for food free of pesticides, hormones, and artificial additives were a significant contributor to the enlargement of Whole Foods. Founder and CEO John Mackey has referred to Whole Foods as a "mission-driven business" whose deepest calling was to "sell the highest quality natural, organic foods in the world."[60] The business donated 5 percent of after-tax profits to not-for-profit organizations. Whole Foods had gone public, experienced 900 percent growth, and become "a billion-dollar juggernaut with 78 stores in 17 states" by the late 1990s.[61] According to observations in *Time* magazine, its prosperity was because Americans remained "a nation of committed Twinkie eaters even while welcoming organic foods to the table." Organic-minded consumers were far from ascetic and appreciated the conveniences of shopping in large stores.[62] Furthermore, shoppers' "unaccountable willingness to pay premiums of up to 175 percent over the regular cost of ordinary supermarket food" resulted in Whole Foods becoming "a giant cash mill of eco-righteousness." Whole Foods Market morphed into "destination retail," hoping to both satisfy and delight customers.[63]

In 2002, *Time* discussed how Whole Foods was selling a feeling of healthy stylishness while "enticing shoppers to gorge on fancy fare." Although the chain phased out all goods with hydrogenated fats, it produced its own organic chocolates and sold organic cheese puffs. A Whole Foods representative said that this apparent incongruity was part of the store's charm for "healthy-chic" customers who wanted nutritious eating options that were not limited solely to brown rice and vegetables.[64] Whole Foods employee Benjamin Wurgaft noted that consumers were willing to pay more for the products because they wanted the assurance that they were "doing no wrong." He described Whole Foods as a descendant of "hippie organic cooperatives of the 1960s and '70s, when the link between food consumption and activism was apparent," and he acknowledged that "some of my customers are as motivated by politics as our store once was." However, others just wished for absolution, and by shopping at Whole Foods, the customer felt that he or she became "part of a culinary and moral elite."[65]

Slow food founder Carlo Petrini asserted that the commencement of the organic movement was mistaken in that "it didn't place any emphasis on pleasure. It had an ideological, almost religious approach," insinuating that carnality was antithetical to health and sustainability.[66] Whole Foods remedied that alleged deficiency. Its organic food was imbued with the aura of bliss. Throughout all the stores were indicators of how virtuous its lovely products were. Whole Foods managed to marry green and healthy with comfort and elegance. Selling organic no longer meant "an unwashed carrot in a shop smelling of mould and patchouli." Instead, Whole Foods signified the "Starbucksification of the supermarket."[67] The *New York Times* described Whole Foods as a "Pleasure Palace without the Guilt." The absence of consumptive contrition stemmed from the knowledge that the store's "gustatory temptations" lacked unnecessary preservatives, hydrogenated oils, artificial colors, and genetically modified ingredients. Subscribing to a religion of "moralistic hedonism," Whole Foods "built its empire . . . on the willingness of consumers to pay more for organic and natural foods."[68] It was indeed an empire—and a marriage of integrity and indulgence. Whole Foods was selling a surfeit of deluxe, high-end food, though it also developed a private-label "365" line, meant to be more affordable and to rival the lower prices at Trader Joe's. Maria Rodale counted herself among the store's fans: "The first time I walked into a Whole Foods I cried. Finally, someone had gotten it right. I tried to imagine what my grandfather would have thought—back then if you wanted organic food you had to grow it yourself and endure the ridicule of your neighbors. Sixty years later you could enter a paradise and buy almost anything organic you wanted."[69]

By 2005, Whole Foods was a Fortune 500 company. The first London store opened in 2006, allowing customers to book facials, exercise in the yoga studio, mix their own cereal from the muesli bar, sample Earl Grey crème brûlée, and have a beer at the organic pub. A study in 2007 revealed that organic consumers were over 200 percent more likely than the average consumer to have shopped at Whole Foods during the past week.[70] Whole Foods generated twice the profit per square foot of any other US supermarket.[71] It had nearly three hundred stores across the United States, Canada, and Britain in 2009. Along the way, it relentlessly acquired competitors: Mrs. Gooch's, Bread and Circus, Wellspring Markets, and Fresh Fields. It bought Wild Oats Market, a comparable natural foods chain, which was also managing stores under the banners of Henry's Farmers Market, Sun Harvest, and Capers Community. Whole Foods served as a highly visible face of the organic industry, and it seemed that the business had succeeded as a stalwart organic pioneer. But the trade-off was that, accompanying the positive press, a backlash against Whole Foods ensued. Several observers accused the store of "selling out," betraying its principles, and making only a superficial commitment to local food producers and small farmers. Some critics indicted Whole Foods of misleading consumers about the products that they were paying through the roof for. Charges of elitism were common, as was the derisive nickname "Whole Paycheck."[72]

Sundry participants in the organic movement presupposed that big was inherently evil, so huge supermarket chains were incompatible with "sustainable, natural food production."[73] Farmer Joel Salatin pronounced that he had "found Whole Foods completely untrustworthy," that "a supermarket is still just a supermarket," and that all supermarkets were part of "an inherently disconnected" and opaque food system.[74] Whole Foods was a convenient scapegoat. Michael Pollan castigated Whole Foods as the epitome of Big (therefore Bad) Organic, because it had adopted the regional distribution platform that other grocery stores used, which made backing small farms impractical. The "organic" label and the store's evocative prose conjured up a rich narrative, dubbed "Supermarket Pastoral," so consumers believed that they were engaging in an authentic, bucolic experience. While posters in the store depicted family farmers, Pollan said that the vegetables on sale came "primarily from the two big corporate organic growers in California, Earthbound Farm and Grimmway Farms," which dominated the American organic produce market.[75] *New York Times* writer Marian Burros noted that Whole Foods was opening new, bigger stores, with "in-store restaurants, spas, concierge shopping services, gelato stands, chocolate fountains and pizza counters." Countless shoppers reveled in the amenities. Yet a more ambivalent band decried Whole Foods for straying from its "original vision," which theoretically included the foundational values of espousing organic agriculture and local farmers.[76] Gargantuan stores seemed like bullies, squeezing the tiny, meek underdogs.

Confronted with harsh attacks about produce transported long distances, the neglect of small farmers, and aloofness from grassroots communities, Whole Foods worked to increase the visibility of its local options and created positions for "Local Food Foragers." Mackey disputed charges of selling out, arguing that he helped bring organic food and responsible business tactics into the mainstream. He noted that there had always been an ongoing battle between "purists" and "pragmatists" in organics, and he was sympathetic to both points of view.[77] Mackey said that he actually wanted the stores to go "beyond organic" and do more to address other ethical and ecological concerns around industrialized food.[78] Whole Foods developed its own fair trade label and continued to adapt to the changing consumer landscape. In 2008, to help counteract its "Whole Paycheck" stereotype in a troubled economy, Whole Foods introduced an advertising campaign that highlighted weekly bargains and inexpensive selections in all the stores. The chain's reputation as a sybaritic organic mecca for "foodies" was hard to shake; still, there was plenty of praise. *Health* magazine named Whole Foods as America's healthiest grocery store in 2008, referring to it as "the Rolls Royce of healthy eating."[79] *Natural Health* magazine gave it a Green Choice Award for being one of ten multinational companies that successfully pursued environmental initiatives. The magazine recognized Whole Foods Market for supporting sustainable agriculture, purchasing offsets for 100 percent of its electricity use, and phasing out the use of plastic bags.[80] The chain was still on a hot streak in 2013, opening dozens of new stores (for a total of over 340) and reporting steady profits and sales growth. Whole Foods had become enthralling to a broad scope of people, not just a devoted nucleus of organic shoppers. Some may have hoped that their modest shopping habits could have an impact on the rest of the world, but it was increasingly difficult to portray food consumption as activism.

GENTRIFICATION OF ORGANICS

Issues of class and income have permeated the organic movement since its inception. Envisioning the untapped market potential that organic food might hold, Rodale declared in an *Organic Gardening* editorial in 1945 that "a large part of our population is not only health-conscious but has the money to pay a little more for quality food that will keep the doctor away." He reckoned that "discriminating purchasers" would gladly pay elevated prices if the indulgence would reward their well-being and taste buds. He also predicted that "the time is not far off when grocers will offer special grades of organically grown fruit, guaranteed to be unsprayed, at higher than regular prices and they will have difficulty meeting the demand."[81] Within a few decades, Rodale's forecast would become a reality. Organic farmer Leonard Dodge noted in 1950 that marketing organic crops to "persons of above-average intelligence and education" was the most promising promotional maneuver and felt that other farmers "should make a special effort to convert this special group" to organics.[82] As such, organic advocates have often preached to well-heeled "enlightened" shoppers who seem disposed to stock up on organic food, rather than evangelizing to the humble "masses" who may have economic restrictions.

When it was inextricably associated with dusty bins of buckwheat flour, droopy heads of lettuce, and self-denial, organic food did not appear snobbish. Over time, though, organic cuisine acquired overtones of upmarket elitism and gentility. Organic nibbles garnered rave reviews at debonair soirées. In 1990, *Time* reported on more modish restaurants providing elegant, urbane organic food. The article noted that, "in contrast to the monotonous vegetarianism of the '60s (steamed carrots, brown rice and beans ruled), today's highbrow organic restaurants not only offer a wide variety of dishes but also often serve meat." An array of fashionable restaurants bridged the gulf between gourmet cuisine and natural food. Although ordering from an organic kitchen entailed exorbitant prices, "growing hordes of patrons obviously believe the result is worth the extra money."[83] Organic food became a form of epicurean ethics, located at the nexus of hedonism and morality. Its aspects of "culinary privilege" were part of what *Bon Appétit* called a "happy utopian foodie future."[84] Gourmands flocked to organics, mesmerized by the golden glow, though this facet of organic food had little bearing on the daily lives of organic farmers.

Restaurant Nora in Washington, DC, is a template of the classy organic wave. Executive chef and owner Nora Pouillon opened the eatery after deciding she could not serve conventional food to her customers when she ate only organic food at home. Some diners were surprised to find fine wineglasses on the white tablecloths and museum-quality antique quilts on the wall at a "health food" establishment. "People told me I was a crazy lady; I was called completely nuts," Pouillon said. She was involved in crafting organic certification standards for restaurants when none existed, and her bistro became the nation's first certified organic restaurant in 1999. Kitchen scraps were composted and energy came from alternative suppliers.[85] Environmentalists and politicians could eat there with a "clear conscience, knowing that what's on their plate hasn't polluted the environment, is healthy for them, and tastes good too," claimed the website.[86] At least 95 percent of everything dished up in Restaurant Nora came from certified organic growers and farmers. One page of the menu—printed with environmentally sound dyes on chlorine-free, 100 percent postconsumer recycled paper—listed the names of the local organic farmers who outfitted the restaurant with produce, bread, grains, dairy products, eggs, and meat. Some of the seasonal main courses have been "Sake Glazed Wild Alaskan Black Cod with Yuchoi, Shitakes, Scallions, Crispy Yams, Ginger Miso Emulsion" ($36); "Applewood Smoked Amish Duck Breast with Farro Risotto, Baby Beets, Grilled Maitakes, Sugar Snaps, Maple Sherry Jus" ($36); and "Grilled Grassfed Ribeye Mignon with Local Tomato & Cucumber Panzanella, Grilled Asparagus, Balsamic Jus" ($35). The $78 tasting menu has included local cherry pie with vanilla bean ice cream for dessert.[87] The servers' uniforms, from Patagonia, were made of 100 percent organic cotton.[88] Sustainably sourced fibers fit perfectly in the mise-en-scène of an organically minded restaurant filled with yuppie diners.

One consumer guide, *Living Organic* (2001), reflected that organic food had "come a long way since the days when it had a reputation for being grubby, eccentric-looking, and usually found lurking in the dark recesses of health food shops." Since then, "a new breed of organic supermarkets and juice bars frequented by wheatgrass-sipping celebrities have helped give the organic image a designer makeover."[89] Organic was "becoming a gold standard for premium foods."[90] As Michael Pollan observed, "The word 'elitist' has stuck to organic food in this country like balsamic vinegar to mache.

Thirty years ago the rap on organic was a little different: back then the stuff was derided as hippie food, crunchy granola and bricklike brown bread for the unshaved set (male and female division)."[91] In a more clean-shaven era, the vegetables were less gnarly and the organic label became a status symbol.

The "Deep Organic" camp has wailed about the organic gentility visible in the media and at chic palaces of consumption. Slow food founder Carlo Petrini generated controversy when he recounted his visit to the Ferry Plaza farmers' market with Alice Waters in 2007. He described it as "an exclusive boutique with fresh, healthy-looking food, all carefully marked *organic*" and said that he was dismayed that "the prices were astronomical." Petrini added that "the amiable ex-hippies and young dropouts-turned-farmers greeted their customers with a smile and offered generous samples of their products to a clientele whose social status was pretty clear: either wealthy or very wealthy."[92] Ironically, slow food chapters themselves have a reputation for being entirely made up of moneyed members, inhospitable to the hoi polloi. It is often the same clique of organic "purists" that has denigrated the inclination of discount stores to offer organic products at low prices.

Organic food has steadily become a covetable menu option. A survey of chefs by the National Restaurant Association found that the top three "hot" items for 2008 were bite-size desserts, locally grown produce, and organic produce.[93] An article in the *Atlantic* in 2009 offhandedly listed the two-parent marriage, along with "fancy schools, tae kwon do lessons, and home-cooked organic food," as another "impressive—and rare—attainment to bestow on our fragile, gifted children."[94] Opulent organic food in glitzy retail outlets illuminates this symbolic trajectory. In most cases, organic fare costs more than its conventional counterpart. Organic foods are luxury items in some circumstances, rather than staples, and eating organic has become associated with the well-to-do. One lavish establishment, GustOrganics in New York, became the first USDA-certified organic bar and began serving organic Latin-inspired cuisine and beverages like Buenos Aires Style Steak ($26), Homemade Turkey Meatballs ($21), Dulce de Leche Martini ($12), and Sambazon-Açaí Smoothie ($4.75)—sumptuousness not exactly on a par with the meager McDonald's Dollar Menu.[95]

Food, like other commodities, can be used as a status indicator. Class-stratified consumption is a hallmark of the postmodern economy, and foods pigeonholed as "gourmet" tend to require cultural and economic assets to obtain them. The florid discourse of gourmet food writing confers high repute upon certain items.[96] Organic food, when situated as haute gastronomy,

Farmers' market price board (Photo courtesy of Colleen Freda Burt)

is often framed as artisanal, authentic, traditional, precious, or glamorous. There is a delegation within the organic movement that prefers honey-glazed roasted organic carrots served at ritzy restaurants to dirt-caked raw organic carrots straight from the farm. Those who savor organic apple compote for dessert rarely know how to make organic compost from apple cores. Many who extol organic heirloom zucchini do not actually want to germinate the seeds and prune the vines themselves. The organic lifestyle has become a mark of refinement, with no dirt under the fingernails required.

The leitmotif of classiness has been paramount among the identities of people who align themselves with organics. A new *Organic Style* magazine that launched in 2008, unrelated to the one Rodale Inc. had previously published, was an online magazine from Organic Style Limited touted as "the premier green-living magazine." Writer-activist Julia Butterfly Hill was on the cover in spring 2008 as an "eco-hero." That issue included an article on Earth Day founder Denis Hayes, advice from PETA on how to throw a dog party, a report on a California biodynamic vineyard, and a piece on the Nature Conservancy's Plant A Billion Trees campaign. The cover also promised "down-to-earth inspiration and advice on gardening, travel, food, fashion, beauty, the environment, giving, and living." Gerald Prolman, founder and CEO of *Organic Style*, discussed organic agriculture in the publisher's note and said that it "thrives because both farmers and consumers are inspired by their love of the earth to make responsible choices. By growing organically, farmers care for the environment, for wildlife, for the people they employ— and for the people who conscientiously purchase their products."[97] The magazine's boutique section featured jewelry, body care products, flowers, food, wine, garden accessories, apparel, dog treats, and other eye-catching goodies from vendors eager to entice conscientious *Organic Style* readers.

Numerous top-notch companies have turned to organics, promising that people can make the world a better place with certain pampering products. M lie Organics Koke'e Body Cream ($32 for 7.5 ounces) is infused with awapuhi ginger, kukui, and macadamia nut oils; a portion of sales is donated to help preserve Hawaii's Koke'e State Park.[98] John Masters Organics Shine On Leave-In hair treatment ($30 for 4 ounces) is made from nine certified organic ingredients, including organic sea kelp, and has marine phytoplankton to help moisturize hair.[99] The Body Deli, in California, has "chefs" who use fresh organic ingredients to concoct skin care products, such as Crème de la Rose moisturizing cream ($75 for two ounces), Sea Cucumber Gelee ($45 for two ounces), Blueberry Fusion Scrub ($36 for two ounces), and Coconut

Cream Body Soufflé ($26 for eight ounces).[100] S. W. Basics makes an exfoliant that, in its "pure kitchen-cabinet awesomeness," could be edible: it is made from organic oat flour, organic almond flour, and Maine sea salt.[101] Upscale food purveyor Harry & David began offering organic fruit in its Fruit-of-the-Month Club and gift baskets; the seasonal organic palette included apples, pears, and grapefruit. The club was meant "for anyone who appreciates the benefits of eating organically grown fruits." Through the Organic Options Club, customers could pay $350 per year to receive the "finest, best-tasting" organic fruit, including clementines in January, cherries in July, and nectarines in September.[102] To serve travelers, many luxury hotels and resorts now operate their own organic gardens. When the CuisinArt Golf Resort & Spa in Anguilla wanted fresh salads for guests, it started a hydroponic farm and an organic vegetable garden that yields peppers, pumpkins, melons, okra, soybeans, and black-eyed peas. The resort's organic orchards produce limes, avocados, guavas, tamarinds, and starfruit. Guests can sample the harvest by ordering the spicy wok-tossed green soy edamame beans ($18) as an appetizer, the signature vegetable club sandwich with avocados ($18) for lunch, or the fruit plate ($10) for dessert.[103]

Kona Brewing Company had to pay six times more to make its Oceanic Organic Belgian-style ale than it did to make its conventional beers, but the result—Hawaii's first certified organic beer—was exceedingly popular, and the market for organic craft beers has been flowering.[104] Hangar 24 Craft Brewery in Redlands, California, uses hundreds of pounds of organic apricots from California's South Desert to make its Polycot beer, which is only available in August.[105] Bainbridge Organic Distillery obtains grain from organic farms west of Walla Walla, Washington; though the other organic ingredients it uses are roughly double the price of conventionally grown ingredients, demand for its USDA-certified organic vodka, gin, and whiskey is high. Benromach Organic Speyside Single Malt Scotch Whiskey, which was the world's first to be certified organic, is brewed in a small Scottish distillery and sells for about $52 per bottle online (plus $32 for shipping to the United States).[106] Prairie Organic Vodka—"made with respect from seed to glass"—is prepared using organic yellow corn from a co-op of nine hundred Minnesota farmers, bottled in recycled glass, labeled with organic ink, and packaged in sustainable wood pulp.[107] The labels for Square One Organic Vodka are printed on paper made from renewable fibers like bamboo and bagasse, and by-products of the organically certified North Dakota–grown rye used to make the vodka are sold as feed to an organic dairy farm; one bottle costs about $75 online.[108] Organic wines, to which no sulfites are added, have also raised their profile in the market. La Riojana Cooperativa, a member co-op of indigenous farmers in Argentina's Famatina Valley, sells organic vegan wines under the Pircas Negras label. Frey Winery in California produces certified organic wines like Organic Dessertage Port ($49), Organic Late Harvest Zin ($25), and Organic Pinot Noir ($18). The vineyard says that its "emphasis is on producing wine of the highest quality while caring for planet and palate alike."[109] These and other examples of organic's prevalence in the "green glamour" industry demonstrate its refined radiance. One can easily picture well-dressed people hobnobbing on yachts, sipping Bonterra's organic chardonnay, and pecking at steak tartare with organic shallots and capers on crostini.

Organic food has, in many respects, become a sign of distinction and prestigious consumption, more representative of the gentleman farmer spreading salted butter on cranberry scones than the gritty homesteader churning his own butter. Organic advertisements designed for the affluent take this reality into account. In advertisements for Bija Omega Truffles made with organic ingredients, the chocolates are portrayed as a luxurious but healthy indulgence, part of the sophisticated standard of living. They come in three "sublime vegetarian" flavors: dark chocolate, milk chocolate hazelnut, and white maple. Organic product promotions often exude the ethos of a prosperous lifestyle of material possessions, wholesome cuisine, and domestic comforts. The strategic endorsement of exclusivity is visible in advertisements for Green & Black's organic chocolate bars. Eco-preneur Craig Sams, the former chairman of Britain's Soil Association, founded Green & Black's in partnership with his wife, Josephine Fairley. This purveyor of costly organic confectionery became a market leader, and multinational candy company Cadbury bought the company in 2005.[110]

One ad in 2008 for Green & Black's Almond chocolate bar announced that it was "made with whole organic Sicilian almonds, pure organic cocoa and just a pinch of obsession." Text beneath this mentioned the importance of world-class organic ingredients: "We insist on Trinitario cocoa beans. And they must be grown organically, ensuring absolutely nothing gets in the way of their intense flavor." On the opposite page was a discussion of which Frei Brothers Reserve wine would best match each class of chocolate bar. Green & Black's Dark 70% was paired with Frei Brothers Reserve Pinot Noir, because "the light, fruity bitterness of the dark chocolate is complex but not too sweet, a perfect complement to the tart raspberry notes in the Pinot."

Appropriately, this particular ad was placed in *Bon Appétit*, a magazine catering to those who appreciate fine food and wine. Kraft Foods purchased Cadbury (and, by extension, Green & Black's) in 2010. In 2012, Green & Black's ads urged people to "live in the &"—"indulging in life" while "respecting it." Consumers could have it all: an organic conscience-soothing product in compliance with fair trade standards, and a mouth-watering chocolate bar; no compromises needed. The Green & Black's Maya Gold Dark 60% bar wrapper in 2013 claimed to follow the lead of "generations of Maya people in Belize" who "flavored their cocoa with spices." It blended orange flavor, organic vanilla extract, and spices with the organic bittersweet chocolate (and a touch of soy lecithin). Ironically, the bar was made in Poland and approved by California Certified Organic Farmers; Kraft Foods was in Illinois, so Belize merely inspired the ambiance for the swish delicacies.

Celebrity chef Wolfgang Puck created a line of organic bottled iced coffees made from blends of organic coffee, organic milk, Tahitian vanilla, European chocolate, and pure cane sugar. The café au lait, vanilla fusion, crème caramel, and double blend mocha flavors were all low-fat, kosher, and more expensive than ready-to-drink (nonorganic) bottled coffees from Starbucks, but Puck believed that coffee aficionados would appreciate the cold brewing process and organic ingredients he used.[111] It seems that entrepreneurs have found a way to make an upmarket organic version of everything. The Zambeezi company uses organic beeswax "from deep in the forests of central Africa" to make its organic tangerine lip balm.[112] Quality Assurance International certifies organic beeswax, jojoba seed oil, and spearmint leaf oil for inclusion in the Aubrey Organics spearmint lip balms. Virgin Vapor offers an extensive line of USDA-certified, organically flavored e-liquids, including organic piña colada and virgin organic kona velvet milkshake, for use in electronic cigarettes.[113]

A National Public Radio piece in 2011 poked fun at companies selling organic bottled water; the USDA specifically excluded water and salt from certification, but one brand professed that its water was organic because it came from beneath certified organic fields and had never been tainted with chemicals.[114] In 2012, Etihad Airways, the national airline of the United Arab Emirates, announced that it would be serving organic eggs and honey from the company's own free-range hens and bees (raised on a farm in Abu Dhabi) in dishes prepared fresh for Diamond First Class passengers by on-board chefs. Etihad also developed a line of organic signature pickles to serve to passengers with warm bread and cheeses.[115] When posh products are explicitly directed at well-off organic consumers, this subtly implies that those who are either uninterested in or unable to afford organic food are morally and intellectually inferior. Organic consumers, concurrently, get to feel luminescent inside and out.

Scores of consumers are willing to splurge for the perceived benefits that organic food provides. Some regard it as almost a necessity. Still, unduly high prices are a significant obstacle to the widespread adoption of organic food. Market research indicates that price is the single most important deterrent to those who do not purchase organics.[116] Many people who claim that they simply can't afford organic food still agree that it is better. Nearly 90 percent of shoppers say that they would buy organic produce if it cost the same as nonorganic but find the elevated cost to be a barrier.[117] Some observers hypothesize that, for farmers, the price premium must be upheld in order to ensure the feasibility of organic agriculture.[118] As early as the 1940s, Rodale told his magazine readers that "at the beginning premiums must be paid" for organically grown food, but eventually there would be a "drastic change in farm practice."[119] Organic food handlers were not getting rich in their business, he said in 1951. Rather, many were "working under hardship, pioneering to hew out a clearing from the wilderness of poor nutrition." When comparing costs, Rodale relayed that people should remember that organically produced foods would "give better health" and eliminate doctor visits.[120] Premiums were indeed paid, but there was no drastic nationwide overhaul of farm practice. Supporters still militantly pronounce that if a surplus of people buy organic, then prices will drop; however, this may not be the case if the premium is value-added, rather than cost-based. In the meantime, a completely organic grocery cart is beyond the budget of most people with low to moderate incomes. When organic food is twice as dear, one implication could be that only rich, enlightened individuals deserve healthy, wholesome food. The wealthy may be privileged enough to treat themselves to unpolluted noni juice and tempura seaweed snacks; the poor are left with "fruit" punch and fried pork rinds that are full of chemicals but more cost-efficient from a calorie-for-calorie perspective. Lower-income and minority neighborhoods are often "food deserts" that have inadequate access to large supermarkets, which correlates with the reduced consumption of fresh fruits and vegetables and more "empty calories." Individuals facing impediments to obtaining affordable, nutritious foods can be malnourished and have more health-related problems. Ironically, many farmworkers in mammoth organic agriculture operations cannot even afford the organic produce they help harvest.

Early studies largely characterized organic consumers as "white, affluent, well-educated, and concerned about health and product quality."[121] Analysis of scanner data from a Nielsen Homescan study in 2004 found that most purchasers of organic milk were "white, high income, and well educated."[122] Organic households were mostly in the West or East of the United States, with annual household incomes of at least $70,000. They were "less likely than conventional households to be Black." The data indicated that organic households had "higher discretionary income than conventional house-holds."[123] Global demand for organics was concentrated in the world's most prosperous countries, where consumers had higher purchasing power and could absorb the price markup.[124] It seemed that organic food was made for an upper-middle-class market. However, additional studies of the "new" organic consumer began to indicate that the demographics had changed. By 2005, Latinos and African Americans were the fastest-growing nub of organic consumers.[125] A Hartman Group study in 2006 showed that core consumers, defined as those committed to an organic lifestyle, were most likely to be Hispanic and black.[126] According to another study published in 2007, there was a popular perception that most organic consumers were white, were wealthy, and had young children. However, the consumer base of organic food had diversified. In fact, the authors showed that "Asian and African Americans tend to purchase organic over conventional produce more than Whites and Hispanics." This study found "little consistent association between per capita expenditures on organic produce and household income."[127] Studies by the USDA also did not tie high household income to organic purchases, despite the price premiums. Nonetheless, consumers still cited expense as the main reason that they did not buy organic foods.[128] Organic strategists need multifarious approaches that are not only aimed at the top socioeconomic echelons.

There have been some attempts to bridge class inequalities in access to organic food. The federal Farmers' Market Nutrition Program (FMNP) was designed to provide families on public assistance with locally grown produce at its peak of freshness. This program for lower-income recipients bequeathed vouchers that could only be redeemed at farmers' markets, encouraging purchases of fresh fruits and vegetables.[129] Some schools and hospitals began to offer healthy, organic menus. Alice Waters started the Edible Schoolyard program at an underprivileged Berkeley middle school in 1994, planting a one-acre organic garden for students to tend that allowed them to eat wholesome food; it has served more than seven thousand students over the years.

Also in the Bay Area, the Marin Organic School Lunch and Gleaning Program acts as a liaison between farmers and schools, enabling students from at least half of Marin's schools to eat locally grown organic food. In 2006, over two thousand hospitals in the United States gained access to natural and organic foods, due to a deal between MedAssets, a leading purchaser for the health care industry, and United Natural Food Incorporated (UNFI), the largest wholesale distributor to the natural and organic foods industry. The Detroit Black Community Food Security network operates a seven-acre farm in Detroit that features organic vegetable plots, mushroom beds, beehives, and a composting operation. The coalition hopes that its urban agriculture projects will help build self-reliance and food security in the city's black community; it also sells organic food at discounted prices through a co-op buying club. In another bid to overcome the food gap, Holcomb Farm, a CSA in Connecticut, began extending subsidized shares to urban families below the poverty level, because farm managers felt that organic produce ought not to be as elitist as it had become.[130]

Several organic food advocates recommend strategies—such as buying in bulk, on sale, from a co-op, in season, or online—that can keep organic food from being cost-prohibitive. *Consumer Reports* noted in 2006 that organic food costs were, on average, 50 percent extra, but they could be 100 percent more for milk and meat. The organization advised readers that it was worth paying more for organic apples, peaches, spinach, milk, and beef; they could pass on asparagus, broccoli, seafood, and cosmetics. To avoid "sticker shock," *Consumer Reports* also suggested comparison shopping, mail-order services, and CSAs for cheaper organic food.[131] *Shape* magazine advised readers in 2009 in the article "Go Organic without Going Broke": choosing store brands, using coupons from organic companies, finding CSAs, or asking the store for samples of new products.[132] One grocery chain, Sunflower Farmers Markets, expanded organic options by opening many new stores around the United States in 2009. CEO Mike Gilliland, who founded the Colorado-based business in 2002, was doubling it to include more than thirty locations. Modeled after farmers' markets, the stores specialized in natural and organic foods but kept prices at rock-bottom levels by minimizing overhead and capitalizing on supplier connections.[133] Gilliland had found that consumers regarded the opportunity to procure high-quality food at lower cost to be a refreshing change. A few years later, Sunflower had over forty stores promising "Serious Food" at "Silly Prices."[134] With scrupulous planning, many people feel that buying organic food doesn't have to blow your budget. Linda Watson's

Wildly Affordable Organic (2011) provided tips, ingredient lists, and menu plans for eating green, healthy meals that averaged less than $5 a day per person.[135] When competing with the historically low conventional food prices that Americans have grown accustomed to, those rooting for organics have exercised their creativity.

CONSUMER SOVEREIGNTY

Along with purity, freshness, exoticism, and succulence, many consumers crave meals with a sprinkling of virtue. The term "green consumerism" describes purchasing practices directed at products that minimize deleterious environmental consequences and lessen consumer exposure to environmental risks. Whereas environmentalists have often implored people to *stop* buying things (for example, fur, meat, or certain types of fuel), marketers feature certain goods as edifying for people, nature, and society. These products carry a moral incandescence, and organics are among those that have earned an ethereal luminosity. "Ethical food" is often juxtaposed to "fast food" or "junk food." There are parallels between the organic movement and other principled food movements that emphasize vegetarianism, fair trade, or local food. All of these may be considered New Social Movements (NSMs), which focus on consumption's place in the political economy. Having gained a growing role in late capitalism, NSMs often treat shopping as an axis for social change. They see "consumptive resistance" as a constructive individual tactic or collective gambit. "Buying green" is frequently described as an alternative consumption practice, driven by conscious reflexivity, in that consumers monitor and reflect upon the outcome of their conduct.[136] "Conscientious consumers" are drawn to the proliferation of goods that they feel righteous about buying, such as organic food. Though some naysayers disdain all consumerism as superficial and materialistic, adherents extol "ethical consumerism" as the best and most progressive method for enacting social insurgency.

Advocates of "consumer sovereignty" postulate that consumers bear the power to choose and even control what is offered in the capitalist marketplace. A consumer is said to be "voting" whenever he or she selects a certain product. Those who are smitten with organic food regularly insist that to vote with your pocketbook, dollars, or fork for organics is to engage in an influential political act. They see organic shoppers as consumer activists.

This archetype of "responsible capitalism" posits that certain companies provide socially and environmentally sustainable goods and services that are worth acquiring. The Environmental Working Group has recommended that consumers "vote with their wallets" by purchasing produce with consistently lower levels of toxic pesticides on them.[137] In *Eating with Conscience* (1997), Michael Fox described how consumers could become "kitchen anarchists" simply by supporting "local, humane organic farmers and market co-ops."[138] Buying power would make a difference, so "we can vote with our food dollars and change our eating habits for our own good and for the good of the animal kingdom, the environment, and caring farmers."[139] The Northeast Organic Farming Association agreed that this was the best course of action, because "by making a few changes in what you purchase and where you shop and by joining our community of organic-agriculture supporters, you cast your vote for a healthier state and a healthier planet."[140] *The Green Food Shopper: An Activist's Guide to Changing the Food System* (1997) advised readers to choose organically produced items when they could be found. The rationale was that, "as a consumer, you can help shape the global economy by what you buy."[141] *The Organic Cookbook* (2000) declared: "Vote with your fork—choose organic."[142] *Living Organic* (2001) noted: "We can vote for better products with our wallets through 'green consumerism' or 'ethical consumerism.'"[143] In *The Best Natural Foods on the Market Today: A Yuppie's Guide to Hippie Food* (2004), Greg Hottinger asserted that organic farmers deserved financial patronage. He wrote, "If you typically give to charitable causes, consider your extra expense of natural foods a donation to a healthier way of producing food."[144] Jane Goodall also acknowledged that organic foods cost more. However, she imagined that some people who paid willingly saw it "as a charity donation—a way to support the health of the planet or the farmers who are trying to do right by the land and their communities," and others saw it as a "health insurance payment, recognizing that by ridding their bodies, and the bodies of their children, of agricultural chemicals they may have fewer medical bills."[145] Organic practitioners, according to this logic, were providing not just crops but a multitude of public reimbursements.

An abundance of guides emphasize how organics benefit the long-term agricultural agenda. Leslie Duram's *Good Growing: Why Organic Farming Works* (2005) said, "Consumers speak with their wallets." Since buying organic food had the potential to address the "ecological, economic, and social concerns that go hand in hand with our global industrial food system,"

Duram thought that buying food produced locally and organically was "the best way to 'speak out' against these problems."[146] *The Organic Cook's Bible* (2006) assented that every piece of organic fruit purchased was another vote for "life-affirming, joyful, and humane farming."[147] The author wrote, "I think of my food dollars as ballots that can be cast either for agribusiness or for small farmers."[148] *Organic Housekeeping* (2006) urged consumers to "vote with your pocketbook for humane treatment for farm animals . . . and for clean water and healthy soil." In the end, paying a bit more for food and buying organic would be "a real bargain" for everyone.[149] *The Organic Food Handbook* (2006) was adamant that "people do make a difference with their food choices. The small ripples created by individuals choosing organic are rising to a tidal wave of change that will transform agriculture and food production, resulting in better human health, a cleaner environment, vital farming communities, a more balanced economy, a greater appreciation for how food is produced, and a renewed connection between farmers and consumers."[150]

Marion Nestle, professor of nutrition and public health, noted that, while businesses exploited public disquiet about health, the best recourse against such manipulation was to "vote with your dollars every time you buy food." She admitted, however, that it was not easy for an individual to "oppose an entire food system." To facilitate better choices, the "food environment" could be renovated in ways that encouraged eating healthfully.[151] Still, Nestle pressed consumers who were alarmed about pesticides or genetically modified foods to buy organics. Although organic produce had not proved to be more nutritious, she said, "there are loads of other good reasons to buy organics, and I do."[152] She viewed the price of organics as a "political choice," because "when you choose organics, you are voting with your fork for a planet with fewer pesticides, richer soil, and cleaner water supplies—all better in the long run."[153] Consumers ogling attractive products that slake their thirst for ethical consumption might also be helping to mitigate soil erosion and pollution, conserve energy, or strengthen communities.

According to those who defend organics, price should not deter shopper-activists. The Natural Resources Defense Council affirmed that organic food merited the added cost and counseled that organic food provided "extra value in the form of safer food that's better for the environment."[154] *Ode* magazine proclaimed in 2007 that "if 2 percent of the population starts paying extra for organic, people notice. Markets change. Behaviours change. Next thing you know, the world has changed."[155] *Food Fight: A Citizen's Guide to a Food and Farm Bill* (2007) affirmed that "every day, we can support or choose not to support a particular aspect of the food and farming sector through our purchases."[156] Michael Pollan's *In Defense of Food* (2008) concurred that "the more eaters who vote with their forks for a different kind of food, the more commonplace and accessible such food will become."[157] *Big Green Purse: Use Your Spending Power to Create a Cleaner, Greener World* (2008) announced that women could use consumer clout to create the world they want.[158] The author's first rule was to "buy less," but she also specified that favoring responsible companies built an incentive for their rivals to follow suit. Although organic food was more expensive, "the more you buy, the cheaper organic food will eventually get."[159] Papa's Organic, an online produce retailer, also predicted that more farms would move toward certification if more people switched to organic, and the cost of organic foods would then be reduced.[160] This maxim that positive upheavals are on the horizon has been repeated often, though it is unclear whether shopper-activism does much good for organic farmers.

Advocates have accentuated the lack of effort required to stage a protest against the callous industrial food system. Wendy Johnson, who spent nearly thirty years as an organic gardener for the San Francisco Zen Center's Green Gulch Farm, expressed her belief that "growing food organically and eating conscientiously are political acts that help to establish and ensure social, economic, and ecological justice."[161] The article "A Delicious Revolution" in *O, the Oprah Magazine* in 2008 stated that "all you have to do to join is pass up the chips and nuggets, and eat a locally grown, organic carrot instead." Though this easy step was, admittedly, far away from lining up for the giant marches and boycotts of the civil rights or antiwar movements in prior decades, the author still categorized those who were dutifully considering what crossed their lips as being actors in "a full-fledged revolution."[162] To change the world, it seems, you only need to switch what you eat. The fact that this insurrection is delectable has certainly helped the cause.

As these examples demonstrate, the organic movement has principally adopted a utilitarian approach, underlining how pesticide-free food provides private benefits. Advisements for consumers to vote with their wallets and choose organic food have notoriously played on fear (for example, risks to personal health and the environment) or sympathy (for example, the plight of livestock and family farmers). In posing organic food as a desirable supplement to the mundane fare, crusaders made it a niche product. As a mouthwatering amenity, it became part of the search for a better standard of living, tied to evolving planes of consumption.[163] This propelled the acceptance of inflated prices for organic products. Meanwhile, those who could not afford organic shiitake mushrooms and micro greens were left with the cheaper, chemically tainted debris. The same "you're worth it" logic extends to other organic goods, such as those available on Rodale Inc.'s own online shopping site, Rodale's, which launched in 2013 with the tagline "where inspired design meets healthy living." Maria Rodale, CEO of Rodale Inc., told visitors in her welcome video that Rodale's was only selling products meeting "rigorous standards for health, safety, and style"; she hoped that it would be "your one stop shop for wonderful." The site explained that its "carefully curated" products would allow you to "invest in your personal well-being and the care of the earth, without sacrificing beauty or quality."[164] These judiciously vetted items included a "Unique Fernwood Necklace" ($710), "Canvas Convertible Tote" bag ($245), "Modern Coffeepot" ($120), "Floppy Raffia Hat" ($80), "Eco-Sleek Paddle Brush" hairbrush ($35), "DIY Goat Cheese Kit" ($28), and "Italian Organic Orange Flower Water" ($18). Rodale's promised to take on all the "hard work" of figuring out what was safe and healthy; a shopper could confidently click away, making a positive impact on personal and planetary health by adding a $460 king-size organic cotton comforter to his or her cart.

Champions of green consumerism argue that it endows individuals who may eschew deeper ecological activities with a space for moderate environmental activism. Examining the paradox of "conscious consumption," environmental consultant Annie Muldoon discussed the extent to which, as a form of participatory democracy, it was a critical first step. It provided a forum in which consumers could actualize environmental convictions through their purchasing choices. Muldoon reasoned that "small, incremental changes may be derided as inconsequential, but they are perhaps the only way that substantial social change begins."[165] Psychologist Daniel Goleman also proposed in *Ecological Intelligence* (2009) that "radical transparency" about the environmental impact of products would enable shopping to become "an opportunity for compassion," generating ripple effects throughout global supply chains.[166] In the face of this chorus about consumer cogency when shopping for a good cause, though, skeptics have exposed weaknesses in the notion of consumer sovereignty. The ideology of "free choice" in a "free market" masks imbalanced power relations. Any act of consumption reinforces, rather than undermines, the capitalist infrastructure in which economic, political, and cultural authority is concentrated.

The truism of "consumer power" falls apart when people do not have genuine choices about the food they eat. Consumer preferences are not always met. Options in public situations—for example, schools, hospitals, workplace cafeterias, and government food coupon programs—are often restricted. Race and class are factors in food access, consumption, and marketplace leverage. Historian Susan Strasser has observed that attempts to underscore consumer agency should not disguise "the fundamental fact" that "the point of capitalist enterprise is to make money." Corporate profit margins succor stockholders; social inequality is propagated through consumption. Clever marketing ploys contribute to the creation of needs and awaken desires that may exceed a person's means.[167] In *New Age Capitalism* (2000), Kimberly Lau also argued that "consumption is not political action. Believing it to be so is perhaps the greatest risk of modernity."[168] When consumers presume that they have the capacity to subvert the systems of global capitalism, this impression may merely allow those systems to thrive.[169]

Rodale contended in 1952 that it was "up to those who are health-conscious to see that their needs and rights are honestly represented in the halls of Congress and in their State legislatures."[170] Yet the organic alliance chiefly focused on convincing consumers to engage in "green consumption," not on formulating policies. A persistent emphasis on consumptive power led to the individualization of responsibility, which ascribed culpability for society's knotty problems to isolated people; these people, in turn, could contritely assuage their eco-remorse by purchasing eco-friendly goods and attaining forgiveness for transgressions. Rather than bolstering systemic reform, this legitimized existing dynamics of consumption and production. Individualization is apolitical and nonconfrontational. Placing the burden on a consumer's shoulders (and wallet) absolves crucial players of blame for social and environmental damage. It enables organizations and government to evade accountability for making agriculture truly sustainable. As a controlling rule, farm legislation has favored the efficiency and uniformity of chemical-industrial monocultures, not ecological alternatives. The abiding viability of organic farms may depend more on restructuring agricultural policies than on cultivating consumer approval. In the meantime, intractable agricultural axioms (and moneyed lobbyists) continue to create the framework for American food.

Consumers can indeed exert significant pressure on the capitalist marketplace. Progressive, enlightened consumerism can provoke change in what corporations offer. However, the widespread presumption that citizens trigger social cataclysms through everyday purchasing patterns needs sharper scrutiny. Buying recycled paper towels does not threaten any formidable edifices. "Conscious commerce" or "voting" with one's fork may have negligible effects or be counterproductive. Creating better products can be a useful response to environmental troubles, but producing and consuming less across the board would be a vaster affront to profligacy. Donating directly to charitable causes might be smarter than paying money for products that donate a portion of their profits to charity. The immense challenge is to revamp the frameworks that sustain overconsumption.[171] Consumer sovereignty is rooted in the supposition that industries robotically respond to shoppers' wants and needs, assuming that companies don't produce unless there is demand.[172] Detractors assert that this hypothesis neglects to consider how consumers do not have complete information about their options and are not immune to the influence of marketers. Global distribution and political-economic commodity chains affect what is actually produced.[173] Individualization ignores the logistics of how behemoth forces shape consumer decisions.[174] The organic movement's conscious consumerism remains only a piecemeal mechanism for prompting structural social revolutions.

ORGANIC MARKET PROJECTIONS

Organic food has been hailed as the most rapidly growing division of food sales in North America. Between 1997 and 2009, the US organic food market quintupled. Fresh organic produce and milk were the top-selling retail categories.[175] Fruits and vegetables dominated the organic food segment, though nascent organic beverages, snacks, cereals, and other products continued to arise. Nonfood organic offerings, such as clothing and cosmetics, grew 39 percent in 2008.[176] The potential for expansion was wide, but that year, when fuel and food prices rocketed beyond the comfort level of many Americans, market research indicated that consumers were curtailing their consumption of organics. Core organic consumers were more attached, but rising commodity costs meant that less-committed consumers felt insecure paying premiums for organic food during a recession.[177] Demand for organic milk softened, the price of organic feed doubled, and organic dairy farmers suffered.[178] In a joint poll by Cooking Light and the CNN Money website, 60 percent of Americans stated that organic foods seemed too expensive to justify buying.[179] The market seemed saturated. After years of striking annual sales growth, the economic downturn may have curbed the organic tide, but it was far from moribund. The Organic Trade Association reported that US sales of organic food rose 17 percent in 2008, despite the economy being in a shambles.[180] Even with the financial slump, the sales increase indicated underlying resilience in the organic market.

Organic chef Jesse Ziff Cool's cookbook, *Simply Organic* (2008), praised modern-day heroes who were carrying forth J. I. Rodale's beliefs, ranging from "the founders of organic food companies to the small local farmers doing their bit, one acre at a time."[181] Martha Stewart declared that she was still "totally entranced with fresh and organic."[182] Natural Foods Merchandiser predicted that organic food would be the top "continuing trend" captivating the natural food industry.[183] The United States overtook Europe as the largest global market of organic food in 2010.[184] The organic food industry was growing seven times faster than total US food sales.[185] By 2011—when the United States was still in an economic recession—organic food was outpacing sales growth in comparable conventionally produced food.[186] An NPR–Thomson Reuters Health Poll reported that a majority of American adults preferred to eat organic food. The bulk of those who "preferred" nonorganic food said that this was only because they thought organic food was too pricey.[187] While a majority of the public did prefer organic food, the retail premium remained a hurdle.[188] Produce Retailer observed in 2011 that the organic sector had been growing for five years, fueled predominantly by a handful of "loyal consumers" who make up "a small percentage of the overall consumer base." Those who believed believed strongly, but price sensitivity was affecting the decision to purchase organic products. Some consumers did not see enough value in organics to warrant paying more. Some were fickle in their shopping habits. Still, organic produce was "a strong and growing element," and the trade journal recommended that retailers utilize meticulous signage to educate shoppers on the benefits of organic fruits and vegetables.[189] The International Herald Tribune reported that sales of organic foods appeared "robust," and analysts projected that the sector would "remain strong in coming years."[190] The sales figures for 2012 were higher still, making organics a prominent target for both compliments and criticism.[191] The organic industry represented only 3.5 percent of total US retail food sales; yet it clutched a disproportionate amount of media attention, and forecasts for the market were bullish.

Despite the rosy outlook, organic sprawl has been a thorny ordeal. Bob Scowcroft, grand statesman of the organic industry, estimated that it had taken thirty years for the organic share of the food market to go from .013 percent to nearly 4 percent. He said, "Now we have to go to 40 percent. What's it going to take?" When asked if that ambition was realistic, Scowcroft replied that it was an "urgent" necessity. He didn't mind the litany of complaints about organics being overrated either, because he said that the movement was all about "continuous improvement."[192] The organic troops were fighting valiantly. In 2012, the United States and the European Union signed an agreement that brought their organic standards into alignment, and this was expected to expand sales of US organic exports abroad. Florida citrus grower Matt Mclean, who was also board president of the Organic Trade Association and president of Uncle Matt's Organic, anticipated that this "monumental agreement" would open new possibilities for organic farmers.[193] Produce industry insider Tom Karst praised the agreement but also predicted that "the future of organic produce will be related to home-grown consumer appreciation and confidence in what organic produce represents."[194] Consumers were not inclined to give up on organics, and retailers were not settling for mercantile mediocrity.

Concerted strategies to hound consumers who have a lower propensity to buy organic could help the sector reach its apogee. The prospect of further growth, however, sparks both alacrity and alarm within and outside movement. Organic food is still bashed as a bogus, unacceptable, or ridiculous racket in many circles. In an interview in 2012, dietitian Manuel Villacorta said, "To be honest, I think the whole organic thing is a marketing scheme."[195] Agribusiness consultant David Leyonhjelm was even more scathing, portraying organic farming as implausible, irrelevant, and unproductive. In a piece for *Stock & Land*, he wrote, "No intelligent person would choose organic food over conventional food on objective grounds," because it was merely supported by "a number of false assumptions" and resembled a religion.[196] These doubting Thomases were not alone. Misinformation, misunderstandings, and misgivings linger. Consequently, the sum of US farmland that is certified organic hovers at just 0.5 percent of pasture and 0.7 percent of cropland.[197]

Organic boosters may not agree on a bedrock definition of "organic," but in the aggregate they have clung to the power of consumers as a higher authority. J. I. Rodale's faith in the reliability of "discriminating purchasers" was bottomless. In 1953, an *Organic Gardening* piece resolved that, if the "crucial crusade" was to "reach the momentum and magnitude necessary to revolutionize things now," "we must all get behind it 100 per cent." To accomplish this, the fledgling magazine's grand stratagem was exhorting each subscriber to pass the issue along to a friend and enlist at least one new subscriber.[198] Even today, individuals who recruit more fervent organic eaters, one by one, abet the grassroots cause—but they do not ineludibly revolutionize anything. Marion Nestle has warned that if organic standards will "continue to mean something in the United States (and I am convinced that they must), it will be because hundreds of thousands of people will demand that nothing be done to weaken them."[199] Beyond individual actions, though, purposeful strides and intransigent principles at a national level are requisites to amplify the movement's mettle. Organic certification, under the aegis of the USDA, needs to be ironclad. Precocious rhetoric, savvy publicity initiatives, and genuine commitment to the movement's raison d'être at the corporate level would also help keep the organic star from fading. In the long run, the organic market could prolong its acceleration—or it could crumble. The cadre of steadfast followers (both gentrified and humble) could intensify—or it could splinter into antagonistic factions. Euphoric organic devotees, striving for personal and planetary well-being, still feel that the "revolution" will take place if cornerstone precepts are not compromised. Contemporaneously, it could be argued that a revolution has already taken place, in terms of polish, professionalism, and profitability.

A "VITAL CAUSE"

J. I. Rodale ordained "organic" to denote "life-giving" soil and food. He felt that the organic movement generated "a spirit of aliveness."[200] Raising consciousness about the teeming benefits of organics was one of his fortes. He had a penchant for setting in motion ideas that naturally gained momentum. Exuding vigor and vivacity, Rodale struck a chord that changed the way people perceived organics. *Organic Gardening* catapulted the movement's growth. The National Sustainable Agriculture Information Service called Rodale Press a "highly visible and accessible source of information" that was "the single greatest influence on the shape and underlying philosophy of mainstream organics."[201] The ebullient Rodale was the consummate public relations expert. Robert Rodale said that his father proffered an abundance of technical advice yet realized that "humus was not an end in itself, but a foundation upon which rested a way of life."[202] J. I. Rodale did not expect the public to embrace the cause because microbial creatures thrived in organic soil and mycorrhizal associations were an indispensable component of soil chemistry. Rather, the movement was about wholesome food, responsible farmers, bounteous human health, poetically ecological landscapes, harmonious living, the lyrical "balance of nature," and other poignant initiatives.

The organic movement, as a form of collective action, has involved solidarity, has been engaged in conflict, and has violated boundaries.[203] Organic farming has historically faced harsh skeptics in the "establishment." J. I. Rodale vented about the USDA's "apathy" and "ingrained policies" in 1952 and said, "I am afraid if we are going to wait for the Department of Agriculture to recommend the organic method instead of the chemical one, we will have to wait a long, long time."[204] The following year, a writer for *Organic Gardening* called the organic crusade to eviscerate chemical fertilizers a "vital cause" working "against great odds," because it was a way of life hitting at "our most powerful pressure groups, the chemical industry, medicine and food processors, and their pocketbooks."[205] Over time, attempts to undermine organic standards came from the Farm Bureau, food corporations, biotech companies, and industry-friendly government agencies. Hostility helped fuel the movement; melodramatic obstacles abetted member bonding and provided a sense of commonality. As outcasts, organics seemed edgy even to the counterculture. Despite hecklers shouting them down and nonbelievers tarring their credibility, organic enthusiasts did not shuffle on the fringes unobtrusively.

The quandary for a social movement is that it may strive for economic or political prowess but lose oppositional clout as it gains traction. When the disparagement of organics from the powers-that-be subsided, some of the camaraderie that underdogs were inclined to share faded, and some of the fans who were rooting for "hometown" organics stopped applauding. As it straddled a chasm between the haute health food platter and the supermarket bargain bin, organics no longer seemed avant-garde. When a social movement matures into something more inclusive and acceptable to the general public, it naturally loses some of its charismatic intensity through diffusion. The movement's creed is often diluted, compromised, or even corrupted. New converts may not be as passionate about social principles as the early coterie. To the disillusioned, as soon as the organic movement won certain concessions, it also dropped some of its integrity and solidarity. Federal certification was a mitigated benediction.

As the organic movement ripened into a consumer-centric bonanza, its actors may have been willing partners in their own "co-optation." Though people waving the organic flag did engage in conflict, they were not unfailingly subversive or adversarial. Organic comrades defied crucial beliefs but also aligned with those in power in order to gain recognition and legitimacy, enabling the movement to touch a broader audience. One writer for the *Organic Farmer* in 1951 urged "aggressive farmers" to "talk restaurant owners into featuring a few organic dishes on their menus."[206] J. I. Rodale discussed two men who were capitalizing on the gleam of organic food that year, "determined to make a big thing in the retail stores" of an organic cooked cereal they were making themselves.[207] These were hardly the most aggressive acts that organic combatants could have undertaken. Though the movement operated within restraints, sometimes the crusaders corralled themselves. Antagonists tend to denigrate the organic movement for being too big, too industrialized, too commercialized, or simply too prosaic. A chronic thread among discontented commentators is that invincible corporations will inexorably hijack diminutive resisters and suppress their rebelliousness. This chorus of lamentation, though, may actually absolve the movement of responsibility for actively struggling toward a structural agro-food insurrection, which seems futile if the corporate bottom line's omnipotence is inevitable.

This book has historicized narrative strategies, ideological formations, and recurring premises in the fabric of the organic movement. These leitmotifs remind us of the prominent role that farming and food play in American culture. One of the organic agenda's most successful elements was a preference for preindustrial farming (in the quixotic "small is beautiful" vein) over "unnatural" advancements (such as chemical pesticides and colossal setups). Many organic farmers still believe in humus, earthworms, Albert Howard's Law of Return, and the supremacy of "Nature's Way." An Eden Foods ad in 2012 flatly stated that "organic agriculture is society's brightest hope for positive change." Some organic growers and eaters truly feel that they are contributing positively to "the Revolution" that J. I. Rodale envisaged. But the organic upheaval could still be a long way off. Classic American road food and neighborhood venues—lobster roll shacks, hot dog stands, po'boy delis, greasy burger diners, fried chicken dives, barbecue joints, take-out pizza purveyors, ice cream trucks, and tiny donut shops—are notoriously not organic (but wildly popular all the same). There have been coups but no full-fledged mutiny in the food structure.

A social movement is an amalgamation of independent psyches, yet it has a mind of its own. While encompassing individual convictions, it also fos-

An inviting farm stand (Photo courtesy of Colleen Freda Burt)

A young organic consumer (Photo courtesy of Colleen Freda Burt)

ters a sense of kinship. In the formative years of organics, there were rifts and moments of unity. There was no blueprint for victory. Discrete steps propelled developments, as did collective actions and cultural context. The organic tour de force encountered internal fractures and external barriers that may have alternately strengthened and diluted its cohesiveness. Not until decades after it was born did national media sources sincerely recognize how organic food had grown up. Once its potential to step out from the shadowy sidelines was tapped, the movement would indeed perform on the main stage of American culture with élan. Formerly dismissed as a marginal hobby, organic farming slogged through the muck, emerging as a craze, a trend, and then a mighty industry. Once castigated as an invidious scam perpetuated by health hucksters, organic edibles subsequently garnered cachet, adulation, and sensual menu descriptions. Organics acquired both believers and hecklers. Paring it down to a single-issue campaign is nearly impossible, but, ultimately, it remained a movement with a pertinent raison d'être. A dynamic combination of resonant values, germane social matters, fluctuating economic factors, and articulate leaders coalesced in the organic movement and propelled its trajectory. It has been simultaneously quirky and corporate. Organic food never saturated supermarkets, but once organic oats and carrots were easy enough for everybody to find, celebratory sips of organic chardonnay seemed appropriate for toasting the triumph. A self-appointed "organic police force" may attempt to keep a tight rein on the requirements for what constitutes a "sincere" organic practitioner, but there is no badge to prove that someone is a card-carrying member of Organic Nation. Large organic operations, small niche growers, profit-hunting marketers, and philosophical weekend gardeners are all part of the movement.

The varying viewpoints and goals encompassed by *American Organic*, in all its complexity, continue to evolve. Organic food has mainly matured as an individual choice within a sweeping social movement that has not brought systemic change to agriculture. J. I. Rodale exemplified the volatile, labyrinthine conditions of the movement from the start. Opposition is itself a key theme throughout this story, as is the war between organic and antiorganic forces. The reality that there are even now people who care passionately about organics is why the essence of the movement—notwithstanding quibbles and fractures—has endured for over seven decades. An organic zenith may still lie ahead. On the other hand, an avalanche of unregulated GMOs and chemical pesticides could flatten every compost heap in the nation. In the perfect planet that J. I. Rodale imagined, perhaps all food would be grown organically and everybody would be supremely healthy. Organic advocates have argued that "the most pressing challenges of our day"—including rising health care costs, global warming, and world hunger—can be met "one organic bite at a time."[208] It is probable that devoted organic "agtivists" will continue to feel that they are inching toward a world-changing revolution with each organic nibble.

Notes

INTRODUCTION

1. J. I. Rodale, "With the Editor: The Principle of Eminent Domain," *Organic Gardening* 10 (1947): 16–18.

2. L. F. Dodge, "Planning Organic Profits," *Organic Farmer* 1 (1950): 15–18, at 15.

3. C. G. King, "Good Nutrition in the Shopper's Basket," in *A Report to the Nation: "The Good in Your Food": Reprinted from the Proceedings of the 23rd Annual Convention of Super Market Institute* (Chicago: Super Market Institute, 1960), 2–5, at 3.

4. R. Goldstein, "Earl L. Butz, Secretary Felled by Racial Remark, Is Dead at 98," *New York Times*, February 4, 2008.

5. Rodale Inc., "Organic Gardening: About the Brand," December 2009, www.rodaleinc.com/brand/organic-gardening.

6. For example, see Clarence J. Glacken, *Traces on the Rhodian Shore: Nature and Culture in Western Thought from Ancient Times to the End of the Eighteenth Century* (1967); Roderick Nash, *Wilderness and the American Mind* (1967); Donald Worster, *Nature's Economy: A History of Ecological Ideas* (1977); Donald Worster, *Dustbowl: The Southern Plains in the 1930s* (1979); Alfred Crosby, *Ecological Imperialism: The Biological Expansion of Europe, 900–1900* (1986); David Arnold, *The Problem of Nature: Environment, Culture, and European Expansion* (1996); Paul Josephson, *Industrialized Nature: Brute Force Technology and the Transformation of the Natural World* (2002); Carolyn Merchant, *Reinventing Eden: The Fate of Nature in Western Culture* (2004).

7. See William Cronon, *Nature's Metropolis: Chicago and the Great West* (1991); and William Cronon, "The Trouble with Wilderness; or, Getting Back to the Wrong Nature," in *Uncommon Ground: Toward Reinventing Nature*, ed. William Cronon (1995).

8. For example, see Bruce Braun, "Towards a New Earth and a New Humanity: Nature, Ontology, Politics," in *David Harvey: A Critical Reader*, ed. Noel Castree and Derek Gregory (2006); Ursula Lehmkuhl and Hermann Wellenreuther, eds., *Historians and Nature: Comparative Approaches to Environmental History* (2007); Michael P. Nelson and J. Baird Callicott, *The Wilderness Debate Rages On: Continuing the Great New Wilderness Debate* (2008); Damian F. White and Chris Wilbert, eds., *Technonatures: Environments, Technologies, Spaces, and Places in the Twenty-First Century* (2009); Christof Mauch, *Natural Disasters, Cultural Responses* (2009); Anthony N. Penna, *The Human Footprint: A Global Environmental History* (2009); and Sarah Pilgrim and Jules Pretty, eds., *Nature and Culture: Rebuilding Lost Connections* (2012).

9. For example, see Mark David Spence, *Dispossessing the Wilderness: Indian Removal and the Making of the National Parks* (1999); William Deverell and Greg Hise, eds., *Land of Sunshine: An Environmental History of Urban Los Angeles* (2005); Michael Lewis, ed., *American Wilderness: A New History* (2007); Eric W. Sanderson, *Manhattan: A Natural History of New York City* (2009).

10. Jean Baudrillard, *The System of Objects* (New York: Verso, 1996), 199–200.

11. M. Douglas and B. Isherwood, *The World of Goods: Towards an Anthropology of Consumption* (New York: Basic Books, 1979), 67, 75.

12. Michel de Certeau, *The Practice of Everyday Life* (Berkeley: University of California Press, 1998), xiii.

13. Ibid., xvii.

14. Pierre Bourdieu, *Distinction: A Social Critique of the Judgement of Taste* (Cambridge, MA: Harvard University Press, 1984), 101.

15. Ibid. 283.

16. Ibid. 316.

17. For example, see R. W. Fox and T. J. Jackson Lears, eds., *The Culture of Consumption: Critical Essays in American History, 1880–1980* (1983); Daniel Horowitz, *The Morality of Spending: Attitudes toward the Consumer Society in America, 1875–1940* (1985); Jeffrey Meikle, *American Plastic: A Cultural History* (1997); Katherine Grier, *Culture and Comfort: Parlor Making and Middle-Class Identity, 1850–1930* (1998); Daniel Horowitz, *The Anxieties of Affluence: Critiques of American Consumer Culture, 1939–1979* (2004); Grant McCracken, *Culture and Consumption II: Markets, Meaning, and Brand Management* (2005).

18. For example, see Rob Shields, ed., *Lifestyle Shopping: The Subject of Consumption* (1992); Barry Schwartz, *The Paradox of Choice: Why More Is Less* (2004); Grant McCracken, *Culture and Consumption II: Markets, Meaning, and Brand Management* (2005); Michael Silverstein and Neil Fiske, *Trading Up: Why Consumers Want New Luxury Goods—and How Companies Create Them* (2005); Allison J. Pugh, *Longing and Belonging: Parents, Children, and Consumer Culture* (2009).

19. For example, see Ernest Dichter, *Handbook of Consumer Motivations* (New York: McGraw Hill, 1964); Stuart Ewen, *Captains of Consciousness: Advertising and the Social Roots of Consumer Culture* (1976); Michael Schudson, *Advertising, the Uneasy Persuasion: Its Dubious Impact on American Society* (1984); Roland Marchand, *Advertising the American Dream: Making Way for Modernity, 1920–1940* (1985); Jackson Lears, *Fables of Abundance: A Cultural History of Advertising in America* (1994); Thomas Frank, *The Conquest of Cool: Business Culture, Counterculture, and the Rise of Hip Consumerism* (1997); Martin Lindstrom, *Brandwashed: Tricks Companies Use to Manipulate Our Minds and Persuade Us to Buy* (2011); and Arthur Asa Berger, *Ads, Fads, and Consumer Culture: Advertising's Impact on American Character and Society* (2011).

20. For example, see Lizabeth Cohen, *A Consumers' Republic: The Politics of Mass Consumption in Postwar America* (2003); Andrew Szasz, *Shopping Our Way to Safety: How We Changed from Protecting the Environment to Protecting Ourselves* (2007); Michele Micheletti, *Political Virtue and Shopping: Individuals, Consumerism, and Collective Action* (2010).

21. For example, see Duane Elgin, *Voluntary Simplicity* (1981); Julie Schor, *The Overspent American: Why We Want What We Don't Need* (1999); John de Graaf, *Affluenza: The All-Consuming Epidemic* (2001).

22. For example, see Diane MacEachern, *Big Green Purse: Use Your Spending Power to Create a Cleaner, Greener World* (2008); Daniel Goleman, *Ecological Intelligence: How Knowing the Hidden Impacts of What We Buy Can Change Everything* (2009); Ellis Jones, *The Better World Shopping Guide: Every Dollar Makes a Difference* (2010).

23. For example, see Thomas Princen, Michael Maniates, and Ken Conca, eds., *Confronting Consumption* (2002); Norman Myers and J. Kent, *The New Consumers: The Influence of Affluence on the Environment* (2004); Peter Dauvergne, *The Shadows of Consumption: Consequences for the Global Environment* (2008); Daniel Miller, *Consumption and Its Consequences* (2012).

24. Roland Barthes, "Toward a Psychosociology of Contemporary Food Consumption," in *Food and Drink in History: Selections from the Annales*, ed. R. Forster and O. Ranum (1979).

25. For example, see Claude Lévi-Strauss, *The Raw and the Cooked* (1964); Carole M. Counihan, *The Anthropology of Food and Body: Gender, Meaning, and Power* (1999); and John Pottier, *Anthropology of Food* (1999).

26. For example, see Carole M. Counihan, ed., *Food in the USA: A Reader* (2002); and Laura Shapiro, *Something from the Oven: Reinventing Dinner in 1950s America* (2004).

27. For example, see M. Conner and C. J. Armitage, *The Social Psychology of Food* (2002); Warren Belasco, *Appetite for Change* (1989); and Warren Belasco, *Meals to Come: A History of the Future of Food* (2006).

28. For example, see Harvey Levenstein, *Revolution at the Table: The Transformation of the American Diet* (1988); Harvey Levenstein, *Paradox of Plenty: Social History of Eating in Modern America* (1993); David Bell and Gill Valentine, *Consuming Geographies: We Are Where We Eat* (1997); Leslie Brenner, *American Appetite: The Coming of Age of a Cuisine* (1999); James McWilliams, *A Revolution in Eating: How the Quest for Food Shaped America* (2005); and Andrew Smith, *Eating History: Thirty Turning Points in the Making of American Cuisine* (2011).

29. For example, see Linda Keller Brown and Kay Mussel, eds., *Ethnic and Regional Foodways in the United States: The Performance of Group Identity* (1984); Laura Shapiro, *Perfection Salad: Women and Cooking at the Turn of the Century* (1986); Barbara G. Shortridge and James R. Shortridge, eds., *The Taste of American Place: A Reader on Regional and Ethnic Foods* (1998); Donna Gabaccia, *We Are What We Eat: Ethnic Food and the Making of Americans* (2000); Sherrie A. Inness, ed., *Kitchen Culture in America: Popular Representations of Food, Gender, and Race* (2000); and Sherrie Inness, *Dinner Roles: American Women and Culinary Culture* (2001).

30. For example, see James L Watson, ed., *Golden Arches East: McDonald's in East Asia* (1997); and David Ingles and Debra Gimlin, eds., *The Globalization of Food* (2010).

31. For example, see Sidney Mintz, *Sweetness and Power: The Place of Sugar in Modern History* (1985); Kathy Neustadt, *Clambake: A History and Celebration of an Amer-*

ican Tradition (1992). Mark Kurlansky, *Cod: A Biography of the Fish That Changed the World* (1997); Virginia Scott Jenkins, *Bananas: An American History* (2000); Mark Pendergrast, *Uncommon Grounds: The History of Coffee and How It Transformed Our World* (1999); Andrew Smith, *Peanuts: The Illustrious History of the Goober Pea* (2002); E. Melanie DuPuis, *Nature's Perfect Food: How Milk Became America's Drink* (2002); Steve Ettlinger, *Twinkie, Deconstructed* (2007); Dan Koeppel, *Banana: The Fate of the Fruit That Changed the World* (2007); and the series by Reaktion Books, including Carol Helstosky, *Pizza: A Global History* (2008); Ken Albala, *Pancake: A Global History* (2008); and William Rubel, *Bread: A Global History* (2011).

32. See Warren Belasco and Roger Horowitz, eds., *Food Chains: From Farmyard to Shopping Cart* (2009); Barry Estabrook, *Tomatoland: How Modern Industrial Agriculture Destroyed Our Most Alluring Fruit* (2011); and Oran Hesterman, *Fair Food: Growing a Healthy, Sustainable Food System for All* (2011).

33. See Eric Schlosser, *Fast Food Nation: The Dark Side of the All-American Meal* (2001); Michael Pollan, *The Omnivore's Dilemma: A Natural History of Four Meals* (2006); Michael Pollan, *In Defense of Food: An Eater's Manifesto* (2009); Michael Pollan and Maira Kalman, *Food Rules: An Eater's Manual* (2011); Marion Nestle, *Food Politics: How the Food Industry Influences Nutrition and Health* (2002); Marion Nestle, *Safe Food: Bacteria, Biotechnology, and Bioterrorism* (2003); Marion Nestle, *What to Eat* (2006); Marion Nestle and Malden Nesheim, *Why Calories Count: From Science to Politics* (2012); Mark Bittman, *Food Matters: A Guide to Conscious Eating with More Than 75 Recipes* (2008); as well as the films *The True Cost of Food* (2002); *King Corn* (2005); *Fast Food Nation* (2006); and *Food, Inc.* (2009).

34. Albert Melucci, *Nomads of the Present: Social Movements and Individual Needs in Contemporary Society* (Philadelphia: Temple University Press, 1989), 29.

35. Stuart Hall, "Who Needs 'Identity'?," in *Questions of Cultural Identity*, ed. S. Hall and P. D. Gay (London: Sage, 1996), 1–17, at 2–4.

36. M. Goldstein, *The Health Movement: Promoting Fitness in America* (New York: Twayne, 1992).

37. D. d. Porta and M. Diani, *Social Movements: An Introduction* (London: Blackwell, 1999), 6, 20.

38. Melucci, *Nomads of the Present*, 23.

39. P. Kristiansen and C. Merfield, "Overview of Organic Agriculture," in *Organic Agriculture: A Global Perspective*, ed. P. Kristiansen, A. Taji, and J. Reganold (Ithaca, NY: Comstock, 2006), 1–23, at 3.

40. Porta and Diani, *Social Movements*, 18.

41. A. P. Cohen, *The Symbolic Construction of Community* (New York: Tavistock, 1985), 118.

42. Ibid., 12.

43. R. Eyerman and A. Jamison, *Social Movements: A Cognitive Approach* (Cambridge: Polity, 1991), 94.

44. J. I. Rodale, "With the Editor: Whither Science?," *Organic Farmer* 4 (1953): 13.

45. J. I. Rodale, "What 'Organically-Grown' Really Means," *Organic Farmer* 5 (1953): 37.

46. J. I. Rodale, "With the Editor: Artificial Insemination," *Organic Gardening* 14 (1949): 12.

47. R. Rodale, "What Is Organic Gardening?," *Organic Gardening* 20 (1952): 14–15, at 14.

48. V. O. Luckock, "You Don't Need Acres 'n' Acres," *Organic Gardening and Farming* 1 (1954): 18–19, at 18.

49. G. Hamilton, *The Organic Garden Book* (New York: DK, 1993), 9.

50. Eliot Coleman, "Can Organics Save the Family Farm?," 2004, www.secretsofthe city.com/magazine/reporting/features/can-organic-save-family-farm.

51. USDA, "National Organic Program: Final Rule," www.ams.usda.gov/nop/NOP /standards.html., 546.

52. Ibid., 20–21.

CHAPTER 1. ORGANIC DESTINY

1. J. I. Rodale, *Pay Dirt: Farming and Gardening with Composts* (New York: Devin-Adair, 1948), 193.

2. Ibid., 33.

3. See, for example, Gay Bryant, "J. I. Rodale: Pollution Prophet," *Penthouse* 2 (1971): 28–32, at 28; Sustainable Agriculture Network, "Transitioning to Organic Production, Sustainable Agriculture Research and Education (SARE) Program" (2007): 1–31, at 3; Dan Sullivan, "Research Makes It Clear: Organic Food Is Best for People and the Planet," *Rootstock* 9, no. 1 (2009): 4–7, at 7; and Steve Solomon, "Organic Gardener's Composting," www.soilandhealth.org/03sov/0302hsted/030202/030202bib .html.

4. J. I. Rodale, "Editorial," *Organic Farmer* 1 (1949): 9–10, at 9.

5. J. I. Rodale, "Editorial: Looking Back, Part IV, The Beginning of Our Experimental Farm," *Organic Gardening* 20 (1952): 10–11, 36–39, at 39.

6. J. I. Rodale, "Introduction to Organic Farming," *Organic Farming and Gardening* 1 (1942): 3–4, at 4.

7. J. I. Rodale, "With the Editor: Is Our Health Related to the Soil?," *Organic Gardening* 5 (1944): 3–8, at 8.

8. J. I. Rodale, "Tenth Anniversary Editorial: Looking Back," *Organic Gardening* 20 (1952): 11–14, 43, at 43.

9. Robert Rodale, "The Heart and Soul of Organic Gardening," *Organic Gardening* 39 (1992): 46.

10. David M. Tucker, *Kitchen Gardening in America: A History* (Ames: Iowa State University Press, 1993), 142.

11. J. I. Rodale, "Tenth Anniversary Editorial: Looking Back, Part II," *Organic Gardening* 20 (1952): 11–12, 37–38, at 11.

12. Wade Greene, "Guru of the Organic Food Cult," *New York Times Magazine*, June 8, 1971, 30, 31, 54, 56, 60, 65, 68, at 30.

13. J. I. Rodale, *The Healthy Hunzas* (Emmaus, PA: Rodale, 1949), 31.

14. James Whorton, *Crusaders for Fitness: The History of American Health Reformers* (Princeton, NJ: Princeton University Press, 1982), 332.

15. Carlton Jackson, *J. I. Rodale: Apostle of Nonconformity* (New York: Pyramid, 1974), 55.

16. J. I. Rodale, "Editorial: Looking Back, Part III, Tradition Throttles Research," *Organic Gardening* 20 (1952): 10–11, at 10.

17. Jackson, *J. I. Rodale*, 61.

18. Albert Howard, *An Agricultural Testament* (New York: Oxford University Press, 1943), 39.

19. Albert Howard, *The Soil and Health: A Study of Organic Agriculture* (New York: Devin-Adair, 1947), v.

20. Ibid., 223.

21. F. H. King, *Farmers of Forty Centuries* (Emmaus, PA: Organic Gardening Press, 1955).

22. Howard, *An Agricultural Testament*, 20.

23. Howard, *The Soil and Health*, 17.

24. Howard, *An Agricultural Testament*, 224.

25. Robert McCarrison, *Nutrition and Health* (London: Faber and Faber, 1953), 14.

26. Ibid., 21.

27. Weston A. Price, *Nutrition and Physical Degeneration: A Comparison of Primitive and Modern Diets and Their Effects* (Redlands, CA: Weston A. Price, 1945), 415.

28. J. I. Rodale, "With the Editor," *Organic Gardening* 7 (1945): 4.

29. William A. Albrecht, "Man and the Soil: Degeneration of Both, Often Feared, Remains to Be Verified," *New York Times*, May 9, 1943.

30. Rodale, *Pay Dirt*, 139.

31. Rodale, "Tenth Anniversary Editorial: Looking Back," 13.

32. J. I. Rodale, "The Soil and Health Foundation," *Organic Gardening* 11 (1947): 31.

33. J. I. Rodale, "With the Editor: Sir Albert Howard: A Tribute," *Organic Gardening* 13 (1948): 13–14, at 14.

34. Eve Balfour, *The Living Soil* (London: Faber and Faber, 1948), 44.

35. Ibid., 137.

36. Ibid., 163.

37. Ibid., 16.

38. Lord Northbourne, *Look to the Land* (London: Dent, 1940), 98.

39. Ibid., 96.

40. Ibid., 170.

41. Lionel Picton, "Medical Testament," in *Nutrition & the Soil: Thoughts on Feeding* (New York: Devin-Adair, 1949), 39–50.

42. Louise E. Howard, *The Earth's Green Carpet* (London: Faber and Faber, 1948), 147, www.journeytoforever.org/farm_library/greencarp/greencarptoc.html.

43. Rudolf Steiner, "Beekeeping: Nine Lectures on Bees," *Biodynamics* 216 (1998): 19–23, at 23.

44. Ehrenfried Pfeiffer, *Bio-Dynamic Farming and Gardening: Soil Fertility, Renewal and Preservation* (New York: Anthroposophic Press, 1938), 210–211.

45. Haydn S. Pearson, "Science Shows Earthworms Are Friends of Gardeners," *New York Times*, September 28, 1941.

46. "Grow a Garden and Be Self-Sufficient, by Ehrenfried Pfeiffer and Erika Ries, Translated by Alice Heckel. New York: Anthroposophic Press," *New York Times*, May 10, 1942.

47. Carey McWilliams, *Factories in the Field: The Story of Migratory Farm Labor in California* (Berkeley: University of California Press, 2000).

48. "Fewer Farms: But They Are Bigger, Produce More Food; Machinery Is the Reason Texan Plows 5,000 Acres with 10 Tractors, Michigan Man Has 1,800 Acres of Potatoes More Owners; Less Tenants Fewer Farms: But They Are Bigger, Produce More Food with Machines," *Wall Street Journal*, December 22, 1945.

49. "Twenty Million Gardens," *New York Times*, March 25, 1945.

50. Mike McGrath, ed., *The Best of Organic Gardening* (Emmaus, PA: Rodale, 1996), viii.

51. Ibid., 8.

52. Rodale, "Introduction to Organic Farming," 4.

53. Rodale, "Tenth Anniversary Editorial: Looking Back," 14.

54. J. I. Rodale, "Health and the Soil," *Organic Farming and Gardening* 1 (1942): 1.

55. F. J. Gardenhire, "The Crime of Abandoned Farms," *Organic Farming and Gardening* 1 (1942): 13–15, at 13.

56. Rodale, "Tenth Anniversary Editorial: Looking Back," 43.

57. J. I. Rodale, "With the Editor," *Organic Gardening* 2 (1943): 2–4, at 2.

58. H. A. Lane, "Reader's Correspondence," *Organic Gardening* 2 (1943): 28–31, at 28–29.

59. J. I. Rodale, "With the Editor: Federal Program, Part II," *Organic Gardening* 3 (1943): 1–3, at 1.

60. J. I. Rodale, "With the Editor: Advantages of Compost Farming," *Organic Gardening* 5 (1944): 1–5.

61. "All the *Extra* Vitamins and Minerals You Need," *Vintage Ads and Stuff*, www .vintageadsandstuff.com/viewfoodovaltine1.jpeg.

62. J. I. Rodale, "With the Editor: Is Our Health Related to the Soil?," *Organic Gardening* 5 (1944): 3–8, at 6–8.

63. Ibid., 8.

64. J. I. Rodale, "With the Editor: Insects, the Censors of Nature," *Organic Gardening* 12 (1948): 16.

65. "Medicine: What Grandfather Ate," *Time*, December 9, 1940, www.time.com /time/magazine/article/0,9171,765032,00.html.

66. Samuel Glasstone and Violette Glasstone, *The Food You Eat: A Practical Guide to Home Nutrition* (Norman: University of Oklahoma Press, 1943), 252–253.

67. Rodale, *The Healthy Hunzas*, 183.

68. J. I. Rodale, "You Can Do Much to Help Your Health!," *Organic Farming and Gardening* 1 (1942): 31.

69. Organic Gardening, "Poison Sprays on Washed Apples," *Organic Gardening* 6 (1945): 27.

70. H. E. Muckler, "Letters," *Organic Gardening* 6 (1945): 28.

71. R. A. Driscoll, "California Compost," *Organic Gardening* 6 (1945): 24.

72. Organic Gardening, "Reader's Correspondence," *Organic Gardening* 7 (1945): 26–29, at 27–29.

73. R. W. Logan, "Results," *Organic Gardening* 6 (1945): 25.

74. J. I. Rodale, "With the Editor: A Debate," *Organic Gardening* 8 (1946): 2–4, at 2.

75. Albert Howard, "Organic Campaign," *Organic Gardening* 10 (1947): 19.

76. J. I. Rodale, "Organic Food Shops," *Organic Gardening* 7 (1945): 9.

77. H. Meyer, "Over the Fence," *Organic Gardening* 7, no. 2 (July 1945): 21–22, at 21.

78. Howard, *The Soil and Health*, 241–243.

79. Ibid., vi.

80. J. I. Rodale, "With the Editor: The Principle of Eminent Domain," *Organic Gardening* 10 (1947): 16–18, at 17.

81. R. H. Calvin, "Club News," *Organic Gardening* 10 (1947): 53.

82. J. I. Rodale, "Memorandum," *Organic Gardening* 10 (1947) 18.

83. J. I. Rodale, "With the Editor: The Rodale Diet, Part II," *Organic Gardening* 11 (1947): 11–13, at 11.

84. J. I. Rodale, "With the Editor: The Rodale Diet," *Organic Gardening* 11 (1947): 12–14.

85. J. I. Rodale, "With the Editor: Cancer—Part III: Primitive Peoples," *Organic Gardening* 15 (1949): 12.

86. J. I. Rodale, "With the Editor: Should the U.S. Government Go into the Chemical Fertilizer Business?," *Organic Gardening* 11 (1947): 12–13, at 13.

87. J. I. Rodale, "With the Editor: The Organiculturist's Creed," *Organic Gardening* 12 (1948): 12–14, at 12.

88. Rodale, *Pay Dirt*, 239.

89. Ibid., 139.

90. Ibid., 240.

91. Randal S. Beeman and James A. Pritchard, *A Green and Permanent Land: Ecology and Agriculture in the Twentieth Century* (Lawrence: University Press of Kansas, 2001), 38.

92. Rodale, *Pay Dirt*, 3.

93. Ibid., 11.

94. Ibid., 203.

95. Ibid., 75.

96. Ibid., 134–135.

97. Ibid., 219.

98. Ibid., 220.

99. Ibid., 89.

100. Ibid., 23.

101. Ibid., 187.

102. Ibid., 171.

103. Ibid., 188.

104. Albert Howard, introduction to *Pay Dirt*, vii.

105. W. M. Teller, "The Garden Book of the Year," *Organic Gardening* 8, no. 6 (1946).

106. Harriet K. Morse, "Of Making Books," *New York Times*, March 16, 1947.

107. J. I. Rodale, "With the Editor: What's It All About?," *Organic Gardening* 21 (1953): 9–13, at 12.

108. S. W. Edwards, "Grindstone Run Empties into the Potomac," *Bio-Dynamics* 4, no. 3 (1948): 20–24, at 21.

109. Rodale, *The Healthy Hunzas*, 248.

110. Organic Gardening, "Pay Dirt in Japan," *Organic Gardening* 19 (1951): 48.

111. Jackson, *J. I. Rodale*, 30.

112. Rebecca Kneale Gould, "Modern Homesteading in America: Religious Quests and the Restraints of Religion," *Social Compass* 44, no. 1 (1997): 157–170, at 162.

113. Henry David Thoreau, *Walden and Civil Disobedience* (New York: Penguin, 1986), 183.

114. Ibid., 157.

115. Ibid., 200.

116. Liberty Hyde Bailey, *The Country-Life Movement in the United States* (New York: Macmillan, 1911), 204.

117. Ibid., 198.

118. Scott T. Peters and Paul A. Morgan, "The Country Life Commission: Reconsidering a Milestone in American Agricultural History," *Agricultural History* 78, no. 3 (Summer 2004): 289–316, at 293.

119. J. C. Marquis, untitled article, *American Economic Review* 1, no. 3 (1911): 567–568, at 568.

120. Jeffrey Jacob, *New Pioneers: The Back-to-the-Land Movement and the Search for a Sustainable Future* (University Park: Pennsylvania State University, 1997), 8.

121. Liberty Hyde Bailey, *The Seven Stars* (New York: Macmillan, 1923), 92–94.

122. Ibid., 158.

123. Ralph Borsodi, *Flight from the City: The Story of a New Way to Family Security* (New York: Harper & Brothers, 1933), xv.

124. Ibid., 2.

125. Ibid., 22.

126. Ibid., 9.

127. Ibid., 72.

128. Rodale, *Pay Dirt*, 90–91.

129. Ibid., 236.

130. Ibid., 237.

131. Ibid., 239.

132. Hugh Hammond Bennett, "Waste by Wind and Water," *Scientific Monthly* 42, no. 2 (February 1936): 172–176, at 175.

133. Kathleen O'Neill, "Reforming Rice: Lundberg's Greener Farms," *E: The Environmental Magazine* 18, no. 1 (January–February 2007): 10.

134. Lundberg Family Farms, "Our Family: History," www.lundberg.com/Family/History.aspx.

135. Ed Robinson and Carolyn Robinson, *The "Have-More" Plan: A Little Land—a Lot of Living* (Pownal, VT: Storey Books, 1973), 2.

136. Ibid., 3.

137. Ibid., 64.

138. Harold S. Richmond, "Story of a Citrus Grove," *Bio-Dynamics* 6, no. 3 (1948): 2–11, at 2.

139. F. H. Billington, *Compost for Garden Plot or Thousand-Acre Farm: A Practical Guide to Modern Methods* (Boston: Charles T. Branford, 1956), 69.

140. Wilfred Wellock, "An Agricultural-Industrial Economy," in *Organic Husbandry: A Symposium*, ed. John Stead Blackburn (London: Biotechnic, 1949), 93–94.

141. R.G.M. Wilson, "I Believe," in Blackburn, *Organic Husbandry*, 90–91.

142. Fairfield Osborn, *Our Plundered Planet* (Boston: Little, Brown, 1948), 201.

143. John S. Cooper, "Soil Savers: Businessmen Crusade for Conservation on Southwest Farmland," *Wall Street Journal*, February 10, 1948.

144. J. I. Rodale, *Our Poisoned Earth and Sky* (Emmaus, PA: Rodale, 1964), 244.

145. Philip Conford, *The Origins of the Organic Movement* (Edinburgh: Floris, 2001), 103.

146. Ibid., 60.

147. Louis Bromfield, *Pleasant Valley* (New York: Harper & Brothers, 1945), vii.

148. Ibid., 296.

149. Louis Bromfield, *Malabar Farm* (New York: Harper & Brothers, 1948), 230.

150. Ibid., 38.

151. Ibid., 230.

152. Ibid., 282.

153. J. I. Rodale, "With the Editor: The Human Health Aspect of Organic Farming," *Organic Gardening* 8 (1945): 2–4, at 2.

154. Bromfield, *Malabar Farm*, 292.

155. Louis Bromfield, *From My Experience: The Pleasures and Miseries of Life on a Farm* (New York: Harper & Brothers, 1955), 175.

156. Ibid., 36.

157. Ibid., 183.

158. J. I. Rodale, "Reader's Correspondence," *Organic Gardening* 6 (1945): 25.

159. L .L. Sherman, "Organic Gardening in Oakland, Cal," *Organic Gardening* 10 (1946): 57–58, at 58.

160. O. Lawrence, "Composting in the Olden Days," *Organic Gardening* 8 (1946): 39–40, at 40.

161. J. W. Hershey, "Organic Farming and Its Influence on the Health of Soil, Plants, Animals and Man," *Bio-Dynamics* 6, no. 3 (1948): 11–19, at 11.

162. J. I. Rodale, "With the Editor: Artificial Insemination," *Organic Gardening* 14 (1949): 12.

163. Bill Briggs, "Going Organic: Enthusiastic Consumers Join Craze," *Denver Post*, August 19, 2001, 1–5.

164. J. I. Rodale, "Solicitation of Members for the Soil and Health Foundation," *Organic Gardening* 11 (1947): 14.

165. J. I. Rodale, "The Soil and Health Foundation," *Organic Gardening* 11 (1947): 31.

166. J. I. Rodale, "With the Editor: Grants to Research Institutions," *Organic Gardening* 18 (1951): 16, 18, at 18.

167. Donald P. Hopkins, *Chemicals, Humus, and the Soil* (Brooklyn, NY: Chemical Publishing Society, 1948), 219, 332.

168. Rodale, *The Healthy Hunzas*, 15.

169. Ibid., 35.

170. Ibid., 20.

171. Ibid., 229.

172. Ibid.

173. Ibid., 235.

174. J. I. Rodale, *The Organic Front* (Emmaus, PA: Rodale, 1948), 199.

175. J. I. Rodale, *Stone Mulching in the Garden* (Emmaus, PA: Rodale, 1949), 27.

176. Ibid., 35.

177. Jonathan Forman, "What Has Been Learned about Soil-Health Relationships at the Conferences," in *Soil, Food and Health*, ed. Jonathan Forman and O. E. Fink (Columbus, OH: Friends of the Land, 1948), 35–99, at 38.

178. Ibid., 45.

179. Ibid., 71.

180. Ibid., 99.

181. Elizabeth C. Hall, "Books—New and Old," *New York Times*, December 12, 1948.

182. Louise E. Howard, *The Earth's Green Carpet* (London: Faber and Faber, 1948), www.journeytoforever.org/farm_library/greencarp/greencarptoc.html.

183. Lionel Picton, *Nutrition & The Soil: Thoughts on Feeding* (New York: Devin-Adair, 1949), 85.

184. Ibid., 348.

185. Ibid., 339–340.

186. Ibid., 127–128.

187. Ibid., 53.

188. Ibid., 344.

189. Rodale, "With the Editor: The Organiculturist's Creed," 12.

190. T. H. Sanderson-Wells, "Time, Population and the Soil," in Blackburn, *Organic Husbandry*, 40–43, at 43.

191. "The Albert Howard Foundation of Organic Husbandry," in Blackburn, *Organic Husbandry*, 138–140.

192. "The Farmer: The Journal of Organic Husbandry," in Blackburn, *Organic Husbandry*, 143.

193. Newman Turner, *Fertility Farming* (London: Faber and Faber, 1951), 21.

194. Rodale, "With the Editor: What's It All About?," 13.

195. J. I. Rodale, "Editorial," *Organic Farmer* 1 (1949): 9, 14, at 14.

196. J. I. Rodale, "Radical Change in Organic Method," *Organic Gardening* 15 (1949): 26–27.

197. J. I. Rodale, "Notice about The Organic Farmer," *Organic Gardening* 15, no. 5 (May 1949): 14.

198. J. I. Rodale, "Editorial," *Organic Farmer* 1 (1949): 9–10, at 10.

199. J. I. Rodale, "With the Editor: The Flea Beetle," *Organic Farmer* 2 (1950): 8–9, at 9.

200. A. E. Lesle, "First Award," *Organic Farmer* 1 (1950): 47.

201. D. A. Van Tuyle, "Letter," *Organic Farmer* 3 (1952): 7.

202. W. H. Allen, "Crucial Crusade," *Organic Gardening* 21 (1953): 21.

203. Committee on the Role of Alternative Farming Methods in Modern Production Agriculture, *Alternative Agriculture* (Washington, DC: National Academy Press, 1989), 25.

204. "To Combat Hunger," *New York Times*, February 20, 1950.

205. Staff Reporter, "Senate Farm Group Considers Use of Food as Cold War Weapon: Flanders Proposes Letting Eisenhower Offer Surplus Goods to Starving Iron Curtain Nations," *Wall Street Journal*, July 17, 1953.

206. John F. Lawrence, "Mechanized Farming," *Wall Street Journal*, September 22, 1959.

207. "The World at Work: Brief Notes of the Week," *Barron's National Business and Financial Weekly*, April 11, 1955.

208. "More Light on DDT: Government Tests Show Where and How It Can Be Used against Pests, Drawbacks of DDT Tree Insects Controlled," *New York Times*, September 16, 1945.

209. Rodale, *Pay Dirt*, 179.

210. Dorothy H. Jenkins, "Around the Garden," *New York Times,* June 11, 1944.

211. Oklahoma State University Extension Service, *Oklahoma Agriculture Today and Tomorrow* (1960), Page H. Belcher Collection, Box 39, Carl Albert Congressional Research and Studies Center.

212. Hartley W. Barclay, "New Products Aid in Farm Economy: Chemicals Developed to Cut 'Stoop Labor' Costs by as Much as 50%," *New York Times*, May 20, 1950, 19.

213. "Prospect of Big Bug Crop Worries Farmers," *News and Courier* (Charleston, SC), March 7, 1950.

214. "NC State College Offers Third Annual Pesticide School," pamphlet, 1951, NCSU Libraries Rare & Unique Digital Collections, http://d.lib.ncsu.edu/collections/catalog/ua100_052–001-bx0001–001–000.

215. Allen Van Cranebrock, "Death Valley Crop," *Wall Street Journal*, September 10, 1954.

216. William A. Clark, "All-Around Element: Versatile Phosphorus Grabs Many New Jobs; Output Climbs Sharply One New Compound Way Rival DDT; Others Cut Costs for Fertilizer Dealers the Story of Hennig Brandt All-Around Element: Phosphorus Grabs New Jobs; Output Climbs," *Wall Street Journal*, March 18, 1955.

217. Staff Reporter, "Free World Agricultural Output This Year May Exceed 1954. Foreign Crop Observers Predict," *Wall Street Journal*, September 19, 1955.

218. Ray Vicker, "Farm Revolution Vegetable Men Apply New Ways, Get Along without Federal Help," *Wall Street Journal*, July 8, 1957.

219. Sam Dawson, "Farming, in Today's Style, Is No Simple Occupation," *Spokane Daily Chronicle*, July 8, 1957.

220. Oklahoma State University Extension Service, *Oklahoma Agriculture Today and Tomorrow.*

221. William Barry Furlong, "Chemical Revolution on the Farm," *New York Times,* October 4, 1959.

222. Ibid.

223. Associated Press, "Opinions Vary on Status of Ezra Benson," *News and Courier* (Charleston, SC), December 26, 1959.

224. Ovid A. Martin, "New Drive Is Afoot to Oust Ezra Benson," *Sarasota Herald-Tribune,* March 2, 1958.

225. "The Benson Rumors," *Mount Airy News,* November 19, 1957.

226. "Benson Learns Way in Survival Battle," *Palm Beach Post-Times,* March 9, 1958.

227. Furlong, "Chemical Revolution on the Farm."

228. Arlen J. Large, "Lift for Lawns: Move to the Suburbs Spurs Boom in Grass and Garden Fertilizers; Food, Drug Stores Stock Up; New Makers Enter Field; Corn Cob Crusher Converts Tung Nuts and Tobacco Stems Lift for Lawns: Move to Suburbs Spurs Boom in Grass Fertilizers," *Wall Street Journal,* July 2, 1957.

229. "Monsanto Develops New Soil Conditioning Resin," *Wall Street Journal,* December 31, 1951.

230. Sydney B. Self, "Soil-Conditioners: Companies Stampede into Production of New Plant Stimulators the 25-Odd Makers May Be Joined by a Dozen More; Garden Potential Is Fat Two-Month Sales: $3 Million Soil-Conditioners: Plant-Stimulant Find Sets Off a Rush into the Field," *Wall Street Journal,* July 25, 1952.

231. Dorothy Thompson, "The Plight of the Farmer," *Spokesman-Review,* January 26, 1954.

232. Thomas L. Stokes, "Plight of Small Farmers," *Toledo Blade,* December 12, 1955.

233. J. I. Rodale, ed., *The Complete Book of Food and Nutrition* (Emmaus, PA: Rodale, 1966), 620.

234. Ibid., 624.

235. Rodale, "With the Editor: What's It All About?," 11.

236. Rodale, *Complete Book of Food and Nutrition,* 619.

237. R. I. Throckmorton, "The Organic Farming Myth," *Country Gentleman* 121, no. 9 (1951): 21, 103, 105, at 21.

238. J. I. Rodale, "With the Editor: This Organic Gardening Bunk, Part 1," *Organic Gardening* 21 (1953): 10–11, 49–54, at 10–11.

239. H. P. Bateman, "Letters," *Organic Gardening* 4 (1953): 6.

240. Arthur B. Beaumont, "Biochemical Gardening," *Horticulture* 30, no. 10 (1952): 388.

241. Wayne Gard, "Organic Farm Cult Blind to Evidence," *Dallas Morning News,* June 8, 1952.

242. J. I. Rodale, "With the Editor: This Organic Gardening Bunk, Part II," *Organic Gardening* 21 (1953): 10–11, 26–27, 34–35, 40, at 10–11.

243. Warren Belasco, *Appetite for Change: How the Counterculture Took on the Food Industry, 1966–1988* (New York: Pantheon, 1989), 16, 71.

244. Ehrenfried Pfeiffer, "The Organic-Chemical Controversy in Agriculture," *Bio-Dynamics* 10, no. 3 (1952): 2–19, at 2.

245. Ibid., 3–5.

246. Rodale, "With the Editor: What's It All About?," 9.

247. J. I. Rodale, "The Mounting Campaign against Organic Farming," *Organic Farmer* 3 (1952): 32.

248. Rodale, "With the Editor: This Organic Gardening Bunk, Part 1," 11.

249. Ibid., 10–11.

250. *New York Times*, December 10, 1950.

251. J. I. Rodale, "Prevention," *Organic Gardening* 16 (1950): 56.

252. Rodale, "Tenth Anniversary Editorial: Looking Back," 43.

253. J. I. Rodale, "Why Chemical Fertilizers Are Bad," *Organic Farmer* 1 (1949): 15–16, at 15.

254. Michael Heasman, and Julian Mellentin, *The Functional Foods Revolution: Healthy People, Healthy Profits?* (Sterling, VA: Earthscan, 2001), 6.

255. Jorian Jenks, *The Stuff Man's Made Of: The Positive Approach to Health through Nutrition* (London: Faber and Faber, 1959), 117.

256. Sterling W. Edwards, "Grindstone Run Becomes a Summer Stream," *Bio-Dynamics* 10, no. 3 (1952): 20–23, at 20–21.

257. Gertrude Springer, "Home on the Range," *Organic Gardening and Farming* 1, no. 8 (1954): 64–65.

258. J. V. Clute, "Even Indians Eat Organically," *Organic Gardening and Farming* 1 (1954): 42–43, at 42.

259. J. I. Rodale, "With the Editor: In Defense of the Organic Method," *Organic Farmer* 3 (1951): 17–19, 49, 51–53, at 18.

260. "J. I. Rodale Dead; Organic Farmer: Espoused the Avoidance of Chemical Fertilizers," *New York Times*, June 8, 1971.

261. J. I. Rodale, "Organic Farming—Bunk?," 18–19.

262. J. I. Rodale, "With the Editor: Progress throughout the Nation," *Organic Gardening* 20 (1952): 11.

263. P. Arena, "Why I Operate an Organic Stand," *Organic Gardening* 20 (1952): 16–17, 46–47, at 46.

264. Rodale, "Tenth Anniversary Editorial: Looking Back," 11.

265. J. I. Rodale, "Miscellany: Looking Forward," *Organic Gardening* 20 (1952): 24–25.

266. Organic Gardening, "Important Announcement," *Organic Gardening* 21 (1953): 13–16, at 15.

267. Rodale, "With the Editor: What's It All About?," 9–13.

268. J. Olds, "Testing Ground for Organics," *Organic Gardening and Farming* 1 (1954): 24–27, at 26.

269. Joseph Cocannouer, *Farming with Nature* (Norman: University of Oklahoma Press, 1954), 169; and Joseph Cocannouer, *Weeds: Guardians of the Soil* (New York: Devin-Adair, 1950), 65.

270. Cocannouer, *Weeds*, 109.

271. Ibid., 15.

272. Cocannouer, *Farming with Nature*, 16.

273. Ibid., 17.

274. Large, "Lift for Lawns."

275. Malcolm Beck, *Lessons in Nature* (Austin, TX: Acres USA, 2005), 11.

276. Ibid., 40.

277. Ibid., 94.

278. Ben Easey, *Practical Organic Gardening* (London: Faber and Faber, 1976), 28.

279. Hugh Corley, *Organic Small Farming* (Pauma Valley, CA: Bargyla and Gylver Rateaver, 1975), 191.

280. Conford, *Origins of the Organic Movement*, 212.

281. Jenks, *The Stuff Man's Made Of*, 7.

282. Ibid., 203.

283. Ibid., 100.

284. Ibid., 9.

285. North Carolina State University, Agricultural Policy Institute, "School of Agriculture, N.C. State College, Information and Curricula, 1960–1961," North Carolina State University, College of Agriculture and Life Sciences, Agricultural Institute Records, UA 100.040, Special Collections Research Center, North Carolina State University Libraries, Raleigh, North Carolina.

286. Louise Hughston, "Crusading Zeal Abounds in Health Food Sales," *Washington Post*, September 27, 1959.

287. Bob Thomas, "Organic Food Lures Stars to Jim Baker's 'Aware Inn,'" *Geneva Times*, April 24, 1959.

288. Bob Thomas, "Stars Go for Organic Food Fad; Make the Aware Inn Prosperous," *Milwaukee Journal*, April 24, 1959.

289. "Better Your Garden," *Publishers Weekly* 246, no. 51 (1999): 77.

290. Rodale, *Complete Book of Food and Nutrition*, xiv.

291. Ibid., 802.

292. Ibid., xv.

293. Ibid., 559.

294. Ibid., 558.

295. Ibid., 625.

296. Ibid., 799.

297. "J. I. Rodale Dead," 42.

298. Rodale, *Complete Book of Food and Nutrition*, xiv, 927.

299. Ibid., 637.

CHAPTER 2. A NOISY SPRING

1. Louis Bromfield, *Pleasant Valley* (New York: Harper & Brothers, 1945), 35.

2. Christopher Bosso, *Environment Inc.: From Grassroots to Beltway* (Lawrence: University Press of Kansas, 2005), 34.

3. John W. Hershey, "Organic Farming and Its Influence on the Health of Soil, Plants, Animals and Man," *Bio-Dynamics* 6, no. 3 (1948): 11–19, at 17.

4. Rachel Carson, *Silent Spring* (Boston: Houghton Mifflin, 1987), 8.

5. Ibid., 99.

6. W. Barrett, "The Organic Way of Gardening and Its Prophet," *Smithsonian* 2 (1971): 52–55.

7. Samuel Hays, *Beauty, Health, and Permanence: Environmental Politics in the United States, 1955–1985* (New York: Cambridge University Press, 1987), 34.

8. Ibid., 263.

9. David M. Tucker, *Kitchen Gardening in America: A History* (Ames: Iowa State University Press, 1993), 151–152.

10. Paul Kristiansen and Charles Merfield, "Overview of Organic Agriculture," in *Organic Agriculture: A Global Perspective*, ed. Paul Kristiansen, Acram Taji, and John Reganold (Ithaca, NY: Comstock, 2006), 1–23, at 6.

11. Mark Stoll, "Rachel Carson's Silent Spring," *Environment & Society Portal*, www.environmentandsociety.org/exhibitions/silent-spring/industrial-and-agricultural-interests-fight-back.

12. "Rachel Carson's Warning," *New York Times*, July 2, 1962.

13. "Rachel Carson Book Is Called One-Sided," *New York Times*, September 14, 1962.

14. Stoll, Mark, "Rachel Carson's Silent Spring," *Environment & Society Portal*, www.environmentandsociety.org/exhibitions/silent-spring/us-federal-government-responds.

15. "Miss Carson Describes Rise in Chemical Poison," *New York Times*, June 7, 1963.

16. Lawrence Galton, "Great Debate Over Pests—And Pesticides," *New York Times*, April 14, 1963.

17. Ibid.

18. Daniel Imhoff, *Farming with the Wild: Enhancing Biodiversity on Farms and Ranches* (San Francisco: Sierra Club Books, 2003), 14.

19. Randal S. Beeman and James A. Pritchard, *A Green and Permanent Land: Ecology and Agriculture in the Twentieth Century* (Lawrence: University Press of Kansas, 2001), 122.

20. J. I. Rodale, *Our Poisoned Earth and Sky* (Emmaus, PA: Rodale, 1964), 332.

21. Ibid., 184.

22. Karen Iacobbo and Michael Iacobbo, *Vegetarian America: A History* (Westport, CT: Praeger, 2004), 170–173.

23. Gillian Flaccus, "California's First Health Guru, Gypsy Boots, Dead at Age 89," *U-T San Diego*, August 9, 2004, www.signonsandiego.com/news/state/20040809-2136-ca-bit-gypsyboots.html.

24. Doug Rossinow, *The Politics of Authenticity: Liberalism, Christianity, and the New Left in America* (New York: Columbia University Press, 1998), 282.

25. Michelle Stacey, *Consumed: Why Americans Love, Hate, and Fear Food* (New York: Simon and Schuster, 1994), 116.

26. East West Journal, *Shopper's Guide to Natural Foods* (Garden City Park, NY: Avery, 1987), 2.

27. Ann Vileisis, *Kitchen Literacy: How We Lost Knowledge of Where Food Comes from and Why We Need to Get It Back* (Washington, DC: Island, 2008), 209.

28. Michael Destries, "Meryl Streep Says Julia Child Was Initially against Organic Foods," *Ecorazzi*, August 12, 2009, www.ecorazzi.com/2009/08/12/meryl-streep-says -julia-child-was-initially-against-organic-foods/.

29. Beatrice Trum Hunter, *The Natural Foods Primer: Help for the Bewildered Beginner* (New York: Simon and Schuster, 1972), 16.

30. Chris Maynard and Bill Scheller, *The Bad for You Cookbook* (New York: Villard, 1992), xiv.

31. Euell Gibbons, *Stalking the Wild Asparagus* (New York: David McKay, 1962), 5.

32. Euell Gibbons, *Stalking the Good Life: My Love Affair with Nature* (New York: David McKay, 1971), 175.

33. Wilson MacDougall, "Organic Food Boom Is Growing," *Cape Girardeau Southeast Missourian*, June 17, 1971.

34. J. I. Rodale, *Rodale's System for Mental Power and Natural Health* (Emmaus, PA: Rodale, 1966), xi.

35. Ibid., 169.

36. "The Kosher of the Counterculture," *Time*, November 16, 1970, www.time.com /time/magazine/article/0,9171,904481,00.html.

37. "The Nation: Windmill Power," *Time*, December 2, 1974, www.time.com/time /magazine/article/0,9171,945280,00.html.

38. Fred Turner, "Where the Counterculture Met the New Economy: The WELL and the Origins of Virtual Community," *Technology and Culture* 46, no. 3 (July 2005): 485–512, at 488.

39. Maria Rodale, *Maria Rodale's Organic Gardening: Your Seasonal Companion to Creating a Beautiful and Delicious Garden* (Emmaus, PA: Rodale, 1998), 72.

40. J. I. Rodale, *The Complete Book of Composting* (Emmaus, PA: Rodale, 1960), 9, 19.

41. Ibid., 5.

42. Eleanor Perényi, *Green Thoughts: A Writer in the Garden* (New York: Random House, 1981), 44.

43. Ibid., 41.

44. Malolm Beck, *Lessons in Nature* (Austin, TX: Acres USA, 2005), 174.

45. Ibid., 239.

46. Ibid., 240.

47. Ibid., 11.

48. Beck, *Lessons in Nature*, 19.

49. Jacquin Sanders, "Back to Nature—by Organic Foods," *Deseret News*, June 20, 1970.

50. "Warning Issued on Food Fad Fantasies," *Sarasota Herald-Tribune*, July 14, 1968.

51. George Grimsrud, "Down-to-Earth Appeal: Organic Farming Gains a Devoted Following," *Wall Street Journal*, December 9, 1969.

52. Sandra Blakeslee, "Challenge to Food Tests: Criticism Grows over Tests to Determine Which Food Additives Are Safe," *New York Times*, November 10, 1969.

53. Ibid.

54. Ibid.

55. Jeanie Darlington, *Grow Your Own: An Introduction to Organic Gardening* (Berkeley, CA: Bookworks, 1970), 2.

56. Ibid., 13.

57. Ibid.

58. Samuel Ogden, *Step-by-Step to Organic Vegetable Growing* (Emmaus, PA: Rodale, 1971), 37.

59. Samuel Ogden, *Straight-Ahead Organic: A Step-by-Step Guide to Growing Great Vegetables in a Less-Than-Perfect World* (White River Junction, VT: Chelsea Green, 1999), 74.

60. Scott Nearing and Helen Nearing, *The Good Life: Helen and Scott Nearing's Sixty Years of Self-Sufficient Living* (New York: Schocken, 1989), 3.

61. Ibid., 149.

62. Ibid., 192.

63. Ibid., 153.

64. J. Krizmanic, "Inch by Inch, Row by Row," *Vegetarian Times* no. 139 (1989): 44–53, 68, at 46.

65. Nearing and Nearing, *The Good Life*, 134.

66. Ibid., 368.

67. Krizmanic, "Inch by Inch, Row by Row," 46.

68. Rebecca Kneale Gould, *At Home in Nature: Modern Homesteading and Spiritual Practice in America* (Berkeley: University of California Press, 2005), 141.

69. Nearing and Nearing, *The Good Life*, 124.

70. Ibid., 391.

71. Scott Nearing, and Helen Nearing, *Building and Using Our Sun-Heated Greenhouse: Grow Vegetables All Year-Round* (Charlotte, VT: Garden Way, 1977), 134.

72. Ibid., 69.

73. Nearing and Nearing, *The Good Life*, 384.

74. Helen Nearing, *Simple Food for the Good Life: An Alternative Cookbook* (New York: Delacorte, 1980), 17.

75. Ibid., 9.

76. Gould, *At Home in Nature*, xvii.

77. Ibid., 76.

78. Vileisis, *Kitchen Literacy*, 210.

79. Beeman and Pritchard, *A Green and Permanent Land*, 107.

80. Ogden, *Step-by-Step to Organic Vegetable Growing*, viii.

81. M. C. Goldman and William H. Hylton, eds., *The Basic Book of Organically Grown Foods* (Emmaus, PA: Rodale, 1972), 306.

82. Ibid., 307.

83. Bonnie J. Hollis, "Sonnewald Homestead," *Green Revolution* 33, no. 11 (1976): 16–17, at 16.

84. Robert Rodale, *Sane Living in a Mad World: A Guide to the Organic Way of Life* (Emmaus, PA: Rodale, 1972), 237.

85. Gene Logsdon, *Homesteading: How to Find Independence on the Land* (Emmaus, PA: Rodale, 1973), 246.

86. Ibid., 221.

87. Gene Logsdon, *The Contrary Farmer* (White River Junction, VT: Chelsea Green, 1994), 19.

88. Ibid., 161.

89. Ibid., 50.

90. George A. Shumway, "Deep Run Farm," *Green Revolution* 33, no. 11 (1976): 9–11, at 10.

91. Arnold Greenberg, "Searching for Alternatives in Education: The Homestead School," *Green Revolution* 35, no. 5 (1978): 19–21, at 21.

92. "Ecology: The New Jeremiahs," *Time*, August 15, 1969, www.time.com/time /magazine/article/0,9171,901238,00.html.

93. MacDougall, "Organic Food Boom Is Growing."

94. "Agriculture Has Big Stake in Crackdown on Pesticides," *Progressive Farmer*, March 1970.

95. J. Gordon Edwards, "DDT Is Great Benefactor of Mankind against Pests," *Texas Agriculture*, March 1970.

96. R.G.V. Buskirk, "Pesticide Formulators and Dealers, Have Confidence in Your Product!," *Farm Chemicals*, March 1970.

97. "Norman Borlaug, D.D.T.," *New York Times*, November 26, 1971.

98. Editorial, "Borlaug Condemns Ban on Pesticides," *New York Times*, November 3, 1971.

99. John C. Devlin, "Borlaug Rebuked by Audubon Chief," *New York Times*, November 18, 1971, 17.

100. Jeff Cox, *The Organic Food Shopper's Guide* (Hoboken, NJ: John Wiley & Sons, 2008), 23.

101. Jeff Cox, *The Organic Cook's Bible: How to Select and Cook the Best Ingredients on the Market* (Hoboken, NJ: John Wiley & Sons, 2006), 21.

102. "The Move to Eat Natural," *Life* 69 (1970): 44–46, at 45.

103. Elaine Marie Lipson, *The Organic Foods Sourcebook* (Chicago: Contemporary Books, 2001), 76.

104. Robert C. Oelhaf, *Organic Agriculture: Economic and Ecological Comparisons with Conventional Methods* (New York: John Wiley & Sons, 1978), 132.

105. Jerome Goldstein, ed., *The Organic Gardening Guide to Organic Living: San Francisco Bay Area Edition* (Emmaus, PA: Rodale, 1970), 7.

106. Ibid., 11.

107. "The Move to Eat Natural," 46.

108. Gaynor Maddox, "Balanced Diet Still Best," *Sarasota Journal* (October 1, 1971): 4B.

109. Art Buchwald, "The Health Nuts," *Meriden Journal* (December 24, 1969): 6.

110. Sanders, "Back to Nature—by Organic Foods."

111. Susan Sward, "Use of 'Natural Foods' Increases with Concern over Insecticides," *Press-Courier* (August 19, 1970): 27.

112. David M. Nowacek and Rebecca S. Nowacek, "The Organic Foods System: Its Discursive Achievements and Prospects," *College English* 70, no. 4 (March 2001): 403–420, at 409.

113. Michael Allaby and Floyd Allen, *Robots behind the Plow: Modern Farming and the Need for an Organic Alternative* (Emmaus, PA: Rodale, 1974), 30.

114. Mike McGrath, ed., *The Best of Organic Gardening* (Emmaus, PA: Rodale, 1996), 10.

115. Goldstein, *Organic Gardening Guide to Organic Living*, 50.

116. Tucker, *Kitchen Gardening in America*, 152.

117. Ibid., 61.

118. Sanders, "Back to Nature—by Organic Foods."

119. Goldstein, *Organic Gardening Guide to Organic Living*, 78.

120. "Catching Up to Rodale Press," *Time*, March 22, 1971, www.time.com/time/magazine/article/0,9171,904923,00.html.

121. Robert Rodale, "Any Food That's Good for You Is Health Food," *Eugene Register-Guard*, November 21, 1971.

122. J. I. Rodale, *The Health Seeker* (Emmaus, PA: Rodale, 1971), 147.

123. Ibid., 404.

124. Jane Howard, "Earth Mother to the Foodists," *Life* 71, no. 17 (October 22, 1971): 67–70.

125. Adelle Davis, *Let's Cook It Right* (New York: Harcourt Brace Jovanovich, 1970), 21.

126. Daniel Yergin, "Let's Get Adelle Davis Right: Supernutritionist," *New York Times*, May 20, 1973.

127. J. I. Rodale, ed., *The Complete Book of Food and Nutrition* (Emmaus, PA: Rodale, 1966), 431.

128. W. Lockeretz, "What Are the Key Issues for Consumers?," *Organic Agriculture: Sustainability, Markets and Policies* (Wallingford, Oxford: CABI, 2003): 239–243, at 241–242.

129. MacDougall, "Organic Food Boom Is Growing."

130. Margaret D. Pacey, "Nature's Bounty: Merchandisers of Health Foods Are Cashing In on It," *Barron's Financial Weekly* (1971), 5.

131. MacDougall, "Organic Food Boom Is Growing."

132. Ecological Food Society, "Caution: Eating May Be Hazardous to Your Health," *Village Voice*, January 14, 1971.

133. Jean Hewitt, *The New York Times Natural Foods Cookbook* (New York: New York Times Book Co., 1971), 2.

134. Ibid., 3.

135. Alicia B. Laurel, *Living on the Earth* (New York: Random House, 1971).

136. Rodale, "Any Food That's Good for You Is Health Food," 14.

137. Frances Moore Lappé, *Diet For a Small Planet: Twentieth Anniversary Edition* (New York: Ballantine, 1991), 12.

138. Charles B. Heiser Jr., *Seed to Civilization: The Story of Man's Food* (San Francisco: W. H. Freeman, 1973), 36.

139. "24 Hours of Organic Food," *Los Angeles Times* (October 8, 1971): I6.

140. Gay Bryant, "J. I. Rodale: Pollution Prophet," *Penthouse* 2 (1971): 28–32, at 32.

141. "The Profitable Earth," *Time*, April 12, 1971, www.time.com/time/magazine/article/0,9171,904999,00.html.

142. MacDougall, "Organic Food Boom Is Growing."

143. Hunter, *The Natural Foods Primer*, 38.

144. Ibid., 70.

145. Bernice Kohn Hunt, *The Organic Living Book* (New York: Viking, 1972), 12.

146. "Eating Organic," *Time*, December 18, 1972, www.time.com/time/magazine/article/0,9171,945186,00.html.

147. "Health and Hucksterism," *Time*, October 23, 1972, www.time.com/time/magazine/article/0,9171,878084,00.html.

148. Goldman and Hylton, *Basic Book of Organically Grown Foods*, 44.

149. Ibid., 62.

150. Alan H. Nittler, *A New Breed of Doctor* (New York: Pyramid, 1972), 16.

151. Ibid., 19.

152. Darryl McLeod, "Urban-Rural Food Alliances: A Perspective on Recent Community Food Organizing," in *Radical Agriculture*, ed. Richard Merrill (New York: New York University Press, 1976), 188–211, at 205.

153. Carlton Jackson, *J. I. Rodale: Apostle of Nonconformity* (New York: Pyramid, 1974), 220.

154. Bryant, "J. I. Rodale: Pollution Prophet," 28.

155. "Catching Up to Rodale Press."

156. Barrett, "The Organic Way of Gardening and Its Prophet," 52–55.

157. J. I. Rodale, *My Own Technique of Eating for Health* (Emmaus, PA: Rodale, 1971).

158. Ibid., 41.

159. Ibid., 68.

160. Ibid., 173.

161. Ibid., 297–298.

162. Ibid., 422.

163. James Whorton, *Crusaders for Fitness: The History of American Health Reformers* (Princeton, NJ: Princeton University Press, 1982), 339.

164. Wade Greene, "Guru of the Organic Food Cult," *New York Times Magazine*, June 6, 1971, 30, 31, 54, 56, 60, 65, 68.

165. Ibid., 31.

166. Ibid., 60.

167. Tucker, *Kitchen Gardening in America*, 154.

168. Jackson, *J. I. Rodale*, 222.

169. Danny Gallagher, "Dick Cavett Show Audience Member Recalls the Day a Guest Died," *Aol TV*, February 25, 2010, www.aoltv.com/2010/02/25/dick-cavett-show-audience-member-recalls-the-day-a-guest-died/.

170. Rodale, *Maria Rodale's Organic Gardening*, 14.

171. Jackson, *J. I. Rodale*, 330.

1. Business Week, "Rodale Reaches Out for the Mainstream," *Business Week* 85 (1980).

2. Robert Rodale, "The Heart and Soul of Organic Gardening," *Organic Gardening* 39 (1992): 46.

3. K. C. Beeson, "Spring Gardens: What about the 'Organic' Way?," *New York Times*, April 16, 1972.

4. Robert Rodale, *Sane Living in a Mad World: A Guide to the Organic Way of Life* (Emmaus, PA: Rodale, 1972), 261.

5. National Health Food Society, "These 12 Health Foods Are Yours to Taste and Enjoy . . . Absolutely Free!," *Life* 71, no. 18 (October 29, 1971): 15.

6. Christopher Lasch, *The Culture of Narcissism: American Life in an Age of Diminishing Expectations* (New York: W. W. Norton, 1978).

7. Adam Fisher, "Freak Folks: An Obscure California Cult Finds a New Following," *New York Times*, April 13, 2008.

8. Jennifer Sharpe, "From Source Restaurant to 'Cosmic' Commune," *National Public Radio*, April 8, 2008, www.npr.org/templates/story/story.php?storyId=894 67276.

9. Jamaica Tourist Board, "Jamaica," *Life* 70, no. 23 (June 18, 1971), 19.

10. Sylvia Porter, "The Organic Living Fad Can Cost You a Bundle," *Modesto Bee*, February 7, 1972.

11. William H. Hylton, ed., *Organically Grown Foods: What They Are and Why You Need Them* (Emmaus, PA: Rodale, 1973), 60.

12. Ibid., 61.

13. Ibid., 76.

14. "Educating Housewives Part of Marketing Organic Food," *Toledo Blade*, October 4, 1972.

15. H. William Gross, "Health Foods," *Life* 3 (October 20, 1972): 31.

16. N. Baltad, "Organic Foods: Skepticism," *Los Angeles Times*, June 30, 1972.

17. Gaynor Maddox, "Nutritionist Raps Food-Fad Trends," *Leader-Herald* (Gloversville, NY), March 8, 1972.

18. "The Perils of Eating, American Style," *Time*, December 18, 1972, www.time.com/time/magazine/article/0,9171,945185,00.html.

19. Associated Press, "Health Foods Overpriced Critics Say," *Montreal Gazette*, December 6, 1977.

20. Earl Butz, "Crisis or Challenge," *Nation's Agriculture* 19 (July–August 1971): 19.

21. H. S. White, "The Organic Foods Movement," *Food Technology* 5, no. 2 (April 1972): 29–33, at 30.

22. George Kuepper and Lance Gegner, "Organic Crop Production Overview," August 2004, http://guamsustainableag.org/organicfarming/organiccrop%20%285%29 .pdf.

23. Murray Cox, "Organic Farm Not So Simple," *Dallas Morning News*, August 6, 1972.

24. *Organic Farming Act of 1982: Hearing* on *H.R. 5618 Before the Subcomm. on Forests, Family Farms, and Energy of the Committee on Agriculture*, 97th Cong. (1982), www.archive.org/stream/organicfarminga00energoog/organicfarminga00energoog_djvu.txt.

25. Wade Greene, "Guru of the Organic Food Cult," *New York Times Magazine* (June 6, 1971): 30, 31, 54, 56, 60, 65, 68.

26. M. C. Goldman and William H. Hylton, eds., *The Basic Book of Organically Grown Foods* (Emmaus, PA: Rodale, 1972), 3.

27. Ibid., 15.

28. Ibid., 84–85.

29. Ibid., 328.

30. Ibid.

31. "Good Earth Grows Luscious Organic Corn," advertisement, *Village Voice*, May 4, 1972.

32. "Natural Food: How to Grow It," advertisement, *Village Voice*, July 13, 1972.

33. "IFOAM," www.ifoam.org/.

34. Goldman and Hylton, *Basic Book of Organically Grown Foods*, 325.

35. Ibid., 206.

36. V. L. Warren, "Organic Foods: Spotting the Real Thing Can Be Tricky," *New York Times*, April 9, 1972.

37. "3 Market Chains Face $40 Million Organic Food Suit," *Los Angeles Times*, March 21, 1972.

38. Goldman and Hylton, *Basic Book of Organically Grown Foods*, 326.

39. Maine Organic Farmers and Gardeners Association, *Fertile Ground: A 40th Anniversary Celebration of the Maine Organic Farmers and Gardeners Association* (Unity, ME: MOFGA, 2011), 16.

40. Roy Reed, "Back-to-Land Movement Seeks Self-Sufficiency," *New York Times*, June 9, 1975.

41. Julie Guthman, "Regulating Meaning, Appropriating Nature: The Codification of California Organic Agriculture," *Antipode* 30, no. 2 (1998): 135–154, at 144.

42. "The History of California Certified Organic Farmers (CCOF)," www.ccof.org/history_ab.php#sec1.

43. Samuel Fromartz, "The (Not So) New Agtivist: Organic Movement Leader Bob Scowcroft Looks Back," *Grist.org*, February 7, 2011, http://grist.org/article/food-2011-02-07-organic-movement-leader-bob-scowcroft-looks-back/.

44. USDA, "National Organic Program: Final Rule," 2007, www.ams.usda.gov/nop/NOP/standards.html, 465.

45. Jeff Cox, *The Organic Cook's Bible: How to Select and Cook the Best Ingredients on the Market* (Hoboken, NJ: John Wiley & Sons, 2006), 32.

46. Robert C. Oelhaf, *Organic Agriculture: Economic and Ecological Comparisons with Conventional Methods* (New York: John Wiley & Sons, 1978), 177.

47. Anna Colamosca, "Health Foods Prosper despite High Prices," *New York Times*, November 17, 1974.

48. Lois D. McBean and Elwood W. Speckmann, "Food Faddism: A Challenge

to Nutritionists and Dietitians," *American Journal of Clinical Nutrition* 27 (October 1974): 1071–1078, at 1073.

49. "Scientists Assail Organic Food Fad," *New York Times*, February 26, 1974, 19.

50. "Organic Food Fad Based on Scientific Nonsense," *Sarasota Herald-Tribune*, February 26, 1974.

51. Thomas H. Jukes, "When Friends or Patients Ask about . . . the Organic Food Myth," *Journal of the American Medical Association* 230 (October 1974): 276–277, at 276.

52. McBean and Speckmann, "Food Faddism," 1071.

53. Ibid., 1074.

54. Edward H. Rynearson, "Americans Love Hogwash," *Nutrition Reviews* 32 (July 1974): 1–14, at 1.

55. Ibid., 10.

56. Ibid., 11.

57. "Fie on Food Fads," *Leader-Herald* (Gloversville-Johnstown, NY), April 18, 1975.

58. Leslie Maitland, "Health Foods Tasting Inflation," *New York Times*, April 9, 1975.

59. Barbara Delatiner, "North Fork Housewives Start Co-Op to Beat Food Prices," *New York Times*, March 2, 1975.

60. Julie Guthman, "The Trouble with 'Organic Lite' in California: A Rejoinder to the 'Conventionalisation' Debate," *Sociologia Ruralis* 44, no. 3 (2004): 301–316, at 303.

61. Julie Guthman, "Regulating Meaning, Appropriating Nature: The Codification of California Organic Agriculture," *Antipode* 30, no. 2 (1998): 135–154, at 140.

62. Julie Guthman, "Fast Food/Organic Food: Reflexive Tastes and the Making of 'Yuppie Chow,'" *Journal of Social and Cultural Geography* 4, no. 1 (2003): 43–56, at 48.

63. Carlo Petrini, *Slow Food Nation: Why Our Food Should Be Good, Clean, and Fair* (New York: Random House, 2007), ix.

64. Thomas McNamee, *Alice Waters and Chez Panisse: The Romantic, Impractical, Often Eccentric, Ultimately Brilliant Making of a Food Revolution* (New York: Penguin, 2007), 136.

65. Guthman, "Fast Food/Organic Food," 49, 54.

66. McNamee, *Alice Waters and Chez Panisse*, 6.

67. Jeffrey Jacob, *New Pioneers: The Back-to-the-Land Movement and the Search for a Sustainable Future* (University Park: Pennsylvania State University Press, 1997), 23–25.

68. Ibid., 29.

69. Jerome Belanger, "Correcting Some Misconceptions about Organic Farming," in *Organic Farming: Yesterday's and Tomorrow's Agriculture*, ed. Ray Wolf (Emmaus, PA: Rodale, 1977), 7–20.

70. Jacob, *New Pioneers*, 25.

71. Sue Robishaw, *Homesteading Adventures: A Guide for Doers and Dreamers* (Cooks, MI: Many Tracks, 1997), 94.

72. Ibid., 32.

73. Reed, "Back-to-Land Movement Seeks Self-Sufficiency."

74. John Seymour and Sally Seymour, *Farming for Self-Sufficiency: Independence on a 5-Acre Farm* (New York: Schocken, 1973), 8.

75. Reed, "Back-to-Land Movement Seeks Self-Sufficiency."

76. J. Hector St. John de Crèvecœur, *Letters from an American Farmer* (New York: Oxford University Press, 1997), 39–41.

77. Ingolf Vogeler, *The Myth of the Family Farm: Agribusiness Dominance of U.S. Agriculture* (Boulder, CO: Westview, 1981), 39.

78. Thomas Jefferson, *Notes on the State of Virginia* (New York: Harper & Row, 1964), 157.

79. Yi-Fu Tuan, *The Good Life* (Madison: University of Wisconsin Press, 1986), 38.

80. Ibid., 116.

81. Ibid., 38.

82. Ibid., 127.

83. Kimberly K. Smith, *Wendell Berry and the Agrarian Tradition: A Common Grace* (Lawrence: University Press of Kansas, 2003).

84. Karl Schwenke, *Successful Small-Scale Farming: An Organic Approach* (Pownal, VT: Storey, 1991), 9–11.

85. Ibid., 47, 91.

86. Wendell Berry, *Home Economics* (San Francisco: North Point, 1987), 184.

87. Ibid., 164.

88. Wendell Berry, *The Art of the Commonplace* (Washington, DC: Counterpoint, 2002), 45.

89. Ibid., 85–86.

90. Ibid., 245.

91. Ibid., 88.

92. Berry, *Home Economics*, 274.

93. Wendell Berry, "In Distrust of Movements," in *In the Presence of Fear: Three Essays for a Changed World* (Great Barrington, MA: Orion Society, 2001), 35–44, at 36.

94. Berry, *The Art of the Commonplace*, 245.

95. Ibid., 203.

96. Earl Butz, "Agriblunders," *Growth and Change* 9, no. 2 (1978): 52.

97. Ibid., 52.

98. Alex Avery, *The Truth about Organic Foods* (Chesterfield, MO: Henderson, 2006), 7.

99. Masanobu Fukuoka, *The One-Straw Revolution: An Introduction to Natural Farming* (Mapusa, Goa, India: Other India Press, 1992), 34.

100. Ibid., 117.

101. Ibid., 104.

102. Ibid., 140.

103. Ibid., 89–91.

104. Arthur Bell, "Barbra Streisand Doesn't," *Village Voice*, April 26, 1976.

105. Elizabeth M. Whelan and Frederick Stare, *Panic in the Pantry: Food Facts, Fads and Fallacies* (New York: Atheneum, 1975), 13.

106. Elizabeth M. Whelan, *The One-Hundred-Percent Natural, Purely Organic, Cholesterol-Free, Megavitamin, Low-Carbohydrate Nutrition Hoax* (New York: Atheneum, 1983), 13.

107. Whelan and Stare, *Panic in the Pantry*, xi.

108. Ibid., 41–43.

109. Ibid., 56.

110. Ibid., 61.

111. Ibid., 126.

112. Ibid., 22.

113. Melissa Clark, "Diet Crazes," *Newsweek*, December 19, 1977, 67.

114. N. R. Kleinfield, "Rodale Press: Successful Organic Venture a Money Loser in Early Years," *New York Times*, November 19, 1979.

115. Ibid.

116. Ibid.

117. See, for example, George Perkins Marsh's *Man and Nature* (1864) and Frieda Knobloch's *The Culture of Wilderness: Agriculture as Colonization in the American West* (1996).

118. Charlie Ryrie and Cindy Engel, *The Gaia Book of Organic Gardening* (London: Gaia Books, 2005), 9.

119. George B. Mueller, "America's Family Farms in the Spotlight on Capitol Hill," *New York Times*, January 18, 1972.

120. USDA, *Structure and Finances of U.S. Farms: 2005 Family Farm Report/EIB-12* (Washington, DC: Economic Research Service, 2005).

121. Linda F. Little, Francine P. Proulx, Julia Marlowe, and Patricia K. Knaub, "The History of Recent Farm Legislation: Implications for Farm Families," *Family Relations* 36, no. 4 (October 1987): 402–406, at 403.

122. Everett G. Smith Jr., "Fragmented Farms in the United States," *Annals of the Association of American Geographers* 65, no. 1 (March 1975): 58–70, at 69.

123. Santa Cruz Organic, "About Us," http://scojuice.com/about_us.

124. "Crisis in Agriculture," *Nebraska Studies*, www.nebraskastudies.org/1000 /stories/1001_0100.html.

125. USDA Study Team on Organic Farming, *Report and Recommendations on Organic Farming* (Washington, DC: USDA, 1980), xiii.

126. Ibid., 82.

127. *Organic Farming Act of 1982.*

128. Ibid.

129. Ibid.

130. Ibid.

131. "Representatives Split on Farming Bill," *Altus Times* (Jackson County, OK), September 2, 1982.

132. Whelan, *Nutrition Hoax*, 8.

133. Ibid., 20.

134. Ibid., 62.

135. Ibid., 138–141.

136. Dale M. Atrens, *Don't Diet* (New York: William Morrow, 1988), 219.

137. Ibid., 232.

138. Ibid., 233.

139. Craig Fox, "Consumers Make It Worthwhile," *Finger Lakes Times* (Geneva, NY), January 11, 1988.

140. Barry Wookey, *Rushall: The Story of an Organic Farm* (Oxford: Blackwell, 1987), 42.

141. Bonnie Gregson and Bob Gregson, *Rebirth of the Small Family Farm: A Handbook for Starting a Successful Organic Farm Based on the Community Supported Agriculture Concept* (Vashon Island, WA: Island Meadow Farm, 1996), 4.

142. Ibid., 19.

143. Ibid., 57.

144. Ibid., 5.

145. Ibid.

146. Julie Guthman, *Agrarian Dreams: The Paradox of Organic Farming in California* (Berkeley: University of California Press, 2004), 312.

147. Paul Keene, *Fear Not to Sow Because of the Birds: Essays on Country Living and Natural Farming from Walnut Acres*, ed. Dorothy Seymour (Chester, CT: Globe Pequot, 1988), 26.

148. Associated Press, "A Natural Food Oasis in Fast-Food World," *Finger Lakes Times* (Geneva, NY), December 21, 1988.

149. Joanna Poncavage, "Walnut Acres: The Farm That Gandhi Grew," *Organic Gardening* 38, no. 2 (February 1991).

150. Associated Press, "A Natural Food Oasis in Fast-Food World."

151. Keene, *Fear Not to Sow Because of the Birds*, 4.

152. Ibid., 11.

153. Ibid., 34.

154. Associated Press, "A Natural Food Oasis in Fast-Food World," 24.

155. Poncavage, "Walnut Acres."

156. Walnut Acres, "Who We Are," www.walnutacres.com/who_we_are.php.

157. Frank Ford, "My Life in Organics," in *Taste Life! The Organic Choice*, ed. David Richard and Dorie Byers (Bloomington, IL: Vital Health, 1998), 70.

158. Arrowhead Mills, www.arrowheadmills.com/.

159. Ford, "My Life in Organics," 72.

160. Berke Sound, "The Story of Grimmway Farms," www.berkesound.com/?p=338.

161. Grimmway Farms, "History of Grimmway Farms," http://grimmway.com/our-family-story/company.php.

162. Jennifer Siegel and Mo Siegel, *Celestial Seasonings Cookbook: Cooking with Tea* (New York: Park Lane, 1996), 11.

163. Ibid., 13.

164. Celestial Seasonings, www.celestialseasonings.com/index.html.

165. "The Perils of Eating, American Style," *Time*, December 18, 1972, www.time.com/time/magazine/article/0,9171,945185,00.html.

166. "All the Ingredients of a Health Co-Op," *New York Times*, August 28, 1983.

167. Eden Foods, "About Eden," www.edenfoods.com/about/.

168. Michael Allaby and Floyd Allen, *Robots behind the Plow: Modern Farming and the Need for an Organic Alternative* (Emmaus, PA: Rodale, 1974), 167.

169. *Organic Farming Act of* 1982.

170. San Gwynne, "Born Green," *Saveur*, May 26, 2009, 27–30.

171. San Gwynne, "Thriving on Health Food," *Time*, February 23, 1998, www.time.com/time/archive. See chapter 6 for more on the growth of Whole Foods.

172. Gary Hirshberg, *Stirring It Up: How to Make Money and Save the World* (New York: Hyperion, 2008), 113–114.

173. Ibid., 113.

174. Myra Goodman, *Food to Live By: The Earthbound Farm Organic Cookbook* (New York: Workman, 2006), ix.

175. Earthbound Farm, www.ebfarm.com/.

176. Goodman, *Food to Live By*, x.

177. Amy's Kitchen, "The Family," www.amys.com/about-us/the-family.

178. "The Perils of Eating, American Style," *Time*, December 18, 1972, www.time.com/time/magazine/article/0,9171,945185,00.html.

179. Michael Heasman and Julian Mellentin, *The Functional Foods Revolution: Healthy People, Healthy Profits?* (Sterling, VA: Earthscan, 2001), 55.

180. USDA Study Team on Organic Farming, *Report and Recommendations on Organic Farming* (Washington, DC: USDA, 1980), 64.

181. Ibid., 65.

182. P. Elmer-DeWitt, "Fat Times: What Health Craze?," *Time*, January 16, 1995, www.time.com/time/archive.

183. East West Journal, *Shopper's Guide to Natural Foods* (Garden City Park, NY: Avery, 1987), 22.

184. Ibid., 61.

185. Ibid., 5.

186. "All the Ingredients of a Health Co-Op."

187. Ibid., 60.

188. Michael Heasman and Julian Mellentin. *The Functional Foods Revolution: Healthy People, Healthy Profits?* (Sterling, VA: Earthscan, 2001), 55.

189. Oelhaf, *Organic Agriculture*, 139–140.

190. Richard Wiles, Kenneth A. Cook, et al., *How 'Bout Them Apples? Pesticides in Children's Food Ten Years after Alar* (Washington, DC: Environmental Working Group, 1999), i.

191. "The History of CCOF," www.ccof.org/history_ab.php#sec1.

192. Robert Davis, *The Healthy Skeptic: Cutting through the Hype about Your Health* (Berkeley: University of California Press, 2008), 146.

193. "Rodale Reaches out for the Mainstream," *Business Week* 85 (1980).

194. J. I. Rodale, "With the Editor: The Organiculturist's Creed," *Organic Gardening* 12 (1948): 12–14, at 12.

CHAPTER 4. LEADERS, LAND LOVERS, LOCAVORES, LABELS, LAWS, AND A LITTLE LUNACY

1. Janice M. Horowitz, "Bye-Bye Tofu; Hello, Truffles!," *Time*, March 19, 1990, www .time.com/time/magazine/article/0,9171,969613,00.html.

2. Samuel Fromartz "The (Not So) New Agtivist: Organic Movement Leader Bob Scowcroft Looks Back," *Grist.org*, February 7, 2011, http://grist.org/article/food-2011 –02–07-organic-movement-leader-bob-scowcroft-looks-back/.

3. J. I. Rodale, "Miscellany: Looking Forward," *Organic Gardening* 20 (1952): 24–25, at 24.

4. Jean M. Rawson, *Organic Agriculture in the United States: Program and Policy Issues* (Washington, DC: Congressional Research Service, 2006): 1–12, at 3.

5. Demeter Association, "Position Paper on Organic Foods Production Act of 1990," *Biodynamics* 203 (1996): 10–11, at 10.

6. Agricultural Marketing Service, "National Organic Standards Board (NOSB)," www.ams.usda.gov.

7. Joanna Poncavage, "MOA & RI = WSAA (and a Better World for Us All)," *Organic Gardening* 38, no. 9 (December 1991).

8. Maria Rodale, *Maria Rodale's Organic Gardening: Your Seasonal Companion to Creating a Beautiful and Delicious Garden* (Emmaus, PA: Rodale, 1998), 15.

9. Nancy Gibbs, "Power Gardening," *Time*, June 19, 1995, www.time.com/time /magazine/article/0,9171,983057,00.html.

10. Poncavage, "MOA & RI = WSAA."

11. John Holusha, "Folksy Rodale Emerges as Hard-Driving Marketer," *New York Times*, June 27, 1992.

12. Mike McGrath, ed., *The Best of Organic Gardening* (Emmaus, PA: Rodale, 1996), vii–viii.

13. Carol Krol, "Rodale Heir Tends New Unit Devoted to Organic Living," *Advertising Age* 70, no. 3 (January 18, 1999).

14. Roy Reed, "Back-to-Land Movement Seeks Self-Sufficiency," *New York Times*, June 9, 1975.

15. Michael Ableman, *Fields of Plenty: A Farmer's Journey in Search of Real Food and the People Who Grow It* (San Francisco: Chronicle, 2005), 175.

16. Eliot Coleman, *Four-Season Harvest: Organic Vegetables from Your Home Garden All Year Long* (White River Junction, VT: Chelsea Green, 1999), xii.

17. Eliot Coleman, *The New Organic Grower: A Master's Manual of Tools and Techniques for the Home and Market Gardener* (White River Junction, VT: Chelsea Green, 1995), 2.

18. Ibid., 278.

19. Ibid., 14.

20. Ibid., 144.

21. Eliot Coleman, "Can Organics Save the Family Farm?," *Secrets of the City*, August 27, 2004, www.secretsofthecity.com/magazine/reporting/features/can-organic -save-family-farm.

22. Barbara Damrosch, *The Garden Primer: The Completely Revised Gardener's Bible* (New York: Workman, 2008), ix.

23. Stephen Orr, "The Good Life," *Martha Stewart Living*, March 2012, 88–95, at 94.

24. Joel Salatin, *Folks, This Ain't Normal: A Farmer's Advice for Happier Hens, Healthier People, and a Better World* (New York: Hachette, 2011), 132.

25. Joel Salatin, *Family Friendly Farming: A Multi-Generational Home-Based Business Testament* (Swoope, VA: Polyface, 2001), 305.

26. Ibid., 75.

27. TreeHugger, "Joel Salatin, America's Most Influential Farmer, Talks Big Organic and the Future of Food," *TreeHugger*, www.treehugger.com/files/2009/08/joel-salatin-americas-most-influential-farmer.php.

28. Polyface Farms, "Polyface Guiding Principles," www.polyfacefarms.com/principles.

29. Salatin, *Family Friendly Farming*, 267.

30. Graeme Sait, *Nutrition Rules! Guidelines from the Master Consultants* (Eumundi, Qld, Australia: Soil Therapy Pty, 2003), 213.

31. Joel Salatin, "'Sound Science' Is Killing Us," *Acres USA* 34, no. 4 (2004): 1, 8, at 8.

32. Todd S. Purdum, "High Priest of the Pasture," *New York Times*, May 1, 2005, www.nytimes.com/2005/05/01/style/tmagazine/pasture.html?oref=login&_r=0.

33. Manohla Dargis, "Meet Your New Farmer: Hungry Corporate Giant," *New York Times*, June 12, 2009, www.nytimes.com/2009/06/12/movies/12food.html.

34. Andrea Gabor, "Inside Polyface Farm, Mecca of Sustainable Agriculture," *Atlantic*, July 25, 2011, www.theatlantic.com/health/archive/2011/07/inside-polyface-farm-mecca-of-sustainable-agriculture/242493/.

35. Masumoto Family Farm, "Family Farm Timeline," http://masumoto.com/organic/timeline.htm.

36. Suzanne Hamlin, "Championing the Imperfect Peach," *New York Times*, June 7, 1995.

37. Dan Barber, "Preface," in *Wisdom of the Last Farmer: Harvesting Legacies from the Land*, ed. David Mas Masumoto (New York: Free Press, 2009), xii.

38. Masumoto Family Farm, "Organic and Sustainable Farm," www.masumoto.com/organic/index.htm.

39. Shiuh-huah Serena Chou, "Pruning the Past, Shaping the Future: David Mas Masumoto and Organic Nothingness," *Ethnicity and Ecocriticism* 34, no. 2 (Summer 2009): 157–174, at 157.

40. David Mas Masumoto, *Wisdom of the Last Farmer: Harvesting Legacies from the Land* (New York: Free Press, 2009), 5.

41. Ibid., 6.

42. Michael Ableman, *On Good Land: The Autobiography of an Urban Farm* (San Francisco: Chronicle, 1998), 6.

43. Ibid., 32.

44. Ibid., 99.

45. Ableman, *Fields of Plenty*, 170.

46. Ibid., 236.

47. Scott Nearing and Helen Nearing, *Building and Using Our Sun-Heated Greenhouse: Grow Vegetables All Year-Round* (Charlotte, VT: Garden Way, 1977), 144.

48. Scott Chaskey, *This Common Ground: Seasons on an Organic Farm* (New York: Viking, 2005), 10.

49. Ibid., 27.

50. John Ikerd, *Small Farms Are Real Farms: Sustaining People through Agriculture* (Austin, TX: Acres USA, 2008), 149.

51. Thomas R. DeGregori, *Origins of the Organic Agriculture Debate* (Ames: Iowa State University Press, 2004), 148.

52. Iowa State University Organic Agriculture, http://extension.agron.iastate.edu /organicag.

53. Lynda Brown, *Organic Living: Simple Solutions for a Better Life* (New York: Dorling Kindersley, 2000), 43.

54. HRH The Prince of Wales and Charles Clover, *Highgrove: An Experiment in Organic Gardening and Farming* (New York: Simon and Schuster, 1993), 135.

55. Sait, *Nutrition Rules!*, 23.

56. M. Allaby and F. Allen, *Robots behind the Plow: Modern Farming and the Need for an Organic Alternative* (Emmaus, PA: Rodale, 1974), 26.

57. S. Fromartz, *Organic, Inc.: Natural Foods and How They Grew* (Orlando, FL: Harcourt, 2006), 6.

58. K. Schwenke, *Successful Small-Scale Farming: An Organic Approach* (Pownal, VT: Storey, 1991), ix.

59. Geoff Hamilton, *The Organic Garden Book* (New York: DK, 1993), 6.

60. Ibid., 8.

61. Jim Minick, *The Blueberry Years: A Memoir of Farm and Family* (New York: St. Martin's, 2010), 161.

62. J. D. Gussow, *This Organic Life: Confessions of a Suburban Homesteader* (White River Junction, VT: Chelsea Green, 2001), 15.

63. Ibid., 107–108.

64. Ibid., 219.

65. J. Ivanko, and Lisa Kivirist, "A Rural Renaissance," *Mother Earth News*, June–July 2004, www.motherearthnews.com/Green-Homes/2004–06–01/A-Rural-Renaissance .aspx?page=2.

66. Ibid.

67. J. Ivanko, and Lisa Kivirist, *Rural Renaissance: Renewing the Quest for the Good Life* (Gabriola Island, BC: New Society, 2004), xvii.

68. Ibid., 73.

69. Inn Seredipity, www.innserendipity.com/.

70. Inn Seredipity, "Who's Farmsteadtarian?," www.innserendipity.com/farmstead chef/farmsteadtarian.html.

71. N. Smith, *Harvest: A Year in the Life of an Organic Farm* (Guilford, CT: Lyons Press, 2004), 46–47.

72. Ibid., 47.

73. Keith Stewart, *It's a Long Road to a Tomato: Tales of an Organic Farmer Who Quit the Big City for the (Not So) Simple Life* (New York: Marlowe, 2006), 2.

74. Ibid., 5.

75. Ibid., 270.

76. Ibid., 92.

77. Kinnikinnick Farm, http://kinnikinnickfarm.com.

78. Weatherbury Farm, www.weatherburyfarm.com/aboutweatherbury.htm.

79. Josh Dorfman, *The Lazy Environmentalist: Your Guide to Easy, Stylish, Green Living* (New York: Stewart, Tabori & Chang, 2007), 185.

80. Click and Grow, www.clickandgrow.com/en/.

81. Encyclopedia Pictura, "Trout Gulch," http://encyclopediapictura.com/the-story.

82. Jessica Vernabe, "19-Year-Old Combines Farming and Tech Experience, Develops iPhone App for Organic Farmers," May 16, 2012, http://seedstock.com /2012/05/16/19-year-old-combines-farming-and-tech-experience-develops-iphone -app-for-organic-farmers/.

83. Oddveig Storstad and Hilde Björkhaug, "Foundations of Production and Consumption of Organic Food in Norway: Common Attitudes among Farmers and Consumers," *Agriculture and Human Values* 20 (2003): 151–163, at 160.

84. Brian Halweil, "Organic Gold Rush," *WorldWatch Magazine* 14, no. 3 (May–June 2001), 1–12, at 5.

85. P. Kristiansen and C. Merfield, "Overview of Organic Agriculture," *Organic Agriculture: A Global Perspective*, ed. P. Kristiansen, A. Taji, and J. Reganold (Ithaca, NY: Comstock, 2006), 1–23, at 16.

86. Ibid., 17.

87. D. P. Baltaz, *Why We Do It: Organic Farmers on Farming* (Ayr, Ontario: Sand Plains, 1998), 47.

88. J. I. Rodale, "With the Editor—the Theory Underlying the Composting Process," *Organic Gardening* 7 (1945): 4–7, at 4.

89. Charles Dowding, *Organic Gardening: The Natural No-Dig Way* (Foxhole, Devon, UK: Green Books, 2007), 45.

90. Ibid., 9.

91. Ibid., 17.

92. Francis Blake, *Organic Farming and Growing* (Wiltshire, UK: Crowood Press, 1990), 10.

93. Ibid., 9.

94. Ibid., 47.

95. D. Richard and D. Byers, eds., *Taste Life! The Organic Choice* (Bloomington, IL: Vital Health, 1998), 158.

96. Baltaz, *Why We Do It*, 35.

97. B. Flowerdew, *The Organic Gardening Bible: Successful Gardening the Natural Way* (Lanham, MD: Taylor, 1998), 7.

98. Ibid., 11.

99. Ibid., 16.

100. Rodale, *Maria Rodale's Organic Gardening*, 11.

101. Ibid., dedication.

102. Ibid., 121.

103. Ibid., 122.

104. Ibid., 23.

105. Pamela C. Ronald and R. W. Adamchak, *Tomorrow's Table: Organic Farming, Genetics, and the Future of Food* (New York: Oxford University Press, 2008), 14.

106. D. S. Conner, "The Organic Label and Sustainable Agriculture: Consumer Preferences and Values" (PhD diss., Cornell University, 2002), 83, 54.

107. USDA Study Team on Organic Farming, *Report and Recommendations on Organic Farming* (Washington, DC: USDA, 1980), xii.

108. J. R. Fairweather, "Understanding How Farmers Choose between Organic and Conventional Production: Results from New Zealand and Policy Implications," *Agriculture and Human Values* 16 (1999): 51–63, at 59.

109. Brown, *Organic Living*, 15.

110. Ibid., 6.

111. A. Clarke, H. Porter, et al., eds., *Living Organic: Easy Steps to an Organic Family Lifestyle* (Naperville, IL: Sourcebooks, 2001), 129–130.

112. FAO/WHO Food Standards Programme, *Codex Alimentarius: Organically Produced Foods* (Rome: Food and Agriculture Organization of the United Nations, World Health Organization, 2001), 6.

113. USDA, "National Organic Program: Final Rule," www.ams.usda.gov/nop/NOP/standards.html, 9.

114. Ibid., 470–471.

115. Ellen Sandbeck, *Eat More Dirt: Diverting and Instructive Tips for Growing and Tending an Organic Garden* (New York: Broadway, 2003), 20.

116. Rodale Institute, "Help Your Garden Kick Its Chemical Dependency—a 12 Step Program," www.rodaleinstitute.org/node/2697.

117. S. Lockie and D. Halpin, "The 'Conventionalisation' Thesis Reconsidered: Structural and Ideological Transformation of Australian Organic Agriculture," *Sociologia Ruralis* 45, no. 4 (2005), 284–307, at 296–304.

118. Cindy Engel and Charlie Ryrie, *The Gaia Book of Organic Gardening* (London: Gaia Books, 2005), 30.

119. Ibid., 48.

120. Ibid., 10.

121. Ibid., 133.

122. Adrian Myers, *Organic Futures: The Case for Organic Farming* (Devon, UK: Green Books, 2005), 17.

123. Ibid., 12.

124. Ibid., 190.

125. Steve Meyerowitz, *The Organic Food Guide: How to Shop Smarter and Eat Healthier* (Guilford, CT: Globe Pequot, 2004), 3.

126. Ibid., 6.

127. Ken Roseboro, *The Organic Food Handbook: A Consumer's Guide to Buying and Eating Organic Food* (Laguna Beach, CA: Basic Health, 2006), 19.

128. Jeff Cox, *The Organic Cook's Bible: How to Select and Cook the Best Ingredients on the Market* (Hoboken, NJ: John Wiley & Sons, 2006), 54.

129. Sustainable Agriculture Network, *Transitioning to Organic Production* (Sustainable Agriculture Research and Education [SARE] Program, 2007), 1–31, at 3.

130. Ibid., 2.

131. Doug Oster, and Jessica Walliser, *Grow Organic: Over 250 Tips and Ideas for Growing Flowers, Veggies, Lawns and More* (Pittsburgh, PA: St. Lyon's, 2007), 2.

132. Wendy Johnson, *Gardening at the Dragon's Gate: At Work in the Wild and Cultivated World* (New York: Bantam, 2008), xiii.

133. Michele Owens, "Yours for the Picking," *O, the Oprah Magazine* 10 (2009): 95–96, at 95.

134. Annie Spiegelman, "How to Live an Organic Life, Even in New York City," *Huffington Post*, November 16, 2010, www.huffingtonpost.com/annie-spiegelman/how-to-live-an-organic-li_b_773502.html.

135. Storstad and Björkhaug, "Foundations of Production and Consumption," 153.

136. Artur Granstedt, and Lars Kjellenberg, "Long-Term Field Experiment in Sweden: Effects of Organic and Inorganic Fertilizers on Soil Fertility and Crop Quality," in *Proceedings of an International Conference in Boston, Tufts University, Agricultural Production and Nutrition* (Boston: Tufts University, 2003), 1–11.

137. Andy Coghlan, "Going Back to Nature Down on the Farm," *New Scientist* 166, no. 2241 (2000): 20.

138. Halweil, "Organic Gold Rush," 5.

139. Graydon Forrer, Alex Avery, and John Carlisle, "Marketing & the Organic Food Industry: A History of Food Fears, Market Manipulation and Misleading Consumers," Center for Global Food Issues, September 2000, 3.

140. Sheryl Eisenberg, "Is Organic Food Worth It?," *This Green Life*, 2007, www.nrdc.org/thisgreenlife/.

141. New Scientist, "Thought for Food: Feeding the World While Nurturing the Planet Doesn't Mean Going Back to Nature. Nor Does It Mean Letting Biotech Giants Run the Whole Show. Smart Farmers Are Learning How to Have the Best of Both Worlds," *New Scientist* 174, no. 2343 (2002): 34. See also Dennis T. Avery, *Saving the Planet with Pesticides and Plastic: The Environmental Triumph of High-Yield Farming* (Indianapolis, IN: Hudson Institute, 1995).

142. Noramn Adams, "Forum: The Case against Organic Farming—Farming with Chemicals May Be Best for Wildlife," *New Scientist* 127, no. 1734 (1990).

143. Anthony Trewavas, "Urban Myths of Organic Farming: Organic Agriculture Began as an Ideology, But Can It Meet Today's Needs?," *Nature* 410 (March 22, 2001): 409–410.

144. DeGregori, *Origins of the Organic Agriculture Debate*, ix–xi.

145. Christopher D. Cook, *Diet for a Dead Planet: How the Food Industry Is Killing Us* (New York: New Press, 2004), 4.

146. Ibid., 243.

147. Ibid., 242.

148. Ibid., 251.

149. Anna Lappé and Bryant Terry, *Grub: Ideas for an Urban Organic Kitchen* (New York: Penguin, 2006), 57.

150. Ibid., 51.

151. Anna Lappé, "An Interview with Timothy LaSalle," 2008, www.takeabite.cc /organic-farming-and-carbon-offsets.

152. D. Sullivan, "Research Makes It Clear: Organic Food Is Best for People and the Planet," *Rootstock* 9, no. 1 (2009): 4–7, at 5.

153. Dennis T. Avery, "The Fallacy of the Organic Utopia," in *Fearing Food: Risk, Health, and Environment*, ed. J. Morris and R. Bate (Boston: Butterworth-Heinemann, 1999): 3–18, at 3.

154. Cornucopia Institute, "Who Is Mischa Popoff?," June 14, 2011, www.cornucopia .org/2011/06/who-is-mischa-popoff/.

155. Alex A. Avery, *The Truth about Organic Foods* (Chesterfield, MO: Henderson, 2006).

156. Ronald and Adamchak, *Tomorrow's Table*, xi.

157. Leopold Center for Sustainable Agriculture, *Organic Practices Outpace Conventional in Long-Term Research* (Ames: Iowa State University, 2007).

158. University of Michigan News Service, "Organic Farming Can Feed the World, U-M Study Shows," July 10, 2007, www.ns.umich.edu/htdos/releases/print.php.

159. J. L. Posner et al., "Organic and Conventional Production Systems in the Wisconsin Integrated Cropping System Trials," *Agronomy Journal* 100, no. 2 (2008).

160. Rob Johnston, "The Great Organic Myths," May 7, 2008, www.redorbit.com /news/science/1375056/the_great_organic_myths/.

161. Katherine Gustafson, *Locavore U.S.A.: How a Local-Food Economy Is Changing One Community* (New York: St. Martin's Griffin, 2012).

162. Stanley Feldman, "Organic Fertilizers Pose More Health Risks Than Pesticides," in *Is Organic Food Better?*, ed. Ronald D. Lankford Jr. (Detroit: Greenhaven, 2011), 35–43, at 42–43.

163. Jeff Gillman, *The Truth about Organic Gardening: Benefits, Drawbacks, and the Bottom Line* (Portland, OR: Timber Press, 2008).

164. J. Hightower, "The Hightower Report," *Austin Chronicle* 28 (2009): 21.

165. CropLife, "MACA Letter to White House about Organic Garden," March 31, 2009, www.croplife.com/article/1984.

166. A. Martin, "Is a Food Revolution Now in Season?," *New York Times*, March 21, 2009.

167. Natasha Gilbert, "Organic Farming Is Rarely Enough," *Nature*, April 25, 2012, www.nature.com/news/organic-farming-is-rarely-enough-1.10519.

168. Bryan Walsh, "Whole Food Blues: Why Organic Agriculture May Not Be So Sustainable," *Time: Ecocentric*, April 26, 2012, http://ecocentric.blogs.time .com/2012/04/26/whole-food-blues-why-organic-agriculture-may-not-be-so -sustainable/.

169. Parke Wilde, "How to Read Organic Agriculture Debates," U.S. Food Policy

(blog), April 27, 2012, www.usfoodpolicy.blogspot.com/2012/04/how-to-read-organic-agriculture-debates.html.

170. Jessica Morey-Collins, "Farm Makes Leap from Conventional to Organic Farming for Health and Profit, Proves Naysayers Wrong," Seedstock website, www.seedstock.com, April 23, 2012.

171. Ari LeVaux, "The War between Organic and Conventional Misses the Point," *Atlantic,* May 16, 2012, www.cornucopia.org/2012/05/the-war-between-organic-and-conventional-farming-misses-the-point/?utm_source=rss&utm_medium=rss&utm_campaign=the-war-between-organic-and-conventional-farming-misses-the-point.

172. Economic Research Service/USDA, "U.S. Farm Policy: The First 200 Years," *Agricultural Outlook,* March 2000, 21–25.

173. Leslie A. Duram, *Good Growing: Why Organic Farming Works* (Lincoln: University of Nebraska Press, 2005), 184.

174. *Organic Farming Act of 1982: Hearing* on *H.R. 5618 Before the Subcomm. on Forests, Family Farms, and Energy of the Committee on Agriculture,* 97th Cong. (1982), www.archive.org/stream/organicfarminga00energoog/organicfarminga00energoog_djvu.txt.

175. Farm and Food Policy Project, "Seeking Balance in U.S. Farm and Food Policy," 2007, www.farmandfoodproject.org, 1–15, at 10.

176. Max Follmer, "The Hidden Costs of the Farm Bill," TakePart.com, June 12, 2012, www.takepart.com/article/2012/06/07/farm-bill-infographic.

177. Farm and Food Policy Project, "Seeking Balance in U.S. Farm and Food Policy," 1.

178. Fred Kirschenmann, "What's News in Organic," *Biodynamics* 203 (1996): 10–12, at 12.

179. G. P. Nabhan, *Coming Home to Eat: The Pleasures and Politics of Local Foods* (New York: W. W. Norton, 2002), 14.

180. Ibid., 303.

181. B. Halweil, "Eating at Home," *Ode* 3 (2005): 34–46, at 36.

182. B. Schildgen, "10 Ways to Eat Well: Mr. Green's Food Commandments," *Sierra,* November–December 2006, www.sierraclub.org.

183. C. Burke, *To Buy or Not to Buy Organic: What You Need to Know to Choose the Healthiest, Safest, Most Earth-Friendly Food* (New York: Marlowe, 2007), xv.

184. J. Cloud, "My Search for the Perfect Apple," *Time,* March 12, 2007, 42–50, at 43.

185. Ibid., 50.

186. Nutrition Report, "Natural Selection," *Women's Health,* 2008, 28.

187. Sunset subsequently published as Margo True and Staff of Sunset Magazine, *The One-Block Feast: An Adventure in Food from Yard to Table* (Berkeley, CA: Ten Speed Press, 2011).

188. E. B. Murray, "Eco Challenge: Eating Local," *Body + Soul* 26 (2009): 52–54.

189. Leda Meredith, *The Locavore's Handbook: The Busy Person's Guide to Eating Local on a Budget* (Guilford, CT: Globe Pequot, 2012), 184.

190. Annie Spiegelman, *Talking Dirt: The Dirt Diva's Down-to-Earth Guide to Organic Gardening* (New York: Penguin, 2010), xiv.

191. Ibid., xv.

192. Gustafson, *Locavore U.S.A.*

193. T. Keane, "A Bitter Reality," *Boston Globe Magazine*, June 28, 2009, 12.

194. C. Foster, K. Green, et al., *Environmental Impacts of Food Production and Consumption: A Report to the Department for Environment, Food and Rural Affairs* (Defra, London: Manchester Business School, 2006), 15.

195. Ibid., 142.

196. Ibid., 15.

197. Pierre Desrochers and Hiroko Shimizu, "Eating Local Hurts the Planet," *Salon.com*, June 16, 2012, www.salon.com/2012/06/16/eating_local_hurts_the_planet /singleton/.

198. Emily Badger, "Debating the Local Food Movement," *Atlantic*, July 3, 2012, www .theatlanticcities.com/arts-and-lifestyle/2012/07/debating-local-food-movement /2435/.

199. New Scientist, "Thought for Food," 34.

200. Foster, Green, et al., "Environmental Impacts of Food Production and Consumption," 95.

201. Ibid., 13.

202. Organic Prairie home page, www.organicprairie.com/.

203. Applegate Farms home page, www.applegatefarms.com.

204. A. Waters, "One Thing to Do about Food: A Forum," *Nation* 283 (2006): 14–21, at 18.

205. P. Singer and J. Mason, *The Way We Eat: Why Our Food Choices Matter* (Emmaus, PA: Rodale, 2006), 241.

206. Tom Ryan, "Grown in the USA!," Retail Wire website, July 7, 2011, www.retail wire.com/discussion/15363/grown-in-the-usa.

207. Naturally Grown website, www.naturallygrown.org.

208. Ayrshire Farm home page, http://store.ayrshirefarm.com.

209. S. Lustgarden, "Organics Take Root," *Vegetarian Times*, June 1993, 72–78, at 76–77.

210. J. Guthman, "Regulating Meaning, Appropriating Nature: The Codification of California Organic Agriculture," *Antipode* 30, no. 2 (1998): 135–154.

211. David Goodman, "Organic and Conventional Agriculture: Materializing Discourse and Agro-Ecological Managerialism," *Agriculture and Human Values* 17 (2000): 215–219.

212. K. Lyons, "From Sandals to Suits: Green Consumers and the Institutionalization of Organic Agriculture," in *Consuming Foods, Sustaining Environments*, ed. S. Lockie and B. Pritchard (Brisbane: Australian Academic Press, 2001), 82–93, at 82.

213. Lockie and Halpin, "The 'Conventionalisation' Thesis Reconsidered," 285.

214. J. Guthman, "The Trouble with 'Organic Lite' in California: A Rejoinder to the 'Conventionalisation' Debate," *Sociologia Ruralis* 44, no. 3 (2004): 301–316.

215. Jim Hightower, "The Hightower Report," *Austin Chronicle* 28 (2009): 21.

216. M. Ingram, "Biology and Beyond: The Science of 'Back to Nature' Farming in

the United States," *Annals of the Association of American Geographers* 97, no. 2 (2007): 298–312, at 299.

217. Lockie and Halpin, "The 'Conventionalisation' Thesis Reconsidered," 286.

218. Kirschenmann, "What's News in Organic," 12.

219. Ibid., 11.

220. Fred Kirschenmann, "Hijacking of Organic Agriculture . . . and How USDA Is Facilitating the Theft," *Ecology and Farming: International IFOAM Magazine*, May 2000.

221. M. Sligh, *Toward Organic Integrity: A Guide to the Development of US Organic Standards*, Rural Advancement Foundation International—USA, 2000, vii.

222. Ibid., xxii.

223. Maryanne Murray Buechner, "A New Cash Cow," *Time*, July 8, 2003.

224. Mark Lipson, *Searching for the "O-Word": Analyzing the USDA Current Research Information System for Pertinence to Organic Farming* (Santa Cruz, CA: Organic Farming Research Foundation, 1997), 29–30.

225. Stewart, *It's a Long Road to a Tomato*, 68.

226. Graydon Forrer, et al., "Marketing & the Organic Food Industry," 4, http://iuc commonsproject.wikispaces.com/file/view/Marketing+and+the+Organic+Food +Industry.pdf.

227. S. F. Moore and A. Mendenhall, "USDA's Proposed Rules for Organic Farming Threaten Biodynamic Farmers," *Biodynamics* 216 (1998): 15–18, at 15–16.

228. Goodman, "Organic and Conventional Agriculture," 215–219.

229. J. D. Doliner, "Growing Our Industry from Within: Meeting an Aggressive Demand Curve with Outside Investment Capital," in *IFOAM 2000—the World Grows Organic: Proceedings of the 13th International IFOAM Scientific Conference*, ed. T. Alföldi, W. Lockeretz, and U. Niggli (Basel, Switzerland: vdf Hochschulverlag AG an der ETH Zurich, 2000), 536.

230. Desmond Jolly, "From Cottage Industry to Conglomerates: The Transformation of the U.S. Organic Foods Industry," paper presented at the International Federation of Organic Agriculture Movements (IFOAM) 2000: The World Grows Organic Conference, in Basel, Switzerland, August 25–September 2, 2000, 512.

231. Michael Pollan, "Naturally: How Organic Became a Marketing Niche and a Multibillion-Dollar Industry," *New York Times Magazine*, May 13, 2001.

232. Halweil, "Organic Gold Rush," 11.

233. William Lockeretz, "What Are the Key Issues for Consumers?," in *Organic Agriculture: Sustainability, Markets and Policies* (Washington, DC: September 23–26, 2002): 239–243, at 243.

234. USDA, "National Organic Program: Final Rule," 2007, www.ams.usda.gov /nop/NOP/standards.html, 514.

235. Ibid., 93.

236. J. M. Rawson, *Organic Agriculture in the United States: Program and Policy Issues* (Washington, DC: Congressional Research Service, 2006), 1–12.

237. Green Valley Organics, www.greenvalleylactosefree.com.

238. Warren Belasco, *Appetite for Change: How the Counterculture Took on the Food Industry, 1966–1988* (New York: Pantheon, 1989), 4.

239. Ibid., 10.

240. Randal S. Beeman and James A. Pritchard, *A Green and Permanent Land: Ecology and Agriculture in the Twentieth Century* (Lawrence: University Press of Kansas, 2001), 72.

241. Ibid., 64.

242. Ibid., 132.

243. Karen Iacobbo and Michael Iacobbo, *Vegetarians and Vegans in America Today* (Westport, CT: Praeger, 2006), 184.

244. Ibid., 39.

245. Examining the rise of "environmentally sound" products, Michael Maniates noted "the relentless ability of contemporary capitalism to commodify dissent and sell it back to dissenters" in "Individualization: Plant a Tree, Buy a Bike, Save the World?," in *Confronting Consumption*, ed. T. Princen, M. Maniates, and K. Conca (Cambridge, Mass.: MIT Press, 2002): 43–66, at 51.

246. Max Weber, *Economy and Society: An Outline of Interpretive Sociology* (Berkeley: University of California Press, 1978), 1121–1123.

247. Adrienne Clarke, Helen Porter, et al., eds. *Living Organic: Easy Steps to an Organic Family Lifestyle* (Naperville, IL: Sourcebooks, 2001), 51.

248. Lockie and Halpin, "The 'Conventionalisation' Thesis Reconsidered," 284.

249. Daniel Imhoff, *Farming with the Wild: Enhancing Biodiversity on Farms and Ranches* (San Francisco: Sierra Club Books, 2003), 138.

250. Organization for Economic Co-Operation and Development, *Organic Agriculture: Sustainability, Markets and Policies* (Wallingford, Oxford: CABI, 2003), 9.

251. Julie Guthman, *Agrarian Dreams: The Paradox of Organic Farming in California* (Berkeley: University of California Press, 2004), 2–3.

252. Kregg Hetherington, *Cultivating Utopia: Organic Farmers in a Conventional Landscape* (Halifax, NS: Fernwood, 2005), 23.

253. Eliot Coleman, *The New Organic Grower: A Master's Manual of Tools and Techniques for the Home and Market Gardener* (White River Junction, VT: Chelsea Green, 1995), 287.

254. Ableman, *Fields of Plenty*, 176.

255. Eliot Coleman, "Can Organics Save the Family Farm?," 2004, www.secretsof thecity.com/magazine/reporting/features/can-organic-save-family-farm.

256. Lyons, "From Sandals to Suits," 82.

257. J. D. Gussow, "The Real Story of 'O,'" *Organic Gardening* 49, no. 5 (September–October 2002): 39.

258. Malcolm Beck, *Lessons in Nature* (Austin, TX: Acres USA, 2005), 11.

259. Stewart, *It's a Long Road to a Tomato*, 164.

260. Ibid., 166.

261. Jane Goodall, *Harvest for Hope: A Guide to Mindful Eating* (New York: Warner, 2005), 166–167.

262. Ibid., 190.

263. Duram, *Good Growing*, 32.

264. Bob Schildgen, "10 Ways to Eat Well: Mr. Green's Food Commandments," *Sierra*, November–December 2006, www.sierraclub.org.

265. Field Maloney, "Is Whole Foods Wholesome? The Dark Secrets of the Organic-Food Movement," *Slate*, March 17, 2006.

266. John Ikerd, "Contradictions of Principles in Organic Farming," in *Organic Agriculture: A Global Perspective*, ed. P. Kristiansen, A. Taji, and J. Reganold (Ithaca, NY: Comstock, 2006), 221–229, at 221.

267. Ibid.

268. Michael Pollan, *The Omnivore's Dilemma: A Natural History of Four Meals* (New York: Penguin, 2006), 139.

269. Michael Pollan, "Mass Natural," *New York Times*, June 4, 2006.

270. Ibid.

271. Roseboro, *The Organic Food Handbook*, 5.

272. Ibid., 1.

273. USDA Economic Research Service, *Data Sets: Organic Production* (USDA, 2009), 1–4.

274. USDA, "National Organic Program: Final Rule," 467–468.

275. Burke, *To Buy or Not to Buy Organic*, 66.

276. Jeff Cox, *The Organic Food Shopper's Guide* (Hoboken, NJ: John Wiley & Sons, 2008), 19.

277. A. Martin, "How to Add Oomph to 'Organic,'" *New York Times*, August 19, 2007.

278. USDA Economic Research Service, *Data Sets: Organic Production*, 1–4.

279. Daniel Imhoff, *Food Fight: A Citizen's Guide to a Food and Farm Bill* (Healdsburg, CA: Watershed Media, 2007).

280. Jessica Morey-Collins, "Farm Makes Leap from Conventional to Organic Farming for Health and Profit, Proves Naysayers Wrong," Seedstock website, www.seedstock.com, April 23, 2012.

281. Washington State University, "Sustainability through Education," http://foundation.wsu.edu/news/.

282. University of Florida, "Center for Organic Agriculture," http://fycs.ifas.ufl.edu/organic/index.htm.

283. Headlines in 2012 from the *New York Times* (July 7), www.nytimes.com/2012/07/08/business/organic-food-purists-worry-about-big-companies-influence.html?_r=1&pagewanted=all; Mother Nature News (July 10), www.mnn.com/food/healthy-eating/blogs/is-organic-labeling-a-victim-of-its-own-success; and *Grist.org*, July 9, http://grist.org/news/multinational-food-corporations-thank-you-for-buying-organic/.

284. Cornucopia Institute, "The Organic Watergate—White Paper," May 2012, 1–75.

285. Antonio Gramsci, "Notes for an Introduction and an Approach to the Study of Philosophy and the History of Culture: Some Preliminary Reference Points," in *Antonio Gramsci Reader*, ed. D. Forgacs (New York: New York University Press, 2000), 323–343.

286. Raymond Williams, *Marxism and Literature* (New York: Oxford University Press, 1977), 114.

287. Raymond Williams, "Base and Superstructure in Marxist Cultural Theory," in *Rethinking Popular Culture: Contemporary Perspectives in Cultural Studies,* ed. C. Mukerji and M. Schudson (Berkeley: University of California Press, 1991): 407–423, at 414.

288. Williams, *Marxism and Literature,* 112.

289. J. I. Rodale, "Notice," *Organic Gardening* 11 (1947): 13.

290. Natahlie Jordi, "The Garden Bus Guys," *Bon Appétit* 5, no. 4 (2009): 26.

291. White House Organic Farm Project home page, www.thewhofarm.org.

292. A. Streep, "Sustainability Complex: Small Things, Done Right: The Next Great Leap Forward?," 2006, www.orion.org.

293. R. Raisfeld and R. Patronite, "Birdbath: Solving the Case of the East Village Bakery without a Name," January 23, 2006, www.nymag.com/nymetro/food/15533/.

294. "City Bakery Brands," www.thecitybakery.com/birdbath.

295. "About INNA jam," http://innajam.com/pages/know.

CHAPTER 5. INDIVIDUAL ORGANIC OPTIMIZATION

1. Kimberly Rider, *The Healthy Home Workbook: Easy Steps for Eco-Friendly Living* (San Francisco: Chronicle, 2006), 44.

2. Ibid., 50.

3. J. I. Rodale, "The 15 Most Pointless Foods in Your Supermarket," *Rodale News,* www.rodale.com/worst-food?cm_mmc=Twitter-_-Rodale-_-Content-Slideshow -_-15PointlessFoods.

4. Mark Bittman, "Eating Food That's Better for You, Organic or Not," *New York Times,* March 22, 2009.

5. Maria Rodale, *Maria Rodale's Organic Gardening: Your Seasonal Companion to Creating a Beautiful and Delicious Garden* (Emmaus, PA: Rodale, 1998), 102.

6. Michael Pollan, "Naturally: How Organic Became a Marketing Niche and a Multibillion-Dollar Industry," *New York Times Magazine,* May 13, 2001.

7. Nicolas Lampkin, *Organic Farming* (Ipswich, UK: Old Pond, 2002), 463.

8. Michael Heasman and Julian Mellentin, *The Functional Foods Revolution: Healthy People, Healthy Profits?* (Sterling, VA: Earthscan, 2001), 255.

9. Andrew Szasz, *Shopping Our Way to Safety: How We Changed from Protecting the Environment to Protecting Ourselves* (Minneapolis: University of Minnesota Press, 2007), 4.

10. Maria Rodale, *Maria Rodale's Organic Gardening Secrets: Summer* (Emmaus, PA: Rodale, 2012).

11. Maria K. Magnusson, Anne Arvola, et al., "Choice of Organic Foods Is Related to Perceived Consequences for Human Health and to Environmentally Friendly Behaviour," *Appetite* 40, no. 2 (2003): 109–117.

12. Robert C. Oelhaf, *Organic Agriculture: Economic and Ecological Comparisons with Conventional Methods* (New York: John Wiley & Sons, 1978), 147.

13. Donna Maurer, *Vegetarianism: Movement or Moment?* (Philadelphia: Temple University Press, 2002), 60–61.

14. S. Ristovski-Slijepcevic, G. E. Chapman, et al., "Engaging with Healthy Eating Discourse(s): Ways of Knowing about Food and Health in Three Ethnocultural Groups in Canada," *Appetite* 50, no. 1 (2008).

15. Bob Ashley, Joanne Hollows, et al., *Food and Cultural Studies* (New York: Routledge, 2004), 61.

16. Hodan Farah Wells and Jean C. Buzby, "Dietary Assessment of Major Trends in U.S. Food Consumption, 1970–2005," *USDA Economic Information Bulletin* 33 (2008): 3.

17. Ristovski-Slijepcevic, Chapman, et al., "Engaging with Healthy Eating Discourse(s)."

18. Ibid., xv.

19. Michael Goldstein, *The Health Movement: Promoting Fitness in America* (New York: Twayne, 1992), 62.

20. Heasman and Mellentin, *The Functional Foods Revolution*, xvi.

21. Ibid., 11–12.

22. Ibid., 254.

23. Ibid., 78.

24. Daren Fonda, "Organic Growth," *Time*, August 4, 2002.

25. Joyce Hendley, "The Sweet & The Sour," *Eating Well* 8 (2009): 40–41.

26. Business Wire, "National Survey: Green Is Officially Mainstream—but Consumers Are Confused, Skeptical about Products," *Business Wire*, 2009, www.business wire.com/news/home/20090630005830/en.

27. Crow Miller and Elizabeth Miller, *Organic Gardening: A Comprehensive Guide to Chemical-Free Growing* (New York: IDG Books, 2000), 23.

28. J. Helmer, "Get Growing!," *Natural Solutions*, May–June 2009, 65–68, at 65.

29. International Food Information Council (IFIC) Foundation, 2008 *Food & Health Survey: Consumer Attitudes toward Food, Nutrition & Health* (Washington, DC: IFIC Foundation, 2008), 54.

30. Michael Pollan, *In Defense of Food: An Eater's Manifesto* (New York: Penguin, 2008), 9.

31. Ibid., 6–8.

32. Ibid., 169.

33. Michael Pollan, *The Omnivore's Dilemma: A Natural History of Four Meals* (New York: Penguin, 2006), 181.

34. Wells and Buzby, "Dietary Assessment of Major Trends," iii–iv.

35. Max Follmer, "The Hidden Costs of the Farm Bill," *TakePart.com*, June 12, 2012, www.takepart.com/article/2012/06/07/farm-bill-infographic.

36. Environmental Working Group, "EWG's 2012 Shopper's Guide to Pesticides in Produce," 2012, www.ewg.org/foodnews/.

37. Richard Wiles, Kenneth A. Cook, et al., *How 'Bout Them Apples? Pesticides in Children's Food Ten Years after Alar* (Washington, DC: Environmental Working Group, 1999), 5.

38. Josef G. Thundiyil, "Acute Pesticide Poisoning: A Proposed Classification

Tool," *Bulletin of the World Health Organization*, www.who.int/bulletin/volumes/86/3/07–041814/en/.

39. Environmental Working Group, "EWG's 2012 Shopper's Guide."

40. US Government, "US Government Facts: Children's Chemical & Pesticide Exposure via Food Products," 2005, 1–2.

41. D. Goodman, "Foodtopia," *Eating Well* 8 (2009): 50–56, 81, at 54.

42. "Parmesan and Rosemary," www.quinnpopcorn.com/popcorn/parmesan-rosemary/.

43. Forrer, Avery, and Carlisle, "Marketing & the Organic Food Industry: A History of Food Fears, Market Manipulation and Misleading Consumers," September 2000, 9, http://iuccommonsproject.wikispaces.com/file/view/Marketing+and+the+Organic+Food+Industry.pdf.

44. Brad Stone, "The Flavr Savr Arrives," *Access Excellence*, May 18, 1994, www.accessexcellence.org/RC/AB/BA/Flavr_Savr_Arrives.php.

45. Ecowatch, "Monsanto's Dark History," http://readersupportednews.org/opinion2/271–38/16828-focus-monsantos-dark-history.

46. USDA Economic Research Service, "Adoption of Genetically Engineered Crops in the U.S," www.ers.usda.gov/data-products/adoption-of-genetically-engineered-crops-in-the-us/recent-trends-in-ge-adoption.aspx.

47. Just Label It website, http://justlabelit.org/.

48. Will Allen, "Monsanto Threatens to Sue Vermont over GMO Labeling Bill," Organic Consumers Association website, www.organicconsumers.org/articles/article_25180.cfm.

49. Alex A. Avery, *The Truth about Organic Foods* (Chesterfield, MO: Henderson, 2006).

50. Sally Fallon, *Nourishing Traditions: The Cookbook That Challenges Politically Correct Nutrition and the Diet Dictocrats* (Washington, DC: New Trends, 2001), xii.

51. Ibid., 50.

52. C. Dimitri and C. Greene, *Recent Growth Patterns in the U.S. Organic Foods Market* (Washington, DC: USDA, 2002), 1–39, at 2.

53. Jon Newton, *Profitable Organic Farming* (Oxford: Blackwell Science, 2004), 142–143.

54. Brian Halweil, "Organic Gold Rush," *WorldWatch Magazine* 14, no. 3 (May–June 2001), 1–12, at 7.

55. M. Sligh and C. Christman, *Who Owns Organic? The Global Status, Prospects and Challenges of a Changing Organic Market* (Pittsboro, NC: Rural Advancement Foundation International [RAFI-USA], 2003), 24.

56. Ibid., 9.

57. D. Bolton, "Costco Nurtures Growth of Organics," 2007, www.naturalfoodnet.com.

58. "Publix Greenwise Market Products," *Publix.com*, www.publix.com/wellness/greenwise/products/ProductDetail.do?id=978.

59. Samuel Fromartz, *Organic, Inc.: Natural Foods and How They Grew* (Orlando, FL: Harcourt, 2006), 185.

60. Daniel Imhoff and Fred Kirschenmann, *Farming with the Wild: Enhancing Biodiversity on Farms and Ranches* (San Francisco: Sierra Club Books, 2003), 138.

61. Hain Pure Foods website. www.hainpurefoods.com/index.php.

62. Hain Celestial Group, 2004 *Annual Report* (Melville, NY: Hain Celestial Group, 2005), 1–58, at 2.

63. Ibid., 4–5.

64. Hain Celestial Group, 2010 *Corporate Social Responsibility Report* (Melville, NY: Hain Celestial Group, 2011), 1–24.

65. Matthew Saltmarsh, "Increasing Appetite for Organic Products Defies a Weak Global Economy; Sector Attracts Investors as Sales in Europe and U.S. Continue to Grow," *International Herald Tribune*, Paris, May 25, 2011.

66. David Goodman, "Culture Change," *Mother Jones* 1 (January–February 2003).

67. A. Martin, "Is a Food Revolution Now in Season?," *New York Times*, March 22, 2009.

68. Marion Nestle, *What to Eat* (New York: North Point, 2006), 106.

69. Courtney Kane, "Stonyfield Farm Tries to Change the World and Sell Some Yogurt," *New York Times*, September 6, 2000.

70. Gary Hirshberg, *Stirring It Up: How to Make Money and Save the World* (New York: Hyperion, 2008), 97.

71. Reed McManus, "Culturing the Organic Revolution," *Sierra*, November–December 2007, 20–21, at 20.

72. Stonyfield Farm blog, www.stonyfield.com/blog/2011/12/09/holiday-ornament-recycling-oikos-foil-lids/.

73. Stonyfield Farm, http://iwillknowmyfood.com/#description.

74. O'Naturals website, www.onaturals.com.

75. Stonyfield Café Facebook page, www.facebook.com/pages/Stonyfield-Caf%C3%A9/327050900676?sk=info.

76. Pollan, "Naturally."

77. Ibid.

78. Cascadian Farm website," www.cascadianfarm.com/home.aspx.

79. LOHAS, "Consumers Prefer Artisanal Foods," www.lohas.com/articles/100992.html.

80. W. Berry, *Home Economics* (San Francisco: North Point, 1987), 326.

81. Laura Mulvey, "Some Thoughts on Theories of Fetishism in the Context of Contemporary Culture," *October* 65 (Summer 1993): 3–20, at 9–10.

82. C. Benbrook, X. Zhao, et al., "New Evidence Confirms the Nutritional Superiority of Plant-Based Organic Foods," Organic Center, 2008, 1–50, at 17.

83. US Government, "US Government Facts: Children's Chemical & Pesticide Exposure via Food Products," 1–2.

84. Kristi Bahrenburg, "Organic for Baby?," 65, no. 5 (June–July 2000): 66.

85. C. Dimitri and K. M. Venezia, "Retail and Consumer Aspects of the Organic Milk Market," USDA, 1–18, at 3.

86. "Denise's Balancing Act," *US Weekly* 947 (April 8, 2013): 56.

87. Soil Association, "Organic Market Report 2009," Bristol, 1–72, at 28, www.soilassociation.org/LinkClick.aspx?fileticket=GPynfoJoPho%3D&tabid=116.

88. Annie Schoening, "Organics for Babies?," *Parenting* 21, no. 4 (May 2007): 153.

89. Anni Daulter and Shanté Lanay, *Organically Raised: Conscious Cooking for Babies and Toddlers* (Emmaus, PA: Rodale, 2010), xvi.

90. Hago Limited, "About Sunval," http://hago-group.com/eng/product.about .sunval.php?bid=2.

91. Plum Organics, "Why Plum?," www.plumorganics.com/why_plum_1.php.

92. Ella's Kitchen, "Helpful Stuff," www.ellaskitchen.com/helpful-stuff.

93. Miessence certified organics, "Organic Baby Care," www.micertifiedorganics .com/certified-organic-baby-products.

94. Avalon Organics, "Shampoo & Body Wash," http://avalonorganics.com/?id =335&pid=407.

95. Nature's Baby Organics, "Products," www.naturesbabyorganics.com/product .html.

96. Nature's Baby Organics, "Organic Baby Oil," www.naturesbabyorganics.com /organic_baby-oil.html.

97. BabyGanics, "Bye, Bye, Dry™" and "About Us," www.babyganics.com/Bye _Bye_Dry_Eczema_Lotion and www.babyganics.com/about_us.

98. Robert W. Sears and Amy Marlow, *HappyBaby: The Organic Guide to Baby's First 24 Months* (New York: Harper, 2009), 24.

99. Little Duck Organics, "Story," http://littleduckorganics.com/story.php.

100. M. C. Goldman and W. H. Hylton, eds., *The Basic Book of Organically Grown Foods* (Emmaus, Pa.: Rodale, 1972), 5.

101. William Lockeretz, "What Are the Key Issues for Consumers?," in *Organic Agriculture: Sustainability, Markets and Policies* (Wallingford, Oxford: CABI, 2003), 239–243, at 242.

102. J. D. Gussow, "Can an Organic Twinkie™ Be Certified?," in *For ALL Generations: Making World Agriculture More Sustainable*, ed. J. Patrick Madden and Scott G. Chaplowe (West Hollywood, CA: World Sustainable Agriculture Association, 1997), 143–153, at 149.

103. Ibid., 151.

104. A. Gramsci, "Notes for an Introduction and an Approach to the Study of Philosophy and the History of Culture: Some Preliminary Reference Points," in *Antonio Gramsci Reader*, ed. D. Forgacs (New York: New York University Press, 2000), 323–343, at 328.

105. Jonathan Leake, "Organic Food Can Make You Fatter," *Sunday Times*, April 10, 2011.

106. Fearless Chocolate website, http://shop.fearlesschocolate.com/70-superfruit/.

107. E. M. DuPuis, *Nature's Perfect Food: How Milk Became America's Drink* (New York: New York University Press, 2002), 220.

108. Farmers Weekly, "Organic Milk for McDonald's at the Olympics," November 4, 2012, www.fwi.co.uk/Articles/04/11/2010/124235/Organic-milk-for-McDonald39s -at-the-Olympics.htm.

109. Real California Milk, "Happy Cows," 2010, www.realcaliforniamilk.com/happy cows.

110. Mark Allen Kastel, "Maintaining the Integrity of Organic Milk," Cornucopia Institute, April 19, 2006, http://cornucopia.org/dairysurvey/OrganicDairyReport /cornucopia_milk_exec.pdf.

111. Dimitri and Venezia, "Retail and Consumer Aspects," 2.

112. Horizon Organic website, www.horizonorganic.com.

113. Cornucopia Institute, "Nation's Largest Corporate Dairy Sues Organic Farmer-Owned Cooperative," July 16, 2012, www.cornucopia.org/2012/07/nations -largest-corporate-dairy-sues-organic-farmer-owned-cooperative/.

114. C. F. Marcy, "Organics in the Supermarket," in *Proceedings of the 14th IFOAM Organic World Congress*, ed. R. Thompson (Ottaway, Ontario: Canadian Organic Growers, 2002), 194.

115. D. Philips, "Organic and Natural Dairy," *Dairy Foods*, June 2007, 30–36, at 32.

116. Cornucopia News. "Profit Over Organics: Nation's Largest Dairy Marketer Sets Up Competing Market Category," July 2, 2009, www.cornucopia.org/2009/07/profit -over-organics-nation%E2%80%99s-largest-dairy-marketer-sets-up-competing -market-category/.

117. Horizon Dairy home page, www.horizondairy.com/.

118. The Organic Cow home page, http://theorganiccow.com/.

119. D. Sullivan, "Research Makes It Clear: Organic Food Is Best for People and the Planet," *Rootstock* 9, no. 1 (2009): 4–7, at 7.

120. Organic Valley, "Our History." www.organicvalley.coop/about-us/overview /our-history/.

121. LOHAS, "Organic Valley Sales at $432.5 Million," March 27, 2008, www.lohas .com.

122. Cornucopia Institute, "Aurora Organic Factory Dairy," www.cornucopia.org /aurora-organic-factory-dairy/.

123. Lynne Buske, "Bush Era Organic Scandal Ends in $7.4 Million Settlement," September 15, 2012, http://readersupportednews.org/news-section2/312–16/13490-bush -era-organic-scandal-ends-in-75-million-settlement.

124. Cornucopia Institute, "Enforcement Hammer Falls on Giant Arizona Organic Factory Farm Dairy," December 15, 2011, www.cornucopia.org/2011/12/enforcement -hammer-falls-on-giant-arizona-organic-factory-farm-dairy/.

125. J. I. Rodale, "With the Editor: Whither Science?," *Organic Farmer* 4 (1953): 13.

126. Bob Flowerdew, *The Organic Gardening Bible: Successful Gardening the Natural Way* (Lanham, MD: Taylor, 1998), 140.

127. C. Benbrook, X. Zhao, et al., "New Evidence Confirms the Nutritional Superiority of Plant-Based Organic Foods," Organic Center, 2008, 1–50, C.

128. E. M. Lipson, *The Organic Foods Sourcebook* (Chicago: Contemporary Books, 2001), 90.

129. Ibid., 92.

130. OrganicAthlete, "Guide to Sports Nutrition," 2001, www.organicathlete.org.

131. Ibid., 30.

132. See, for example, A. Coghlan, "Digging the Dirt: Fans Say Organic Foods Are Best, but Are They Just Full of Manure?," *New Scientist* 171, no. 2303 (2001): 15;

V. Worthington, "Nutritional Quality of Organic Versus Conventional Fruits, Vegetables, and Grains," *Journal of Alternative and Complementary Medicine* 7, no. 2 (2001): 161–173; R. Edwards, "The Natural Choice: Organic Food Has More of What It Takes to Keep You Healthy," *New Scientist* 173, no. 2334 (2002): 10; S. Gwynne, "Born Green," *Saveur*, May 26, 2009, 27–30; C. Benbrook, "Elevating Antioxidant Levels in Food through Organic Farming and Food Processing," *State of Science Review*, the Organic Center, 2005, 1–6; Organic Center, *Core Truths: Serving up the Science behind Organic Agriculture*, Organic Center, 2006; S. Y. Wang, C.-T. Chen, et al., "Fruit Quality, Antioxidant Capacity, and Flavonoid Content of Organically and Conventionally Grown Blueberries," *Journal of Agricultural and Food Chemistry* 56 (2008): 5788–5794; and J. Cox, *The Organic Food Shopper's Guide* (Hoboken, NJ: John Wiley & Sons, 2008).

133. Organic Center, *Core Truths*, 11, 52.

134. P. Jaret, "A Growing Trend," *Cooking Light* 22 (2008): 30–34, at 32.

135. R. C. Theuer, "Do Organic Fruits and Vegetables Taste Better Than Conventional Fruits and Vegetables?," Organic Center, 2006.

136. Tara Parker-Pope, "For Three Years, Every Bite Organic," *New York Times*, December 1, 2008, www.nytimes.com/2008/12/02/health/02well.html?_r=1.

137. Sullivan, "Research Makes It Clear," 4.

138. C. Benbrook, X. Zhao, et al., "New Evidence Confirms the Nutritional Superiority of Plant-Based Organic Foods," Organic Center, 2008, 1–50.

139. T. R. DeGregori, *Origins of the Organic Agriculture Debate* (Ames: Iowa State University Press, 2004), 98.

140. M. Ingram, "Biology and Beyond: The Science of 'Back to Nature' Farming in the United States," *Annals of the Association of American Geographers* 97, no. 2 (2007): 298–312.

141. Avery, *The Truth about Organic Foods*, 76.

142. Joseph D. Rosen, *Claims of Organic Food's Nutritional Superiority: A Critical Review* (New York: American Council on Science and Health, 2008), 1–15, at 12.

143. Alan D. Dangour, Sakhi K. Dohia, Arabella Hayter, et al., "Nutritional Quality of Organic Foods: A Systematic Review," *American Journal of Clinical Nutrition* 90, no. 3 (September 2009): 680–685, www.ncbi.nlm.nih.gov/pubmed/19640946.

144. Rob Johnston, "The Great Organic Myths," *Red Orbit*, May 7, 2008, www.redorbit.com/news/science/1375056/the_great_organic_myths/.

145. Gary Hirshberg, "UK Study Misleads Public by Ignoring Documented Health and Environmental Benefits of Organic Food," *Huffington Post*, July 31, 2009, www.huffingtonpost.com/gary-hirshberg/.

146. Stanley Feldman, "Organic Fertilizers Pose More Health Risks Than Pesticides," in *Is Organic Food Better?*, ed. Ronald D. Lankford Jr., 35–43 (Detroit: Greenhaven Press, 2011), 42–43.

147. Ibid., 37.

148. Mischa Popoff, "Beware of Organic Crusaders," *National Post*, April 11, 2011.

149. Mischa Popoff, "Is It Organic?," http://isitorganic.ca/.

150. Cornucopia Institute, "Who Is Mischa Popoff?," June 14, 2011, www.cornucopia.org/2011/06/who-is-mischa-popoff/.

151. Pirjo Honkanen, Bas Verplanken, et al., "Ethical Values and Motives Driving Organic Food Choice," *Journal of Consumer Behaviour* 5 (September–October 2006): 420–430, at 421.

152. Nancy Shute, "Organic Isn't Always Safer When It Comes to Botulism," *The Salt: NPR's Food Blog*, November 7, 2011, www.npr.org/blogs/thesalt/2011/11/07/142110648 /organic-isnt-always-safer-when-it-comes-to-botulism.

153. Diet-Weight-Lose, "Celebrity Diet: Nicole Kidman," www.diet-weight-lose .com/celebrity/nicole-kidman.php.

154. Sarah Bailey, "Gwyneth Unveiled," *Harper's Bazaar*, May 2013, 228–231, at 266.

155. K. Roderick, *Organic Bath: Creating a Natural, Healthy Haven* (New York: Melcher Media, 2007), 9.

156. Ibid., 12.

157. Heather C. Flores, *Food Not Lawns: How to Turn Your Yard into a Garden and Your Neighborhood into a Community* (White River Junction, VT: Chelsea Green, 2006), 193.

158. Goldstein, *The Health Movement*, 157.

159. Digital Detox, "Registration," http://thedigitaldetox.org/registration/.

160. Valerie Tejeda, "6 Fitness Secrets of Latina Stars," *Latina*, June 11, 2012, www .latina.com/lifestyle/health/celebrity-fitness-secrets-workouts.

161. Amazing Grass, "In the Press," April 2012, http://amazinggrass.com/in_the _press/6553/April-2012—Marie-Claire-Magazine.html.

162. Goop, "Organic Avenue," http://goop.com/newsletter/64/en.

163. Joan Lang, "20% of Daily Biz at Rodale Press: Organics Play Growing Role," *FoodService Director* 12, no. 8 (August 15, 1999).

164. Bob Moseley, "Rodale's Era of Upheaval," *Folio: The Magazine for Magazine Management*, 29, no. 4 (April 1, 2000).

165. Rodale Institute, www.rodaleinstitute.org/.

166. Maria Rodale and Maya Rodale, *It's My Pleasure: A Revolutionary Plan to Free Yourself from Guilt and Create the Life You Want* (New York: Free Press, 2005), xx.

167. J. Walker, "Editors at New Magazines Give Pitch Tips," *O'Dwyer's PR Services Report* (New York: J. R. O'Dwyer, 2005).

168. Text from subscription order letters for *Organic Style* in 2004.

169. S. D. Smith, "Rodale to Shutter Four-Year-Old Organic Style," *Media Week*, www.mediaweek.com/mw/news/recent_display.jsp?vnu_content_id=1001053674.

170. Maria Rodale indicated that she would be stepping down to COO in 2013 and seeking a new CEO.

171. Susan Harris, "Garden Rant: Ethne Clarke and the Makeover of Organic Gardening, *Garden Rant*, January 13, 2010, www.gardenrant.com/my_weblog/2010/01 /ethne-clark-and-og-mag.html.

172. Rodale Inc., "Organic Gardening Relaunches with February/March 2010 Issue," January 4, 2010, www.rodaleinc.com/newsroom/iorganic-gardeningi-relaunches -februarymarch-2010-issue.

173. Rodale Inc., "Rodale Inc. Promotes Matt Bean to VP, Digital Product Development," March 6, 2012, www.rodaleinc.com/newsroom/rodale-inc-promotes-matt -bean-vp-digital-product-development.

174. Rodale and Rodale, *It's My Pleasure*, xix.

175. Rodale, "With the Editor: Whither Science?," 13.

176. J. I. Rodale, "With the Editor: The Organiculturist's Creed," *Organic Gardening* 12 (1948): 12–14, at 14.

177. OrganicMatch, "About Us," www.organicmatch.com/about_us.php.

178. Williams-Sonoma, www.williams-sonoma.com/shop/agrarian-garden/?cm_type=lnav.

179. "Wanderlust," http://wanderlustfestival.com/.

180. J. I. Rodale, editorial, *Organic Farmer* 1 (1949): 9–10, at 9.

181. L. F. Dodge, "Planning Organic Profits," *Organic Farmer* 1 (1950): 15–18, at 18.

CHAPTER 6. ORGANIC CONSUMERS

1. Jane Goodall, *Harvest for Hope: A Guide to Mindful Eating* (New York: Warner, 2005), 159.

2. Ibid., xxiii.

3. National Center for Public Policy, "Organic Labeling Study," 2000, www.nationalcenter.org/OrganicLabe1500.html.

4. Steve Meyerowitz, *The Organic Food Guide: How to Shop Smarter and Eat Healthier* (Guilford, CT: Globe Pequot, 2004), 35.

5. Organization for Economic Co-Operation and Development, *Organic Agriculture: Sustainability, Markets and Policies* (Wallingford, Oxford: CABI Publishing, 2003), 10.

6. Marcia Mogelonsky, "Organic Food and Drink," *Prepared Foods*, June 1, 2008, 21–26, at 26.

7. Natural Marketing Institute, "Organic Food & Beverage Sales Increase 18%; Household Penetration Decreases," February 23, 2005, www.NMIsolutions.com.

8. Stewart Lockie, "Capturing the Sustainability Agenda: Organic Foods and Media Discourses on Food Scares, Environment, Genetic Engineering and Health," *Agriculture and Human Values* 23, no. 3 (2006): 248–249.

9. Georgina Holt, "A Conceptual Model of Willingness to Pay for Organic Food in the UK," in *Sociological Perspectives of Organic Agriculture: From Pioneer to Policy*, ed. Georgiana Holt and Matthew Reed (Oxfordshire, UK: CAB International, 2006), 88–106.

10. Felix Ureña, Rodolfo Bernabéu, et al., "Women, Men and Organic Food: Differences in Their Attitudes and Willingness to Pay. A Spanish Case Study," *International Journal of Consumer Studies* 32, no. 1 (2008): 18–26.

11. Anne Arvola, Marco Vassallo, et al., "Predicting Intentions to Purchase Organic Food: The Role of Affective and Moral Attitudes in the Theory of Planned Behaviour," *Appetite* 50, no. 2–3 (March–May 2008), 443–454.

12. International Food Information Council (IFIC) Foundation, 2008 *Food & Health Survey: Consumer Attitudes toward Food, Nutrition & Health* (Washington, DC: International Food Information Council [IFIC] Foundation, 2008).

13. Jeff Cox, *The Organic Cook's Bible: How to Select and Cook the Best Ingredients on the Market* (Hoboken, NJ: John Wiley & Sons, 2006), 21.

14. Jeff Cox, *The Organic Food Shopper's Guide* (Hoboken, NJ: John Wiley & Sons, 2008), vii.

15. Jesse Ziff Cool, *Simply Organic: A Cookbook for Sustainable, Seasonal, and Local Ingredients* (San Francisco: Chronicle Books, 2008), 16.

16. "Top 12 Reasons to Go Organic," *Dr.Greene.com*, www.drgreene.com/perspec tives/2011/08/22/top-12-reasons-go-organic.

17. Chipotle, "Food with Integrity," www.chipotle.com/en-us/fwi/environment /environment.aspx.

18. L. E. Annett, V. Muralidharan, et al., "Influence of Health and Environmental Information on Hedonic Evaluation of Organic and Conventional Bread," *Journal of Food Science* 73, no. 4 (2008): 1–14, at 7.

19. Paul Sparks and Richard Shepherd, "Self-Identity and the Theory of Planned Behavior: Assessing the Role of Identification with 'Green Consumerism,'" *Social Psychology Quarterly* 55, no. 4 (December 1992): 388–399, at 397.

20. David Scott Conner, "The Organic Label and Sustainable Agriculture: Consumer Preferences and Values" (PhD diss., Cornell University, 2002), 26, http://agecon search.umn.edu/bitstream/27137/1/35010034.pdf.

21. Sparks and Shepherd, "Self-Identity and the Theory of Planned Behavior," 388–399.

22. Nina Michaelidou and Louise M. Hassan, "The Role of Health Consciousness, Food Safety Concern and Ethical Identity on Attitudes and Intentions towards Organic Food," *International Journal of Consumer Studies* 32 (2008): 163–170.

23. Pirjo Honkanen, Bas Verplanken, et al., "Ethical Values and Motives Driving Organic Food Choice," *Journal of Consumer Behaviour* 5, no. 5 (September–October 2006): 420–430.

24. S. Waldman and V. Reiss, "It's a Lohasian Moment," *Newsweek*, June 5, 2006, www.msnbc.msn.com/id/13004986/site/newsweek/Beliefwatch: Lohasians.

25. Marion Nestle, *What to Eat* (New York: North Point, 2007), 449.

26. Stephanie Tourles, *Organic Body Care Recipes: 175 Homemade Herbal Formulas for Glowing Skin & a Vibrant Self* (North Adams, MA: Storey, 2007), 4.

27. Ibid., 32.

28. Michael J. Silverstein, Neil Fiske, et al., *Trading Up: Why Consumers Want New Luxury Goods—and How Companies Create Them* (New York: Portfolio, 2005), 1.

29. Ibid., 5.

30. Ibid., 49.

31. "Our Popcorn," 479° Popcorn website, www.479popcorn.com/our_popcorn .html?id=24WEpkWQ.

32. "Pimentòn de La Vera," 479° Popcorn website, www.479popcorn.com/flavor .html?mv_arg=PDV.

33. Silverstein and Fiske, *Trading Up*, 28.

34. LOHAS, "Wal-Mart Supercenter Tops among Organics Shoppers: Study," 2007, www.lohas.com/articles/100733.html.

35. Silverstein and Fiske, *Trading Up*, 121.

36. Trader Joe's, *Fearless Flyer* (Monrovia, CA: Trader Joe's, 2007), 1.

37. Silverstein and Fiske, *Trading Up*, 122–124.

38. Trader Joe's, *Fearless Flyer*, 11.

39. Silverstein and Fiske, *Trading Up*, 121.

40. Trader Joe's, *Fearless Flyer*, 6.

41. Bob Ashley, Joanne Hollows, et al., *Food and Cultural Studies* (New York: Routledge, 2004), 106.

42. Ibid., 117.

43. Louis Bromfield, *Malabar Farm* (New York: Harper & Brothers, 1948), 314–315.

44. Carolyn Dimitri and Catherine Greene, *Recent Growth Patterns in the U.S. Organic Foods Market* (Washington, DC: USDA, 2002): 1–39, at 2.

45. Amy Kremen, Cathrine Greene, et al., *Organic Produce, Price Premiums, and Eco-Labeling in U.S. Farmers' Markets* (Washington, DC: USDA, 2003), 1–12, at 6.

46. Ibid., 2.

47. Ibid., 6.

48. Kim Darby, Marvin T. Batte, et al., "Willingness to Pay for Locally Produced Foods: A Customer Intercept Study of Direct Market and Grocery Store Shoppers," *American Agricultural Economics Association Annual Meeting*, Long Beach, California, 2006, 11.

49. Soil Association, "Organic Market Report 2009," Bristol, 1–72, at 22.

50. Miranda Smith and E. Henderson, eds., *The Real Dirt: Farmers Tell about Organic and Low-Input Practices in the Northeast* (Burlington, VT: Northeast Regional Sustainable Agriculture Research and Education Program, 1998).

51. Thomas A. Lyson, *Civic Agriculture: Reconnecting Farm, Food, and Community* (Medford, MA: Tufts University Press, 2004), 31.

52. E. Henderson, R. Mandelbaum, et al., *Toward Social Justice and Economic Equity in the Food System: A Call for Social Stewardship Standards in Sustainable and Organic Agriculture* (Pittsboro, NC: Rural Advancement Foundation International [RAFI-USA], 2003), 12.

53. Philip McMichael, "The Power of Food," *Agriculture and Human Values* 17 (2000): 21–33, at 23.

54. Ingolf Vogeler, *The Myth of the Family Farm: Agribusiness Dominance of U.S. Agriculture* (Boulder, CO: Westview, 1981), 6.

55. Lyson, *Civic Agriculture: Reconnecting Farm, Food, and Community*, xiii.

56. Jules Pretty and Peggy F. Barlett, "Concluding Remarks: Nature and Health in the Urban Environment," in *Urban Place: Reconnecting with the Natural World*, ed. Peggy F. Barlett (Cambridge, MA: MIT Press, 2005), 299–319, at 307.

57. Heather Flores, *Food Not Lawns: How to Turn Your Yard into a Garden and Your Neighborhood into a Community* (White River Junction, VT: Chelsea Green, 2006), 2.

58. Deborah Schneebeli-Morrell, *Organic Crops in Pots: How to Grow Your Own Vegetables, Fruits, and Herbs* (New York: Cico Books, 2009), 8, 10.

59. "Red Rood Herb & Vegetable Farm," *Local Harvest*, www.localharvest.org/red-root-herb-vegetable-farm-M11385?p=2.

60. National Public Radio, "John Mackey on Whole Foods' Growth," *Marketplace*, February 26, 2007, http://marketplace.publicradio.org/shows/2007/02/26/PM 200702266.html.

61. San Gwynne, "Thriving on Health Food," *Time*, February 23, 1998.

62. Ibid.

63. San Gwynne, "Retail," *Texas Monthly* 34 (2006): 116–121, 191–193, at 120.

64. Daren Fonda, "Organic Growth," *Time*, August 4, 2002.

65. Benjamin Aldes Wurgaft, "East of Eden: Sin and Redemption at the Whole Foods Market," *Gastronomica* 2, no. 3 (2002): 87–89.

66. Carlo Petrini, "Speech at the W. K. Kellogg Foundation Conference," April 28, 2005, www.slowfoodusa.org/events/carlo_petrini_speech.html.

67. Alex Renton, "Ripe Target," *Guardian*, March 27, 2007, www.guardian.co.uk /supermarkets/story/0,,2043674,00.html.

68. William Grimes, "A Pleasure Palace without the Guilt," *New York Times*, February 18, 2004.

69. Maria Rodale and Maya Rodale, *It's My Pleasure: A Revolutionary Plan to Free Yourself from Guilt and Create the Life You Want* (New York: Free Press, 2005), xx.

70. LOHAS, "Wal-Mart Supercenter Tops among Organics Shoppers."

71. Renton, "Ripe Target."

72. Field Maloney, "Is Whole Foods Wholesome? The Dark Secrets of the Organic-Food Movement," *Slate*, March 17, 2006, www.slate.com/articles/arts/culture box/2006/03/is_whole_foods_wholesome.html.

73. Renton, "Ripe Target."

74. TreeHugger, "Joel Salatin, America's Most Influential Farmer, Talks Big Organic and the Future of Food," *Tree Hugger*, August 5, 2009, www.treehugger.com /files/2009/08/joel-salatin-americas-most-influential-farmer.php.

75. Michael Pollan, *The Omnivore's Dilemma: A Natural History of Four Meals* (New York: Penguin, 2006), 137–138.

76. Marian Burros, "Is Whole Foods Straying from Its Roots?," *New York Times*, February 28, 2007, www.nytimes.com/2007/02/28/dining/28whole.html?pagewanted =all&_r=0.

77. National Public Radio, "John Mackey on Whole Foods' Growth."

78. Renton, "Ripe Target."

79. Pamela Paul, "America's Healthiest Grocery Stores," *Health* 22 (2008): 114–118, at 114.

80. Daniel Mazori "The 2009 Natural Health Green Choice Awards," *Natural Health* 39 (2009): 58–65.

81. J. I. Rodale, "With the Editor: Orchard Practices," *Organic Gardening* 6 (1945): 7.

82. L. F. Dodge, "Planning Organic Profits," *Organic Farmer* 1 (1950): 15–18, at 15.

83. Janice M. Horowitz, "Bye-Bye Tofu; Hello, Truffles!," *Time*, March 19, 1990.

84. Nathalie Jordi, "Food's Golden State," *Bon Appétit* 54 (March 2009): 116–123, at 118.

85. Organic Connections Magazine, "Nora Pouillon: A Pioneer's Odyssey to Organic."

86. Restaurant Nora, "About Us," www.noras.com/nora/about/.

87. Restaurant Nora, "Our Menus," www.noras.com/menu/.

88. On a related note, as interest in eco-fashion has grown, high-end retailers have increasingly requested organic cotton. Patagonia decided to convert its entire cotton line of outdoor apparel to organic in 1994, and Nike committed to using more organic fibers in its clothing; both are now at the apex of the world's organic cotton markets. Most clothing in the United States is derived from conventional cotton and cheap (overseas) labor, but the Global Organic Textile Standard certifies garments made with at least 70 percent organic fibers and fair labor practices.

89. Adrienne Clarke, Helen Porter, et al., eds., *Living Organic: Easy Steps to an Organic Family Lifestyle* (Naperville, IL: Sourcebooks, 2001), 10.

90. Ibid., 24.

91. Michael Pollan, "Mass Natural," *New York Times*, June 4, 2006.

92. Carlo Petrini, *Slow Food Nation: Why Our Food Should Be Good, Clean, and Fair* (New York: Random House, 2007), 130.

93. A. Elizabeth Sloan, "What, When, and Where America Eats," *Food Technology* (2008): 20–29, at 25.

94. Sandra Tsing Loh, "Let's Call the Whole Thing Off," *Atlantic* (July–August 2009): 116–126, at 126.

95. GustOrganics, http://gustorganicsnyc.com.

96. Josée Johnston and Shyon Baumann, "Democracy versus Distinction: A Study of Omnivorousness in Gourmet Food Writing," *American Journal of Sociology* 113, no. 1 (2007): 165–204.

97. Organic Style, www.organicstyle.com/.

98. Mālie Organics, www.malie.com/.

99. John Masters Organics, www.johnmasters.com/so.htm.

100. Body Deli, https://thebodydeli.com/.

101. "Exfoliant," http://store.swbasicsofbk.com/products/exfoliant.

102. Harry & David, "Organic Options Club," www.harryanddavid.com.

103. CuisinArt Golf Resort and Spa, www.cuisinartresort.com/index.php?catID=33.

104. Jonny Fullpint, "Kona Brewing," *Full Pint* website, December 17, 2009, http://thefullpint.com/beer-news/kona-brewing-introduces-hawaii%E2%80%99s-first-certified-organic-beer/.

105. "Hangar 24 Polycot," http://hangar24brewery.com/co_local_polycot.htm.

106. Master of Malt, www.masterofmalt.com/whiskies/benromach-organic-whisky/.

107. Prairie Vodka, http://prairievodka.com/.

108. Square One Organic Sprits, www.squareoneorganicspirits.com/Singular Spirit/SSPIRIT_whyOrganic.html; Spirits.com.

109. Frey Vineyards, www.freywine.com/. All other prices obtained from company websites between 2010 and 2012.

110. Joe Dolce, "Mister Cool," *Gourmet* 28 (August 2008): 58–61, 118, at 61.

111. www.wolfgangpuckicedcoffee.com/benefits.html.

112. Zambeezi, "Our Product," www.zambeezi.com/our_product.

113. Virgin Vapor, "Organically Flavored E-Liquid," www.virginvapor.com /collections/organic-e-liquid.

114. Allison Aubrey and Jessica Goldstein, "Organic Water: A New Marketing Wave," *National Public Radio Health Blog*, July 13, 2011, www.npr.org/blogs/health /2011/07/13/137796144/organic-water-a-new-marketing-wave.

115. Ben Mutzabaugh, "Etihad Airways Makes Unusual Pitch: Grow Its Own Food," *USA Today*, June 25, 2012, http://travel.usatoday.com/flights/post/2012/06 /etihad-airline-food/788928/1.

116. Martin Cottingham and Elisabeth Winkler, "The Organic Consumer," in *The Handbook of Organic and Fair Trade Food Marketing*, ed. Simon Wright and Diane McCrea (Hoboken, NJ: John Wiley & Sons, 2007), 25–50, at 46.

117. John F. Wasik, *Green Marketing & Management: A Global Perspective* (Cambridge, MA: Blackwell, 1996), 144.

118. M. Sligh and C. Christman, *Who Owns Organic? The Global Status, Prospects and Challenges of a Changing Organic Market* (Pittsboro, NC: Rural Advancement Foundation International [RAFI-USA], 2003), 14.

119. J. I. Rodale, "With the Editor—The Work of Weston A. Price," *Organic Gardening* 7 (1945): 4–6, at 6.

120. J. I. Rodale, "Expensive Organic Foods," *Organic Gardening* 18, no. 1 (January 1951): 37.

121. Carolyn Dimitri and Kathryn M. Venezia, "Retail and Consumer Aspects of the Organic Milk Market," USDA, 2007, 1–18, at 3.

122. Ibid., 1.

123. Ibid., 11.

124. Amarijit Sahota, "The International Market for Organic and Fair Trade Food and Drink," in Wright and McCrea, *The Handbook of Organic and Fair Trade Food Marketing*, 1–24, at 25.

125. Cindy Burke, *To Buy or Not to Buy Organic: What You Need to Know to Choose the Healthiest, Safest, Most Earth-Friendly Food* (New York: Marlowe, 2009), 1.

126. Dimitri and Venezia, "Retail and Consumer Aspects," 1–18, at 3.

127. John Stevens-Garmon, Chung L. Huang, et al., "Organic Demand: A Profile of Consumers in the Fresh Produce Market," *CHOICES: The Magazine of Food, Farm, and Resource Issues* 22, no. 2 (2007): 109–132, at 110–111.

128. Catherine Greene, Carolyn Dimitri, et al., "Emerging Issues in the U.S. Organic Industry," USDA, 2009, 1–36, at 16.

129. Keith Stewart, *It's a Long Road to a Tomato: Tales of an Organic Farmer Who Quit the Big City for the (Not So) Simple Life* (New York: Marlowe, 2006), 19.

130. M. Wine, "The Food Gap," *Orion* 24, no. 5 (2005): 60–67, at 62.

131. Consumer Reports, "When It Pays to Buy Organic," *Consumer Reports*, February 2006, 12–17.

132. Shape, "Go Organic without Going Broke," *Shape* 28 (2009): 126.

133. S. Novak, "Sunflower Plans to Take Root in Austin's Natural Foods Market," *Austin American-Statesman*, June 3, 2008.

134. Sunflower Farmers Market, www.sunflowermarkets.com/.

135. Linda Watson, *Wildly Affordable Organic: Eat Fabulous Food, Get Healthy, and Save the Planet All on $5 a Day or Less* (Cambridge, MA: De Capo, 2011).

136. Guthman, "Fast Food/Organic Food," *Social & Cultural Geography* 4, no. 1 (2003): 43–56, at 45.

137. Environmental Working Group, *A Shopper's Guide to Pesticides in Produce* (Washington, DC: Environmental Working Group, 1995), 2.

138. Michael W. Fox, *Eating with Conscience: The Bioethics of Food* (Troutdale, OR: NewSage, 1997), 12.

139. Ibid., 166.

140. Fran McManus, ed., *Eating Fresh from the Organic Garden State: A Year-Round Guide to Cooking & Buying Local Organic Products* (Pennington, NJ: Northeast Organic Farming Association—New Jersey, 1997), ix.

141. Mothers & Others for a Livable Planet, *The Green Food Shopper: An Activist's Guide to Changing the Food System* (New York: Mothers & Others for a Livable Planet, 1997), 88.

142. Renee Elliott and Eric Treuillé, *The Organic Cookbook: Naturally Good Food* (New York: Dorling Kindersley, 2001), 7–9.

143. Clarke, Porter, et al., *Living Organic*, 106.

144. Greg Hottinger, *The Best Natural Foods on the Market Today: A Yuppie's Guide to Hippie Food* (Boulder, CO: Huckleberry Mountain Press, 2004), 1:24.

145. Goodall, *Harvest for Hope*, 169.

146. Leslie A. Duram, *Good Growing: Why Organic Farming Works* (Lincoln: University of Nebraska Press, 2005), x.

147. Cox, *The Organic Cook's Bible*, 217.

148. Ibid., 10.

149. Ellen Sandbeck, *Organic Housekeeping: In Which the Nontoxic Avenger Shows You How to Improve Your Health and That of Your Family While You Save Time, Money, and, Perhaps, Your Sanity* (New York: Scribner, 2006), 114.

150. Ken Roseboro, *The Organic Food Handbook: A Consumer's Guide to Buying and Eating Organic Food* (Laguna Beach, CA: Basic Health, 2007), 69.

151. Nestle, *What to Eat*, 521.

152. Ibid., 55.

153. Ibid., 66.

154. Sheryl Eisenberg, "Is Organic Food Worth It?," *This Green Life*, www.nrdc.org/thisgreenlife/.

155. S. Godin, "Organic Top 20," *Ode* 5, no. 10 (December 2007): 60–69, at 60.

156. Daniel Imhoff, *Food Fight: A Citizen's Guide to a Food and Farm Bill* (Healdsburg, CA: Watershed Media, 2012), 140.

157. Michael Pollan, *In Defense of Food: An Eater's Manifesto* (New York: Penguin, 2008), 14.

158. Diane MacEachern, *Big Green Purse: Use Your Spending Power to Create a Cleaner, Greener World* (New York: Avery, 2008), x.

159. Ibid., 164.

160. Papa's Organic, "Frequently Asked Questions," http://papasorganic.com/t-faq.aspx?#wheredoesyourproducecomefrom?

161. Wendy Johnson, *Gardening at the Dragon's Gate: At Work in the Wild and Cultivated World* (New York: Bantam, 2008), xiii.

162. Celia Barbour, "A Delicious Revolution," *O, the Oprah Magazine* 9 (2008): 292–299, at 294.

163. Samuel Hays, *Beauty, Health, and Permanence: Environmental Politics in the United States, 1955–1985* (New York: Cambridge University Press, 1989).

164. "Why Rodale's," www.rodales.com/why-rodales.html.

165. Annie Muldoon, "Where the Green Is: Examining the Paradox of Environmentally Conscious Consumption," *Electronic Green Journal* 23 (April 2006).

166. Daniel Goleman, *Ecological Intelligence: How Knowing the Hidden Impacts of What We Buy Can Change Everything* (New York: Broadway, 2009), 245.

167. Susan Strasser, "Making Consumption Conspicuous: Transgressive Topics Go Mainstream," *Technology and Culture* 43, no. 4 (October 2002): 755–770.

168. Kimberly Lau, *New Age Capitalism: Making Money East of Eden* (Philadelphia: University of Pennsylvania Press, 2000), 140.

169. Ibid., 14.

170. J. I. Rodale, "Miscellany: Looking Forward," *Organic Gardening* 20 (1952): 24–25, at 25.

171. Thomas Princen, Michael Maniates, et al., eds., *Confronting Consumption* (Cambridge, MA: MIT Press, 2002), 328.

172. Ibid., 321.

173. Ibid., 322, 325.

174. Ibid., 15.

175. Greene, Dimitri, et al., *Emerging Issues in the U.S. Organic Industry*, iii–iv.

176. Organic Trade Association, "U.S. Organic Sales Grow by a Whopping 17.1 Percent in 2008," Organic Trade Association, 2009, www.organicnewsroom.com/2009/05/us_organic_sales.

177. Keith Naughton, "Natural Response," *Newsweek*, May 3, 2008, www.newsweek.com/id/135377/output.

178. Katie Zezima, "Organic Dairies Watch the Good Times Turn Bad," *New York Times*, May 28, 2009.

179. "The Economy and You: More Home Cooking, Less Organic," *Cooking Light* 23 (2009): 66.

180. Organic Trade Association, "U.S. Organic Sales Grow."

181. Cool, *Simply Organic*, 14.

182. Terri Trespicio, "Martha Gets Real," *Body + Soul* (2009): 93.

183. Clara Hopkins, "Fads That Last: Experts Reveal Continuing Trends for 2010," Natural Foods Merchandiser, 2009, http://naturalfoodsmerchandiser.com/tabId/107/itemId/4360/Fads-that-last-Experts-reveal-continuing-trends-f.aspx.

184. Matthew Saltmarsh, "Increasing Appetite for Organic Products Defies a Weak Global Economy; Sector Attracts Investors as Sales in Europe and U.S. Continue to Grow," *International Herald Tribune*, Paris, May 25, 2011.

185. Anonymous, "Organic Farming Grows to $29-billion Industry," *Western Farm Press*, April 26, 2011.

186. Organic Trade Association, "2012 Press Releases," www.organicnewsroom.com /2012/04/us_consumerdriven_organic_mark.html.

187. Scott Hensley, "Organic Foods Have Broad Appeal, but Costs Temper Demand," *NPR Health* blog, July 20, 2011, www.npr.org/blogs/health/2011/07/20/138534183 /organic-foods-have-broad-appeal-but-costs-temper-demand.

188. Fred Wilkinson, "Survey Finds Deep Appeal for Organics," *Packer*, July 28, 2011, www.thepacker.com/opinion/Survey-finds-deep-appeal-for-organics—126321513 .html.

189. Produce Retailer, "Category Spotlight: Organic Produce," November 1, 2011, *Produce Retailer*, www.produceretailer.com/produce-retailer-categories/CATEGORY -SPOTLIGHT-Organic-Produce-132947073.html.

190. Saltmarsh, "Increasing Appetite for Organic Products," 19.

191. Mary Clare Jalonick, "Organic Food Industry Gains Clout on Capitol Hill, Causing Tensions within Congress," *Huffington Post*, May 17, 2013, www.huffington post.com/2013/05/17/organic-food-industry_n_3291908.html?utm_hp_ref=green.

192. Samuel Fromartz, "The (Not So) New Agtivist: Organic Movement Leader Bob Scowcroft Looks Back," *Grist.org*, February 7, 2011, http://grist.org/article/food-2011 −02−07-organic-movement-leader-bob-scowcroft-looks-back/.

193. Tom Karst, "'Monumental' Organic Agreement Signed by U.S., E.U.," *Packer*, February 15, 2012, www.thepacker.com/fruit-vegetable-enewsletter/organics-insider /Monumental-organic-agreement-signed-by-US-EU-139369043.html.

194. Tom Karst, "Still Waiting for Organic to Jump the Shark," *Packer*, February 24, 2012, www.thepacker.com/fruit-vegetable-enewsletter/organics-insider/Still -waiting-for-organic-to-jump-the-shark-140295703.html.

195. Celia San Miguel, "Ending Yo-Yo Dieting," *Latina* 16, no. 8 (June–July 2012): 60–62, at 62.

196. David Leyonhjelm, "Organic Food—It's a Religion," *Stock & Land*, July 3, 2012, http://sl.farmonline.com.au/blogs/agribuzz-with-david-leyonhjelm/organic-food -its-a-religion/2611131.aspx?storypage=0.

197. USDA Economic Research Service, "Data Sets: Organic Production," www .ers.usda.gov/Data/organic.

198. W. H. Allen, "Crucial Crusade," *Organic Gardening* 21 (1953): 21.

199. Nestle, *What to Eat*, 523.

200. J. I. Rodale, "An Open Letter to Readers," *Organic Gardening and Farming* 1 (1954): 53.

201. G. Kuepper and L. Gegner. "Organic Crop Production Overview," August 2004, http://guamsustainableag.org/organicfarming/organiccrop%20%285%2 9.pdf, 2.

202. Robert Rodale, "The Heart and Soul of Organic Gardening," *Organic Gardening* 39 (1992), 46.

203. Alberto Melucci, *Nomads of the Present: Social Movements and Individual Needs in Contemporary Society* (Philadelphia: Temple University Press, 1989), 29.

204. J. I. Rodale, "Editorial: Looking Back, Part III, Tradition Throttles Research," *Organic Gardening* 20 (1952): 10–11, at 11.

205. Allen, "Crucial Crusade," 21.

206. J. V. Chute, "Be a Salesman," *Organic Farmer* 3 (1951): 26–28, at 27.

207. J. I. Rodale, "Organic Food Crashes the Retail Market," *Organic Farmer* 2 (1951): 61.

208. Dan Sullivan, "Research Makes It Clear: Organic Food Is Best for People and the Planet," *Rootstock* 9, no. 1 (2009), 4–7, at 7.

Bibliography

Ableman, Michael. *Fields of Plenty: A Farmer's Journey in Search of Real Food and the People Who Grow It.* San Francisco: Chronicle, 2005.

———. *On Good Land: The Autobiography of an Urban Farm.* San Francisco, Chronicle, 1998.

"About INNA jam." http://innajam.com/pages/know.

Adams, N. "Forum: The Case against Organic Farming—Farming with Chemicals May Be Best for Wildlife." *New Scientist* 127, no. 1734 (1990).

Allaby, Michael, and Floyd Allen. *Robots behind the Plow: Modern Farming and the Need for an Organic Alternative.* Emmaus, PA: Rodale, 1974.

Allen, W. H. "Crucial Crusade." *Organic Gardening* 21 (1953): 21.

Althusser, Louis. "Ideology and Ideological State Apparatuses." In *Lenin and Philosophy, and Other Essays*, 85–126. New York: Monthly Review Press, 2001.

Annett, L. E., V. Muralidharan, et al. "Influence of Health and Environmental Information on Hedonic Evaluation of Organic and Conventional Bread." *Journal of Food Science* 73, no. 4 (2008): 1–14.

Arena, P. "Why I Operate an Organic Stand." *Organic Gardening* 20 (1952): 16–17, 46–47.

Arrowhead Mills website. www.arrowheadmills.com/.

Arvola, Anne, Marco Vassallo, et al. "Predicting Intentions to Purchase Organic Food: The Role of Affective and Moral Attitudes in the Theory of Planned Behaviour." *Appetite* 50, nos. 2/3 (March 2008): 443–454.

Ashley, Bob, Joanne Hollows, et al. *Food and Cultural Studies.* New York: Routledge, 2004.

Atrens, Dale M. *Don't Diet.* New York: William Morrow, 1988.

Avery, Alex A. *The Truth about Organic Foods.* Chesterfield, MO: Henderson, 2006.

Avery, Dennis T. "The Fallacy of the Organic Utopia." In *Fearing Food: Risk, Health, and Environment*, ed. J. Morris and R. Bate, 3–18. Boston: Butterworth-Heinemann, 1999.

———. *Saving the Planet with Pesticides and Plastic: The Environmental Triumph of High-Yield Farming.* Indianapolis, IN: Hudson Institute, 1995.

Bailey, L. H. *The Country-Life Movement in the United States.* New York: Macmillan, 1911.

Bailey, Sarah. "Gwyneth Unveiled." *Harper's Bazaar*, May 2013, 228–231, 266.

Balfour, Eve B. *The Living Soil.* London: Faber and Faber, 1948.

Baltad, N. "Organic Foods: Skepticism." *Los Angeles Times*, June 30, 1972, 8.

Baltaz, Diane P. *Why We Do It: Organic Farmers on Farming*. Ayr, Ontario: Sand Plains, 1998.

Barbour, Celia. "A Delicious Revolution." *O, the Oprah Magazine* 9 (2008): 292–299.

Barclay, Hartley W. "New Products Aid in Farm Economy: Chemicals Developed to Cut 'Stoop Labor' Costs by as Much as 50% Products Seen at Plant Exhibit Part of Vast Program of American Cyanamid to Mechanize Agriculture." *New York Times*, May 20, 1950.

Barrett, W. "The Organic Way of Gardening and Its Prophet." *Smithsonian* 2 (1971): 52–55.

Barthes, Roland. *Mythologies*. New York: Hill and Wang, 1995.

Bateman, H. P. "Letters." *Organic Farmer* 4 (1953): 6.

Baudrillard, Jean. *The System of Objects*. New York: Verso, 1996.

Beaumont, A. B. "Biochemical Gardening." *Horticulture* 30, no. 10 (1952): 388.

Beck, Malcolm. *Lessons in Nature*. Austin, TX: Acres USA, 2005.

Beeman, Randal S., and James A. Pritchard. *A Green and Permanent Land: Ecology and Agriculture in the Twentieth Century*. Lawrence: University Press of Kansas, 2001.

Beeson, K. C. "Spring Gardens: What about the 'Organic' Way?" *New York Times*, April 16, 1972.

Belanger, Jerome. "Correcting Some Misconceptions about Organic Farming." *Organic Farming: Yesterday's and Tomorrow's Agriculture*, ed. R. Wolf, 7–20. Emmaus, PA: Rodale, 1977.

Belasco, Warren. *Appetite for Change: How the Counterculture Took on the Food Industry, 1966–1988*. New York: Pantheon, 1989.

Benbrook, C. "Elevating Antioxidant Levels in Food through Organic Farming and Food Processing." *State of Science Review*, Organic Center (2005): 1–6.

Benbrook, C., X. Zhao, et al. "New Evidence Confirms the Nutritional Superiority of Plant-Based Organic Foods." Organic Center (2008): 1–50.

Berry, Wendall. *The Art of the Commonplace*. Washington, DC: Counterpoint, 2002.

———. *Home Economics*. San Francisco: North Point, 1987.

———. "In Distrust of Movements." In *In the Presence of Fear: Three Essays for a Changed World*, 35–44. Great Barrington, MA: Orion Society 2001.

Billington, F. H. *Compost for Garden Plot or Thousand-Acre Farm: A Practical Guide to Modern Methods*. Boston: Charles T. Branford, 1956.

Bittman, Mark. "Eating Food That's Better for You, Organic or Not." *New York Times*, March 22, 2009.

Blake, Francis. *Organic Farming and Growing*. Wiltshire, UK: Crowood, 1990.

The Body Deli website. https://thebodydeli.com/.

Bolton, D. "Costco Nurtures Growth of Organics." www.naturalfoodnet.com.

Borsodi, Ralph. *Flight from the City: The Story of a New Way to Family Security*. New York: Harper & Brothers, 1933.

Bosso, Christopher J. *Environment, Inc.: From Grassroots to Beltway*. Lawrence: University Press of Kansas, 2005.

Bourdieu, Pierre. *Distinction: A Social Critique of the Judgement of Taste.* Cambridge, MA: Harvard University Press, 1984.

Bové, Jose, and Francois DuFour. *The World Is Not for Sale: Farmers against Junk Food.* New York: Verso, 2001.

Briggs, B. "Going Organic: Enthusiastic Consumers Join Craze." *Denver Post*, August 19, 2001, 1–5.

Bromfield, Louis. *From My Experience: The Pleasures and Miseries of Life on a Farm.* New York: Harper & Brothers, 1955.

———. *Malabar Farm.* New York: Harper & Brothers, 1948.

———. *Pleasant Valley.* New York: Harper & Brothers, 1945.

Brown, Louis. *Organic Living: Simple Solutions for a Better Life.* New York: Dorling Kindersley, 2000.

Bryant, G. "J. I. Rodale: Pollution Prophet." *Penthouse* 2 (1971): 28–32.

Buechner, M. M. "A New Cash Cow." *Time*, July 8, 2003.

Burke, Cindy. *To Buy or Not to Buy Organic: What You Need to Know to Choose the Healthiest, Safest, Most Earth-Friendly Food.* New York: Marlowe, 2007.

Burros, Marian. "Is Whole Foods Straying from Its Roots?" *New York Times*, February 28, 2007.

Business Week. "Rodale Reaches Out for the Mainstream." *Business Week* (October 27, 1980): 85.

Business Wire. "National Survey: Green Is Officially Mainstream—but Consumers Are Confused, Skeptical about Products." *Business Wire*, June 30, 2009. www .businesswire.com/news/home/20090630005830/en.

Buskirk, R. G. V. "Pesticide Formulators and Dealers, Have Confidence in Your Product!" *Farm Chemicals*, March 1970.

Butz, Earl. "Agriblunders." *Growth and Change* 9, no. 2 (1978): 52.

———. "Crisis or Challenge." *Nation's Agriculture* 19 (July–August 1971): 19.

Calvin, R. H. "Club News." *Organic Gardening.* 10 (1947): 53.

Cascadian Farm website. www.cascadianfarm.com/home.aspx.

Castree, N. "Socializing Nature: Theory, Practice, and Politics." In *Social Nature: Theory, Practice and Politics*, ed. N. Castree and B. Braun. Oxford: Blackwell, 2001.

Celestial Seasonings website. www.celestialseasonings.com/index.html.

Cerulo, K. A. "Identity Construction: New Issues, New Directions." *Annual Review of Sociology* 23 (1997): 385–409.

Chaskey, Scott. *This Common Ground: Seasons on an Organic Farm.* New York: Viking, 2005.

Chipotle website. "Food With Integrity." www.chipotle.com/en-us/fwi/environment /environment.aspx.

Chute, J. V. "Be a Salesman." *Organic Farmer* 3 (1951): 26–28.

"City Bakery Brands." www.thecitybakery.com/birdbath.

Clark, Matt. "Diet Crazes." *Newsweek*, December 19, 1977, 67.

Clark, William A. "All-Around Element: Versatile Phosphorus Grabs Many New Jobs; Output Climbs Sharply One New Compound Way Rival DDT; Others Cut Costs for Fertilizer Dealers the Story of Hennig Brandt All-Around Element: Phosphorus Grabs New Jobs; Output Climbs." *Wall Street Journal*, March 18, 1955.

Clarke, Adrienne, Helen Porter, et al., eds. *Living Organic: Easy Steps to an Organic Family Lifestyle*. Naperville, IL: Sourcebooks, 2001.

Claval, P. "Reading the Rural Landscapes." *Landscape and Urban Planning* 70 (2005): 17.

Cloud, J. "My Search for the Perfect Apple." *Time* 169 (2007): 42–50.

Clute, J. V. "Even Indians Eat Organically." *Organic Gardening and Farming* 1 (1954): 42–43.

Cocannouer, Joseph. *Farming with Nature*. Norman: University of Oklahoma Press, 1954.

———. *Weeds: Guardians of the Soil*. New York: Devin-Adair, 1950.

Coghlan, A. "Digging the Dirt: Fans Say Organic Foods Are Best, but Are They Just Full of Manure?" *New Scientist* 171, no. 2303 (2001): 15.

———. "Going Back to Nature Down on the Farm." *New Scientist* 166, no. 2241 (2000): 20.

Cohen, Anthony P. *The Symbolic Construction of Community*. New York: Tavistock, 1985.

Colamosca, A. "Health Foods Prosper despite High Prices." *New York Times*, November 17, 1974, 205.

Coleman, Eliot. "Can Organics Save the Family Farm?" *The Rake* (2004). www.secretsofthecity.com/magazine/reporting/features/can-organics-save-family-farm.

Coleman, Eliot, and Sheri Amsel. *The New Organic Grower: A Master's Manual of Tools and Techniques for the Home and Market Gardener*. White River Junction, VT: Chelsea Green, 1995.

Coleman, Eliot, and Barbara Damrosch. *Four-Season Harvest: Organic Vegetables from Your Home Garden All Year Long*. White River Junction, VT, Chelsea Green, 1999.

Committee on the Role of Alternative Farming Methods in Modern Production Agriculture. *Alternative Agriculture*. Washington, DC, National Academy Press, 1989.

Conford, Philip, and Jonathan Dimbleby. *The Origins of the Organic Movement*. Edinburgh: Floris, 2001.

Conner, D. S. *The Organic Label and Sustainable Agriculture: Consumer Preferences and Values*. PhD diss., Cornell University, 2002.

Consumer Reports. "When It Pays to Buy Organic." *Consumer Reports* (2006): 12–17.

Cook, Christopher D. *Diet for a Dead Planet: How the Food Industry Is Killing Us*. New York: New Press, 2004.

Cool, Jesse Ziff, and France Ruffenach. *Simply Organic: A Cookbook for Sustainable, Seasonal, and Local Ingredients*. San Francisco: Chronicle, 2008.

Corley, Hugh. *Organic Small Farming*. Pauma Valley, CA: Bargyla and Gylver Rateaver, 1975.

Cottingham, Martin, and Elisabeth Winkler. "The Organic Consumer." In *The Handbook of Organic and Fair Trade Food Marketing*, ed. Simon Wright and Diane McCrea, 25–50. Hoboken, NJ: John Wiley & Sons, 2007.

Cox, Jeff. *The Organic Cook's Bible: How to Select and Cook the Best Ingredients on the Market.* Hoboken, NJ: John Wiley & Sons, 2006.

——. *The Organic Food Shopper's Guide.* Hoboken, NJ: John Wiley & Sons, 2008.

Cranebrock, Allen Van. "Death Valley Crop." *Wall Street Journal,* September 10, 1954.

Cronon, W. "A Place for Stories: Nature, History, and Narrative." *Journal of American History* 78, no. 4 (1992).

——. "The Uses of Environmental History." *Environmental History Review* 17, no. 3 (1993).

Cussler, Margaret, and Mary L. DeGive. *'Twixt the Cup and the Lip: Psychological and Socio-Cultural Factors Affecting Food Habits.* New York: Twayne, 1952.

Damrosch, Barbara. *The Garden Primer: The Completely Revised Gardener's Bible.* New York: Workman, 2008.

Darby, Kim, Marvin T. Batte, et al. "Willingness to Pay for Locally Produced Foods: A Customer Intercept Study of Direct Market and Grocery Store Shoppers." *American Agricultural Economics Association Annual Meeting.* Long Beach, California, 2006.

Dargis, M. "Meet Your New Farmer: Hungry Corporate Giant." *New York Times,* June 12, 2009.

Darlington, Jeanie. *Grow Your Own: An Introduction to Organic Gardening.* Berkeley, CA: Bookworks, 1970.

Davis, Adelle. *Let's Cook It Right.* New York: Harcourt Brace Jovanovich, 1970.

Davis, Robert J. *The Healthy Skeptic: Cutting through the Hype about Your Health.* Berkeley: University of California Press, 2008.

De Certeau, Michael. *The Practice of Everyday Life.* Berkeley: University of California Press, 1988.

DeGregori, Thomas R. *Origins of the Organic Agriculture Debate.* Ames: Iowa State University Press, 2004.

Demeritt, D. "Being Constructive about Nature." In *Social Nature: Theory, Practice and Politics,* ed. N. Castree and B. Braun, 21–40. Oxford: Blackwell, 2001.

Demeter Association. "Position Paper on Organic Foods Production Act of 1990." *Biodynamics* 203 (1996): 10–11.

"Denise's Balancing Act." *US Weekly* 947 (April 8, 2013): 56.

Dichter, Ernest. *Handbook of Consumer Motivations.* New York: McGraw Hill, 1964.

Dimitri, Carolyn, and Catherine Greene. *Recent Growth Patterns in the U.S. Organic Foods Market.* Washington, DC, USDA, 2002.

Dimitri, Carolyn, and Kathryn M. Venezia. "Retail and Consumer Aspects of the Organic Milk Market." USDA, 2007.

Dodge, L. F. "Planning Organic Profits." *Organic Farmer* 1 (1950): 15–18.

Dolce, Joe. "Mister Cool." *Gourmet* 28 (2008): 58–61, 118.

Doliner, J. D. "Growing Our Industry from Within: Meeting an Aggressive Demand Curve with Outside Investment Capital." In *IFOAM 2000—the World Grows Organic: Proceedings of the 13th International IFOAM Scientific Conference,* ed. T. Alföldi, W. Lockeretz, and U. Niggli. Basel, Switzerland: vdf Hochschulverlag AG an der ETH Zurich, 2000.

Dorfman, Josh. *The Lazy Environmentalist: Your Guide to Easy, Stylish, Green Living.* New York: Stewart, Tabori & Chang, 2007.

Douglas, Mark, and Baron Isherwood. *The World of Goods: Towards an Anthropology of Consumption.* New York: Basic, 1979.

Dowding, Charles. *Organic Gardening: The Natural No-Dig Way.* Foxhole, Devon: Green Books, 2007.

Driscoll, R. A. "California Compost." *Organic Gardening* 6 (1945): 24.

Duchy Originals. www.duchyoriginals.com/.

DuPuis, E. Melanie. *Nature's Perfect Food: How Milk Became America's Drink.* New York: New York University Press, 2002.

Duram, Leslie A. *Good Growing: Why Organic Farming Works.* Lincoln: University of Nebraska Press, 2005.

Earthbound Farm website. www.ebfarm.com/.

Easey, Ben. *Practical Organic Gardening.* London: Faber and Faber, 1976.

East West Journal. *Shopper's Guide to Natural Foods.* Garden City Park, NY: Avery, 1987.

"The Economy and You: More Home Cooking, Less Organic." *Cooking Light* 23 (2009): 66.

Ecowatch. "Monsanto's Dark History." http://readersupportednews.org/opinion2/271 –38/16828-focus-monsantos-dark-history.

Eden Foods, "About Eden." www.edenfoods.com/about/.

Edwards, J. G. "DDT Is Great Benefactor of Mankind against Pests." *Texas Agriculture,* March 1970.

Edwards, R. "The Natural Choice: Organic Food Has More of What It Takes to Keep You Healthy." *New Scientist* 173, no. 2334 (2002): 10.

Edwards, S. W. "Grindstone Run Becomes a Summer Stream." *Bio-Dynamics* 10, no. 3 (1952): 20–23.

———. "Grindstone Run Empties into the Potomac." *Bio-Dynamics* 4, no. 3 (1948): 20–24.

Eisenberg, Sheryl. "Is Organic Food Worth It?" *This Green Life,* 2007. www.nrdc.org /thisgreenlife/.

Elliott, Renee J., and Eric Treuillé. *The Organic Cookbook: Naturally Good Food.* New York: Dorling Kindersley, 2000.

Elmer-DeWitt, P. "Fat Times: What Health Craze?" *Time,* January 16, 1995.

Engel, Cindy. *The Gaia Book of Organic Gardening.* London: Gaia Books, 2005.

Environmental Working Group. "EWG's 2012 Shopper's Guide to Pesticides in Produce." 2012. www.ewg.org/foodnews/.

———. *A Shopper's Guide to Pesticides in Produce.* Washington, DC: Environmental Working Group, 1995.

Eyerman, Ron, and Andrew Jamison. *Social Movements: A Cognitive Approach.* Cambridge: Polity, 1991.

Fairweather, J. R. "Understanding How Farmers Choose between Organic and Conventional Production: Results from New Zealand and Policy Implications." *Agriculture and Human Values* 16 (1999): 51–63.

Fallon, Sally. *Nourishing Traditions: The Cookbook That Challenges Politically Correct Nutrition and the Diet Dictocrats.* Washington, DC: New Trends, 2001.

FAO/WHO Food Standards Programme. *Codex Alimentarius: Organically Produced Foods.* Rome: Food and Agriculture Organization of the United Nations World Health Organization, 2001.

Farm and Food Policy Project. Seeking Balance in U.S. Farm and Food Policy. 2007. www.farmandfoodproject.org.

Fearless Chocolate website. http://shop.fearlesschocolate.com/70-superfruit/.

Flaccus, G. "California's First Health Guru, Gypsy Boots, Dead at Age 89." *Sign On San Diego*, August 9, 2004. www.signonsandiego.com/news/state/20040809-2136 -ca-bit-gypsyboots.html.

Flores, Heather C. *Food Not Lawns: How to Turn Your Yard into a Garden and Your Neighborhood into a Community.* White River Junction, VT: Chelsea Green, 2006.

Flowerdew, Bob. *The Organic Gardening Bible: Successful Gardening the Natural Way.* Lanham, MD: Taylor Trade, 1998.

Fonda, Daren. "Organic Growth." *Time*, May 12, 2002.

Ford, Frank. "My Life in Organics." In *Taste Life! The Organic Choice*, ed. David Richard and Dorie Byers. Bloomington, IL: Vital Health, 1998.

Forrer, Graydon, Alex Avery, and John Carlisle. "Marketing & The Organic Food Industry: A History of Food Fears, Market Manipulation and Misleading Consumers." September 2000.

Foster, C., K. Green, et al. *Environmental Impacts of Food Production and Consumption: A Report to the Department for Environment, Food and Rural Affairs.* Defra, London: Manchester Business School, 2006.

Foucault, Michel. *The History of Sexuality.* Vol. 1, *An Introduction.* New York: Vintage, 1990.

Fox, Michael W. *Eating with Conscience: The Bioethics of Food.* Troutdale, OR: NewSage, 1997.

Frey Vineyards website. www.freywine.com/.

Fromartz, Samuel. *Organic, Inc.: Natural Foods and How They Grew.* Orlando, FL: Harcourt, 2006.

Fukuoka, Masanobu. *The One-Straw Revolution: An Introduction to Natural Farming.* Mapusa, Goa, India: Other India Press, 1992.

Gardenhire, F. J. "The Crime of Abandoned Farms." *Organic Farming and Gardening* 1 (1942): 13–15.

Garden Organic. *Grow Organic.* New York: DK Adult, 2008.

Gardner, Frank D. *Traditional American Farming Techniques.* Guilford, CT: Lyons, 2001.

Gibbons, Euell. *Stalking the Good Life: My Love Affair with Nature.* New York: David McKay Company, 1971.

———. *Stalking the Wild Asparagus.* New York: David McKay, 1962.

Gibbs, N. "Power Gardening." *Time*, May 12, 1995.

Gillman, Jeff. *The Truth about Organic Gardening: Benefits, Drawbacks, and the Bottom Line.* Portland, OR: Timber, 2008.

Glacken, Clarence J. *Traces on the Rhodian Shore: Nature and Culture in Western*

Thought from Ancient Times to the End of the Eighteenth Century. Berkeley: University of California Press, 1967.

Glasstone, Samuel, and Violette Glasstone. *The Food You Eat: A Practical Guide to Home Nutrition.* Norman: University of Oklahoma Press, 1943.

Godin, S. "Organic Top 20." *Ode* 5, no. 10 (December 2007): 60–69.

Goldman, M. C., and William H. Hylton, eds. *The Basic Book of Organically Grown Foods.* Emmaus, PA: Rodale, 1972.

Goldstein, Jerome, ed. *The Organic Gardening Guide to Organic Living: San Francisco Bay Area Edition.* Emmaus, PA: Rodale, 1970.

Goldstein, Michael. *The Health Movement: Promoting Fitness in America.* New York: Twayne, 1992.

Goldstein, R. "Earl L. Butz, Secretary Felled by Racial Remark, Is Dead at 98." *New York Times,* February 4, 2008.

Goleman, Daniel. *Ecological Intelligence: How Knowing the Hidden Impacts of What We Buy Can Change Everything.* New York: Broadway, 2009.

Goodall, Jane. *Harvest for Hope: A Guide to Mindful Eating.* New York: Warner, 2005.

Goodman, D. "Foodtopia." *Eating Well* 8 (2009): 50–56, 81.

———. "Organic and Conventional Agriculture: Materializing Discourse and Agro-Ecological Managerialism." *Agriculture and Human Values* 17 (2000): 215–219.

Goodman, Myra. *Food to Live By: The Earthbound Farm Organic Cookbook.* New York: Workman, 2006.

Gould, Rebecca Kneale. *At Home in Nature: Modern Homesteading and Spiritual Practice in America.* Berkeley: University of California Press, 2005.

———. "Modern Homesteading in America: Religious Quests and the Restraints of Religion." *Social Compass* 44, no. 1 (1997): 157–170.

Gramsci, Antonio. "Notes for an Introduction and an Approach to the Study of Philosophy and the History of Culture: Some Preliminary Reference Points." In *The Antonio Gramsci Reader,* ed. D. Forgacs, 323–343. New York: New York University Press, 2000.

———. *Selections from the Prison Notebooks of Antonio Gramsci.* New York: International, 1971.

Granstedt, A., and L. Kjellenberg. "Long-Term Field Experiment in Sweden: Effects of Organic and Inorganic Fertilizers on Soil Fertility and Crop Quality." In *Proceedings of an International Conference in Boston, Tufts University, Agricultural Production and Nutrition,* 1–11. Boston: Tufts University, 1997.

Greenburg, A. "Searching for Alternatives in Education: The Homestead School." *Green Revolution* 35, no. 5 (1978): 19–21.

Greene, Catherine, Carolyn Dimitri, et al. "Emerging Issues in the U.S. Organic Industry." USDA, 2009.

Greene, Wade. "Guru of the Organic Food Cult." *New York Times Magazine,* June 8, 1971, 30, 31, 54, 56, 60, 65, 68.

Gregson, Bob, and Bonnie Gregson. *Rebirth of the Small Family Farm: A Handbook for Starting a Successful Organic Farm Based on the Community Supported Agriculture Concept.* Vashon Island, WA: Island Meadow Farm, 1996.

Grimes, William. "A Pleasure Palace without the Guilt." *New York Times*, 2004.

Gussow, Joan Dye. "Can an Organic Twinkie™ Be Certified?" In *For ALL Generations: Making World Agriculture More Sustainable*, ed. J. Patrick Madden and Scott G. Chaplowe, 143–153. West Hollywood, CA: World Sustainable Agriculture Association, 1997.

———. *This Organic Life: Confessions of a Suburban Homesteader*. White River Junction, VT: Chelsea Green, 2001.

———. "The Real Story of 'O.'" *Organic Gardening* 49, no. 5 (2002): 49.

GustOrganics website. http://gustorganicsnyc.com.

Guthman, Julie. *Agrarian Dreams: The Paradox of Organic Farming in California*. Berkeley: University of California Press, 2004.

———. (2003). "Fast Food/ Organic Food: Reflexive Tastes and the Making of 'Yuppie Chow.'" *Journal of Social and Cultural Geography* 4, no. 1 (2003): 43–56.

———. "Regulating Meaning, Appropriating Nature: The Codification of California Organic Agriculture." *Antipode* 30, no. 2 (1998): 135–154.

———. "The Trouble with 'Organic Lite' in California: A Rejoinder to the 'Conventionalisation' Debate." *Sociologia Ruralis* 44, no. 3 (2004): 301–316.

Gwynne, San. "Born Green." *Saveur*, May 26, 2009, 27–30.

———. "Retail." *Texas Monthly* 34 (2006): 116–121, 191–193.

———. "Thriving on Health Food." *Time*, February 23, 1998.

Hain Celestial Group. 2004 Annual Report. Melville, NY: Hain Celestial Group, 2005.

Hain Pure Foods website. www.hainpurefoods.com/index.php.

Hall, S. "Notes on Deconstructing 'the Popular.'" In *People's History and Socialist Theory*, ed. R. Samuel, 227–240. London: Routledge & Kegan Paul, 1981.

———. "Who Needs 'Identity'?" In *Questions of Cultural Identity*, ed. S. Hall and P. D. Gay, 1–17. London: Sage, 1996.

Halweil, B. "Eating at Home." *Ode* 3 (2005): 34–46.

———. "Organic Gold Rush." Washington, DC: Worldwatch Institute, 2001.

Hamilton, Geoff. *The Organic Garden Book*. New York: DK, 1993.

"Hangar 24 Polycot." http://hangar24brewery.com/co_local_polycot.htm.

Hanson, Victor Davis. *The Land Was Everything: Letters from an American Farmer*. New York: Free Press, 2000.

Harris, Susan. "Garden Rant: Ethne Clarke and the Makeover of Organic Gardening." 2010. www.gardenrant.com/my_weblog/2010/01/ethne-clark-and-og-mag.html.

Harry & David. "Organic Options Club." 2008. www.harryanddavid.com.

Hays, Samuel. *Beauty, Health, and Permanence: Environmental Politics in the United States, 1955–1985*. New York: Cambridge University Press, 1987.

Heasman, Michael, and Julian Mellentin. *The Functional Foods Revolution: Healthy People, Healthy Profits?* Sterling, VA: Earthscan, 2001.

Heiser, Charles B., Jr. *Seed to Civilization: The Story of Man's Food*. San Francisco: W. H. Freeman, 1973.

Helmer, J. "Get Growing!" *Natural Solutions* 117 (June 2009): 65–68.

Henderson, E., R. Mandelbaum, et al. *Toward Social Justice and Economic Equity in the Food System: A Call for Social Stewardship Standards in Sustainable and Or-*

ganic Agriculture. Pittsboro, NC: Rural Advancement Foundation International (RAFI-USA), 2003.

Hendley, J. "The Sweet & The Sour." *Eating Well* 8 (2009): 40–41.

Hershey, J. W. "Organic Farming and Its Influence on the Health of Soil, Plants, Animals and Man." *Bio-Dynamics* 6, no. 3 (1948): 11–19.

Hetherington, Kregg. *Cultivating Utopia: Organic Farmers in a Conventional Landscape*. Halifax, NS: Fernwood, 2005.

Hewitt, Jean *The New York Times Natural Foods Cookbook*. New York: New York Times Book, 1971.

Hightower, J. "The Hightower Report." *Austin Chronicle* 28 (2009): 21.

Hirshberg, Gary. *Stirring It Up: How to Make Money and Save the World*. New York: Hyperion, 2008.

———. "UK Study Misleads Public by Ignoring Documented Health and Environmental Benefits of Organic Food." 2009. www.huffingtonpost.com/gary-hirshberg/.

Hollis, B. J. "Sonnewald Homestead." *Green Revolution* 33, no. 11 (1976): 16–17.

Holt, Georgiana. "A Conceptual Model of Willingness to Pay for Organic food in the UK." In *Sociological Perspectives of Organic Agriculture: From Pioneer to Policy*, ed. Georgiana Holt and Matthew Reed, 88–106. Oxfordshire, UK: CAB International, 2006.

Holusha, J. "Folksy Rodale Emerges as Hard-Driving Marketer." *New York Times*, June 27, 1992.

Honkanen, Piro, Bas Verplanken, et al. "Ethical Values and Motives Driving Organic Food Choice." *Journal of Consumer Behaviour* 5 (September/October 2006): 420–430.

Hopkins, C. "Fads That Last: Experts Reveal Continuing Trends for 2010." http://naturalfoodsmerchandiser.com/tabId/107/itemId/4360/Fads-that-last-Experts-reveal-continuing-trends-f.aspx.

Horizon Dairy. www.horizondairy.com/.

Horizon Organic website. www.horizonorganic.com/.

Horowitz, Janice M. "Bye-Bye Tofu; Hello, Truffles!" *Time*, March 19, 1990.

Hottinger, Gregg. *The Best Natural Foods on the Market Today: A Yuppie's Guide to Hippie Food*. Vol. 1. Boulder, CO: Huckleberry Mountain Press, 2004.

Howard, Albert. *An Agricultural Testament*. New York: Oxford University Press, 1943.

———. "Introduction." In *Pay Dirt: Farming and Gardening with Composts*, vii. New York: Devin-Adair, 1948.

———. "Organic Campaign." *Organic Gardening* 10 (1947): 19.

———. *The Soil and Health: A Study of Organic Agriculture*. New York: Devin-Adair, 1947.

HRH The Prince of Wales and Charles Clover. *Highgrove: An Experiment in Organic Gardening and Farming*. New York: Simon & Schuster, 1993.

HRH The Prince of Wales and Stephanie Donaldson. *The Elements of Organic Gardening: Highgrove, Clarence House, Birkhall*. Carlsbad, CA: Kales, 2007.

Hughston, L. "Crusading Zeal Abounds in Health Food Sales." *Washington Post*, September 27, 1959.

Hunter, Beatrice Trum. *The Natural Foods Primer: Help for the Bewildered Beginner.* New York: Simon and Schuster, 1972.

Hylton, William H., ed. *Organically Grown Foods: What They Are and Why You Need Them.* Emmaus, PA: Rodale, 1973.

Iacobbo, Karen, and Michael Iacobbo. *Vegetarian America: A History.* Westport, CT: Praeger, 2004.

———. *Vegetarians and Vegans in America Today.* Westport, CT: Praeger, 2006.

IFOAM website. www.ifoam.org/.

Ikerd, J. "Contradictions of Principles in Organic Farming." In *Organic Agriculture: A Global Perspective*, ed. P. Kristiansen, A. Taji, and J. Reganold, 221–229. Ithaca, NY: Comstock, 2006.

———. *Small Farms Are Real Farms: Sustaining People through Agriculture.* Austin, TX: Acres USA, 2008.

Imhoff, Daniel. *Farming with the Wild: Enhancing Biodiversity on Farms and Ranches.* San Francisco: Sierra Club Books, 2003.

———. *Food Fight: A Citizen's Guide to a Food and Farm Bill.* Healdsburg, CA: Watershed Media, 2007.

Ingram, M. "Biology and Beyond: The Science of 'Back to Nature' Farming in the United States." *Annals of the Association of American Geographers* 97, no. 2 (2007): 298–312.

International Food Information Council (IFIC) Foundation. *2008 Food & Health Survey: Consumer Attitudes toward Food, Nutrition & Health.* Washington, DC: IFIC Foundation, 2008.

Iowa State University. "Iowa State University Organic Agriculture website." http://extension.agron.iastate.edu/organicag/.

Ivanko, John, and Lisa Kivirist. *Rural Renaissance: Renewing the Quest for the Good Life.* Gabriola Island, BC: New Society, 2004.

Jackson, Carlton. *J. I. Rodale: Apostle of Nonconformity.* New York: Pyramid, 1974.

Jacob, Jeffery Carl. *New Pioneers: The Back-to-the-Land Movement and the Search for a Sustainable Future.* University Park: Pennsylvania State University Press, 1997.

Jalonick, Mary Clare. "Organic Food Industry Gains Clout on Capitol Hill, Causing Tensions within Congress." *Huffington Post*, May 17, 2013. www.huffingtonpost.com/2013/05/17/organic-food-industry_n_3291908.html?utm_hp_ref=green.

Jaret, P. "A Growing Trend." *Cooking Light* 22 (2008): 30–34.

Jefferson, Thomas. *Notes on the State of Virginia.* New York: Harper & Row, 1964.

Jenkins, Dorothy H. "AROUND THE GARDEN." *New York Times*, June 11, 1944.

Jenks, Jorian. *The Stuff Man's Made Of: The Positive Approach to Health through Nutrition.* London: Faber and Faber, 1959.

John Masters Organics website. www.johnmasters.com/so.htm.

Johnson, Wendy. *Gardening at the Dragon's Gate: At Work in the Wild and Cultivated World.* New York: Bantam, 2008.

Johnston, Josée, and Shyon Baumann. "Democracy versus Distinction: A Study of Omnivorousness in Gourmet Food Writing." *American Journal of Sociology* 113, no. 1 (2007): 165–204.

Jolly, D. "From Cottage Industry to Conglomerates: The Transformation of the U.S. Organic Foods Industry." In *IFOAM 2000—the World Grows Organic: Proceedings of the 13th International IFOAM Scientific Conference*, ed. T. Alföldi, W. Lockeretz, and U. Niggli. Basel, Switzerland: vdf Hochschulverlag AG an der ETH Zurich, 2000.

Jordi, Nathalie. "Food's Golden State." *Bon Appétit* 54 (2009): 116–123.

———. "The Garden Bus Guys." *Bon Appétit* 54 (2009): 26.

Keane, T. "A Bitter Reality." *Boston Globe Magazine*, June 28, 2009, 12.

King, C. G. "Good Nutrition in the Shopper's Basket." In *A Report to the Nation: "The Good in Your Food": Reprinted from the Proceedings of the 23rd Annual Convention of Super Market Institute*, 2–5. Chicago: Super Market Institute, 1960.

King, Franklin Hiram. *Farmers of Forty Centuries*. Emmaus, PA: Organic Gardening Press, 1955.

Kirk, Andrew G. *Counterculture Green: The Whole Earth Catalog and American Environmentalism*. Lawrence: University Press of Kansas, 2007.

Kirschenmann, F. "Hijacking of Organic Agriculture . . . and How USDA Is Facilitating the Theft." *Ecology and Farming: International IFOAM magazine*, May 2000.

———. "What's News in Organic." *Biodynamics* 203 (1996): 10–12.

Kleinfeld, N. R. "Rodale Press: Organic Venture." *New York Times*, November 19, 1979.

Kohn, Bernice. *The Organic Living Book*. New York: Viking, 1972.

Kremen, Amy, Catherine Greene, et al. *Organic Produce, Price Premiums, and Eco-Labeling in U.S. Farmers' Markets*. Washington, DC: USDA, 2003.

Kristiansen, Paul, and Charles Merfield. "Overview of Organic Agriculture." In *Organic Agriculture: A Global Perspective*, ed. Paul Kristiansen, Acram Taji, and John Reganold, 1–23. Ithaca, NY: Comstock, 2006.

Krizmanic, J. "Inch by Inch, Row by Row." *Vegetarian Times* no. 139, 1989, 44–53, 68.

Kuepper, G., and L. Gegner. "Organic Crop Production Overview." 2004.

Lampkin, Nicolas. *Organic Farming*. Ipswich, UK: Old Pond, 2002.

Lane, H. A. "Reader's Correspondence." *Organic Gardening* 2 (1943): 28–31.

Lappé, A. "An Interview with Timothy LaSalle." *Take a Bite*, April 15, 2008. www .takeabite.cc/organic-farming-and-carbon-offsets.

Lappé, Anna, and Bryant Terry. *Grub: Ideas for an Urban Organic Kitchen*. New York: Penguin, 2006.

Lappé, Francis Moore. *Diet for a Small Planet: Twentieth Anniversary Edition*. New York: Ballantine, 1991.

Lau, Kimberly J. *New Age Capitalism: Making Money East of Eden*. Philadelphia: University of Pennsylvania Press, 2000.

Laurel, Alicia Bay. *Living on the Earth*. New York: Random House, 1971.

Lawrence, John F. "Mechanized Farming." *Wall Street Journal*, September 22, 1959.

Lawrence, O. "Composting in the Olden Days." *Organic Gardening* 8 (1946): 39–40.

Leopold Center for Sustainable Agriculture. "Organic Practices Outpace Conventional in Long-Term Research." Ames: Iowa State University, 2007.

Lesle, A. E. "First Award." *Organic Farmer* 1 (1950): 47.

Levy, N. "Foucault's Unnatural Ecology." In *Discourses of the Environment*, ed. E. Darier. Malden, MA: Blackwell, 1999.

Life. "The Move to Eat Natural." *Life* 69 (1970): 44–46.

Lipson, Elaine Marie. *The Organic Foods Sourcebook*. Chicago: Contemporary Books, 2001.

Lipson, Mark. *Searching for the "O-Word": Analyzing the USDA Current Research Information System for Pertinence to Organic Farming*. Santa Cruz, CA: Organic Farming Research Foundation, 1997.

Little Duck Organics. "Story." http://littleduckorganics.com/story.php.

Lockeretz, W. "What Are the Key Issues for Consumers?" In *Organic Agriculture: Sustainability, Markets and Policies*, 239–243. Wallingford, Oxford: CABI Publishing, 2003.

Lockie, Stewart. "Capturing the Sustainability Agenda: Organic Foods and Media Discourses on Food Scares, Environment, Genetic Engineering and Health." *Agriculture and Human Values* 23 (2006).

Lockie, Stewart, and Darren Halpin. "The 'Conventionalisation' Thesis Reconsidered: Structural and Ideological Transformation of Australian Organic Agriculture." *Sociologia Ruralis* 45, no. 4 (2005): 284–307.

Logan, R. W. "Results." *Organic Gardening* 6 (1945): 25.

Logsdon, Gene. *The Contrary Farmer*. White River Junction, VT: Chelsea Green, 1994.

———. *Homesteading: How to Find Independence on the Land*. Emmaus, PA: Rodale, 1973.

Loh, Sandra Tsing. "Let's Call the Whole Thing Off." *Atlantic* 304 (2009): 116–126.

LOHAS. "Consumers Prefer Artisanal Foods." 2008. www.lohas.com/articles/100992.html.

———. "Organic Valley Sales at $432.5 Million." 2008. www.lohas.com.

———. "Wal-Mart Supercenter Tops among Organics Shoppers: Study." 2007. www.lohas.com/articles/100733.html.

Los Angeles Times. "3 Market Chains Face $40 Million Organic Food Suit." *Los Angeles Times*, March 21, 1972.

———. "24 Hours of Organic Food." *Los Angeles Times*, October 8, 1971.

Luckock, V. O. "You Don't Need Acres 'n' Acres." *Organic Gardening and Farming* 1 (1954): 18–19.

Lustgarden, S. "Organics Take Root." *Vegetarian Times*, no. 190 (June 1993): 72–78.

Lyons, Kristen. "From Sandals to Suits: Green Consumers and the Institutionalization of Organic Agriculture." In *Consuming Foods, Sustaining Environments*, ed. Stewart Lockie and B. Pritchard, 82–93. Brisbane: Australian Academic Press, 2001.

Lyson, Thomas A. *Civic Agriculture: Reconnecting Farm, Food, and Community*. Medford, MA: Tufts University Press, 2004.

MacEachern, Diane. *Big Green Purse: Use Your Spending Power to Create a Cleaner, Greener World*. New York: Avery, 2008.

Magnusson, Maria K., Anne Arvola, et al. "Choice of Organic Foods Is Related to Perceived Consequences for Human Health and to Environmentally Friendly Behaviour." *Appetite* 40, no. 2 (2003): 109–117.

Mālie Organics website. www.malie.com/.

Maloney, Field. "Is Whole Foods Wholesome? The Dark Secrets of the Organic-Food Movement." *Washington Post*, March 17, 2006. www.WashingtonPost.com.

Maniates, M. "Individualization: Plant a Tree, Buy a Bike, Save the World?" In *Confronting Consumption*, ed. Thomas Princen, Michael Maniates, and K. Conca, 43–66. Cambridge, MA: MIT Press, 2002.

Marcy, C. F. "Organics in the Supermarket." In *Proceedings of the 14th IFOAM Organic World Congress*, ed. R. Thompson. Ottawa, ON: Canadian Organic Growers, 2002.

Marquis, J. C. Untitled article. *American Economic Review* 1, no 3 (1911): 567–568.

Martin, A. "How to Add Oomph to 'Organic.'" *New York Times*, August 19, 2007.

———. "Is a Food Revolution Now in Season?" *New York Times*, March 21, 2009.

Master of Malt website. www.masterofmalt.com/whiskies/benromach-organic -whisky/.

Maurer, Donna. *Vegetarianism: Movement or Moment?* Philadelphia: Temple University Press, 2002.

Maynard, Chris, and Bill Scheller. *The Bad for You Cookbook.* New York: Villard, 1992.

Mazori, Daniel. "The 2009 Natural Health Green Choice Awards." *Natural Health* 39 (2009): 58–65.

McCarrison, Robert. *Nutrition and Health.* London: Faber and Faber, 1953.

McDowell, Michael J. "The Bakhtinian Road to Ecological Insight." In *The Ecocriticism Reader: Landmarks in Literary Ecology*, ed. Cheryll Glotfelty and Harold Fromm, 371–391. Athens: University of Georgia Press, 1996.

McGrath, Mike, ed. *The Best of Organic Gardening.* Emmaus, PA: Rodale, 1996.

McLeod, Darryl. "Urban-Rural Food Alliances: A Perspective on Recent Community Food Organizing." In *Radical Agriculture*, ed. Richard Merrill, 188–211. New York: New York University Press, 1976.

McManus, Fran, ed. *Eating Fresh from the Organic Garden State: A Year-Round Guide to Cooking & Buying Local Organic Products.* Pennington, NJ: Northeast Organic Farming Association—New Jersey, 1997.

McMichael, Philip. "The Power of Food." *Agriculture and Human Values* 17 (2000): 21–33.

McNamee, Thomas. *Alice Waters and Chez Panisse: The Romantic, Impractical, Often Eccentric, Ultimately Brilliant Making of a Food Revolution.* New York: Penguin, 2007.

McWilliams, Carey. *Factories in the Field: The Story of Migratory Farm Labor in California.* Berkeley: University of California Press, 2000.

Melucci, Alberto. *Nomads of the Present: Social Movements and Individual Needs in Contemporary Society.* Philadelphia: Temple University Press, 1989.

Meyer, H. "Over the Fence." *Organic Gardening.* 7 (1945): 21–22.

Meyerowitz, Steve. *The Organic Food Guide: How to Shop Smarter and Eat Healthier.* Guilford, CT: Globe Pequot, 2004.

Michaelidou, Nina, and Louise M. Hassan. "The Role of Health Consciousness, Food Safety Concern and Ethical Identity on Attitudes and Intentions towards Organic Food." *International Journal of Consumer Studies* 32 (2008): 163–170.

Miller, Crow, and Elizabeth Miller. *Organic Gardening: A Comprehensive Guide to Chemical-Free Growing.* New York: IDG, 2000.

Milton, Kay. "Introduction: Environmentalism and Anthropology." In *Environmentalism: The View from Anthropology,* ed. Kay Milton. New York: Routledge, 1993.

Mogelonsky, M. "Organic Food and Drink." *Prepared Foods,* April 2008, 21–26.

Moore, S. F., and A. Mendenhall. "USDA's Proposed Rules for Organic Farming Threaten Biodynamic Farmers." *Biodynamics* 216 (1998): 15–18.

Moran, M. "A Sustainable World." *Gourmet Retailer* 28, no. 3 (2007): 84.

"MORE LIGHT ON DDT: Government Tests Show Where and How It Can Be Used against Pests Drawbacks of DDT Tree Insects Controlled." *New York Times,* September 16, 1945.

Mothers & Others for a Livable Planet. *The Green Food Shopper: An Activist's Guide to Changing the Food System.* New York: Mothers & Others for a Livable Planet, 1997.

Muckler, H. E. "Letters." *Organic Gardening* 6 (1945): 28.

Muldoon, Annie. "Where the Green Is: Examining the Paradox of Environmentally Conscious Consumption." *Electronic Green Journal* 23 (2006).

Mulvey, Laura. "Some Thoughts on Theories of Fetishism in the Context of Contemporary Culture." *October* 65 (Summer 1993): 3–20.

Murray, E. B. "Eco Challenge: Eating Local." *Body + Soul* 26 (2009): 52–54.

Myers, Adrian. *Organic Futures: The Case for Organic Farming.* Devon, UK: Green Books, 2005.

Nabhan, Gary Paul. *Coming Home to Eat: The Pleasures and Politics of Local Foods.* New York: W. W. Norton, 2002.

National Center for Public Policy. "Organic Labeling Study." 2000. www.nationalcenter.org/OrganicLabe1500.html.

National Public Radio. "John Mackey on Whole Foods' Growth." *Marketplace,* February 26, 2007. http://marketplace.publicradio.org/shows/2007/02/26/PM200702266.html.

Naturally Grown website. www.naturallygrown.org.

Natural Marketing Institute. "Organic Food & Beverage Sales Increase 18%; Household Penetration Decreases." February 23, 2005. www.NMIsolutions.com.

Naughton, Keith. "Natural Response." *Newsweek,* May 12, 2008, www.newsweek.com/id/135377/output.

"NC State College Offers Third Annual Pesticide School," pamphlet, 1951. NCSU Libraries Rare & Unique Digital Collections. http://d.lib.ncsu.edu/collections/catalog/ua100_052–001-bx0001–001–000.

Nearing, Helen. *Simple Food for the Good Life: An Alternative Cookbook.* New York: Delacorte, 1980.

Nearing, Scott, and Helen Nearing. *Building and Using Our Sun-Heated Greenhouse: Grow Vegetables All Year-Round.* Charlotte, VT: Garden Way, 1977.

———. *The Good Life: Helen and Scott Nearing's Sixty Years of Self-Sufficient Living.* New York: Schocken, 1989.

Nestle, Marion. *What To Eat.* New York: North Point, 2006.

New Scientist. "Thought for Food: Feeding the World While Nurturing the Planet

Doesn't Mean Going Back to Nature. Nor Does It Mean Letting Biotech Giants Run the Whole Show. Smart Farmers Are Learning How to Have the Best of Both Worlds." *New Scientist* 174, no. 2343 (2002): 34.

Newton, Jon. *Profitable Organic Farming.* Oxford, UK: Blackwell Science, 2004.

New York Times. "Scientists Assail Organic Food Fad." *New York Times,* February 26, 1974.

Nittler, Alan H. *A New Breed of Doctor.* New York: Pyramid, 1972.

Northbourne, Lord. *Look to the Land.* London: Dent, 1940.

North Carolina State University. Agricultural Policy Institute. "School of Agriculture, N.C. State College, Information and Curricula, 1960–1961." North Carolina State University, College of Agriculture and Life Sciences, Agricultural Institute Records, UA 100.040, Special Collections Research Center, North Carolina State University Libraries, Raleigh, North Carolina.

Novak, S. "Sunflower Plans to Take Root in Austin's Natural Foods Market." *Austin American-Statesman,* June 3, 2008.

Nutrition Report. "Natural Selection." *Women's Health,* June 2008.

Oelhaf, Robert C. *Organic Agriculture: Economic and Ecological Comparisons with Conventional Methods.* New York: John Wiley & Sons, 1978.

Ogden, Samuel. *Step-by-Step to Organic Vegetable Growing.* Emmaus, PA: Rodale Press, 1971.

———. *Straight-Ahead Organic: A Step-by-Step Guide to Growing Great Vegetables in a Less-Than-Perfect World.* White River Junction, VT: Chelsea Green, 1999.

Ohmann, Richard. *Selling Culture: Magazines, Markets, and Class at the Turn of the Century.* New York: Verso, 1996.

Oklahoma State University Extension Service. *Oklahoma Agriculture Today and Tomorrow.* 1960. Page Henry Belcher Collection, Box 39, Carl Albert Congressional Research and Studies Center.

Olds, J. "Testing Ground for Organics." *Organic Gardening and Farming* 1 (1954): 24–27.

O'Naturals website. www.onaturals.com/. 2009.

OrganicAthlete. "Guide to Sports Nutrition." 2007. www.organicathlete.org.

Organic Center. *Core Truths: Serving up the Science behind Organic Agriculture.* Washington, DC: Organic Center, 2006.

Organic Gardening. "Important Announcement." *Organic Gardening* 21 (1953): 13–16.

———. "Pay Dirt in Japan." *Organic Gardening* 19 (1951): 48.

———. "Poison Sprays on Washed Apples." *Organic Gardening* 6 (1945): 27.

———. "Reader's Correspondence." *Organic Gardening* 7 (1945): 26–29.

Organic Style website. www.organicstyle.com/.

Organic Trade Association. "U.S. Organic Sales Grow by a Whopping 17.1 Percent in 2008." *Organic Newsroom,* May 2009, www.organicnewsroom.com/2009/05/us _organic_sales.

Organization for Economic Co-Operation and Development. *Organic Agriculture: Sustainability, Markets and Policies.* Wallingford, Oxford: CABI Publishing, 2003.

Osborn, Fairfield. *Our Plundered Planet.* Boston: Little, Brown, 1948.

Oster, Doug, and Jessica Walliser. *Grow Organic: Over 250 Tips and Ideas for Growing Flowers, Veggies, Lawns and More.* Pittsburgh, PA: St. Lyon's, 2007.

"Our Popcorn." 479° Popcorn website. www.479popcorn.com/our_popcorn.html?id =24WEpkWQ.

Owens, M. "Yours for the Picking." *O, the Oprah Magazine* 10 (2009): 95–96.

Pacey, M. D. "Nature's Bounty: Merchandisers of Health Foods Are Cashing in on It." *Barron's Financial Weekly*, May 10, 1971.

"Parmesan and Rosemary." www.quinnpopcorn.com/popcorn/parmesan-rosemary/.

Paul, Pamela. "America's Healthiest Grocery Stores." *Health* 22 (2008): 114–118.

Perényi, Eleanor. *Green Thoughts: A Writer in the Garden.* New York: Random House, 1981.

Peter, G., M. M. Bell, et al. "Coming Back across the Fence: Masculinity and the Transition to Sustainable Agriculture." *Rural Sociology* 65, no. 2 (2000): 215–233.

Petrini, Carlo. *Slow Food Nation: Why Our Food Should Be Good, Clean, and Fair.* New York: Random House, 2007.

———. "Speech at the W.K. Kellogg Foundation Conference." 2005. www.slowfood usa.org/events/carlo_petrini_speech.html.

Pfeiffer, Ehrenfried. *Bio-Dynamic Farming and Gardening: Soil Fertility, Renewal and Preservation.* New York: Anthroposophic Press, 1938.

———. "The Organic-Chemical Controversy in Agriculture." *Bio-Dynamics* 10, no. 3 (1952): 2–19.

Philips, D. "Organic and Natural Dairy." *Dairy Foods*, June 2007, 30–36.

Pollan, Michael. *In Defense of Food: An Eater's Manifesto.* New York: Penguin, 2008.

———. "Mass Natural." *New York Times*, June 4, 2006.

———. "Naturally: How Organic Became a Marketing Niche and a Multibillion-Dollar Industry." *New York Times Magazine*, 2001.

———. *The Omnivore's Dilemma: A Natural History of Four Meals.* New York: Penguin, 2006.

Porta, Donatella D., and Mario Diani. *Social Movements: An Introduction.* London: Wiley-Blackwell, 1999.

Posner, J. L., et al. "Organic and Conventional Production Systems in the Wisconsin Integrated Cropping System Trials." *Agronomy Journal* 100, no. 2 (2008).

Prairie Vodka website. http://prairievodka.com/.

Pretty, Jules, and Peggy Barlett. "Concluding Remarks: Nature and Health in the Urban Environment." In *Urban Place: Reconnecting with the Natural World*, ed. Peggy Barlett, 299–319. Cambridge, MA: MIT Press, 2005.

Price, Weston A. *Nutrition and Physical Degeneration: A Comparison of Primitive and Modern Diets and Their Effects.* Redlands, CA: Weston A. Price, 1945.

Princen, Thomas, Michael Maniates, et al., eds. *Confronting Consumption.* Cambridge, MA: MIT Press, 2002.

Progressive Farmer. "Agriculture Has Big Stake in Crackdown on Pesticides." *Progressive Farmer*, March 1970.

"Prospect of Big Bug Crop Worries Farmers." *News and Courier* (Charleston S.C.), March 7, 1950.

Purdum, T. S. "High Priest of the Pasture." *Time*, May 1, 2005.

Raisfeld, R. and R. Patronite. "Birdbath: Solving the Case of the East Village Bakery Without a Name." *New York Magazine*, January 23, 2006. www.nymag.com/ny metro/food/15533/.

Rawson, J. M. "Organic Agriculture in the United States: Program and Policy Issues." Washington, DC: Congressional Research Service, 2006.

Real California Milk. "Happy Cows." www.realcaliforniamilk.com/happycows.

Renton, Alex. "Ripe Target." *Guardian*, March 27, 2007. www.guardian.co.uk/super markets/story/0,,2043674,00.html.

Restaurant Nora website. www.noras.com/nora/.

Richard, David, and Dorie Byers, eds. *Taste Life! The Organic Choice.* Bloomington, IL: Vital Health, 1998.

Richmond, H. S. "Story of a Citrus Grove." *Bio-Dynamics* 6, no. 3 (1948): 2–11.

Rider, Kimberly. *The Healthy Home Workbook: Easy Steps for Eco-Friendly Living.* San Francisco: Chronicle, 2006.

Ristovski-Slijepcevic, S., G. E. Chapman, et al. "Engaging with Healthy Eating Discourse(s): Ways of Knowing about Food and Health in Three Ethnocultural Groups in Canada." *Appetite* 50, no. 1 (2008).

Robinson, Ed, and Carolyn Robinson. *The "Have-More" Plan: A Little Land—a Lot of Living.* Pownal, VT: Storey, 1973.

Robishaw, Sue. *Homesteading Adventures: A Guide for Doers and Dreamers.* Cooks, MI: Many Tracks, 1997.

Rodale, J. I., ed. *The Complete Book of Food and Nutrition.* Emmaus, PA: Rodale, 1966.

———. "Editorial." *Organic Farmer* 1 (1949): 9–10.

———. "Editorial: Looking Back Part III, Tradition Throttles Research." *Organic Gardening* 20 (1952): 10–11.

———. "Editorial: Looking Back, Part IV, The Beginning of Our Experimental Farm." *Organic Gardening* 20 (1952): 10–11, 36–39.

———. "Expensive Organic Foods." *Organic Gardening* 18 (1951): 37.

———. "Health and the Soil." *Organic Farming and Gardening* 1 (1942): 1.

———. *The Health Seeker.* Emmaus, PA: Rodale, 1971.

———. *The Healthy Hunzas.* Emmaus, PA: Rodale, 1949.

———. "Introduction to Organic Farming." *Organic Farming and Gardening* 1 (1942): 3–4.

———. "Organic Food Shops." *Organic Gardening* 7 (1945): 9.

———. "Memorandum." *Organic Gardening* 10 (1947): 18.

———. "Miscellany: Looking Forward." *Organic Gardening* 20 (1952): 24–25.

———. "The Mounting Campaign against Organic Farming." *Organic Farmer* 3 (1952): 32.

———. *My Own Technique of Eating for Health.* Emmaus, PA: Rodale, 1971.

———. "Notice." *Organic Gardening* 11 (1947): 13.

———. "Notice about The Organic Farmer." *Organic Gardening* 14, no. 5 (1949).

———. "An Open Letter to Readers." *Organic Gardening and Farming* 1 (1954): 53.

———. "Organic Farming—Bunk?" *Organic Farmer* 4 (1952): 18–19.

———. "Organic Food Crashes the Retail Market." *Organic Farmer* 2 (1951): 61.

———. *Our Poisoned Earth and Sky.* Emmaus, PA: Rodale, 1964.

———. *Pay Dirt: Farming and Gardening with Composts.* New York: Devin-Adair, 1948.

———. "Prevention." *Organic Gardening* 16 (1950): 56.

———. "Radical Change in Organic Method." *Organic Gardening* 15 (1949): 26–27.

———. "Reader's Correspondence." *Organic Gardening* 6 (1945): 25.

———. *Rodale's System for Mental Power and Natural Health.* Emmaus, PA: Rodale, 1966.

———. "The Soil and Health Foundation." *Organic Gardening* 11 (1947): 31.

———. "Solicitation of Members for the Soil and Health Foundation." *Organic Gardening* 11 (1947): 14.

———. "Tenth Anniversary Editorial: Looking Back" *Organic Gardening* 20 (1952): 11–14, 43.

———. "Tenth Anniversary Editorial: Looking Back, Part II." *Organic Gardening* 20 (1952): 11–12, 37–38.

———. "What 'Organically-Grown' Really Means." *Organic Farmer* 5 (1953): 37.

———. "With the Editor." *Organic Gardening* 2 (1943): 2–4.

———. "With the Editor." *Organic Gardening* 7 (1945): 4.

———. "With the Editor: A Debate." *Organic Gardening* 8 (1946): 2–4.

———. "With the Editor: Advantages of Compost Farming." *Organic Gardening* 5 (1944): 1–5.

———. "With the Editor: Artificial Insemination." *Organic Gardening* 14 (1949): 12.

———. "With the Editor: Cancer—Part III: Primitive Peoples." *Organic Gardening* 15 (1949): 12.

———. "With the Editor: Federal Program, Part II." *Organic Gardening* 3 (1943): 1–3.

———. "With the Editor: The Flea Beetle." *Organic Farmer* 2 (1950): 8–9.

———. "With the Editor: Grants to Research Institutions." *Organic Gardening* 18 (1951): 16, 18.

———. "With the Editor: The Human Health Aspect of Organic Farming." *Organic Gardening.* 8 (1945): 2–4.

———. "With the Editor: In Defense of the Organic Method." *Organic Farmer* 3 (1951): 17–19, 49, 51–53.

———. "With the Editor: Insects, The Censors of Nature." *Organic Gardening* 12 (1948): 16.

———. "With the Editor: Is Our Health Related to the Soil?" *Organic Gardening* 5 (1944): 3–8.

———. "With the Editor: Orchard Practices." *Organic Gardening* 6 (1945): 7.

———. "With the Editor: The Organiculturist's Creed." *Organic Gardening* 12 (1948): 12–14.

———. "With the Editor: The Principle of Eminent Domain." *Organic Gardening* 10 (1947): 16–18.

———. "With the Editor: Progress throughout the Nation." *Organic Gardening* 20 (1952): 11.

———. "With the Editor: The Rodale Diet." *Organic Gardening* 11 (1947): 12–14.

———. "With the Editor: The Rodale Diet, Part II." *Organic Gardening* 11 (1947): 11–13.

———. "With the Editor: Should the U.S. Government Go Into the Chemical Fertilizer Business?" *Organic Gardening* 11 (1947): 12–13.

———. "With the Editor: Sir Albert Howard: A Tribute." *Organic Gardening* 13 (1948): 13–14.

———. "With the Editor—the Theory Underlying the Composting Process." *Organic Gardening* 7 (1945): 4–7.

———. "With the Editor—the Work of Weston A. Price." *Organic Gardening* 7 (1945): 4–6.

———. "With the Editor: This Organic Gardening Bunk, Part 1." *Organic Gardening* 21 (1953): 10–11, 49–54.

———. "With the Editor: This Organic Gardening Bunk, Part II." *Organic Gardening* 21 (1953): 10–11, 26–27, 34–35, 40.

———. "With the Editor: What's It All About?" *Organic Gardening* 21 (1953): 9–13.

———. "With the Editor: Whither Science?" *Organic Farmer* 4(1953): 13.

———. "Why Chemical Fertilizers Are Bad." *Organic Farmer* 1 (1949): 15–16.

———. "You Can Do Much to Help Your Health!" *Organic Farming and Gardening* 1 (1942): 31.

Rodale, Maria. *Maria Rodale's Organic Gardening: Your Seasonal Companion to Creating a Beautiful and Delicious Garden.* Emmaus, PA: Rodale, 1998.

Rodale, Maria, and Maya Rodale. *It's My Pleasure: A Revolutionary Plan to Free Yourself from Guilt and Create the Life You Want.* New York: Free Press, 2005.

Rodale, Robert. "The Heart and Soul of Organic Gardening." *Organic Gardening* 39 (1992): 46.

———. *Sane Living in a Mad World: A Guide to the Organic Way of Life.* Emmaus, PA: Rodale, 1972.

———. "What Is Organic Gardening?" *Organic Gardening* 20 (1952): 14–15.

Rodale Inc. "Organic Gardening: About the Brand." 2009. www.rodaleinc.com/brand /organic-gardening.

———. "Organic Gardening Relaunches with February/March 2010 Issue." Rodale, 2010. www.rodaleinc.com/newsroom/iorganic-gardeningi-relaunches-february march-2010-issue.

Rodale Institute website. www.rodaleinstitute.org/.

Roderick, Kyle. *Organic Bath: Creating a Natural, Healthy Haven.* New York: Melcher Media, 2007.

Ronald, Pamela C., and Raoul W. Adamchak. *Tomorrow's Table: Organic Farming, Genetics, and the Future of Food.* New York: Oxford University Press, 2008.

Roseboro, Ken. *The Organic Food Handbook: A Consumer's Guide to Buying and Eating Organic Food.* Laguna Beach, CA: Basic Health, 2006.

Rosen, Joseph D. "Claims of Organic Food's Nutritional Superiority: A Critical Review." New York: American Council on Science and Health, 2008.

Rossinow, Doug. *The Politics of Authenticity: Liberalism, Christianity, and the New Left in America.* New York: Columbia University Press, 1998.

Sachs, Carolyn E. *Gendered Fields: Rural Women, Agriculture, and the Environment.* Boulder, CO: Westview, 1996.

Sahota, Amarijit. "The International Market for Organic and Fair Trade Food and Drink." In *The Handbook of Organic and Fair Trade Food Marketing,* ed. Simon Wright and Diane McCrea, 1–24. Hoboken, NJ: John Wiley & Sons, 2007.

Sait, Graeme. *Nutrition Rules! Guidelines from the Master Consultants.* Eumundi, Qld, Australia: Soil Therapy Pty, 2003.

Salatin, Joel. *Family Friendly Farming: A Multi-Generational Home-Based Business Testament.* Swoope, VA: Polyface, 2001.

———. "'Sound Science' Is Killing Us." *Acres USA* 34, no. 4 (2004): 1, 8.

Sams, C. "Introduction." In *Handbook of Organic Food Processing and Production,* ed. Simon Wright and Diane McCrea, 1–15. Malden, MA: Blackwell Science, 2000.

Sandbeck, Ellen. *Eat More Dirt: Diverting and Instructive Tips for Growing and Tending an Organic Garden.* New York: Broadway, 2003.

———. *Organic Housekeeping: In Which the Nontoxic Avenger Shows You How to Improve Your Health and That of Your Family While You Save Time, Money, and, Perhaps, Your Sanity.* New York: Scribner, 2006.

Schildgen, B. "10 Ways to Eat Well: Mr. Green's Food Commandments." *Sierra,* November–December 2006.

Schudson, Michael. *Advertising, the Uneasy Persuasion: Its Dubious Impact on American Society.* New York: Basic Books, 1984.

Schwenke, Karl. *Successful Small-Scale Farming: An Organic Approach.* Pownal, VT: Storey, 1991.

Scoones, I. "New Ecology and the Social Sciences: What Prospects for a Fruitful Engagement?" *Annual Review of Anthropology* 28 (1999): 479–507.

"Senate Farm Group Considers Use of Food as Cold War Weapon: Flanders Proposes Letting Eisenhower Offer Surplus Goods to Starving Iron Curtain Nations." *Wall Street Journal,* July 17, 1953.

Seymour, John, and Sally Seymour. *Farming for Self-Sufficiency: Independence on a 5-Acre Farm.* New York: Schocken, 1973.

Shape. "Go Organic without Going Broke." *Shape* 28 (2009): 126.

Sherman, L. L. "Organic Gardening in Oakland, Cal." *Organic Gardening* 10 (1946): 57–58.

Shiva, Vandana. *Stolen Harvest: The Hijacking of the Global Food Supply.* Cambridge, MA: South End Press, 2000.

Shumway, A. "Deep Run Farm." *Green Revolution* 33, no. 11 (1976): 9–11.

Siegel, Jennifer, and Mo Siegel. *Celestial Seasonings Cookbook: Cooking with Tea.* New York: Park Lane Press, 1996.

Silverstein, Michael J., Neil Fiske, et al. *Trading Up: Why Consumers Want New Luxury Goods—and How Companies Create Them.* New York: Portfolio, 2005.

Singer, Peter, and Jim Mason. *The Way We Eat: Why Our Food Choices Matter.* Emmaus, PA: Rodale, 2006.

Sligh, M. *Toward Organic Integrity: A Guide to the Development of US Organic Standards*. Rural Advancement Foundation International—USA, 2007.

Sligh, M., and C. Christman. *Who Owns Organic? The Global Status, Prospects and Challenges of a Changing Organic Market*. Pittsboro, NC, Rural Advancement Foundation International (RAFI-USA), 2003.

Sloan, A. Elizabeth. "What, When, and Where America Eats." *Food Technology* 64, no. 1 (2008): 20–29.

Smith, Kimberly. *Wendell Berry and the Agrarian Tradition: A Common Grace*. Lawrence: University Press of Kansas, 2003.

Smith, Miranda, and E. Henderson, eds. *The Real Dirt: Farmers Tell about Organic and Low-Input Practices in the Northeast*. Burlington, VT: Northeast Regional Sustainable Agriculture Research and Education Program, 1998.

Smith, Nicola. *Harvest: A Year in the Life of an Organic Farm*. Guilford, CT: Lyons, 2004.

Smith, S. D. "Rodale to Shutter Four-Year-Old Organic Style." *Media Week*, 2005. www.mediaweek.com/mw/news/recent_display.jsp?vnu_content_id=1001053674.

Soil Association. *Organic Market Report*. 2009. Bristol. http://www.soilassociation .org/LinkClick.aspx?fileticket=GPynfoJoPho%3D&tabid=116.

Sparks, Paul, and Richard Shepherd. "Self-Identity and the Theory of Planned Behavior: Assessing the Role of Identification with 'Green Consumerism.'" *Social Psychology Quarterly* 55, no. 4 (1992): 388–399.

Springer, G. "Home on the Range." *Organic Gardening and Farming* 1 (1954): 64–65.

Sprugel, D. G. "Disturbance, Equilibrium and Environmental Variability: What Is 'Natural' Vegetation in a Changing Environment?" *Biological Conservation* 58 (1991): 1–18.

St. John de Crèvecœur, J. H. *Letters from an American Farmer*. New York: Oxford University Press, 1997.

Stacey, Michelle. *Consumed: Why Americans Love, Hate, and Fear Food*. New York: Simon & Schuster, 1994.

Steiner, R. "Beekeeping: Nine Lectures on Bees." *Biodynamics* 216 (1998): 19–23.

Stevens-Garmon, John, Chung L. Huang, et al. "Organic Demand: A Profile of Consumers in the Fresh Produce Market." *CHOICES: The Magazine of Food, Farm, and Resource Issues* 22, no. 2 (2007): 109–132.

Stewart, Keith. *It's a Long Road to a Tomato: Tales of an Organic Farmer Who Quit the Big City for the (Not So) Simple Life*. New York: Marlowe, 2006.

Stewart, M. A. "Environmental History: Profile of a Developing Field." *History Teacher* 31, no. 3 (1998).

Storstad, O., and H. Björkhaug. "Foundations of Production and Consumption of Organic Food in Norway: Common Attitudes among Farmers and Consumers." *Agriculture and Human Values* 20 (2003): 151–163.

Strasser, Susan. "Making Consumption Conspicuous: Transgressive Topics Go Mainstream." *Technology and Culture* 43, no. 4 (2002): 755–770.

Streep, A. "Sustainability Complex: Small Things, Done Right. The Next Great Leap Forward?" *Orion* (2006). www.orion.org.

Sullivan, Dan. "Research Makes It Clear: Organic Food Is Best for People and the Planet." *Rootstock* 9, no. 1 (2009): 4–7.

Sustainable Agriculture Network. "Transitioning to Organic Production, Sustainable Agriculture Research and Education (SARE) Program." 2007.

Swift, J. "Desertification: Narratives, Winners and Losers." In *The Lie of the Land: Challenging Received Wisdom on the African Environment*, ed. Melissa Leach and Robin Mearns. London: International African Institute, 1996.

Szasz, Andrew. *Shopping Our Way to Safety: How We Changed from Protecting the Environment to Protecting Ourselves*. Minneapolis: University of Minnesota Press, 2007.

Telaroli, G. "Martha Stewart Tweets about Food, Inc." Take Part, 2009. www.takepart.com/news/2009/03/27/martha-stewart-tweets-about-food-inc/.

Teller, W. M. "The Garden Book of the Year." *Organic Gardening* 8, no. 6 (1946).

Theuer, R. C. *Do Organic Fruits and Vegetables Taste Better than Conventional Fruits and Vegetables?* Washington, DC: Organic Center, 2006.

Thoreau, Henry David. *Walden and Civil Disobedience*. New York: Penguin, 1986.

Throckmorton, R. I. "The Organic Farming Myth." *Country Gentleman* 121, no. 9 (1951): 21, 103, 105.

Time. "Catching Up to Rodale Press." *Time*, March 22, 1971.

———. "Eating Organic." *Time*, December 18, 1972.

———. "Ecology: The New Jeremiahs." *Time*, August 15, 1969.

———. "Health and Hucksterism." *Time*, October 23, 1972.

———. "The Kosher of the Counterculture." *Time*, November 16, 1970.

———. "The Perils of Eating, American Style." *Time*, December 18, 1972.

———. "The Profitable Earth." *Time*, April 12, 1971.

———. "What Grandfather Ate." *Time*, December 9, 1940.

———. "Windmill Power." *Time*, December 2, 1974.

"To Combat Hunger," *New York Times*, February 20, 1950.

Tourles, Stephanie. *Organic Body Care Recipes: 175 Homemade Herbal Formulas for Glowing Skin & a Vibrant Self*. North Adams, MA: Storey, 2007.

Trader Joe's, *Fearless Flyer*. Monrovia, CA: Trader Joe's, 2007.

TreeHugger. "Joel Salatin, America's Most Influential Farmer, Talks Big Organic and the Future of Food." www.treehugger.com/files/2009/08/joel-salatin-americas-most-influential-farmer.php.

Trespicio, Terri. "Martha Gets Real." *Body + Soul* 93 (2009).

Trewavas, A. "Urban Myths of Organic Farming: Organic Agriculture Began as an Ideology, but Can It Meet Today's Needs?" *Nature* 410, no. 22 (March 2001): 409–410.

Tuan, Yi-Fu. *The Good Life*. Madison: University of Wisconsin Press, 1986.

Tucker, David M. *Kitchen Gardening in America: A History*. Ames: Iowa State University Press, 1993.

Turner, Newman. *Fertility Farming*. London: Faber and Faber, 1951.

University of Michigan News Service. "Organic Farming Can Feed the World, U-M Study Shows." 2007. www.ns.umich.edu/htdos/releases/print.php.

Ureña, Felix, Rodolfo Bernabéu, et al. "Women, Men and Organic Food: Differences in Their Attitudes and Willingness to Pay. A Spanish Case Study." *International Journal of Consumer Studies* 32 (2008): 18–26.

USDA. "National Organic Program: Final Rule." 2007. www.ams.usda.gov/nop/NOP /standards.html.

————. Organic Vegetable Growers Surveyed in 1994. *AREI Updates*. 2006. 4:1–4.

USDA Economic Research Service. Data Sets: Organic Production, USDA, 2009, 1–4.

USDA Study Team on Organic Farming. *Report and Recommendations on Organic Farming*. Washington, DC: USDA, 1980.

US Government, US Government Facts: Children's Chemical & Pesticide Exposure via Food Products, 2005, 1–2.

Van Tuyle, D. A. "Letter." *Organic Farmer* 3 (1952): 7.

Vileisis, Ann. *Kitchen Literacy: How We Lost Knowledge of Where Food Comes from and Why We Need to Get It Back*. Washington, DC: Island Press, 2008.

Vogeler, Ingolf. *The Myth of the Family Farm: Agribusiness Dominance of U.S. Agriculture*. Boulder, CO: Westview, 1981.

Waldman, S., and V. Reiss. "It's a Lohasian Moment." *MSNBC*, 2006. www.msnbc .msn.com/id/13004986/site/newsweek/Beliefwatch: Lohasians.

Walker, J. "Editors at New Magazines Give Pitch Tips." *O'Dwyer's PR Services Report*. New York: J. R. O'Dwyer, 2005.

Wanderlust. http://wanderlustfestival.com/.

Wang, S. Y., C.-T. Chen, et al. "Fruit Quality, Antioxidant Capacity, and Flavonoid Content of Organically and Conventionally Grown Blueberries." *Journal of Agricultural and Food Chemistry* 56 (2008): 5788–5794.

Warren, V. L. "Organic Foods: Spotting the Real Thing Can Be Tricky." *New York Times*, April 9, 1972.

Wasik, John F. *Green Marketing & Management: A Global Perspective*. Cambridge, MA: Blackwell, 1996.

Waters, A. "One Thing to Do about Food: A Forum." *Nation* 283 (2006): 14–21.

Weber, Max. *Economy and Society: An Outline of Interpretive Sociology*. Berkeley: University of California Press, 1978.

Wells, Hodan Farah, and Jean C. Buzby. "Dietary Assessment of Major Trends in U.S. Food Consumption, 1970–2005." *USDA Economic Information Bulletin* 33 (2008).

Whelan, Elizabeth M. *The One-Hundred-Percent Natural, Purely Organic, Cholesterol-Free, Megavitamin, Low-Carbohydrate Nutrition Hoax*. New York: Atheneum, 1983.

————. *Panic in the Pantry: Food Facts, Fads and Fallacies*. New York: Atheneum, 1975.

White, H. S. "The Organic Foods Movement." *Food Technology* (April 1972): 29–33.

Whorton, James. *Crusaders for Fitness: The History of American Health Reformers*. Princeton, NJ: Princeton University Press, 1982.

"Why Rodale's." *Rodale's*, www.rodales.com/why-rodales.html.

Wiles, Richard, Kenneth A. Cook, et al. "How 'Bout Them Apples? Pesticides in Children's Food Ten Years after Alar." Washington, DC: Environmental Working Group, 1999.

Williams, Raymond. "Base and Superstructure in Marxist Cultural Theory." In *Rethinking Popular Culture: Contemporary Perspectives in Cultural Studies*, ed. Chandra Mukerji and Michael Schudson, 407–423. Berkeley: University of California Press, 1991.

———. *Marxism and Literature.* New York: Oxford University Press, 1977.

Wine, M. "The Food Gap." *Orion* 24, no. 5 (2005): 60–67.

Wookey, Barry. *Rushall: The Story of an Organic Farm.* Oxford: Blackwell, 1987.

"The World at Work: Brief Notes of the Week." *Barron's National Business and Financial Weekly*, April 11, 1955.

Worthington, V. "Nutritional Quality of Organic versus Conventional Fruits, Vegetables, and Grains." *Journal of Alternative and Complementary Medicine* 7, no. 2 (2001): 161–173.

Wurgaft, Benjamin Aldes. "East of Eden: Sin and Redemption at the Whole Foods Market." *Gastronomica* 2, no. 3 (2002): 87–89.

Yergin, Daniel. "Let's Get Adelle Davis Right: Supernutritionist." *New York Times*, May 20, 1973.

Zezima, Katie. "Organic Dairies Watch the Good Times Turn Bad." *New York Times*, May 28, 2009.

Zwerdling, D. "In India, Bucking the 'Revolution' by Going Organic." *National Public Radio*, June 1, 2009, www.npr.org/templates/story.

Index

Clements, Frederic, 33
Cloud, John, on local/organic, 161
CMA. *See* California Medical
    Association
CNN Money, poll by, 259
Cocannouer, Joseph, 48, 61
Cohen, Anthony, 10
Cohen, Jerome Irving. *See* Rodale,
    Jerome Irving
Colaciccio, Daniel, 117
Cole, Nat King, 70
Coleman, Eliot, 136–137, 140
    on chemicals, 137
    deep-organic farmers and, 175
    Four Season Farm and, 137
    on organic farming, 13
    organic movement and, 174–175
Collier's, 37
Colony Collapse Disorder, 193
Columbia University, nutrition center
    at, 51–52
Coming Home to Eat (Nabhan), 160
Committee on Nutrition (AAP), 202
Commoner, Barry, 83, 95
Common Ground Country Fair, 145
Community Supported Agriculture
    (CSA), 121, 140, 144, 236, 237,
    238, 252
Complete Book of Composting, The
    (Rodale), 74, 137
Complete Book of Food and Nutrition,
    The (Rodale), 63–64
Complete Book of Self-Sufficiency
    (Seymour), 107
Composting, 17, 35, 42, 45, 50, 61, 62,
    74, 106, 144, 188, 236
Compost News Letter, The, 24
Compost Science, 69
Comprehensive Catalog of Organic
    Products, The (Ecological Food
    Society), 89
ConAgra, 167

Conference on Economic Progress, 56
Confined animal feeding operations
    (CAFOs), 212, 214, 216
Congressional Research Service,
    OFPA and, 134
Consciousness
    contradictory, 208
    divided, 179–182
    ecological, 144
Consumerism, 6, 7, 9, 126, 170
    conscious, 259
    ethical, 253, 254
    green, 5, 14, 232, 253, 257
    progressive/enlightened, 258
Consumer Reports, 252
Consumer sovereignty, 253, 257, 259
Consumption, 10, 233, 253
    activism and, 239, 241–242
    cause-driven, 9
    conscious, 257
    externalities of, 7–8
    green, 9, 176, 253, 258
    organic, 8, 9, 228, 229
    patterns, 186, 189
    production and, 258
    race/class and, 7, 258
    stratified, 244, 246
Conventional agriculture, 16, 62, 147,
    153
    organic farming and, 113
    organic movement and, 180
    supplanting, 15
Conventionalization thesis, 167–168
Cook, Christopher, organic revolution
    and, 154
Cookbooks, 79, 89, 114, 129, 254, 260
Cooking Light, poll by, 259
Cooking with Paula Deen, 145
Cool, Jesse Ziff, 105, 231, 260
Cooperative Regions of Organic
    Producer Pools (CROPP), goal
    of, 213–214

Monoculture, 172, 258
Monosodium glutamate (MSG), 157, 234
Monsanto, 55–56, 119, 155, 192, 193, 211, 219
artificial hormones and, 210
Monsanto Protection Act (2013), 192–193
Montana-Farmer-Stockman, 57
Morales, Betty, 75
Mother Earth, 49, 81
Mother Earth News, 107
Mothering, 114
Mother Jones, 233
Mothers for Natural Law, 170
Mrs. Gooch's, 126, 240
Muir, John, 138
Muldoon, Annie, 257
Murray, Erin Byers, 161
Myers, Adrian, 151
My Own Technique for Eating for Health (Rodale), 93

Nabhan, Gary Paul, 160
Nader, Ralph, 83
Nation, Allan, 138
National Academy of Sciences, 68
National Agricultural Chemical Association, 67
National Audubon Society, 84
National Center for Public Policy (NCPP), 229
National Corn Growers Association, 157
National Farmers Organization, 99
National Health Food Society, 98
National Mall, organic growing on, 155
National Nutritional Foods Association, 119, 126
National Nutrition Conference, 48
National Organic Program (NOP), 14, 135, 171, 175, 178, 179, 216

National Organic Standards, 150, 171, 212, 224
National Organic Standards Board (NOSB), 135, 156–157, 168–169, 171, 179
National Parks Foundation, 155
National Public Radio, 249
National Resources Defense Council (NRDC), 132
National Restaurant Association, 244
National Science Foundation, 178
National Sustainable Agriculture Information Service, 262
National Wartime Nutrition Guide (UDSA), 28
NativEnergy, 199
Natural Food Associates (NFA), 59–60
Natural Foods Merchandiser, 260
Natural food stores, 71, 85, 112
Natural Health, 241
Natural Living, 81
Naturally Grown, 166
Natural Marketing Institute (NMI), 201, 230
Natural Organic Farmers' Association of New York, 120
Natural Resources Defense Council (NRDC), 132, 153, 255
Nature, 21–22, 45, 48, 80, 105–111
balance of, 12, 13, 34, 74, 263
cooperating with, 13, 61
copying, 50
culture and, 6, 114
farming and, 44
laws of life/health of, 22
organic farming and, 141, 152
organic food and, 35, 51
popular constructions of, 9
as self-organizing, 151
urban-industrial life and, 6
Nature, 153, 157
"Nature Boy" (Cole), 70

Nature Conservancy, 246
Nature's Baby Organics, 206
Nature's Path, 147, 214
Nature's Way, 61, 86, 264
Navitas Naturals, 234
Nearing, Helen, 82, 136, 142, 143
   counterculture and, 80
   dietary habits of, 78
   organic good life and, 76–80
   organic movement and, 140
   unprocessed foods and, 77
   vegetarianism and, 77
Nearing, Scott, 82, 136, 142, 143
   counterculture and, 80
   dietary habits of, 78
   homesteading and, 78
   organic good life and, 76–80
   organic movement and, 140
   unprocessed foods and, 77
Nelson, Betty, 73
Nestle, Marion, 8, 197, 255, 262
New Age Capitalism (Lau), 258
New Agrarians, 109
New Breed of Doctor, A (Nittler), 92
New Luxuries, 233, 234, 235
Newman, Nell, 194
Newman, Paul, 194
Newman's Own Organics, 194, 201
"New Science of Miniature Farming,
   The" (Robinson and Robinson),
   41
New Social Movements (NSMs), 253
Newsweek, 126
   Lohasians and, 232, 233
   on organic food, 112
Newton, Jon, 195
New York Botanical Garden, 48, 188
New Yorker, 67
New York Times, 35, 97, 103, 170–171,
   177, 183, 240
   bio-kinetic farming and, 25
   on Carson, 67
   on chemicals/food, 75

   on Davis, 89
   on organic advertisements, 58
   on organic food, 102
   on Rodale, 95, 113
   on Salatin, 138
   Tolman in, 157
   on Whole Foods, 239
New York Times Magazine, on Rodale,
   94
*New York Times Natural Foods
   Cookbook*, 89
Nichols, Joe, 60
Nielsen Homescan, 203, 251
Nitrogen, 19, 64, 106, 218
Nittler, Alan, 92
Nixon, Richard M., 88
Non-GMO Project, 193, 197
NOP. *See* National Organic Program
Norman, Gurney, on organic
   gardening, 87
Northbourne, Lord, 24, 27
North Carolina Agricultural Institute,
   63
North Carolina State College,
   Pesticide School and, 53
Northeast Organic Farming
   Association, 254
NOSB. *See* National Organic
   Standards Board
NPK dogma, 19, 22, 23
NPR–Thompson Reuters Health Poll,
   260
Nutrition, 3, 8, 9, 23, 28, 29, 69, 80, 88,
   92, 112, 126, 185, 187, 209, 218
   basic, 186
   clinical, 30
   concerns about, 19, 90, 189
   cycle of, 62
   health and, 34
   organic food and, 12, 89, 100, 101,
   104, 183, 210, 217
   pseudoscience and, 98–101
   research on, 22

Rodale, Maria, 46, 185, 223, 224, 240
  on grandfather, 95
  organic gardening and, 148–149
  on *Organic Gardening*, 136
  organic lifestyle and, 225
  Organic Living and, 136
  vision of, 257
Rodale, Robert, 90, 120, 135, 149, 262
  described, 7
  organically grown food and, 208
  organic homestead and, 82
  regenerative agriculture and, 113
  social/environmental messages
    and, 101
  writing of, 97
Rodale Diet, 31
Rodale Experimental Farm, 60
Rodale Health blog, 183
Rodale Inc., 222–223, 246
  organic life force and, 224
  publishing by, 223, 225
  tagline of, 224, 257
Rodale Institute, 135, 150, 154, 219, 224
  experimental farm by, 223
  Farming Systems Trial and, 223
  motto of, 113
  Organic Valley and, 214
Rodale Institute Farming System Trial
  (FST), 113
Rodale Organic Farm, 149
Rodale Organic Garden certification
  guidelines, 102
Rodale Organic Method, 149
Rodale Press, 48, 75, 76, 85, 89, 98, 111,
    113, 119, 222
  birth of, 21, 60
  certification and, 87
  described, 262
  environmental living and, 88
  information from, 121
  organic expertise and, 90
  publications by, 3, 109
  revenues for, 135

Rodale Research Center, 119, 158
Rodale's Organic Life, 225
*Rodale's System for Mental Power and
    Natural Health* (Rodale), 72
Roosevelt, Theodore, Country Life
    Commission and, 37
Roseboro, Ken, 177
Rose Valley Farm, 236
Rossinow, Doug, cooperatives and, 71
Roundup, 16, 192
Royal Society of Arts, 22
Rubin, Jordan, 220
Rubin, Maury, 181
Runner's World, 223
Rural New Yorker, 57
Rural Renaissance Network, 143
Rushall: The Story of an Organic Farm
    (Wookey), 120
Rynearson, Edward, 104

S. W. Basics, 247
SafeLawns, 155
Safer Way Natural Foods, 127
Safety, food, 59, 89, 92, 132, 218, 229
Safeway, 102, 126, 195, 216
Salatin, Joel, 136, 137–138, 140, 188, 240
Salmonella, 104, 219
Sambazon, 218
Sams, Craig, 248
Sam's Club, 154, 195
Sandbeck, Ellen, 150
Sand County Almanac, A (Leopold), 35
Sandoz, 119
*Sane Living in a Mad World: A Guide
    to the Organic Way of Life*
    (Rodale), 97
San Francisco Zen Center, 152, 256
Santa Cruz Organic, advertising by,
    115–116
Satisfaction Guaranteed (Strasser), 7
Schiffer, Claudia, 2
Schimp, Alex, 146
Schlosser, Eric, 8, 199